MW01005475

POLITICS, RELIGION AND POPULARITY IN EARLY STUART BRITAIN

Revisionism has had a far-reaching impact upon the history of politics and religion in early Stuart Britain. The essays collected here set out to assess this impact and develop further some of the central themes highlighted in the work of the historian Conrad Russell.

The subject matter ranges from high-political narrative to the study of rumour, gossip and print culture. The essays are organised around a series of related questions. What was the impact of 'the British Problem' on the politics of James I's accession and his project for union? How did the 'functional breakdown' in royal finance affect the working of the English state? What was the place of a parliament, and how did its proceedings influence contemporary political culture? How did the legacy of religious division bequeathed by the English Reformation harden into ideological differences during the 1630s and 1640s? And what was the role played by fear of popularity in contemporary political thought and action? The essays identify some of the most fruitful directions for future research in the field, as well as making an important contribution to the ongoing debate about the causes of the English Civil War.

THOMAS COGSWELL is Professor of History, University of California, Riverside.

RICHARD CUST is Senior Lecturer in Modern History, University of Birmingham.

PETER LAKE is Professor of History, Princeton University.

Conrad Russell (the Earl Russell). (Photograph by kind permission of Derry Moore.)

POLITICS, RELIGION AND POPULARITY IN EARLY STUART BRITAIN

Essays in Honour of Conrad Russell

EDITED BY

THOMAS COGSWELL

RICHARD CUST

AND

PETER LAKE

CAMBRIDGE
UNIVERSITY PRESS

PUBLISHED BY THE PRESS SYNDICATE OF THE UNIVERSITY OF CAMBRIDGE
The Pitt Building, Trumpington Street, Cambridge, United Kingdom

CAMBRIDGE UNIVERSITY PRESS
The Edinburgh Building, Cambridge CB2 2RU, UK
40 West 20th Street, New York, NY 10011-4211, USA
477 Williamstown Road, Port Melbourne, VIC 3207, Australia
Ruiz de Alarcón 13, 28014 Madrid, Spain
Dock House, The Waterfront, Cape Town 8001, South Africa

http://www.cambridge.org

© Cambridge University Press 2002

This book is in copyright. Subject to statutory exception
and to the provisions of relevant collective licensing agreements,
no reproduction of any part may take place without
the written permission of Cambridge University Press.

First published 2002

Printed in the United Kingdom at the University Press, Cambridge

Typeface Baskerville Monotype 11 / 12.5 pt   *System* LATEX 2ε   [TB]

A catalogue record for this book is available from the British Library

Library of Congress Cataloguing in Publication data

Politics, religion, and popularity in early Stuart Britain : essays in honour of Conrad Russell/
edited by Thomas Cogswell, Richard Cust, and Peter Lake.
p.   cm.
Includes bibliographical references and index.
ISBN 0 521 80700 x (hardback)
1. Great Britain – Politics and government – 1603–1649.   2. Religion and politics –
Great Britain – History – 17th century.   3. Public opinion – Great Britain – History –
17th century.   4. Great Britain – Church history – 17th century.   I. Cogswell, Thomas, 1952–
II. Cust, Richard.   III. Lake, Peter.   IV. Russell, Conrad.

DA390 .P65   2002
941.06 – dc21   2002020168

ISBN 0 521 80700 x hardback

Contents

v

Preface

This book is a tribute to the Earl Russell and his work as a historian. We are very conscious that Conrad is a man of many parts – Liberal Democrat spokesman in the House of Lords and one of the most effective advocates of liberal values in modern public life, as well as Professor of History at King's College, London – and we cannot do justice to all of these. But, as he reaches his sixty-fifth birthday, we wanted to celebrate his contribution to the study of early Stuart history.

The essays have been commissioned from a cross-section of his many friends on both sides of the Atlantic. Two of us were taught by him as undergraduates at London University and were fortunate enough to be members of the inaugural class of the special subject which he ran with Nicholas Tyacke on 'Parliament and Society in England, 1603–1629'. This was a memorable experience. Even as naive undergraduates we realised that something dramatic was happening to the field, especially on one occasion when the paper giver failed to materialise and Conrad gave a first outing to what became 'Parliamentary history in perspective, 1604–1629'. Eight of us were supervised by him as research students, benefiting from his sense of excitement about the subject and his powers of motivation. He had a wonderful ability to make us feel that there were big questions out there and the work we were doing at the time might just provide the key to unlocking one of them. All of us have been participants in the Monday evening Tudor and Stuart seminar at the Institute of Historical Research. He and Nicholas Tyacke joined Joel Hustfield in running this in 1975 and he has been associated with it ever since. For many of us the seminar has played a formative role in our development as historians. It helped to teach us that history is great fun, with Conrad's memorable impersonations (which somehow always seem to sound like his rendition of Sir Edward Coke) a constant reminder of this. It has repeatedly demonstrated the value of archival research, the way in which large issues can hinge on that crucial reference uncovered by painstaking investigation. Above all, it has taught us that the study of history is essentially a collective and co-operative enterprise, something to be shared between friends. Conrad's generosity in passing on references and commenting on the work of others is legendary; but, perhaps, even more of an inspiration has been his insistence that as much work goes on in the pub afterwards as during the seminar itself. The present volume, and much other recent writing on the period, is testimony to this.

It is well known that not all the contributors to this volume necessarily 'agree' with Conrad in his interpretation of the period. But we do all share a common appreciation of the magnitude of his contribution, of the scope, ambition and achievement of the intellectual project on which he has been engaged and which he has in different ways shared with us. We are also immensely grateful for the spirit of generosity and open-mindedness that he has always brought to his work. He has the priceless knack of being able to welcome disagreement and stimulate genuinely uninhibited debate. We know that even where we take issue with him, his work is an unerring guide to where the really important issues and questions are. Working through his arguments and discussing the points of difference has proved, and is still proving, an incredibly fruitful way to advance our understanding. We all appreciate his achievement as an intellectual presence and his stature as a scholar; we all owe him a personal debt of gratitude and we have contributed to the volume to acknowledge that fact.

Finally we would like to thank Elizabeth Russell. She has supported this collection from the start and has contributed to it in all sorts of ways. She has been a generous friend to all of us over the years and, in spite of her over-modest valuation of her own powers as a historian, she too has helped us to understand what the important questions are and how we might tackle them.

THOMAS COGSWELL
RICHARD CUST
PETER LAKE

Abbreviations

APC	*Acts of the Privy Council*
BIHR	*Bulletin of the Institute of Historical Research*
BL	British Library
Bod. Lib.	Bodleian Library
CJ	*Commons Journals*
CSPD	*Calendar of State Papers Domestic*
CSPSp	*Calendar of State Papers Spanish*
CSPV	*Calendar of State Papers Venetian*
CUL	Cambridge University Library
DNB	*Dictionary of National Biography*
EcHR	*Economic History Review*
ESTC	*English Short Title Catalogue*
EHR	*English Historical Review*
GEC	*The Complete Peerage*
HEHL	Henry E. Huntington Library
Hist	*History*
HJ	*Historical Journal*
HLQ	*Huntington Library Quarterly*
HLRO	House of Lord Record Office
HMC	Historical Manuscripts Commission
HR	*Historical Research*
JBS	*Journal of British Studies*
JEH	*Journal of Ecclesiastical History*
LJ	*Lords Journals*
NLS	National Library of Scotland
NLW	National Library of Wales
N&Q	*Notes and Queries*
PBA	*Proceedings of the British Academy*
PH	*Parliamentary History*

P&P	*Past and Present*
PRO	Public Record Office
SC	*The Seventeenth Century*
SR	*Statutes of the Realm* (1810–1828)
ST	*State Trials* (1816)
STC	*Short Title Catalogue of Early English Books 1475–1640*
TRHS	*Transactions of the Royal Historical Society*
VCH	*Victoria County History*
WCA	Westminster City Archive

Place of publication is London unless otherwise stated.

Revisionism and its legacies: the work of Conrad Russell

Thomas Cogswell, Richard Cust and Peter Lake

'The unity of the revisionists in the 1970s was always built around a series of negative propositions.' Conrad Russell's comment highlights the extent to which 'revisionism' arose out of a sense of dissatisfaction with the assumptions and approaches which still dominated the study of early Stuart history at this time. Two of the assumptions stood out, as Russell himself looking back on this period, explains: firstly, the supposition which permeated Whig and Marxist historiography that 'there were two sides to every division' and that change necessarily took place through the clash of opposites; and secondly, the belief, rooted in Victorian ideas about progress, that the basic task of the historian was to explain why events led to a particular conclusion.[1] The rejection of a dialectical framework, and the determination to avoid the use of hindsight, led revisionists back to the task of constructing a political narrative for the early Stuart period.

During the early 1970s this was still taken as more or less read, having been put together by S. R. Gardiner and not substantially changed since the late nineteenth century. The assumption underlying much of the most influential historical writing from this period was that the basic story was already well known and that the historian's task was to discover the social and intellectual roots of what could be regarded as a crucial phase in the drive towards modernisation.[2] This tended to mean the creation of a number of different narratives of social and cultural change which were taken to relate the political crises of the 1620s and more particularly of the 1640s and 1650s to broader processes of transition from one sort of society (traditional, feudal, patrimonial) to another (modern,

---

[1] C. S. R. Russell, *Parliaments and English Politics 1621–1629* (Oxford, 1979), 5; C. S. R. Russell, *Unrevolutionary England* (1990), ix–xi.

[2] For further discussion of this point see, Peter Lake, 'Retrospective: Wentworth's political world in revisionist and post-revisionist perspective', in J. F. Merritt (ed.), *The Political World of Thomas Wentworth, Earl of Strafford, 1621–1641* (1996), 253–7.

commercial, individualist). The forms which this search took were various. Some of them were organised around the notion of the rise of the gentry or the linked notion, famously developed by Lawrence Stone, of the *Crisis of the Aristocracy*, of a variety of socio-economic, as well as culturally constructed, notions of 'court' and 'country'. Others centred on the rise of the middling sort in town and country and the attendant religious and cultural changes (organised under the sign of 'puritanism' seen as a movement reflective of the class interests and social trajectory of that group) and here, of course, we are referring to the works of the middle-period Christopher Hill.[3] Others still – and here the prime example is Michael Walzer, using models taken from political science rather than social theory – portrayed puritanism not as the ideology of an emergent social group so much as a nascently modern revolutionary movement, a direct precursor of Jacobinism and bolshevism.[4] All these accounts of the period were centred on the events of the 1640s, events which they termed relatively unproblematically the English Revolution, often placing it at the start of a series as the 'first modern revolution'.

All this served to concentrate a great deal of attention on the nature of the events of the 1640s. If social explanations, that is to say explanations in terms of the social origins and interests of the parties to these struggles, were to be made to stick, then agreement had to be reached as to who 'the real revolutionaries' were. Taking the regicide as the revolutionary event, and the regime that followed it as the real revolutionary regime, some of the most distinguished political histories of the revolution – in particular David Underdown's magisterial account of *Pride's Purge* and Austin Woolrych's analysis of the Barebones parliament[5] – doubled as extended tests of a variety of social characterisations, and even explanations, of the Revolution. At roughly the same time Christopher Hill was trying to provide a social profile and explanation of those whom he regarded as the real revolutionaries – the radical thinkers and incendiary evangelists who inhabited the world turned upside down of the 1650s, a group which Hill identified with the shifting plebeian population of the wastelands and forest regions.[6] These attempts at a variety of social and structural explanations of the sides and parties to the Civil War and Revolution continued into the early 1970s, when they received

[3] C. Hill, *Society and Puritanism in Pre-Revolutionary England* (1964); C. Hill, *Puritanism and Revolution* (1958).
[4] M. Walzer, *The Revolution of the Saints* (Cambridge, Mass., 1965).
[5] A. Woolrych, *Commonwealth to Protectorate* (1982).
[6] C. Hill, *The World Turned Upside Down* (1972); C. Hill, *Milton and the English Revolution* (1977).

a magisterial summation in Lawrence Stone's synthetic overview *The Causes of the English Revolution.*

In short, a great deal of the most distinguished writing on the political and religious history of the period was centred on questions about the long-term social and economic causes and nature of the English Revolution. In many ways what we were seeing here was the fag end, the long death, of the gentry controversy. And here, of course, was one of the central sites for the generation of what was to become revisionism. For in testing claims about rising and falling gentry, historians had been forced into extended local studies of gentry society, politics and what would later come to be known (under the influence of certain sorts of anthropological writing) as culture. In so doing not only had they so muddied the economic and social waters as to make any generalisations about the political opinions or actions of rising or falling, 'court' or 'country', nobility or gentry virtually impossible to make stick, they also started to produce a very different model of gentry social and political life. This was centred on the county community in which the majority of the landed class lived out their lives, dominated by local issues and the need to maintain local order and further local interests. It was a world to which the sort of political and ideological passions, the side-taking over issues of ideological or constitutional principle, the jockeying for political advantage and office that characterised the conventional accounts of the political history of the period had virtually no place. In this world we were dealing not with the first modern revolution but rather with the Great Rebellion, an event unwanted and unwilled by the majority of the local gentry who populated and ran the English shires. This was a vision of provincial life first developed by Alan Everitt in his extraordinarily influential *The Community of Kent and the Great Rebellion* and then applied by a variety of other historians to other counties before being generalised to all England in John Morrill's seminal overview *The Revolt of the Provinces.*

Other straws in what would become the revisionist wind could be found in both the religious and intellectual history being written during the 1960s. Crucial here was J. G. A. Pocock's account of *The Ancient Constitution and the Feudal Law*, a book which, in stressing the insularity of English legal thought, and the dominance of English political and legal culture by the notion of a common law based on immemorial custom and untainted by any originary act of either royal or parliamentary sovereignty, removed the basis of a great deal of earlier writing on the constitutional divisions and principles said to have divided early Stuart England into rival camps labelled 'government and opposition'. Here was an inherently conservative way of looking at the world dominated by ancient precedents and immemorial custom, a unitary realm of discourse outside of which anyone trained within the English legal tradition was in effect unable to think. Increasingly it provided the conceptual limits within which early Stuart Englishmen conducted their political disputes and disagreements. Of course, disagreement could and did occur within the discursive structures laid down by the common-law mind, but Pocock was anxious to point out that there was a common-law case to be made for the king as well as his opponents and contemporaries were well aware of that. On this account, non-negotiable arguments about, or self-conscious struggles for, sovereignty lay in the future; they were a consequence rather than a cause of political conflict and revolution.

Parallel to Pocock's work on political and legal ideology came a similarly sceptical account of the revolutionary potential of 'puritanism'. Here a key text, the significance of which is not perhaps often enough recognised, was William Lamont's study of *Marginal Prynne*. Prynne was the classic point where the radical, even revolutionary, potential within both the common law and puritanism came together to forge the quintessential puritan revolutionary lawyer. That, however, was not how Prynne emerged from Lamont's study of him, but rather as a far more conservative figure. Intensely erastian, committed to the norms and forms of both the common law and what he took to be the Elizabethan and Jacobean church, on Lamont's account, Prynne was only gradually converted to the need for ecclesiastical reform by what he perceived as the 'innovations' being foisted on the church by a clique of Arminians and papists. Lamont's work was followed, of course, by Nicholas Tyacke's hugely influential 1969 Oxford D.Phil. thesis, 'Arminianism in England, in religion and politics, 1604 to 1640', which again did much to undermine the notion of an inherently radical or revolutionary puritanism, placing its emphasis instead on the revolutionary impact of Arminianism. Similar was the purport, if not the immediate impact, of Patrick Collinson's seminal and enigmatic masterpiece, *The Elizabethan Puritan Movement*. The product of a 1957 London thesis, the book came out in 1967 and seemed at first reading to confirm Sir John Neale's vision of a radical, indeed proto-revolutionary, puritan movement under Elizabeth; a predictable precursor of what was to arrive red in tooth and claw in the late 1630s and early 1640s. And yet a close reading of that text shows that Collinson had adduced a vast range of evidence to enable a radical reevaluation of the English church as a reformed or Calvinist church and of 'puritanism' as, in many of its most distinctive forms and at many times, a distinctly establishment creed. In a crucial footnote Collinson cited Tyacke's thesis in a way that showed which way his views were tending and in a series of articles published in the mid 1970s he started to draw out insights that had been left implicit in the book into explicit arguments. These fugitive pieces signalled a basic change in the hitherto ostensibly Nealean tenor of his work, a trend that reached its height with the publication in 1982 of the more or less explicitly revisionist text *The Religion of Protestants*.

The claim being made here is not that either Pocock or Lamont's (and still less Collinson's) books were in any meaningful sense 'revisionist books'; in fact the work of all three men went on to have a decidedly ambiguous, even at times adversarial, relationship to what subsequently emerged as the revisionist interpretation of the period. It is, however, to argue that by the mid to late 1960s, in a number of disparate fields – local and religious history, the history of 'political thought' – many of the central aspects of what was to become revisionism were already available in the literature. To these books one might add several studies of 'high politics'. J. N. Ball and T. G. Barnes's work on Sir John Eliot and Sir Robert Phelips respectively showed that these MPs did not fit easily into models of conflict based on 'court' v. 'country' or government v. opposition, and G. R. Elton's analysis of the Commons' Apology of 1604 challenged one of the accepted milestones on 'the High Road to Civil War'.[7] Arguably, most important of all was Menna Prestwich's magisterial book on *Cranfield* which insisted on the importance, for any sensible account of the central politics of the period, of issues of court favour and patronage and, of course, of royal finance.

Across the scholarly world, starting from very different places, using different sorts of sources, to answer very different questions, we can, in retrospect, see a number of scholars arriving at conclusions none of which quite fitted within the conventional wisdom and all or many of which seemed to be tending in the same general direction. Many, therefore, of the empirical and interpretative materials necessary to launch a challenge to the dominant modes of viewing the period or framing research upon it were available by the late 1960s. But they had not been brought together into anything like a coherent assault and still less into anything resembling an alternative master narrative or interpretation.

[7] J. N. Ball, 'Sir John Eliot at the Oxford Parliament, 1625', *BIHR*, 28 (1955), 113–27; T. G. Barnes, *Somerset 1625–1640* (Oxford, 1961); T. G. Barnes, 'County politics and a puritan cause célèbre: Somerset churchales, 1633', *TRHS*, 5th ser., 9 (1959), 103–22; G. R. Elton, 'A high road to civil war', in his *Studies in Tudor and Stuart Politics and Government*, 2 vols. (1974), II, 164–82.

Nicholas Tyacke tells a fascinating story about his efforts to continue to teach a long-standing course in English constitutional history at University College, London. Having encountered increasing difficulties in maintaining the intellectual integrity of the course, he was forced finally to give up; a decision that Joel Hurstfield found both regrettable and incomprehensible. Something, in short, was about to give. We might speak, in retrospect, therefore, of a revisionist or perhaps of a pre-revisionist moment, poised uneasily between old and new approaches and paradigms.

This was a decidedly odd moment, betwixt and between different historiographical worlds; 'the court' and 'the country', having ceased to be identifiable socio-economic interests or groups, were enjoying an afterlife as ideologically and politically defined connections or cultural archetypes; a now canonical division between centre and localities was sometimes being mapped onto and sometimes juxtaposed against these polarities. The distinctive products of this period were perhaps Perez Zagorin's *The Court and the Country* or Derek Hirst's *Representative of the People?*, the latter divided between a revisionist localism and an account of rising levels of political conflict and popular participation in elections that would sit awkwardly with the revisionist account of the period. Even *Faction and Parliament*, the famously 'revisionist' collection of essays edited by Kevin Sharpe, shows something of this mood. For, despite the self-proclaimedly revisionist rhetoric deployed in the introduction (the existing version of the period did not so much need touching up as a complete reworking, Sharpe argued), the actual essays contained in the book were strewn across the interpretative map, with some, like those by Christopher Thompson or Simon Adams, fitting extremely ill with what was emerging as the revisionist account of the period.[8]

Something of the atmosphere of the time can be gained from the reviewing activities of Geoffrey Elton. He characterised Stone's *Causes of the English Revolution* with a finely measured and modulated disappointment, even derision, as 'a handsome restatement of the traditional explanations'. He responded, however, to Conrad Russell's edited volume on *The Origins of the English Civil War* with considerably more enthusiasm; here, he claimed, was the antidote to Stone. 'Any historians who were depressed by the enthusiastic reception given to L. Stone's recent rehashing of outworn notions of "the causes of the English revolution" may

---

[8] S. L. Adams, 'Foreign policy and the Parliaments of 1621 and 1624' and C. Thompson, 'The divided leadership of the House of Commons in 1629', in K. Sharpe (ed.), *Faction and Parliament* (Oxford, 1978), 139–71, 245–84.

take heart. The New Look has arrived.' The collection, Elton opined, was not yet 'the magisterial revision of the kind that must surely be on the way, sweeping whig, marxist, high tory and social disruption models (and their builders) into oblivion', but it was nevertheless a firm indication of which way the wind was blowing. 'What we have here is a truly welcome prospectus for that very necessary revolution in historical thinking.'[9]

And in this, Elton was surely right. For with the publication of Russell's edited volume in 1973 (and in particular of his own two essays and the seminal piece by Nicholas Tyacke on 'Puritanism, Arminianism and counter-revolution') revisionism, as we have come to know it, had finally started to arrive on the historiographical scene. Thereafter, full fig revisionism emerged with a rush. The staging posts are well known: Russell's own iconoclastic essay on 'Parliamentary history in perspective' and Morrill's *Revolt of the Provinces*, both of 1976; Kevin Sharpe's edited collection *Faction and Parliament* of 1978; Mark Kishlansky's *Rise of the New Model Army* and Russell's first major book, *Parliaments and English Politics, 1621–29*, both of 1979. The crystallisation of the revisionist view was rapid and its success at first almost complete. As Tom Cogswell has observed, many of the central contentions of the revisionist case were translated into textbook truisms almost over night.[10] Truly this had been an historiographical revolution waiting to happen.

It did not, however, happen of its own accord, and it was Russell, more than anyone, who drew the disparate elements of research, argument and assertion, outlined above, together into a compelling new synthesis; and, in particular, it was Russell who, having done so, led the assault on the last redoubt of 'Whiggery', the high-political and parliamentary narratives themselves. For perhaps the greatest benefit conferred on the field by revisionism was the freeing of the domain of the political from a whole series of determinisms, of petty inevitabilities, of tacitly assumed we-already-know-thats, comprised, first, by the familiarity of the traditional renditions of the tale and, second, by multifarious implicit connections to other notionally 'more profound' economic, social or, latterly, 'cultural' factors. By acknowledging, indeed even celebrating, the breakdown of existing social-change explanations of political conflict, revisionism rendered the political interesting again. It was interesting, of course, because the direction, or even the outcome, of the political process under study

---

[9] G. R. Elton, 'Review of Stone, *Causes of the English Revolution*', *HJ*, 16 (1973), 205–8; 'Review of Russell, *Origins of the English Civil War*', *HJ*, 17 (1974), 213–16.

[10] T. E. Cogswell, 'A low road to extinction? Supply and redress of grievances in the parliaments of the 1620s', *HJ*, 33 (1990), 284–5.

was no longer always already known. For the first time probably since Gardiner the politics of early Stuart England had become an open-ended subject for research. The issue was no longer to find deeper, more long-term causes for a process of political change the course of which was already known; rather, the question was how best to reconstitute, to retell (and interconnect) the basic (both high and low, national and local) political narrative/s.

All this Russell set out to do. If the traditional Russellian stories are true, he had started by intending to write a biography of John Pym. But such a project only made sense within the traditional political narrative. For Pym was a figure whose significance was underwritten by the telling of a certain story about the politics of the period, a story about the rise of parliamentary opposition, about the continuties of issue, rhetoric and personnel that linked the crises of the 1620s to those of the Civil War. As those traditional narrative templates ceased to make sense, so too did the initial Pym project. Thus did the early chapters of a Pym biography transmute into *Parliaments and English Politics, 1621–29*. Where a biography about Pym would inevitably have tended to privilege a story of continuity between the 1620s and the 1640s, now what was emerging was a story of discontinuity, as the attempt to reconstruct the political world of the 1620s served to render one in which a civil war could break out unimaginably strange and remote.

What Russell did in the book on the 1620s was to synthesise existing or emergent accounts of the political and religious culture of the period – accounts which, with Pocock, Lamont and Tyacke, were far more con-sensual than anything the existing Whig narratives would lead one to believe – with his own peerless knowledge of the parliamentary sources, to produce a high political narrative entirely different from anything that had passed for current before. Through the unique connection between centre and localities that was parliament the Everittian and Morrillian localism of the local gentry was now allowed to penetrate to the very centre of the high political story. As inflation ate into the real value of traditional sources of royal revenue, the unwillingness of localist MPs to meet the mounting (but unacknowledged and misunderstood) costs of royal government in general and of war in particular, became central. So too was the assumed conservatism of Calvinist MPs in the face of Arminian and Caroline innovation, which replaced, in the revisionist version of these events, traditional accounts of puritan activism in the face of a static Anglican establishment. But perhaps the most daring in-novation introduced into an account still centred on events in parliament, and founded on parliamentary sources, was the claim, based logically enough on the materials and assumptions summarised above, that parliament was an event not an institution. The focal point of the entire Whig narrative was redescribed as an epiphenomenon, an effect rather than a cause of a political narrative, the real causal factors behind which were based elsewhere, based, in fact, where, in a personal monarchy, one might well expect them to be based, at the king's court.

It was often claimed by the early opponents of revisionism that all this amounted to little more than high-political antiquarianism, that the revisionists had reduced the history of the period to a one-damn-thing-after-another retelling of contingent high-political events and interactions. This claim was often combined with the assertion that they had stripped the ideology out of contemporary politics.[11] Whilst it is certainly true that revisionists have insisted that the high-political narrative needed to be redone from the sources up and denounced the teleological tendencies of their opponents, it is simply not the case that they have eschewed long-term structural analysis or ignored issues of ideology. Indeed, one of the criticisms one might make of the wider movement is that after its initial programmatic statements of intent, revisionists have not written enough narratives. With the exception of Russell himself (and, of course, Mark Kishlansky's seminal early text, *The Rise of the New Model Army*) political narrative has not been the distinctive revisionist genre. They have, if anything, tended to favour the analytic essay and the topically arranged overview.

As for Russell himself, his exercises in narrative have always been set in densely argued structural contexts. These were laid out as early as *The Origins of the English Civil War* and were certainly placed at the very centre of the explanatory structure of *Parliaments and English Politics*. They comprise, of course, the so-called 'functional breakdown' – a phrase that Russell appropriated from Gerald Aylmer and made his own as a short-hand label for the long-term fiscal sclerosis of the early Stuart state.[12] This was predicated on the long-term impact of inflation on many of the relatively fixed revenues of the crown interacting with the entrenched localism of the ruling class. It was compounded by a second factor, the financial consequences and effects of 'the military revolution'.

---

[11] L. Stone, 'The revival of narrative: reflections on a new old history', *P&P*, 85 (1979), 3–24; T. K. Rabb, 'Revisionism revised: the role of the Commons', *P&P*, 92 (1981); D. Cannadine, 'British history: past, present – and future?', *P&P*, 116 (1987), 169–91.

[12] The term emerged out of his tape-recorded discussion with Aylmer in: 'Parliamentarianism 1604–1642', in W. Lamont (ed.), *Sussex Tapes* (1976), 135–53.

Here Russell's parliamentary narrative intersected with Everittian and Morrillian local history to produce a new account of the political reactions and values of the landed class both in Westminister and at home in the counties. The third long-term structural feature of Russell's analysis was the impact on a political and religious culture obsessed with unity of the brute fact of post-Reformation religious division. Latterly, these three long-term structural tensions or points of contradiction have been joined by the issue of multiple monarchies – the so-called British Problem. As the presence in *The Origins* of a piece by John Elliott shows,[13] all these various aspects of the case were present *in potentia* at least from the early 1970s and all in their turn were based on or worked out against comparisons with the structure and history of a variety of European monarchies. Here a seminal influence, which Russell has often acknowledged, was Elliott's *Revolt of the Catalans*.

Nor have revisionists eschewed issues of ideology; rather they have recategorised what they take to be the dominant ideological norms, assumptions and expectations of contemporaries in terms of the desire for, and assumption of, consensus, rather than in terms of conflict. In so doing they greatly broadened the range of sources and sorts of places in which one might look for 'ideology'. No longer to be found solely in programmatic statements of principle and argument, in treatises, sermons, parliamentary speeches – the classic places in which that curious beast 'political thought' has always been studied – in the revisionists' hands it would be fair to say that 'ideology' came to be redefined more broadly as the operating assumptions, the often implicit, only partially articulated, beliefs and expectations that underpinned the workings of the polity. Such bodies of belief and assumption could best, indeed could only, be properly reconstructed with reference to a whole variety of texts and practices, not usually examined by historians of political ideology. That surely was what localism was – an attempt to reconstitute from out of the basic structures of their social and political lives the underlying political values and priorities of the provincial gentry. Again that was what Russell was doing in the opening eighty pages of *Parliaments and English Politics*. This is a brilliant analytic essay on the operating assumptions, the ideological structures or culture of the polity of early Stuart England. In fact, a case could be made that – without ever quite admitting or formulating it in this way – revisionism was operating with a notion of political culture (rather than of ideology). Latterly, of course, some

---

[13] J. H. Elliott, 'England and Europe: a common malady?', in C. S. R. Russell (ed.), *The Origins of the English Civil War* (1973).

revisionist historians, most notably Kevin Sharpe, have foregrounded and developed this aspect of the project, raising it to new levels of self-consciousness.[14]

The notion of culture in play here in Russell's work was, in fact, a very sophisticated one. Unlike some revisonist accounts of essentially the same subject matter, it did not collapse all contemporary political culture into its normative aspirations towards unity, consensus and order, but in fact allowed for the existence of contradictory notions of and impulses toward different (and sometimes mutually exclusive) ideals of order or unity to be at work within the same society. Russell's engagement with, and analysis of, such contradictions and paradoxes was at its most self-conscious in his treatment of religion, but was present, by implication at least, in his discussion of a whole range of other 'secular' issues. Here one thinks of his subtle account of the contradictory responses of MPs who were both vocally anti-Catholic and viscerally localist, to the fiscal problems of the crown and the prospect and the experience of anti-Spanish war; or again of the response of both courtiers and parliament men to the 'corruption' of the crown's servants. Or again one thinks of his account of the almost unbearable conceptual and emotional tensions which a common adherence to 'the rule of law' and a rhetoric of divine right could arouse in contemporaries as they faced fiscal/administrative breakdown and concerted political disagreement; breakdowns and disagreements which their own attitudes and expectations had helped to bring about, but which those same attitudes and beliefs were almost entirely unable satisfactorily to contain or explain.

While in *Parliament and English Politics* the two dominant aspects of his work (the long-term analysis of structural contradictions and the high-political narrative) were intertwined, the former both emerging through and subtly shaping the latter, in his later work the two have been split part. The structural analysis is laid out in his *Causes of the English Civil War* and the narrative part contained in *The Fall of the British Monarchies*. Similarly, by the time we reach these last two books Russell has come clean about the long-term goal of the whole project – the laying-bare of the causes of the English Civil War – what, in a telling phrase, he terms the English historians' equivalent of the ascent of Everest.[15] If revisionists complained of the obsessive concern of traditional accounts of the period (like, say, Stone's) with the events of the early 1640s, that did not mean that, in

---

[14] K. Sharpe and P. G. Lake, 'Introduction', in Sharpe and Lake (eds.), *Culture and Politics in Early Stuart England* (1994), 1–20; K.Sharpe, *Reading Revolutions* (2001), esp. ch. 1.
[15] C. S. R. Russell, *The Causes of the English Civil War* (Oxford, 1990), 1.

the long run, they too were not to prove just as concerned with the holy grail of the causes of the Civil War. Certainly the issue of the extent and nature of the continuities linking, say, the politics of the 1620s with those of the 1640s was a live issue in Russell's work as early as the appendix dedicated to precisely that purpose in *Parliaments and English Politics*. All of which might be taken to imply not that revisionists regarded any and every attempt to establish such continuities and connections as *ipso facto* illegitimate, but rather that they held that previous attempts to establish such long-term continuities and causal links had been botched; that is to say that 'Whig' or 'Marxist' historians had too easily assumed or too readily asserted certain continuities between one period and another in their search for the causes of the Civil War, rather than that all such attempts were, by definition, illegitimately 'teleological' or 'Whiggish'. In short, the argument was that the job had been done badly, not that it should not be done at all. And a great deal of Russell's work has been an attempt to sort through these issues.

And so, *pace* the claims of his critics, Russell's work has not eschewed long-term structural argument or explanation. It has not omitted questions of ideology. It has not been solely dedicated to or even dominated by the production of minutely detailed high political narratives centred in Whitehall and Westminister. Russell's argument does indeed at times turn on such narratives, but those moments of detailed, even microscopic, examination of high political interaction and manoeuvre are always carefully placed within other, wider argumentative and structural contexts and purposes. In short, however narrow or particular their immediate focus, even Russell's densest narrative passages always serve far wider interpretative goals and explanatory ambitions. They are designed not only or even mainly to answer the seemingly innocent question 'what happened next?', but to address what remain for Russell the big questions – what sort of event was the English Civil War and what might be taken to have caused it? The answers for those questions are certainly sought, in part, in political, often very high-political, narrative – what Elton called 'the study of men in events' – but they are also sought in the high-political narratives of three nations and in the interactions between those narratives. Moreover, those political narratives are always already located within an analytic context that stretches back at least as far as the Henrician Reformation and is informed by a frame of reference that goes back farther still – to the precedents and crises of the high Middle Ages to which, as Russell himself emphasises, contemporaries themselves turned, as they tried to explain and control their own political and polemical circumstances. Moreover, that analytic framework is itself the result of a series of comparisons made between the nature and course of English, indeed, of 'British' (i.e. of English, Scottish and Irish) state formation and parallel developments amongst the multiple monarchical states of Europe. Whatever this is, it is not antiquarianism. Neither is it the systematic privileging of contingency, of the short-term cause and the accidental conjuncture, of which revisionism has so often been accused.

All of which raises, of course, the basic question of why this body of historical writing, in general, and Russell's œuvre, in particular, has been so often misconceived and misdescribed. On the one hand, the answer to that question lies in the polemical circumstances in which revisionism announced itself to the world. Anxious to renounce what it took to be both the social and economic determinism and the Whiggish progressivism of existing accounts, early revisionism embraced contingency, the free play of high political manoeuvre and circumstance, and denounced what it claimed were the inherently 'teleological' aspects of 'current orthodoxy'. These early claims were, of course, underpinned by a parallel appeal from what were characterised as inherently distorting 'printed sources' – upon which a good deal of the existing literature was said to be based – to the essentially 'primary' manuscript sources, upon which revisionist accounts of the period claimed to be written. These assertions led, in turn, to the accusations of high-political antiquarianism, and obsession with accident and contingency, that characterised the earliest critiques of revisionism. As revisionism wrapped itself in the flag of 'real' (manuscript) research and tended to defend itself with the rhetoric of the obscure (manuscript) source and the contingent political event, its opponents wrapped themselves in the flag of theory, of big questions, and of the long-term, deep-lying cause. These, of course, were, for the most part, false oppositions and dichotomies, self-serving polemical claims doomed to generate far more heat than light. To that extent, they paralleled the early revisionist drive not so much to qualify or controvert but simply to invert the central contentions of what had calcified, in myriad text books and undergraduate essays, as conventional ('Whig') orthodoxy. Thus parliament was not 'rising', it was 'declining' in power; puritanism was not only not part of a radical opposition, it was, in fact, the leading edge of a conservative reaction against an Arminian revolution; far from seeking a more active role in determining the fate of the nation, the landed class were in localist retreat from any genuine responsibility for the future of the English state.

Such polemical inversions, such brutal either/or interpretative choices are perhaps an inevitable part of any genuine historiographical revolution. It is, however, one of the more unfortunate effects of the embattled origins of the revisionist initiative that such choices and polarities continue to cast a shadow over the current historiographical scene. It might be possible to argue that the difference between so-called 'post-' and 'anti-revisionism' is the capacity to acknowledge the real nature and achievement of the revisionist intervention. Paradoxically, this means acknowledging not only the novelty of the revisionist project but also the continuities that link it with the interpretations which it was trying to supersede. In other words, we need to place the extreme and distorting claims made both for and against revisionism in the immediate polemical and, indeed, political (for the academy has its own, largely unacknowledged, both ideological and inter-generational, politics) contexts which produced them. Having done so, we will be in an altogether better position to subject the œuvre of Conrad Russell to the sort of detailed and critical interpretation that an intellectual project of its scope deserves. We will also be able to evaluate the significance of the real advances made by revisionism and convert them into an array of new research agendas designed to test, confirm, reject and extend the considerable insights and advances vouchsafed to us by the initial project.

There are clear signs that this is happening to be found in recent writing, particularly on the late seventeenth century. At first sight this may seem a strange claim, since in his own work Russell has never ventured much past 1642, let alone 1660. But then Russell's analysis has always operated at a number of different levels of causation and periodisation and the appropriate periods for the further study of his long-term structural analyses of the causes of the Civil War have never been the same as those suitable to the more intense bursts of high-political narrative for which he is justly famous. If, however, one wishes to follow through the structural logic of his more long-term arguments to their natural conclusions, a very long chronological span is often called for. In the case of the interaction between 'the functional breakdown' and the 'military revolution' the appropriate period might be thought to stretch from Agincourt to Blenheim. To trace the impact of religious pluralism and confessional conflict on a religio-political culture obsessed with the need for unity and consensus, the relevant chronological unit might extend, if not from Lollardy to the Toleration Act, then certainly from the Henrician Reformation to the Convocation Controversy. For 'the British Problem' the appropriate period might be taken to run from the so-called 'Elizabethan exclusion crisis' to the Act of Union and beyond to the collapse of Jacobitism. Similarly, what one might term Russell's long-term cultural problematic, the adaptation of a political culture built on consensus and assumptions of organic unity and hierarchy to the increasingly frequent incidence of political conflict – what, adopting Mark Kishlansky's phrase, one might term the 'rise of adversary politics' (or otherwise) – demands a long-term treatment, running from the newly ideologised politics of the 1530s to the 'rage of party'. If its final resolution is to be effectively located and explained, Russell's 'crisis of parliaments' demands a similarly *longue durée*, one stretching from what Andrew Thrush terms below 'the personal rule of James I' to the 1690s. Even the Civil War and Revolution do not provide logical or sufficient *termini ad quem* for any of Russell's long-term causes of the Civil War. Any adequate account of what these causes caused, of where they went or led, must, in short, encompass the long seventeenth century.

Russell himself has never attempted to supply such accounts, and small wonder, since his overall historiographical project has always been precisely to explain the outbreak of the Civil War. This leaves an historiographical legacy ripe for critique, development and exploitation, which is precisely what it is in the process of receiving from a new generation of historians at work on the later seventeenth century. Thus, Mike Braddick's seminal work on the development of the English state through the long seventeenth century might be viewed as a playing-with and playing-out of Russell's analysis of the functional breakdown, only now run through the transforming effects of the revolutionary decades.[16] So too might aspects of Steven Pincus's work on the decades between the 1650s and 1690s, as both a post- and proto-revolutionary period. Something similar might also be said of Tim Harris's forthcoming study of the British aspects of the Restoration settlement in three kingdoms and indeed of the Glorious Revolution; whilst Mark Knights' current research on the cultural impact of 'the rage of party' speaks precisely to and indeed transforms by finishing a Russellian and Kishlanskyian story about the incremental 'rise of adversary politics' over the long post-Reformation seventeenth century.[17] Nicholas Tyacke's pioneering, and strangely neglected, work on 'toleration' over the same sort of period also picks up and plays out a Russellian problematic about the relations between post-Reformation religious division and confessional conflict and

---

[16] M. J. Braddick, *State Formation in Early Modern England, c.1550–1700* (Cambridge, 2001).
[17] Much of this work was previewed and discussed at a conference at Chicago in November 2001 on 'England's Revolutionary Century?', organised by Steven Pincus and Adrian John.

a variety of decidedly univocal definitions of political and ecclesiastical order.[18]

Of course, much of this work is still in progress and so its precise tone and impact remains to be seen. It may well be that the conclusions and consequences that emerge will at first sight appear to be anything but 'revisionist' as that term has come to be used as a short-hand description of certain styles or modes of interpretation of early modern England. But that, of course, merely highlights the significance and profundity of the initial (revisionist and Russellian) interventions and insights, and also demonstrates the extent to which we are all working in the ruins of an historiographical world shattered by revisionism, all beneficiaries of the recapture of the political domain as a fit object of study and of political narrative as a central historical genre.

It is with these considerations very much in mind that the current collection of essays has been assembled. The focus is on Russell's own period – the 1590s to the 1640s – and again the aim is to follow through the logic of his arguments and develop the insights which his work has provided. The section on politics begins with two studies which explore different aspects of the British Problem. Nicholas Tyacke uses an analysis of a puritan 'opposition' grouping's involvement with the Scottish reversionary interest of the 1590s and the reform programme of 1603 to re-examine the implications of 'opposition' within contemporary political culture; and Lori Ferrell investigates how a notable Anglo/Scottish court wedding in 1606/7 was promoted through print and public display in an effort to bolster James's collapsing project for union. Pauline Croft takes as her starting point parliament's status as 'an event' and explores some of the ways in which this developed an increasing sense of cohesion between the centre and localities and also within the House of Commons itself. Andrew Thrush investigates the start of Russell's 'crisis of parliaments' by analysing the period when parliament's future first came into question as a result of James's hostility and the financial exigencies of the crown. David Hebb also explores some of the ramifications of 'the functional breakdown', demonstrating how the crown's efforts to exploit the sea spawned a culture of profiteering and corruption which added to the unsavoury reputation of the court and made financial reform harder to achieve. Finally, in this section, Cynthia Herrup analyses the role of parliamentary pardons as symbols of unity within a political culture which highlighted the pursuit of harmony and consensus.

[18] N. R. N. Tyacke, 'The rise of Puritanism and the legalizing of dissent, 1571–1719', in Tyacke, *Aspects of English Protestantism* (Manchester, 2001).

Each of the essays on religion addresses a different aspect of the legacy of religious division which emerged out of the English Reformation. Julia Merritt's study of the Jacobean pedagogue Robert Hill highlights the tensions and dilemmas faced by a puritan operating within the eccle- siastical establishment. Anthony Milton examines the ways in which Laudian polemicists, such as Peter Heylyn, fashioned a distinctive iden- tity for themselves and in the process helped consolidate and harden religious differences. And Jacqueline Eales demonstrates how these same differences continued to provide much of the raw material which fuelled the side-taking of the English Civil War.

The final section on popularity looks at one of the ways in which contemporaries sought to explain the existence of conflict within a po- litical culture built on consensus and unity. Popularity was one of those rhetorical themes which, as Russell puts it, helped to identify who 'was to blame and who should be punished'.[19] Tom Cogswell's piece investigates how the Duke of Buckingham attempted to play the dangerous double game of harnessing popular forces while denying he was doing so, and in the process helped to enlarge the 'public sphere' of informed political debate and discussion. Richard Cust's study of Charles I argues that fear of popularity exerted a powerful influence on the mind-set of the king and shaped his policies and decision making at critical junctures. Finally Peter Lake's study of Sir Thomas Aston's role in pre-Civil War Cheshire highlights the contradictions inherent in a royalist politics which identi- fied popularity as the root cause of the many of the evils it was fighting against whilst recognising that the changing context required politicians to play the 'popular' game. The range of the topics covered is a tribute to the breadth and significance of Russell's scholarly achievements.

---

[19] Russell, *Unrevolutionary England*, xvii.

Politics

Puritan politicians and King James VI and I, 1587–1604

Nicholas Tyacke

I

Profound changes have overtaken the writing of Elizabethan and early Stuart political history since the days when J. E. Neale and Wallace Notestein presided over the subject – like the heavenly twins 'Castor and Pollux', as one of them described it.[1] Indeed their model of an increasingly organised opposition in the House of Commons and associated growth of the power of English parliaments now seemingly lies in ruins. Much of this demolition work has, of course, been at the hands of another pair of historians, G. R. Elton and Conrad Russell. They have rightly pointed out the problematic nature of the concept of opposition and the danger of reading parliamentary history backwards from the revolutionary events of the mid seventeenth century. In many cases MPs portrayed as opponents of the regime by those writing in the Neale-Notestein tradition turn out to have government links, while attention has been redirected to the English court as the real centre of politics. At the same time it is clear that puritanism cannot bear the interpretative weight which Neale especially placed upon it.[2] Yet if the notion of a 'puritan choir' has proved fallacious, there were undoubtedly puritan MPs willing to oppose government policies and, moreover, to combine secular with religious grievances in a powerful critique.[3] The challenge,

For general advice and help concerning specific points, I am grateful to Andrew Boyle, James Burns, Barbara Coulton, Simon Healy, Elizabeth McGrath, Andrew Thrush, Hans van Wees and Jenny Wormald.

[1] J. E. Neale, *The Elizabethan House of Commons* (1949), 11.

[2] J. E. Neale, *Elizabeth I and Her Parliaments*, 2 vols. (1953–7); W. Notestein, 'The winning of the initiative by the House of Commons', *PBA*, 11 (1924–5), 125–75; G. R. Elton, 'Parliament in the sixteenth century: functions and fortunes', *HJ*, 22 (1979), 255–78, and *The Parliament of England 1559–1581* (Cambridge, 1986); C. Russell, 'Parliamentary history in perspective, 1604–1629', *Hist*, 61 (1976), 1–27, and *Parliaments and English Politics 1621–1629* (Oxford, 1979); see also M. A. R. Graves, 'The management of the Elizabethan House of Commons: the Council's "men-of-business"', *PH*, 2 (1983), 11–38.

[3] J. E. Neale, 'Peter Wentworth', *EHR*, 39 (1924), 36–54, 175–205.

therefore, remains how best to fit this phenomenon into the new historiographical framework.

Whereas for Neale the activities of the Elizabehan MP and puritan
Peter Wentworth, and his like, were fraught with significance, Elton
came to regard such individuals as marginal to the politics of the day
and, judged at least by the criterion of practical achievement, the latter
would appear to have the better of the argument. But here we do well
to recall some remarks made by Russell, on the subject of 'opposition':

> It is the first characteristic of an opposition that it represents an alternative
> government, and therefore an alternative power base . . . There are only two
> ways in which serious political opposition is possible under a monarchy. One
> is through possession of a pretender or a reversionary interest to the throne,
> who may provide the necessary alternative source of power, and it is one of
> the peculiarities of the early Stuart period that no pretender was available. The
> other way is through the use of an army, and that was not available until August
> 1640.[4]

Between 1587 and 1603, however, the most plausible reversionary interest and alternative power base was represented by King James VI of
Scotland. Prior to this a nightmare scenario, from the standpoint of committed Protestants, was the possibility that his mother, the Catholic Mary
Queen of Scots, would succeed Elizabeth, because in strict hereditary
terms she was the next in line – by descent from Margaret Tudor, sister of
Henry VIII. Hence the considerable time and energy expended by both
members of the government and the wider political nation in seeking to
prevent such an outcome.[5] With Mary's execution in 1587 there came an
inevitable change of gear, albeit complicated by the refusal of Elizabeth
to have the Protestant James formally acknowledged as her successor.
It now made increasing sense, particularly for those dissatisfied with the
status quo, to curry favour with the presumed heir, an added attraction
for puritans being that Scotland had undergone a much more thorough-
going Reformation than England and might provide a religious model
in the future.

Despite his modern reputation as an impractical idealist, Peter
Wentworth was among the first to grasp some of the potentialities of
the new situation. Having campaigned unsuccessfully during most of the
1570s and 1580s for church reform, and freedom of speech partly as
a means to that end, thereafter the succession became his consuming

---

[4] C. Russell, *Unrevolutionary England, 1603–1642* (1990), xiii. A less restrictive definition of opposition
is, of course, possible.
[5] P. Collinson, 'The Elizabethan exclusion crisis and the Elizabethan polity', *PBA*, 84 (1994), 51–92.

passion. By the time this last-named cause had landed him once more in the Tower of London, in 1593, Wentworth was almost certainly a supporter of James's claim and may have been so as early as the writing of his *Pithie Exhortation* in 1587, although the declared aim remained simply to have the succession determined by parliament in the interests of national security. Not until his *Discourse*, probably written in 1596, did Wentworth come out openly in favour of the hereditary right of James to the English throne.[6] Still a prisoner in the Tower, he remained there until his death in November 1597. The following year, 1598, the *Pithie Exhortation* and *Discourse* were printed together at Edinburgh by Robert Waldegrave, Scottish royal employee and English puritan exile.[7]

Wentworth made no explicit link between church reform and the Stuart succession in his various writings, arguing instead that lack of an agreed heir would lead to civil war and the imperilling of true religion. Yet this was at the very time that Elizabethan puritanism was entering on the nadir of its domestic fortunes, with the deaths of leading friends in high places such as Leicester, Mildmay and Walsingham, betwen 1588 and 1590, and an associated intensification of persecution.[8] North of the border, by contrast, not only did the Scottish Church, in 1590, order prayers for the 'afflicted brethrein' of England, who were suffering for the 'puritie' of religion, but the king also lent his support. Already in 1589 James had intimated his disapproval of Richard Bancroft's well-known sermon attacking presbyterianism, and the following year he went so far as to tell the General Assembly that 'our neighbour kirk in England' was saddled with 'an evill said masse in English, wanting nothing but the liftings'. Furthermore, in 1591, he wrote to Elizabeth on behalf of Thomas Cartwright and other puritan clergy imprisoned 'for their conscience'.[9] Against this background, a puritan vote for James involved more just than a heightened sense of civic duty.

Apart from Wentworth, three other MPs were gaoled in 1593 for dealing in the matter of the succession: Sir Henry Bromley, Richard Stephens and William Walsh. Stephens, already an acquaintance of Wentworth, was related by marriage to Bromley and had, according to his subsequent

---

[6] Neale, 'Peter Wentworth', 182, 197–8; for my redating of the *Discourse* to 1596, see 31 below.
[7] W. L. Rutton, *Three Branches of the Family of Wentworth* (1897), 242; P. Wentworth, *A Pithie Exhortation to her Majestie for establishing her Successors to the Crowne, whereunto is added a Discourse containing the Author's Opinion of the True and Lawfull Successor to her Majestie* (Edinburgh, 1598); W. J. Couper, *Robert Waldegrave, King's Printer for Scotland* (Glasgow, 1916).
[8] P. Collinson, *The Elizabethan Puritan Movement* (1967), 385–431.
[9] D. Calderwood, *The True History of the Kirk of Scotland*, ed. T. Thomson (Edinburgh, 1842–9), v, 88, 106; O. Chadwick, 'Richard Bancroft's submission', *JEH*, 3 (1952), 58–73; A. F. Scott Pearson, *Thomas Cartwright and Elizabethan Puritanism 1535–1603* (Cambridge, 1925), 463–4.

confession, involved him in Wentworth's plans. Bromley in turn probably recruited Walsh, his fellow member for Worcestershire. A further
four MPs were also questioned at this time about a conference they had
attended at Lincoln's Inn with Wentworth, to discuss his proposed parliamentary campaign. They were Henry Apsley, Richard Blount, Oliver
St John of Bedfordshire and Humphrey Winch.[10]

In so far as any common thread can be discerned linking this group
together, apart from the succession question, it is religion. Of the four
imprisoned members, at least three were strong puritans: Bromley,
Stephens and Wentworth. Bromley married as his second wife, in 1591,
the widowed Mrs Elizabeth Palmer (*née* Verney) of Parham in Sussex,
whom Stephens describes in family letters as his 'sister'; a number of
marriage suitors had been considered, and apart from the conventional
bargaining over money matters they were in addition subjected to intense
religious scrutiny. Thus, Sir William Bowes, who made the initial running, was eventually rejected, partly on the grounds of being 'unsound'
on the doctrine of justification and that he 'erred' concerning church
government. In reaching their decision Mrs Palmer and her 'brother'
Stephens, the latter acting in an advisory role, had consulted some of the
leading lights of the Elizabethan puritan movement, including Thomas
Cartwright, Stephen Egerton and Walter Travers. The fact that in the
event it was Bromley who won out speaks volumes for his standing among
the godly.[11] As regards the puritanism of Wentworth there is most obviously the evidence of his parliamentary career, especially his involvement
in the presbyterian scheme of 1587; also by the late 1570s his home at
Lillingstone Lovell – then in Oxfordshire – had become noted as a centre
for puritan worship.[12]

Of the four remaining MPs involved with Wentworth in 1593, three
again have demonstrable puritan affinities. Apsley, who lived at Ore in
Sussex, had introduced a parliamentary bill in 1589 against pluralities
and non-residence, and in 1603 can be found agitating in the cause of
further reformation.[13] Blount's household at Dedisham, also in Sussex,
was later to be described in glowing terms by Edward Topsell, a cleric
of distinctly puritan stripe, as a place where 'we had Christ at the table
every day, I mean the holy scriptures'. Topsell went on to say of Blount

---

[10] Neale, 'Peter Wentworth', 187–95; BL, Harleian MS 6846, fos. 65–108. Also involved, although
not an MP, was 'Black' Oliver St John of Wiltshire.
[11] West Sussex RO, Par 147/2/1, p. 5 (26 November 1591); HMC, *Sixth Report*, 345–6. The financial
aspects too of the marriage contract were vetted by these puritan clergy.
[12] Neale, 'Peter Wentworth', 46–52.
[13] P. W. Hasler (ed.), *The History of Parliament: The House of Commons 1558–1603* (1981), I, 347–8.

himself that 'you have ever loved our nation, I mean the preachers' and 'unto your commendation do al the prophets, and the children of the prophets, give testimony'.[14] In 1608, the year before Topsell's comments were published, a posthumous work by William Perkins had appeared in print with a dedication to St John, by the nonconformist divine Thomas Pierson.[15]

Nevertheless, of the seven MPs associated with Wentworth and the succession question in 1593 only one, as we shall see, looks to have stayed the course. This was Sir Henry Bromley, eldest son of Lord Chancellor Bromley, who had died in 1587. Released from prison after the end of the 1593 parliament, the following year Bromley was a member of the official English embassy sent to Scotland for the christening of Prince Henry. Led by Robert Ratcliffe, fifth Earl of Sussex, and Philip, third Lord Wharton, Bromley was the third most senior of this twelve-man delegation. It also included two of Bromley's brothers-in-law, Oliver Cromwell and Edward Greville.[16] Bromley, Cromwell and Greville may all three have owed their presence in Scotland to Robert Devereux, second Earl of Essex. Certainly, Mrs Palmer can be found entertaining Essex at Parham in 1590, the year before her marriage to Bromley and the latter was to emerge as a committed follower of the earl by the time of his rebellion in 1601 – being imprisoned as a result.[17] Moreover, the likelihood that Essex was acting as the patron of Bromley and his brothers-in-law in 1594 is strengthened by the knowledge that at this very time the earl was in direct communication with the Scottish king.[18]

---

[14] E. Topsell, *The House-holder: or, Perfect Man* (1609), sigs. A4v–A6v. For the puritan sympathies of Topsell see N. Tyacke, *Aspects of English Protestantism c. 1530–1700* (Manchester, 2001), 16, 90–110.

[15] W. Perkins, *A Godly and Learned Exposition of Christs Sermon on the Mount* (Cambridge, 1608), sigs. ¶ 3–¶ 4v; J. Eales, 'Thomas Pierson and the transmission of the moderate puritan tradition', *Midland History*, 20 (1995), 75–102.

[16] Hasler, *The House of Commons 1558–1603*, I, 491. Unfortunately this biography is seriously in error as regards the wives of Sir Henry Bromley. His third wife was the widowed Mrs Anne Knatchbull, daughter of Sir Thomas Scott of Scot's Hall in Kent, *not* Anne Beswick. Evidently Bromley had a penchant for marrying widows. Thus Mrs Anne Offley (*née* Beswick), *not* 'Appleby', was his fourth and final wife: J. R. Scott, *Memorials of the Family of Scott, of Scot's Hall, in the County of Kent* (1876), 227, 254–5; T. Habington, *A Survey of Worcestershire*, ed. J. Amphlett (1895–9), II, 122–3; *CSP Scotland, 1593–5*, 418; G. Grazebrook and J. P. Rylands (eds.), *The Visitation of Shropshire . . . 1623* (Harleian Society, 28, 1889), 78.

[17] HMC, *Sixth Report*, 346; Hasler, *The House of Commons 1558–1603*, I, 491. Another brother-in-law of Bromley, John Littleton, was condemned to death for his part in Essex's rebellion – dying in prison: Grazebrook and Rylands (eds.), *The Visitation of Shropshire . . . 1623*, 78; *CSPD, 1601–3*, 89.

[18] T. Birch, *Memoirs of the Reign of Queen Elizabeth* (1754), I, 175–6; P. E. J. Hammer, *The Polarization of English Politics. The Political Career of Robert Devereux, 2nd Earl of Essex, 1585–1597* (Cambridge, 2000), 168–73. The fifth Earl of Sussex was also to be involved in Essex's rebellion: L. Stone, *The Crisis of the Aristocracy 1558–1641* (Oxford, 1965), 484.

Given the diplomatic sensitivity of the occasion, the presence of Bromley at the baptism of Prince Henry, first-born son of James VI and by implication eventual heir to Elizabeth, is on the face of it remarkable. Nevertheless, the position of the English government itself was highly ambiguous, the queen refusing to recognise James as her successor while promising not to do anything which might prejudice his title.[19] At the christening ceremony, on 30 August 1594 in Stirling Castle, Sussex played a central role as the representative of the queen, carrying the infant Prince Henry to the chapel and again during the baptismal service. (Apart from Robert Bowes, the resident ambassador, Wharton and Bromley were the only other English present in the chapel.) Patrick Galloway preached the sermon and Bishop David Cunningham of Aberdeen, who performed the actual baptism, delivered an oration. Cunningham, however, in his remarks touched on James's claim to the English throne, provoking a subsequent protest to the king by ambassador Bowes.[20] But even more provocative from the official English point of view was a congratulatory poem published at this time by the Scottish presbyterian leader Andrew Melville. Entitled *Principis Scoti-Britannorum Natalia* and published at Edinburgh by Waldegrave, Melville's verses allude to Henry as ultimate ruler of the two kingdoms. The poem also has an engraved title-page, featuring a haloed female figure with a book and candle in either hand and the motto '*veritas vincet tandem*'. The '*veritas*' in question was presumably that of religion, whose victories from a presbyterian point of view were still to win in England rather than Scotland. King James had given permission to publish these verses of Melville, although when challenged by Bowes denied having read them. As to their content and the oration by Bishop Cunningham, the king expressed the view that 'being descended as he was, he could not but make claim to the Crown of England after the decease of her Majesty'.[21] More generally, of course, the very name Henry was a standing reminder of the Tudor lineage of the Scottish royal house.[22]

Sussex set out back to England on 12 September 1594, Bromley and his brothers-in-law one assumes going with him. In light of later events,

---

[19] H. G. Stafford, *James VI of Scotland and the Throne of England* (New York, 1940), 10. According to some accounts, Elizabeth had not originally intended to send a special representative to the christening of Prince Henry: T. Birch, *The Life of Henry Prince of Wales* (1760), 14.

[20] T. Rymer, *Foedera* (1739–45), VII, pt i, 157; *CSP Scotland, 1593–5*, 422, 431.

[21] A. Melville, *Principis Scoti-Britannorum Natalia* (Edinburgh, 1594); *CSP Scotland, 1593–5*, 430–1.

[22] Prince Henry's paternal grandfather was Henry Lord Darnley, himself the great-grandson of Henry VII.

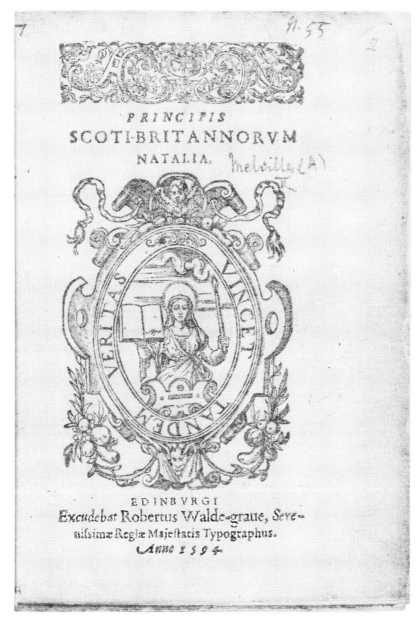

Title-page of Andrew Melville's *Principis Scoti-Britannorum Natalia* (Edinburgh, 1594).
Reproduced by permission of the British Library: shelfmark 1213. 1. 9. (2).

however, some of the Scottish contacts made by Bromley while on this embassy would appear to have been maintained during the remainder of Elizabeth's reign. Moreover, he now acquired as a member of his household a Scot, John Hay, who was probably used for carrying messages. By his own account, Hay was the grandson of a laird and a former student of Robert Rollock at Edinburgh University. He had been recommended to Bromley, so he said, by Bowes. In 1600 Hay was to be arrested at Durham on suspicion of being a Catholic priest, while journeying to Scotland, which is how these details survive.[23] By the eve of Essex's rebellion Bromley was sufficiently well known in Scottish circles for his name to be enciphered in code along with that of Anthony Bacon, secretary to Essex.[24]

Indirect but none the less suggestive evidence of the thinking of Bromley and his circle in these years is furnished by a work printed in 1595. Entitled *Bromleion*, its author was a puritan preacher who simply signs himself with the initials S. I. At the present time of writing the identity of S. I. continues to prove elusive, despite his apparently having published three separate works between 1595 and 1601.[25] Sir Henry Bromley is the principal dedicatee of *Bromleion*, which is largely taken up with a Calvinist theological exposition of justification and predestination, the author acknowledging both him and his father, the late Lord Chancellor, as patrons. S. I. prays to God that Sir Henry, 'his great frend and favourer', might 'rise from credit, to worship, and honour, and princely favour, that you might match, or at lestwise come as neare as might be, to that high degree, which your noble father possessed'. But he also holds up the model of Francis Russell, second Earl of Bedford, who had died in 1585:

wishing that your name and credit may be such as was that of the right honourable the earle of Bedford, who had deservedly gotten this title – the good earl of Bedford, that in religion to God, and to the Church, in loialtie and faithfulnesse to the prince and the realme, in love and liberalitie to learning and poore scholars, in care and bountifulnesse to the poore and needie, you may according to your deserts carrie the godlie and honourable title in the mouthes of all men, that when they name you they may so report of you to be the good knight Sir Henry Bromley.[26]

[23] *CSP Scotland, 1593–5*, 438; *Calendar of Border Papers, 1595–1603*, 680–1; *CSP Scotland, 1597–1603*, 920.

[24] J. Bruce (ed.), *Correspondence of James VI of Scotland with Sir Robert Cecil and Others in England, during the Reign of Queen Elizabeth* (Camden Society, 78, 1861), 88.

[25] S. I., *Bromleion. A Discourse of the Most Substantial Points of Divinity* (1595), *Two Treatises. One of the Latter Day of Judgement, the Other of the Joyes of Heaven* (1600), *Certaine Godlie and Learned Sermons. Made upon Six Parables* (1601).

[26] S. I., *Bromleion*, sigs. *2–*3.

In his 1585 funeral sermon Thomas Sparke does indeed confirm that Bedford was 'commonly' known as the 'good', elaborating on how he 'hated the least rag, relick and clout of the Romishe harlot, every day more and more unto his death'. No 'vaine and prophane politike', Bedford was also, according to Sparke, a 'trustie . . . patron of the commonweale'.[27]

Although Bromley's estates were located in both Shropshire and Worcestershire, the connections of S. I. seem to have been predominantly with the former county. Thus, two of the subsidiary dedications in his *Bromleion* are to the Shropshire JPs Rowland Barker and Francis Newport, the latter being described as one of his 'chiefest friends'. He also refers to Lady Margaret Newport, the mother of Francis and a Bromley by birth, as having 'bountifully relieved and comforted my father and mother', adding that 'many householdes in Shropshire, especially in Shrewsbury, may saie the same'.[28] In his last published work, a collection of sermons which appeared in 1601, S. I. writes of himself as living in the 'neighbour diocesse' to Worcester – which probably implies that of Hereford.[29]

The puritanism of S. I. is revealed not so much by the enthusiastic terms in which he endorses the views of Theodore Beza on predestination, as by some of his dedicatory remarks. Rowland Barker, for instance, is lauded as 'a great favourer of the gospell' in Shropshire, whereas 'most gentlemen are set against it'. In urging Barker to 'promote and further the same more and more', S. I. also refers to Hezekiah, who 'caused the brazen serpent to be pulled down', and Nebuchadnezzar, who was 'a notable meane to deface idolatrie'. As for bishops, 'would to God the reverend fathers of the land . . . had that care as Bishop Hooper and Bishop Latimer had to see the people taught and instructed in everie parish throughout their diocese'. Dedicating his sermons of 1601 to Bishop Gervase Babington, recently appointed Bishop of Worcester, he returned to the same subject. Rumours of Babington being a favourer of 'a learned ministry' had gone before him and S. I. now adjured him to keep back unlearned candidates from ordination 'till they be sufficient, or debar them'. Unlearned clergy already beneficed should be made 'to bestowe some part of their living uppon sufficient and able men', in order to help them 'discharge that waightie dutie which lyeth upon them'. This and a further dedication in *Bromleion* to Dean Alexander

---

[27] T. Sparke, *A Sermon preached at Cheanies . . . 1585* (1585), 78–80. During the late 1580s Sparke was to assist Wentworth in revising the manuscript of his *Pithie Exhortation*: BL, Harleian MS 6846, fo. 101r–v.

[28] Hasler, *The House of Commons 1558–1603*, I, 491; S. I., *Bromleion*, 351–5, 415–16; Grazebrook and Rylands (eds.), *Visitation of Shropshire . . . 1623*, 77.

[29] S. I. *Certaine Godlie and Learned Sermons*, sig. ¶ 4.

Nowell of St Paul's, 'praying God to keepe such men as your selfe long among us', would suggest that S. I. at least was not an uncompromising presbyterian.[30]

In some ways most interesting, however, is the concluding peroration of *Bromleion*, which stands by itself and bears the initials R. T. Its theme is that of England as a beleaguered isle, the fate of which hangs by the thread of the life of Queen Elizabeth, 'under the shadow of whose wings, by the great providence of God, we have these thirtie seven yeares bene shrouded from many daungers and mightily protected from suddaine perilles, at home and abroad'. Yet 'the mallice of the whole world and the hatred of the greatest princes and men of might is kindled and inflamed against us, partlie through envie of our wealth, and partly for the hate they have of true religion'. In consequence the demise of the queen, whenever it occurs,

> cannot be but the end of our prosperitie, whose day of death shall be the beginning of our wofull wretchednesse, whose rest with God in eternall peace our entrance into troubles in this commonwealth, her yeelding to nature . . . the first steppe and degree as it were to our miserable calamitie.

There are distinct echoes here of the kind of arguments deployed by Wentworth in his quest to have the heir to the throne officially declared during Elizabeth's lifetime, although the author understandably offers no such resolution of the problem so dramatically highlighted. Even if the censorship could have been evaded, the likely punishment for thus arguing in print would have been imprisonment.[31]

II

Of those gaoled back in 1593 for their activities concerning the succession all had been freed within the year save Peter Wentworth. This partly reflects the fact that he was the recognised ringleader but also, as the years passed, his continued refusal to accept the conditions attached to being released. For Wentworth resolutely denied any wrongdoing; nor was he prepared to abandon the cause which had led to this latest period of detention.[32] Nevertheless, from May 1593 onwards Wentworth enjoyed the 'libertie' of the Tower, provided that a servant of the lieutenant accompanied him on such walks. Similarly his 'sonnes, freindes, and phisicions' were permitted to visit him, although their conversations

---

[30] S. I., *Bromleion*, sig. *2v, 351–5, 453–6, *Certaine Godlie and Learned Sermons*, sigs. ¶ 3–¶ 6v.
[31] S. I., *Bromleion*, 563–4; Wentworth, *Pithie Exhortation*, *passim*.
[32] Neale, 'Peter Wentworth', 200–2.

were supposed to be monitored. He was also attended by 'one of his owne servants', and subsequently his wife Elizabeth was allowed to join him.[33] It is also clear from surviving letters and petitions, along with a poem, that Wentworth had access to writing materials.[34] Freshly aroused suspicion on the part of the authorities led to a search of his room in July 1596, but this only turned up a copy of the 1587 *Pithie Exhortation*.[35] By then, however, he had almost certainly written and safely dispatched a new clandestine work – his *Discourse* in reply to *A Conference about the Next Succession to the Crowne of Ingland*.

The *Conference*, widely ascribed at the time and since to the Jesuit Robert Parsons writing under the pseudonym of R. Doleman, may in fact have been the product of more than one author. It carries the date 1594 on the title page, yet appears not actually to have been published until about September 1595, at Antwerp, when the English government first came to hear of it.[36] The book is a masterly piece of writing, which very cleverly exploits, in the Catholic interest, the by now notorious unwillingness of Elizabeth to name her successor. Purporting to relate a series of discussions among a religiously mixed group of mainly English and Irish at Amsterdam, during the months of April and May 1593, the *Conference* is set against the background of the English parliament meeting at this time. An initial assumption, we are told, was that 'some thing would be determined . . . in that parliament' as regards the succession. Instead, however, news came that 'nothing at all had bin done therin, but rather that one or two . . . had bin checked or committed for speaking in the same'. (Here a marginal note in the text reads: 'Mr Bromely. Mr Wentworth'.) A debate allegedly then ensued, among those at Amsterdam, about the reasons for this turn of events, the conclusion being that any such declaration of a successor in Elizabeth's lifetime was indeed politically unsafe and hence the wisdom in leaving the matter unresolved. There followed by general request, so the narrative goes on to claim, two expositions, both by lawyers, one about the laws of succession and the other concerning the pros and cons of the various existing 'pretenders' to the English throne.[37]

---

[33] *APC, 1592–3*, 269. Elizabeth Wentworth, sister of the late Sir Francis Walsingham, was apparently living in the Tower by November 1595 and certainly died there in July 1596: Neale, 'Peter Wentworth', 198–9, Rutton, *Three Branches of the Family of Wentworth*, 242.

[34] Neale, 'Peter Wentworth', 200–2; BL, Egerton MS 3139 B.

[35] HMC, *Salisbury*, VII, 284, 288–9.

[36] R. Doleman, *A Conference about the Next Succession to the Crowne of Ingland* (n.p. 1594); L. Hicks, 'Father Robert Parsons S. J. and the book of the succession', *Recusant History*, 4: 3 (1957), 104–37; A. Collins (ed.), *Letters and Memorials of State* (1746), I, 350; F. Peck, *Desiderata Curiosa* (1732), I, bk v, 8–9.

[37] Doleman, *Conference*, sigs. B–B5v.

The first of these expositions, comprising part one of Doleman's *Conference*, argues that 'propinquitie or ancestry of blood alone' is 'not sufficient to be admitted to a crowne, without other conditions and circumstances'. It transpires that fitness to rule must be the overriding consideration, and the possible grounds for disqualification include religion.[38] This, of course, was especially designed to undermine the hereditary claim of the Protestant James VI in the eyes of Catholics and the second exposition elaborates the case against him. Few English or Scots are said to desire such a union of crowns, believing that the disadvantages outweigh any likely gains. England, for example, would acquire an economically impoverished partner and Scotland lose its independence. Furthermore, the Protestant argument in terms of 'true religion' is fatally flawed because of the nature of Scottish Presbyterianism.

And when the archbishopes, bishopes, deanes, archdeacons, and other such of ecclesiastical and honorable dignities of Ingland, shal consider that no such dignity or promotion is left now standing in Scotland, no nor any cathedral or collegiate church is remayned on foote, with the rents and dignities thereunto apperteyning, and when our nobilytie shal remember how the nobilitie of Scotland is subject at this day to a few ordinary and common ministers, without any head, who in their synodes and assemblies have authority to put to the horne [i.e. outlaw], and drive out of the realme any noble man whatsoever without remedie or redresse, except he will yeald and humble himselfe to them, and that the king himselfe standeth in awe of this exorbitant and popular power of his ministers, and is content to yeld therunto: it is to be thought . . . that few Inglish, be they of what religion or opinion so-ever, will show themselves forward to receave such a king, in respect of his religion, that hath no better order in his own house.[39]

According to the *Conference* there are 'three religions in England', consisting of 'protestants, puritanes, and papistes'. Fighting will almost certainly break out among these groups when Elizabeth dies. In general, the Protestants are the people currently in power. Although they have no agreed candidate, Arabella Stuart has considerable support – including that of William Cecil, Lord Burghley.[40] The English puritans on the whole favour Henry Hastings, third Earl of Huntingdon and a Yorkist descendant, rather than King James. Likely to side with them are both the City of London and the French. 'The puritan partye at home in Ingland is thought to be most vigorouse of any other, that is to say most ardent, quick, bold, resolute, and to have a great part of the best

38 Doleman, *Conference*, title-page *verso* and pt i, 212–20.
39 Doleman, *Conference*, pt ii, 118–19, 123.   40 Doleman, *Conference*, pt ii, 236, 239–41.

captaines and soldiers on their side'. They also command a significant following in the 'navy'.[41] Lastly there are the Catholics, especially 'great and stronge' in country districts, whose primary commitment is to a Catholic successor. Their best bet, so the argument runs, is the Infanta Isabella of Spain, daughter of Philip II and Elizabeth of Valois, whose claim to the English throne derives from William the Conqueror as well as John of Gaunt.[42]

The *Conference* concludes that an English civil war is virtually inevitable, but to declare the heir in advance of Elizabeth's death would merely precipitate the crisis. Probably no all-out winner, however, will emerge from the coming succession struggle. Instead the result is likely to be a 'composition' or 'agreement', of the kind currently being hammered out in France as the Wars of Religion drew to a close.[43] Yet regardless of who ended up tolerating whom, the implication is that the king of Scots will play no part. Moreover, as a final piece of mischief, this remarkable *tour de force* was dedicated to the Earl of Essex. 'No man is in more high and eminent place or dignitie at this day in our realme' and none 'like to have a greater part or sway in deciding of this great affaire, when tyme shall come for that determination'. Privately, the Parsons circle were in little doubt that Burghley, not Essex, 'ruled the roost' at the English Court.[44] Nor can they have entertained much hope that Essex would come to back a Catholic claimant. As with the case of James VI, the object was seemingly to sow maximum confusion among the Protestant ranks.

The cautious stance of the English government as regards the succession had in effect played into the hands of the Catholics, allowing the author or authors of the *Conference* to claim that the whole matter was 'extreme doubtful'. A fog of uncertainty had been allowed to descend, as a result of failing to assert the strict hereditary principle. In these circumstances it is unsurprising that Wentworth and certain of his associates concluded that something must be done to dispel the 'darknes' now enveloping the 'light and right of succession'.[45] Specifically King James, the candidate whom allegedly few in England supported, needed rescuing as the true heir. This required both drawing a veil over the religious divisions among Protestants and winning round the radicals. Who better qualified to attempt this feat than Wentworth, with his impressive

---

[41] Doleman, *Conference*, pt ii, 242–4.   [42] Doleman, *Conference*, pt ii, 244–8, 263–4.

[43] Doleman, *Conference*, pt ii, 258–63.

[44] Doleman, *Conference*, sigs. *2-*3; A. G. Petti (ed.), *The Letters and Despatches of Richard Verstegan (c. 1550–1640)*, (Catholic Record Society, 52, 1959), xxx; Elizabeth was reportedly angered by the dedication of Doleman's *Conference* to Essex: *Letters and Memorials of State*, 357, 360.

[45] Doleman, *Conference*, title-page *verso*; Wentworth, *Pithie Exhortation*, pt ii, 2.

parliamentary and prison record concerning the succession question? Certainly some such thinking helps to explain the action of those who now undertook the potentially very hazardous task of conveying a copy of Doleman's *Conference* into the Tower for Wentworth to read, persuading him to write a reply, and then smuggling this out. As regards the identity of the courier, an obvious candidate would seem to be Mrs Elizabeth Wentworth.[46]

The reply of Wentworth to the *Conference*, his so-called *Discourse*, takes the form of a letter. It reveals that he and his correspondent had previously discussed the succession and that Wentworth had not always been of the same opinion. Somewhat confusingly, he refers to both 'your' and 'our freinds' whose doubts his reply is aimed at resolving. (Are we dealing here with two distict albeit overlapping groups?) The main thrust of the letter is to defend the hereditary right of James to succeed Elizabeth, as a person who can be trusted to uphold 'our religion and lawes'.[47] This undertaking was undoubtedly made easier by the fact that the third Earl of Huntingdon had died in December 1595, and the fourth Earl lacked the godly reputation of his predecessor.[48] In so far as Wentworth dealt with the issue of church reform and what the coming of the Scottish king might bode, his attitude was that the succession took priority.

I have not a litle stoode with some of my friends, whither this [latter] question was more to be regarded then the matter of discipline. And I thinke by such practises [as Doleman's *Conference*] we have sufficient proofe that this is the foundation and pillar, on which the realme and religion doth rest.

Accordingly all Protestants should rally as a matter of life or death to the cause of James.[49]

Whether Wentworth's *Discourse* initially circulated in manuscript is unclear. As we have remarked, it and the *Pithie Exhortation* were printed together posthumously in 1598. No one apparently ever claimed overall responsibilty, but the whole production looks to have been carefully orchestrated. Thus the book came out in print, according to the title page, the year after the death of Wentworth, when it could do him no harm,

---

[46] Since Mrs Wentworth was present in the Tower voluntarily, she presumably could come and go relatively freely.
[47] Wentworth, *Pithie Exhortation*, pt ii, 2, 6, 8, 48. Space does not permit an analysis of the sophisticated legal and political arguments advanced by Wentworth.
[48] C. Cross, *The Puritan Earl. The Life of Henry Hastings Third Earl of Huntingdon 1536–1595* (1966), 271, 274.
[49] Wentworth, *Pithie Exhortation*, pt ii, 5 and *passim*.

with a highly crafted introductory preface and extensive marginal notes –
both supplied by the editor, who was clearly English.[50] The decision to
publish in Scotland, rather than for example in the Netherlands, is also
striking. Although neither publisher nor place of printing are indicated,
the Waldegrave press in Edinburgh was soon identified as the source.[51]
Even if it is argued that Robert Waldegrave himself was the editor, he
would still have needed briefing as well as furnishing with the manuscript
copy; above all, the political stakes involved strongly suggest that he was
acting under instructions. Indeed, the Scottish court, perhaps at the top-
most level, must have played some part in this putting of Wentworth onto
the public stage. But what of the English intermediaries? Waldegrave's
own contacts were probably too lowly to have supplied the channel. More
likely is that those who had persuaded Wentworth once more to take up
his pen in the cause of succession retained a controlling interest.[52]

In this connection Sir Henry Bromley has to be a prime suspect. Quite
apart from the fact that Doleman's *Conference* singled him out along with
Wentworth, he was a man with the requisite Scottish links – having
worshipped so to say in the land of the rising sun, in 1594, when he had
attended the christening of Prince Henry. A case can also be made that
Bromley personally prepared Wentworth's manuscript for publication.
Thus, the editor writes: 'I have thought it expedient that hee who hath
spoken in the Parliament with so great regarde and good liking of all
the hearers should nowe as it were with his owne mouth speak to all the
subjects of England'. Among the seven MPs involved with Wentworth
in 1593 only Bromley had sat in parliament as early as 1587 and could
therefore have heard his last recorded speech.[53] Moreover, the editor,
on three separate occasions, glosses statements by Wentworth in the
Pithie Exhortation as having reference to King James, on the grounds of
'being acquainted with his meaning' and this certainly suggests a close
confidant. The mask, however, never truly slips, although the declared

---

[50] *Ibid.*, preface, where Elizabeth is referred to as 'our gracious and soveraigne ladie'.
[51] *CSP Scotland, 1597–1603*, 583, 587. Wentworth's book would appear from this correspondence
not actually to have been published until late 1599.
[52] In February 1598 David Foulis can be found negotiating with Waldegrave, on behalf of King
James, about the projected publication of a Latin treatise on the succession: *CSP Scotland,
1597–1603*, 167. As early as 1594 Foulis was on close terms with members of Essex's inner
circle, and between March and October 1596 he resided in London as Scottish ambassador: BL,
Add. MS 4125, fos. 38, 41, 157, 160–70, 172, *CSP Scotland, 1595–7*, 160, 338. Did Wentworth's
manuscript travel with Foulis to Scotland, in the diplomatic bag?
[53] Wentworth, *Pithie Exhortation*, preface; Hasler, *The House of Commons 1558–1603*, I, 347–8, 450,
491; III, 324, 444–5, 570, 600, 632–3.

motives for publishing the book are said to include the 'preservation and *advancement* of religion', which hints at an underlying puritan agenda.[54]

III

In retrospect one might think that the trust reposed in James VI by the 'freinds' of Peter Wentworth was naive. Not only had Scottish religious policy lurched from the Black Acts of 1584 to the Golden Act of 1592, but it has been claimed that between 1596 and 1612 'the crown advanced inexorably to overturn presbyterian dominance'. Yet at the time puritan reformers could take courage from Beza's encomium on James, written from Geneva in November 1596 and published at Edinburgh the following year by Waldegrave, where the king is described as having 'joined to his singular and admirable care and watchfulness in defending the gospel, and preserving the purity and unspotted sincerity' of the Scottish church, 'so great and exact knowledge of the Christian religion, from the very grounds and principles thereof, that the Lord it seems hath made his majesty both a prince and preacher to his people'.[55] Also, the mixed polity which emerged in early-seventeenth-century Scotland, combining elements of presbytery with episcopacy, remained more radical than anything obtaining in England until the Civil War of the 1640s.[56]

During the 1590s there indeed appeared a great deal still to play for, many of the fears expressed in Doleman's *Conference* mirroring the hopes of English puritans. Nor should we conclude that, because James succeeded Elizabeth peacefully in 1603, the anxieties earlier expressed on this score were simply paranoid. Arguably crucial here was the decision of Spain, in the event, not to field a Catholic candidate.[57] Moreover, just as Scottish developments were linked to the rivalries of court factions so in England the emerging split, in the last decade of the sixteenth century, between the followers of Essex and the Cecils had far-reaching implications. Essex, in fact, became a magnet for all those dissatisfied with their existing lot, including the puritans. At the same time he increasingly identified himself with the cause of James VI, and had the attempted rebellion

---

[54] Wentworth, *Pithie Exhortation*, preface and pt i, 37, 71, 93. My italics

[55] J. Goodare, *State and Society in Early Modern Scotland* (Oxford, 1999), 194–6; R. Rollock, *Select Works*, ed. W. M. Gunn (Edinburgh, 1844–9), I, 1–12. Originally published in Latin, with a dedication to James VI, an English version of this work by Rollock appeared at London in 1603.

[56] W. R. Foster, *The Church before the Covenants. The Church of Scotland 1596–1638* (Edinburgh, 1975), esp. chs. 4–5.

[57] A. J. Loomie, *Guy Fawkes in Spain: the 'Spanish Treason' in Spanish Documents* (*BIHR* Supplement no. 9, 1971), 4–17.

or *coup*, as it is better described, of February 1601 succeeded this would apparently have been followed by a formal recognition of the Scottish king as heir to the English throne. Essex also posed as a champion of domestic reform, although the details remained vague.[58]

Among those faced with ruin or worse as a result of the failure of Essex's rebellion was Bromley, who had played a potentially key role in trying to raise armed suppport in London. Consigned to prison for his activities, he was not released until over a year later – in May 1602.[59] Far from this putting a damper on his political scheming, however, when Elizabeth finally died on 24 March 1603 Bromley was among those who rode post-haste to Scotland, as did his brother-in-law Oliver Cromwell. They may well have been joined there by Bromley's other brother-in-law Edward Greville. Certainly, all three had been appointed gentlemen of the English Privy Chamber by May 1603, which strongly suggests that the links with James VI, established ten years earlier at the time of Prince Henry's christening, had been maintained.[60] It was Cromwell also who entertained the new king at Hinchingbrooke, in Huntingdonshire, between 27 and 29 April, so magnificently, according to the contemporary account of the royal progress south, 'as the like had not beene seene in any place . . . since his first setting forward out of Scotland'.[61]

---

[58] Hammer *Polarization of English Politics*, 389–404; J. Guy (ed.), *The Reign of Elizabeth I. Court and Culture in the Last Decade* (Cambridge,1995), 46–86; Collinson, *Elizabethan Puritan Movement*, 444–7; Stafford, *James VI of Scotland and the Throne of England*, 198–224; *CSPD, 1598–1601*, 554, 556–7, 566, *CSPD, 1601–3*, 2; cf. M. James, 'At a crossroads of the political culture: the Essex Revolt, 1601', in his *Society, Politics and Culture. Studies in Early Modern England* (Cambridge, 1986), 416–65. In the immediate aftermath of the Essex rebellion, the English Privy Council got wind of what they assumed was a new Dutch edition of Wentworth's book on the succession: *APC, 1600–1601*, 216, PRO, SP 84/61, fos. 81v–82, 87. The printer involved was Richard Schilders, who over a long career produced a stream of works by English puritans, but no copy of such an edition is known to survive and Schilders may in this instance have simply been acting as a distributor of the 1598 Scottish edition: N. Japikse (ed.), *Resolutiën der Staten-General, 1600–1601* (The Hague, 1941), 475–6, J. Dover Wilson, 'Richard Schilders and the English puritans', *Transactions of the Bibliographical Society*, 11 (1909–11), 65–134. Nevertheless the date of this 1601 initiative remains highly significant.

[59] *CSPD, 1598–1601*, 559; *CSPD, 1601–33*, 4. Yet another brother-in-law of Bromley, Sir John Scott, was party to his abortive attempt: *CSPD, 1598–1601*, 559, *CSPD, 1601–3*, 4, Scott, *Memorials of the Family of Scott*, 254–5. N. E. McClure (ed.), *The Letters of John Chamberlain*, 2 vols. (Philadelphia, 1939), I, 145.

[60] McClure *Letters of John Chamberlain*, I, 189; HMC, *Salisbury*, XV, 19; HMC, *Seventh Report*, 526; BL, Harleian MS 6166, fo. 68v; N. Cuddy, 'Anglo-Scottish Union and the court of James I, 1603–1625', *TRHS*, 39 (1989), 109–10.

[61] J. Nichols (ed.), *The Progresses, Processions and Magnificent Festivities of King James the First*, I, 96–101. Cromwell owed part of his wealth to having married the widow of Sir Horatio Palavicino in July 1601. This marriage had the approval of Robert Cecil, in his capacity of overseer of Palavicino's will, but it does not follow that Cromwell was therefore the 'political ally' of Cecil: L. Stone, *An Elizabethan: Sir Horatio Palavicino* (Oxford, 1958), 299–310.

In addition Henry Wriothesley, third Earl of Southampton and recently released Essex conspirator, was chosen by the king to bear 'the sword before him . . . to Maister Oliver Cromwell's house'.[62]

How far Bromley, Cromwell and Greville were operating as a team at this point remains uncertain. But for Bromley, at any rate, more than simply personal ambition was at stake, as emerges from a diary entry by the London lawyer John Manningham, dated 10 April 1603, who writes that

> there is a foolishe rime runnes up and downe in the court of Sir Henry Bromley, Lord Thomas Haward [Howard], Lord Cobham, and the Deane of Canterbury, Dr Nevil, that eache should goe to move the king for what they like:
>> Nevil for the protestant, Lord Thomas for the papist,
>> Bromley for the puritan, and Lord Cobham for the atheist.

On the face of it, this reference to Bromley is surprising because his name does not otherwise feature in the puritan agitation for church reform then being mounted. The explanation, however, may well be that for Bromley and his associates religious change in 1603 was only one facet of a grander design the lineaments of which dated back at least to the 1601 Essex rebellion, when it had been planned both to remove the Cecilians from power and to reform the commonwealth.[63]

Such a puritan blueprint in fact survives among the State Papers Domestic, but because of its anonymity and the extremely brief calendar entry – a mere three lines – the evidence until now has been largely ignored.[64] The nineteenth-century editor ascribed this 'memorial' to

---

[62] The sword in question was that of the borough of Huntingdon, and in the normal course of events would have been returned by the king directly to the senior bailiff: Nichols, *Progresses, Processions*, I, 98. Southampton had joined the royal party at Burghley on the evening of 24 April: HMC, *Salisbury*, xv, 58. He may have been privy to the scheme discussed in the remainder of this essay. For a treatment of his political career see N. Cuddy 'The conflicting loyalties of a "vulger counselor": the third Earl of Southampton, 1597–1624', in J. Morrill, P. Slack and D. Woolf (eds.), *Public Duty and Private Conscience in Seventeenth-Century England* (Oxford, 1993), 154–80.

[63] J. Bruce (ed.), *Diary of John Manningham, of the Middle Temple, and of Bradbourne, Kent, Barrister-at-Law, 1602–3* (Camden Society, 99, 1868), 168; BL, Harleian MS 5353, fo. 127v. For a glimpse of the Bromley family in political action, during the Worcestershire election of 1604, see PRO, STAC 8/201/17. At the time Sir Henry Bromley was described as being 'of greatest power and authoritie in court': T. R. Nash, *Collections for the History and Antiquities of Worcestershire* (1781–99), I, xxviii.

[64] An exception must be made for Roger Munden, who ventured some very perceptive remarks in his essay 'James I and "the growth of mutual distrust": King, Commons, and reform, 1603–1604', in K. Sharpe (ed.), *Faction and Parliament. Essays on Early Stuart History* (Oxford, 1978), 44–52; *CSPD, 1603–10*, 7; PRO, SP 14/1, fos. 127–32. This document, which I plan to edit for publication, was the starting point of the present investigation, while Manningham's 'foolishe rime' alerted me to the activities of Bromley.

May 1603, although April or even the end of March seems more likely.[65] Addressed to the new king, the document runs to nine pages and falls into two distinct halves covering 'comonwealth' and 'churche' grievances respectively. There is no preamble, although this may once have existed. Written in the first person and in the same hand throughout, it also contains some clues as to possible authorship. Thus, for example, the writer is particularly well informed about the Court of Chancery, providing details concerning both 'sales of offices' there and the introduction of 'niew fees'. Again, at the end of a list of 'pluralities of offices' comes 'the treasurership of the navie, clerkship of your highnes counsell in the Welch Borders, and secretaryship of the same counsell, with one other office [all] held by one'. (The person being referred to here is Fulke Greville.) As the son of a former Lord Chancellor, Bromley was likely still to have had some chancery contacts, and his own estates lay within the jurisdiction of the Council in the Marches of Wales.[66]

Yet the nature and scope of this 1603 memorial suggest that in reality it was more of a collaborative effort than the product of any single individual. That the document is written in the first person, and was presumably presented by the ostensible author, may indeed be a conscious ploy to avoid allegations of conspiracy.[67] Especially striking in this connection is the wholesale attack on the existing administration as being corrupt. Pluralists are identified by their 'dualities and trialities of great offices, whereof every one is sufficient to mainteyne the honor and expenses of the severall officer', and the accusation levelled that profits which ought to go to the crown are being siphoned off by ministers and their underlings – an example of this being the farm of the 'impost of wynes'. 'Abuses' and 'extortion' are said to be rife. Robert Cecil heads the list of pluralists, as Chief Secretary and Master of the Court of Wards, his 'gayne' from the latter being deemed 'over great for anie subiect'. Wards are sold 'att the second hand, as men do horse and other cattell', often

---

[65] The dating of this memorial is discussed below: 41. Someone has subsequently endorsed it on the back, appropriately enough, as 'A Puritans Plott': PRO, SP 14/1, fo. 132v.

[66] PRO, SP 14/1, fos. 127, 128v. Fulke Greville was to lose the Treasurership of the Navy in 1603 and only retained his Welsh offices with difficulty: R. A. Rebholz, *The Life of Fulke Greville, First Lord Brooke* (Oxford, 1971), 154–80.

[67] The possible involvement of Southampton has been suggested above (fn. 62), although his religious sympathies tended at this time towards Catholicism: *CSPV, 1603–7*, 42. A more probable collaborator would appear to be Sir Henry Neville, of Billingbear in Berkshire, another Essex conspirator and released like Southampton in April 1603. In 1599 Neville was described as 'a puritan and entirely Scottish': Hasler, *The House of Commons, 1558–1603*, III, 122–4; *CSPD, 1598–1601*, 356. Essex, at the time of his rebellion, had considered Neville as a possible secretary of state: *CSPD, 1601–3*, 2.

'forceinge the younge ward to unfytt marriage or to redeeme himself by fyne'. Lord Keeper Egerton and Lord Treasurer Buckhurst are also singled out, along with Sir Walter Raleigh, either as pluralists or vendors of office.[68]

Apart from wardship, other specified burdens on the subject include patents of monopoly, protections for debt, excessive legal fees and purveyance. But redress was not seen simply in terms of a return to 'former tymes', and of particular interest, in the light of subsequent developments, are the proposals for reforming the Court of Wards. King James was offered a number of options, the first involving a 'composition for the payment of a yerelie some . . . rateable by everie one to the value of there lands held *in capite*'. Alternatively a salaried official should be put in charge, 'as is used in the collectting of the customes'. Either way, the revenue to the crown will increase as a result. While a preference was expressed for the first option, the alternative indicates a prejudice in favour of direct customs administration, as opposed to farming, and this is elaborated elsewhere in the memorial. If, however, it is decided after all to retain the Court of Wards, 'one special use maie be made of yt by contractinge the Englishe wards with Scottish gentlemen and gentlewomen . . . whereby both nations maie *coalescere*'. As regards monopolies, fifteen patents are listed as 'not revoked' by the proclamation of 1601, 'but referred to remedy of law, whereby the complaynants are put to great trouble and excessive charge'. The implication is that these fifteen should go the way of the others which had been 'revoked the last Parliament upon the earnest complaint of the lower house'. Apropos purveyors, their 'violent dealinge' with 'poore farmers and countrie people' needs to be brought under control and a fair price paid for what they 'take up'.[69]

Granted that reform of both church and state was very much in the air at the accession of James I in 1603, the two categories have usually been treated as quite distinct. There is indeed contemporary warrant for doing this, not least because religious and secular concerns were often pursued in different venues. A notable feature of the 1603 memorial, however, is that the second section is taken up with religious reform.

---

[68] PRO, SP 14/1, fos. 127–8r. On the growth of corruption generally, from the 1590s onwards, and its political implications see L. L. Peck, *Court Patronage and Corruption in Early Stuart England* (1990).

[69] PRO, SP 14/1, fos. 127–8v; P. L. Hughes and J. F. Larkin (eds.), *Tudor Royal Proclamations* (Newhaven and London, 1964–9), III, 235–8. As regards the customs administration the memorial states that 'the fittest men to informe your highnes . . . are Sir Henry Billingsley, Alderman, Mr Middleton and Mr Carmarden' – a further indication of the collaborative nature of the document: PRO, SP 14/1, fo. 127v.

The first item on this list of church grievances concerns the terms of 'subscription' imposed on the clergy, concluding that 'the groundes and reasons of their refusall to subscribe . . . shal be delivered to your highness in a severall [i.e. separate]'. This last sounds like a reference to what has come to be known as the Millenary Petition, presented to James in April 1603 allegedly in the name of a thousand ministers, and which was instrumental in bringing about the Hampton Court Conference, in 1604, between puritan clergy and members of the ecclesiastical hierarchy. The memorial proceeds to itemise unpreaching ministers, pluralism, non-residence, prophanation of the sabbath, excommunication, the oath *ex officio*, offensive ceremonies, 'exactions of money from poore ministers', licence to marry without banns and prohibition of marriage at certain times of the year, all of which feature too in the Millenary Petition.[70] Yet the former document casts its net far wider, including allegations of simony, attacks on the Court of Faculties, recusancy fines, a request that harsher penalties be imposed for fornication and adultery, 'disorder of noblemen etc. in not cohabiting with their wyves', and abuses involved in touching for the King's Evil. Corruption, in both religion and society, is the common thread running through the two halves of the memorial.[71]

Not only does the apparent anticipation of the Millenary Petition point to an early date for the memorial but the latter most likely helped trigger a letter written on 10 April by James, then at Newcastle, to the English Privy Council, which talks of 'complaints of abuses and corruptions exercised by sundry ministers in the charges committed to them for the government of our people'. The king went on to give instructions that a proclamation be issued promising 'speedy redresse' and announcing his related intention to call a parliament, the chief end of which would be 'the relief of all grievances'. He even included a 'blanck signed with our hand' for the purpose. Although this particular proclamation failed to materialise, one was issued by James in person, on 7 May, at Theobalds, Robert Cecil's country seat and the place that the royal party had then reached on its progress to London. At first sight something of a rag-bag, the Theobalds proclamation can also be read at least in part as a response to concerns raised by the memorial – covering as it does monopolies, protections for debt, excessive fees, purveyance and prophanation of

---

[70] PRO, SP 14/1, fos. 129–31; J. P. Kenyon, *The Stuart Constitution 1603–1688* (Cambridge, 1966, 2nd edn 1986), 117–19.

[71] PRO, SP14/1, fos. 129v, 130v–131. Again individuals are named, including 'La[dy] R[ich]' living apart 'from her husband'. Lady Penelope Rich was, of course, the sister of Essex and in this case religious considerations look to have proved stronger than any possible factional allegiance.

the sabbath.[72] The enthusiastic reaction to the proclamation in puritan circles also tends to confirm this interpretation. 'We joy from our hearts', wrote Andrew Willet, 'to see what reformation your majestie hath begun in the commonwealth'.[73]

IV

The 1603 memorial, with its sweeping plans for change, is an extraordinary document. Probably emanating from the puritan wing of the former Essex faction, the object clearly was to seize the initiative from the Elizabethan old guard in the period of transition following the queen's death on 24 March. With the Privy Council in London and James in Edinburgh something of a political vacuum initially existed and, whereas Bromley and others arrived at the Scottish court within a few days, it was almost a fortnight before the English government had a senior representative at the king's side in the person of Lord Henry Howard, who joined the royal cavalcade at Berwick on 7 April. Robert Cecil did not personally meet up with James until about 17 April, at York, and as late as the Theobalds proclamation of 7 May critics of the regime would appear still to have been making much of the running.[74] Highly effective in the short term, the thinking behind the memorial was, however, strategically flawed and perhaps fatally so, because of false assumptions about the relationship of Robert Cecil and King James. At the time of Essex's rebellion, in February 1601, Cecil was deeply distrusted by James, the king even believing him to be a supporter of the Infanta Isabella. But since then the chief minister of Elizabeth and the Scottish ruler had entered into a secret understanding, as is plain from their surviving correspondence, with the result that Cecil had been transformed from an enemy into a firm friend.[75]

With few exceptions, the English councillors inherited by James from Elizabeth remained safe in their posts and to that extent it was business as usual.[76] Government policy, however, was another matter. Thus,

<hr>

[72] Bod. Lib., Ashmole MS 1729, fos. 68r–v; P. L. Hughes and J. F. Larkin (eds.), *Stuart Royal Proclamations* (Oxford, 1973–83), I, 11–14.
[73] A. Willet, *An Antilogie or Counterplea to an Apologicall Epistle* (1603), sig. *4; N. Tyacke, *Anti-Calvinists. The Rise of English Arminianism c. 1590–1640* (Oxford, 1987, 2nd edn 1990), 12.
[74] Nichols, *Progresses, Processions*, I, 52, 66; HMC, *Salisbury*, xv, 50.
[75] Bruce, *Correspondence of King James VI of Scotland with Sir Robert Cecil*, 5 and *passim*; Stafford, *James VI of Scotland and the Throne of England*, 223.
[76] Lord Keeper Egerton and Sir John Fortescue lost respectively the Mastership of the Rolls and the Chancellorship of the Exchequer, both to Scots. Although a pluralist, Fortescue is not mentioned

there is little evidence that Cecil and his fellow ministers had a reform programme already worked out in advance of the accession of James. Rather, they came to adopt, with varying degrees of conviction, a mix of measures many of which seem to have originated from outside ministerial circles. A case in point is wardship, with Cecil announcing in August 1603 that 'he was to have wardes torned to a certain annual rent – to be propounded in Parliament'.[77] Moreover, it was the king who looks to have been the main driving force at the centre, setting up a commission to investigate monopolies and protections on 4 May and reiterating his reforming intentions in another proclamation the following month. James also summoned a conference to discuss the question of church reform.[78]

Yet by the time parliament met in March 1604 the reformist credentials of the government were wearing thin. The puritan clergy had already been rebuffed at the Hampton Court Conference that January, and the king's opening address to the assembled MPs rubbed salt into this particular wound while containing no reference at all to grievances of the commonwealth.[79] Negotiations about wardship and purveyance did get under way, but discussion of the former ground to a halt at the end of May amidst mutual recriminations. This in turn led to the famous Apology being drawn up by a Commons committee, its members including both Bromley and Greville and which sought to justify the entire proceedings of the lower house – religious as well as secular.[80] Among other things the Apology was a requiem for the hopes enshrined in the memorial of the previous year. The reformers had failed to secure a new administration, and the initial enthusiasm expressed for their proposals by James had proved an insufficient counterweight to the inherited forces of conservatism.[81]

in the 1603 memorial; he also happened to be Bromley's uncle: Hasler, *The House of Commons 1558–1603*, I, 491.

[77] H. Spencer (ed.), 'The journal of Sir Roger Wilbraham, Solicitor-General in Ireland and Master of Requests . . . 1593–1616', *Camden Miscellany*, 10 (1902), 63; see 40 above; cf. N. Tyacke, 'Wroth, Cecil and the Parliamentary Session of 1604', *BIHR*, 50 (1977), 120–5, which argues a rather different case to that presented here.

[78] *APC, 1601–4*, 497; *Stuart Royal Proclamations*, I, 28–9, 60–3.

[79] P. Collinson, 'The Jacobean religious settlement; the Hampton Court Conference', in H. Tomlinson (ed.), *Before the English Civil War* (1983), 27–51; *CJ*, I, 142–6.

[80] *Ibid.*, 222, 227–8, 230–1; HMC, *Salisbury*, XXIII, 130–52. Bromley's brother-in-law Sir John Scott was also involved in these committee proceedings. In addition, Bromley, Greville and Scott, were all members of the original Commons committee set up in March 1604 to consider wardship and other issues: *CJ*, I, 491.

[81] Cf. G. R. Elton, 'A high road to Civil War?', in his *Studies in Tudor and Stuart Government* (Cambridge, 1974–92), II, 164–82. Despite his revisionist argument, Elton wrote of the Apology that it 'preached Peter Wentworth's extreme doctrine of free speech': *ibid.*, 170.

Instead of office and influence, obscurity was to be the individual fate of the 'freinds' of Peter Wentworth – assuming that Bromley and his relatives were such.[82] Nevertheless, the developments which we have analysed in this essay were to leave a very important legacy behind them. During the 1590s court faction in the context of the Scottish reversionary interest had served to focus a previously somewhat inchoate puritan opposition. The resulting programme ultimately proved unacceptable to James VI and I, but in the very process of rejection a new kind of adversary politics was born. Although the details might change, the broad outlines of an alternative politico-religious platform to that of the government henceforth existed, around which dissident elements would be able to rally in the decades ahead when 'free speech' in parliament came increasingly to be perceived, in Wentworth's words, as 'the onely salve to heale all the sores of this common wealth'.[83]

---

[82] As well as becoming a gentleman of the Privy Chamber Bromley was appointed a member of the Council in the Marches of Wales in about 1603, but progressed no further: HMC, *Salisbury*, xv, 391–2; R. H. Clive (ed.), *Documents connected with the History of Ludlow* (1841), 259. He died in 1615: *CSPD, 1611–18*, 344. For the downward spiral of the later careers of both Cromwell and Greville see respectively Stone, *An Elizabethan: Sir Horatio Palavicino*, 299–310, and A. F. Upton, *Sir Arthur Ingram c. 1565–1642. A Study of the Origins of an English Landed Family* (Oxford, 1961), 19–20, 71, 157–9.

[83] T. Hartley (ed.), *Proceedings in the Parliaments of Elizabeth* (Leicester, 1981–95), I, 425. My intention is to pursue some of these more general questions elsewhere. Already, however, it begins to look as if Neale's focus on Peter Wentworth was not so mistaken after all.

2

The sacred, the profane, and the Union: politics of sermon and masque at the court wedding of Lord and Lady Hay

Lori Anne Ferrell

In 1971, Conrad Russell noted the proximate and disproportionate force of early modern Anglo-Scottish relations. 'Though Scotland was not a major power,' he wryly commented, 'it was big enough to occupy most of England's attention.'[1] This essay explores the polemics of Union[2] in the early days of James VI of Scotland's career as James I of England, a period profoundly marked by his inability to create a united kingdom. The king's failure exemplifies Russell's observation. For James's new English subjects, full political Union with Scotland was a concept both too irrelevant to take seriously and too threatening to consider fully. This examination of the paradoxical politics of Anglo-Scottish union thus pays tribute to Professor Russell's appreciation of the antithetical nature of early modern England's 'British Problem'.

James VI and I arrived in England with an ambition to rule Great Britain. To this end, he argued for a 'perfect' incorporation of the kingdoms of England and Scotland despite parliamentary lack of interest, distraction and downright opposition. To the king's initial chagrin and increasing irritation, his English MPs did little more than acknowledge that James had the right to rule two separate kingdoms. Indeed, at the beginning of his English reign, they found even this limited 'union of crowns' threatening. Union of the two kingdoms would lead, they feared, to the wholesale plundering of England's offices and riches by impoverished and improvident Scots.

The historical occasion that inspires this essay is the wedding at Whitehall of an impoverished and improvident Scot, James, Lord Hay, to an English heiress, Honora Denny, daughter of Sir Edward Denny,

---

[1] Conrad Russell, *The Crisis of Parliaments* (Oxford, 1971), 25–6.
[2] Following the example set by Roger Munden, and in order to make the difference clear between the union of crowns established by James's accession and the king's more ambitious plan to unite his two kingdoms fully, I will capitalise the word 'Union' when I refer to James's 1603–7 project: 'James I and "the growth of mutual distrust": King, Commons, and reform, 1603–1604', in Kevin Sharpe (ed.), *Faction and Parliament* (Oxford, 1978), 43–72.

on Twelfth Night 1606/7. The marriage represented the king's express wish: not simply that Scottish nobles should marry wealthy English-women, but that such marriages would be seen as public symbols of the fuller Union he had been working for since his accession. Graced by the royal presence, the Hay wedding was lavish in its ceremonial trappings and rhetorics. Two performances, a witty sermon preached by Robert Wilkinson and an ingenious masque written by Thomas Campion, es-tablished its political meanings in enduring fashion; sermon and masque were both published in 1607. Here, documented almost solely in liter-ary artifact, is an extraordinary convergence of issues – political and personal, formal and unscripted, theoretical and occasional – all issuing from a single day at the English court and all centering around what might reasonably be considered the most significant issue of James's early reign.

Wilkinson's *The Merchant Royall* and Campion's *Lord Hayes Masque* provide the basis for the analysis this essay undertakes. It will not attempt to reconstruct an actual event at the Jacobean court, although it will concentrate on the printed texts' intentions to do just that. It treats ser-mon and masque as formal political interventions, albeit ones danger-ously close to their sell-by dates. For by the winter of 1606/7, it was clear to most observers that James's Union campaign was languishing *in extremis* in the English parliament, with anti-Scottish feeling running high (and waxing eloquent) amongst MPs.[3] The polemics of the Hay–Denny match were constructed so late in the day of the Union project that their utility to that particular enterprise could be no more than tran-sient. This is not to say, however, that this rhetoric became outmoded or irrelevant. The certainty of the union of crowns and the uncertainty of Anglo-Scottish Protestantism allowed James's political theology of union[4] to assume a new relevancy in the years after 1607.

A court wedding provided the perfect setting for a doctrine that pro-claimed the divine rightness of union in biblical and sacramental lan-guage. But the story of this particular promotion of a royal project begins inauspiciously, with the chequered public and personal early career of James, Lord Hay. Hay has been described as 'never uniquely in the royal favour' yet 'seldom out of it',[5] a cosseted favourite who possessed not

---

[3] Conrad Russell, *The Causes of the English Civil War* (Oxford, 1990), 45 and 'Parliamentary history in perspective, 1604–1629', *Hist*, 61 (1976), reprinted in *Unrevolutionary England 1603–1642* (1990), 13–14; Bruce Galloway, *The Union of England and Scotland, 1603–1608* (Edinburgh, 1986), 94–120.

[4] Many thanks to Malcolm Smuts for this expression.

[5] Timothy Raylor, *The Essex House Masque of 1621* (Pittsburgh, 2000), 48.

only charm but also genuine political talent. Contemporary commentary reckoned him a 'true Courtier', a man with 'language enough to be *real* as well as *formal*', a rare gift in a politico.[6] His knowledge of French culture and European politics attracted the notice of James VI, and he came south to England with its new king in 1603 (during which trip he probably met Honora Denny's father).[7] But Hay's early years in England as a Scottish émigré in the king's entourage has produced less historiographical commentary than the events of his later career in foreign service as, first, Viscount Doncaster and, then, Earl of Carlisle. This is due to the nature of the historical archive: between 1603 and 1607, when Hay does appear in State Papers Domestic, it is as the recipient of royal largesse and debt restructuring.[8]

This 'proof' of Hay's improvidence (coupled with entries from the same period that appear to indicate that James made financial and titular awards to Edward Denny contingent upon his daughter's marriage to Hay) led historians from the seventeenth century on to postulate that the father was understandably reluctant to marry his daughter to a feckless and beggarly Scot.[9] This made for speculative, scurrilous narrative of the Sir Anthony Weldon School: a father's entirely justified fears finally overcome by the corrupt combination of personal cupidity and royal might; a resisted marriage signifying the larger cultural implications of a ineffective and ill-considered political campaign.

And it *was* a good story – featuring a spendthrift Rake, a damsel in distress, and an imprudent and impatient king – but one entirely reflective of Whiggish contempt for the character of James I and a lack of interest in the political issues of his northern kingdom. Recently, however, Bruce Galloway and Brian Levack have given detailed accounts of the administrative chronology, cultural impact and political significance of the king's abortive project of 1603–7.[10] James's desire to unite his kingdoms now appears neither foolhardy nor egomaniacal but practical and prescient – an intelligent, genuinely innovative royal initiative. At the same time, parliamentary historians point to Union as the most unsuccessful political issue of a crucial period of mutual acquaintance.[11] Perhaps because of

[6] Arthur Wilson, *History of Great Britain* (1653), quoted in Raylor, *Essex House Masque*, 48.

[7] Denny first came to James's notice by providing him with a sumptuously equipped horse when the king stopped at Royston: John Nichols, *The Progresses of James I* (1828), I, 104–5.

[8] See entries in *CSPD*.

[9] See, for example, Clarendon's *History of the Rebellion*, ed. W. Dunn Macray (1888), I, 115; the *DNB* entry for Hay; and the report of Nichols in *The Progresses of James I*, II, 100, 103–5.

[10] Galloway, *Union*; Brian Levack, *The Formation of the British State* (Oxford, 1987).

[11] For example, see the remarks of Neil Cuddy: 'The revival of the entourage', in David Starkey (ed.), *The English Court* (Harlow, 1987), 202–3.

these interpretive contradictions, the Union campaign of 1603–7 has never been completely reintegrated into the larger revisionist (or even post-revisionist) picture of the Jacobean period.[12] It continues to function for most historians as a kind of intriguing political anomaly, a royal brainchild that failed to thrive: worthy of study as a snap-shot perspective on James VI and I's governing character but rarely seen as influential in long view. Professor Russell himself banished it in 1994 to that notorious revisionist outpost, the lonely realm of the dog in the night-time.[13]

It may be, however, that we have simply been barking up the wrong tree. Investigations that also take into account the polemical productions associated with the Union project allow for a very different view of its political viability and cultural significance. Stephen Orgel's detailed study of the staging and financing of Inigo Jones's work challenges the long-standing assumption that Campion's *Lord Hayes Masque* was paid for by the king simply because the Hay wedding was in the royal interest. Orgel and David Lindley both suggest that wealthy friends, in which cohort they include Thomas Howard and Thomas and Robert Cecil, financed the masque.[14] These findings (coupled with Lindley's commonsense observation that the bride was not old enough to marry until 1607) dispel our last lingering attachment to the nineteenth-century romance of a father wooed not wisely but too wealthily and provide us with the final substantial historical referent underpinning the political theology of Union. The Hay wedding represents the achievement of another kind of arranged marriage at court: the political and fiscal collaboration of two powerful rival families, united in the service of a new king.[15]

The hard work of promoting a project at once so dear to the royal heart and so vastly unpopular (and in the shifting and uncertain political milieu created by James's accession) called for just such an expensive show of courtly patronage.[16] From 1604, the king and his spokesmen had laboured to imprint, onto a stubbornly sceptical kingdom, the principles

---

[12] Galloway, *Union*, 137.
[13] Conrad Russell, 'The Anglo-Scottish Union 1603–1643: a success?' in Anthony Fletcher and Peter Roberts (eds.), *Religion, Culture and Society in Early Modern Britain* (Cambridge, 1994), 240.
[14] David Lindley, 'Who paid for Campion's Lord Hay's masque?', *Notes and Queries*, new series, 26, 2 (April 1979), 144–5. The Howards were artistic patrons of Campion and both families had well-established political connections with Edward Denny, the Cecils claiming blood relation to Honora Denny. Lindley and Orgel's accounts decidedly counter the account in the *DNB* entry for James Hay.
[15] Lindley, 'Lord Hay's masque', 145. For the significance of such a coalition, see Cuddy, 'Revival of entourage', 174–5.
[16] Pauline Croft, 'Robert Cecil and the early Jacobean court', in Linda Peck (ed.), *The Mental World of the Jacobean Court* (Cambridge, 1991), 143–4.

of a 'court culture of Union'.[17] These were values derived from two foundational components: the political ideology of Great Britain, which was unfamiliar (and thus likely to be resisted by a parliament wary of setting precedent), and the socio-religious ideologies of marriage, which were familiar (and thus destined to be the polemical delivery systems for the concept Great Britain). And so, what might be seen as the least politically substantial of the king's personal initiatives had the potential to wield the strongest cultural impress: James worked to unite his dual kingdoms one couple at a time, sponsoring a number of Anglo-Scottish marriages, of which the Hay wedding may be counted as the most spectacular and publicly elaborated.[18]

It was an elaboration built upon three years of official nuptial rhetoric, originating from the throne. James VI and I unveiled the political theology of union in his maiden speech to his English parliament, 19 March 1604. Never one to pass up a patriarchal trope when describing the royal prerogative, this time the king had hit upon a project tailor-made for the marriage topos. James was quick to recognize its metaphoric possibilities in a Protestant age when 'holy matrimony' was no longer strictly a sacramental, but still a religious matter: like Union, marriage was 'not only a civil and politic, but also a divine and spiritual conjunction.'[19] Borrowing extensively from the biblical language and ritual cadence of the wedding service in the Book of Common Prayer (to the point of concluding with the phrase 'what God hath conjoined then, let no man separate'),[20] James described the marriage of his kingdoms as presaged in the integrity of his own body and the sanctity of his married state. Most historians of political thought have been struck by James's use of this imagery, but few have done more than note it. It may have its roots in Celtic tradition; it certainly betrays a certain precocious if underdeveloped imperial ambition.[21] But it is the combination of the Pauline analogy of the church ('For just as the body is one and has many members, and all the members of the body, though many, are one body, so it is with Christ') with the ceremonial language of the Book of Common

---

[17] Galloway, *Union*, 82.

[18] Roy E. Schreiber, *The First Carlisle* (Philadelphia: Transactions of the Royal Philosophical Society, vol. 74, 1984), 9. Brian Levack considers this initiative unsuccessful due to the relatively small numbers of Anglo-Scottish marriages outside the Borders: *Formation*, 186–7.

[19] Matthew Griffith, *A Forme for Families* (1633), quoted in David Cressy, *Birth, Marriage and Death* (Oxford, 1997), 294–5.

[20] The reference is to Matthew 19:6.

[21] For a brief survey of historians' thought on the matter, as well as the argument for the Celtic origins of James's rhetoric, see Michael J. Enright, 'King James and his island', *Scottish Historical Review*, 55, 1, 159 (April 1976), 29–40.

Prayer that makes this commonplace so beautifully suited to its rhetorical task and its political setting.[22]

For one thing, it made a memorable calling card. Brian Levack has pointed out that the simple, regal union created by the accession of a Scottish king to the English throne was 'the ultimate product' of an arranged marriage; fittingly, the marriage analogy initially worked to introduce the king to his new subjects.[23] It described the king's project by way of describing the king himself: binding Union, in a set of memorable and ascending associations, to every aspect of James's complex identity as husband, father, Scottish monarch, and Elizabeth I's successor. From this beginning, the king moved swiftly and logically to make a novel request. The institution of a full incorporating Union between his two kingdoms, James claimed, would not merely reflect the peace and stability already figured in his own person and married state; agreeing to 'perfect union' would demonstrate that his English subjects had bound themselves to their new king in love and fidelity.[24] Indeed, he was 'assured that in hearts and minds [they] all applaud[ed]' his feelings on the matter.

The English court and its literary-religious auxiliary were happy to perform their own assurances. The list of advocates reads like a roll of English worthies: Francis Bacon, Robert Cotton, the Howards, the Cecils, bishops, court preachers. The project provided many of James's more important new subjects with a chance to catch the king's ear, and one sure way to catch it was with the king's own words. The fast track to royal favour was soon littered with pro-union tracts, sermons and panegyrics: all tricked out in epithalamial imagery; most shamelessly cribbing James's 1604 speech directly or employing phrases or texts that called forth the imagery of the marriage-bed. In 1604, the Earl of Northampton defended the union to sceptical Scottish commissioners with *quod deus coniunxit homo non separet*; in 1606, Anthony Maxey preached to the court (if not the choir) on the erotically charged second chapter of the Song of Solomon ('stir not up, nor waken my love till he please').[25] But as time passed and no progress was made on the Union front, James's rhetoric became less uxorious and more jealously suspicious.

Consider another royal speech to parliament on 31 March 1607, less than three months after the Hay–Denny wedding and more than three

[22] Johann Sommerville, *Politics and Ideology in England 1603–1640* (Harlow, 1986), 48–9. The reference is to 1 Corinthians 12:12.
[23] Levack, *Formation*, 3.
[24] Johann Sommerville (ed.), *King James VI and I: Political Writings* (Cambridge, 1994), 133.
[25] Linda Levy Peck, *Northampton* (1982), 190; Lori Anne Ferrell, *Government by Polemic* (Stanford, 1998), 53.

years after James had first unveiled his pet project. James's 1607 speech borrows extensively from the language of the English prayer book, continuing the rhetorical trend he had begun in his remarks on Union in 1604. He opens with a direct reference to the marriage service, which begins 'holy matrimony . . . is an honorable estate . . . which Christ adorned and beautified with his presence and first miracle that he wrought in Cana . . .':

> All men at the beginning of a Feast bring forth good wine first, and, after, worse. This was the saying of the Governor of the Feast at Cana in Galilee, where Christ wrought his first miracle by changing water into wine. But in this case now whereof I am to speak unto you, I must follow that Governors rule, and not Christ's example, in giving you the worst and sourest wine last.[26]

Christ's miracle at Cana symbolized both Eucharistic practice and the divine institution of marriage; in referring to Cana wine, then, the king sanctified his scheme for Union, making his parliament appear to be resisting not simply his personal desires but God's intended design.[27] Throughout this speech, James returns to the underlying theme of the Johannine story: the requirements of hospitality, and the mutual (if inequitable) obligations of familial love. 'I claim nothing but with acknowledgement of my Bond to you,' James told his parliament, 'that as ye owe me subjection and obedience: So my Sovereignty obligeth me to yield to you love, government, and protection.'[28] Here, in a characteristic polemical strategy, the king softens the edge of what is otherwise harsh rhetoric, courting his parliament with flattering expressions of confidence that they can still surpass his expectations by bringing out the good wine of assent late in the day of the Union campaign.

The Union debate, adjourned abruptly in 1605 with the discovery of the Gunpowder Plot, had returned to the parliamentary docket in November 1606, but to little purpose.[29] The king characterized parliament's work on the Union as coyly evasive: 'many crossings, long disputations, strange questions, and nothing done'. How much longer, he demanded, did this deliberative body intend to drag 'leaden feet' on an issue that (now they were well acquainted with his wisdom and benevolence) was clearly indisputable? 'Union is a marriage,' James rather predictably informed them, going on to stress that he had taken pains not to press his own three-year suit inappropriately or impetuously:

---

[26] Sommerville, *King James VI and I*, 159. The reference is to John 2: 1–12.
[27] David Lyle Jeffrey (ed.), *A Dictionary of Biblical Tradition in English Literature* (Grand Rapids, 1992), 124–6.
[28] Sommerville, *King James VI and I*, 161.   [29] Galloway, *Union*, 93–6.

'[W]ould he not be thought absurd that, furthering of a marriage between two friends of his, would make his first motion to have the two parties be laid in bed together . . . must there not precede the mutual sight and acquaintance of the parties?'[30] James makes a distinction between his taking the proper time to present an honourable and reasonable case and parliament's taking far too much time to consider it. Significant here is the fact that he calls upon the English liturgical tradition to underscore his point about the contradictory nature of Union politics. His earthy remarks invoke the tone of warning that prefaced the 'form of solemnization of matrimony' in the Book of Common Prayer, repeated in every contemporary wedding sermon: marriage is 'not to be enterprised nor taken in hand unadvisedly . . . to satisfy men's carnal lusts and appetites . . . but reverently, discreetly, advisedly, soberly'. The king draws on the tensions inherent in the meaning of the marriage service itself – the ritual argument that passion must be restrained by the institution of the church – in order to stress that his own desire for Union is already wisely governed and thus needs no tempering (or dampening) by his subjects.

By now James's expectation of refusal was as well founded as his polemical response to it had become, perhaps, over-developed.[31] As might be expected, the Union issue divided court and country, but it also raised the spectre of clandestine opposition at the heart of the court itself. That there were peers willing to appear supportive of the project before James but not in the House was an open secret, discussed by gossipy foreign ambassadors and disgusted members alike. Indeed, it was widely believed that certain courtiers and counsellors charged with supporting the Union were in fact double-dealing king *and* Commons. In 1604, Sir John Holles complained of the duplicity of the peers in a letter to Lord Burghley:

We like countrymen, they like statesmen more covertly and with ceremony, whence though proceeding one and the same effect, I mean the adjournment of resolutions till further debate, yet they clad angel-like were received into Abraham's bosom while we fried in the furnace of the king's displeasure.[32]

---

[30] Sommerville, *King James VI and I*, 163.
[31] See, for example, the comments of the Venetian ambassador Zorzi Giustinian, who, in a dispatch dated 16 May 1607, said, 'The king is now forced to desire the Union not only because it is useful, but also for his own reputation's sake. Like all great minds opposition fires him.' *CSPV, 1603–1607*, 498.
[32] PRO, SP 14/8/93, quoted in Munden, 'James I', 71. Holles was MP for Nottinghamshire when he wrote this letter.

Significant here is Holles's acknowledgment of the paradoxical procedural tactics that would prompt James three years later to chide his
parliament for leaden-footed progress on the Union. The cloaked but
effective hostility the MP describes surely accounts for the king's persis-
tent, bewildered complaint in public and private that despite his many
persuasive arguments for Union, his subjects continued to behave as
though they were confused about its nature and value.

The Hay wedding thus provided a brilliantly allusive setting for another, perhaps more persuasive, elaboration of James's political theology
to those subjects who (as Holles complained) continued to be entertained in the bosom of the king despite their opposition to his scheme.[33]
Its polemical significance begins with its date, confirmed on the title
pages of both *Merchant Royall* and *Lord Hayes Masque*: 6 January, Twelfth
Night. Ecclesiastically speaking, 6 January was also the feast-day of the
Epiphany. Twelfth Night may have marked the conclusion of Christmas
festivities, but the Epiphany signalled the end of the Advent prohibition
on marriage.[34] In the Jacobean court, where one could always enjoy
a splendid mix of the politicized pleasures of the sacred and the profane, the Hay wedding supplied both the occasion for an 'aristocratic
knees-up'[35] and a venue for the king to express impatience for *his* 'great
intended Union' to commence.

Epiphany was also the date traditionally assigned to the wedding
at Cana,[36] which begs another question about James's own pointed
reference to Cana wine to parliament three months later. For Robert
Wilkinson's sermon for the Hay wedding takes up the theme of the dangers of covert and obstructive disloyalty at close quarters in unmistakable
fashion. *The Merchant Royall* is a sermonic tour de force, a witty and well-
wrought exposition on Proverbs 31:14 ('She is like a merchant's ship,
she bringeth her food from afar') by a preacher already known for his
winning touch with homiletic. (*A Jewell for the Eare*, a 1594 sermon by
Wilkinson, had already been printed several times by 1607; reprinted
five times between 1607 and 1615, *Merchant Royall* would prove to be
Wilkinson's second-best seller in this period.)[37]

---

33 The biblical-literary image of 'Abraham's bosom' originates in the concept of courtly hospitality:
   Jeffrey, *Dictionary of Biblical Tradition*, 11.
34 Cressy, *Birth, Marriage and Death*, 298–305.
35 This charming expression is David Lindley's: David Lindley (ed.), *Court Masques* (Oxford, 1995), x.
36 This ecclesiastical tradition was well known; it should be noted, however, that in the medieval
   calendar the incident at Cana was finally assigned another date in January for observance:
   Jeffrey, *Dictionary of Biblical Tradition*, 124.
37 Ian Green, *Print and Protestantism* (Oxford, 2000), 670.

An attractive woodcut illustration of a stately galleon, sails billowing, flags flying proudly, graces *The Merchant Royall's* title page. In the sermon that follows, the nautical theme calls up a rich store of biblical images and an equally rich and allusive host of exegetical traditions: Noah's Ark, for example, with its evocation of animals and people in more or less happily co-operative pairings, or, related to this, the notion of the church as a ship for the transport of souls. The imagery was particularly well-suited to the polemical work of a sermon that had to discuss the significance of the Hay marriage through the lenses provided by (in ascending order) the moral failings of women, the protections of marriage, the relationship of Christ to his church, the power of the king, and the excellence of the Union project. What is of interest here is how a wedding sermon could lecture Honora Denny on her duties to her brand-new husband and at the same time reprove courtiers on theirs to a nearly new king.

The Merchant Royall's considerable stylishness reflects Wilkinson's skill in drawing out the complex metaphor *a woman is a ship* over nearly forty pages of print. He opens by reminding the couple, the king, and his courtly audience that the world itself is as capricious as the ocean: 'transitory and brittle as glasse, tumultuous and troublesome'. In an uncertain world, marriage should function as a bulwark protecting the couple from dissention, discord and, most importantly, disloyalty: 'the contentions and unquietness of them that live among us, the sharp assaults and oppositions of them that hate us, but chiefly the unfaithfulness and treachery of them that seem to love us'.[38] In this vast sea of betrayals, the woman provides safety, security and direction:

[I]f she be good, she is like a Ship indeed and to nothing so like as to a Ship; for she sits at the stern and by discretion as by card and compass shapes her course; her countenance and conversation are ballasted with soberness and gravity; her sails are full of wind, as if some wisdom from above had inspired or blown upon her; she standeth in the shrouds and calleth out her lead, and when she hath sounded, she telleth (*as Michol did to David*) of depth and danger. If by default she be grounded she casteth out her anchors (*as Rahab did*) and by winding of herself, she gets afloat again. If she spy any within her kenning, any trouble to be nigh, either she makes forward, if she find herself able, or else with *Pilate's wife* she sets sail away; she commands, and countermands each man to his charge . . . as if she, and none but she were Captain, Owner, Master of the Ship; and yet she is not Master, but the Master's mate . . .[39]

[38] Robert Wilkinson, *The Merchant Royall. A Sermon Preached at Whitehall before the Kings Majestie.* (1607), STC 25657, 6. I have analysed this passage elsewhere: *Government by Polemic*, 38–40.
[39] Wilkinson, *Merchant Royall*, 7.

And so we have the attributes of a good wife: skilled, sedate and smart, she should be able to detect and steer clear of danger or doldrums. Her efforts should always be directed towards her husband's interest, for she exercises authority in his name alone. Recognizing this and acting accordingly, she gains his love and admiration. And yet Wilkinson's choice of exemplary women might at first glance seem antithetical: Michol, who mocked King David; Rahab the harlot; Pilate's wife, who in medieval tradition was enlisted by Satan to halt the divine plan of redemption.

It seems likely, however, that Wilkinson chose these contradictory *exempla* precisely for their faulty natures, thereby tempering his commendation with words more monitory. They justify the preacher's argument that, essentially helpful as she can be, the one thing a woman must never do is overestimate the bounds of her power. Her inherent failings and weaknesses make her ultimately subject to another's dominion. 'Of moveable instruments, a ship is the hugest and the greatest, and yet commanded . . . by the helm or stern, a small piece of wood,' Wilkinson pointed out. 'So ought the wife (although a great commander in the house) yet to be turned and ruled by a word of her husband.'[40] Here, with the pointed comment about *great command in the house*, Wilkinson holds up a mirror for courtiers, one in which they see reflected their own talent to advise and protect, and are at the same time reminded of their subordinate place.

Wilkinson's achievement in *The Merchant Royall* is to enlarge the king's nuptial rhetoric beyond its analogical boundaries. He opens up the king's standard trope ('I am the husband, and this whole island is my wife'), moving to the related image, *the king is the captain*, and then invoking a logical corollary, the political commonplace *a state is a ship*. Contained within the rhetoric of wives-or courtiers-as shipmates is the ingratiating notion of their own sagacity, ingenuity and influence. These qualities define not simply the courtier but the courtier-lobbyist, and so the work of early modern government of king-in-parliament, that paradoxical blend of negotiated and absolute powers.

The already contradictory nature of a style of government that was both arbitrary and collaborative would have only been further confused by the king's foreignness (or, for that matter, by his propensity to enact by proclamation what he could not immediately obtain from his parliament in the matters of Union). Addressing this problem, Wilkinson closes with an application to the king that contains a sharp heads-up to the court:

[40] *Ibid.*, 11.

[Y]our Majesty is to us indeed a royal Merchant, not only for the union of holy marriage, which yokes and couples one sex with another, but . . . for knitting and combining one kingdom with another . . . if it be so gracious in God's eyes to do right and justice to a stranger, how much more to love a stranger, but most of all to take away the name of a stranger? The King of Kings be Pilot of your ship, yea thrice blessed and happy be your Majesties endeavor therein.[41]

Note here the striking marital image *taking away the name of a stranger*; it expands upon the image of James as one who 'marries' both persons and kingdoms. With this reference to the king's new title to Great Britain, Wilkinson reminds king and court that, as they share a common name, so they also are bound in a common endeavour: the royal merchant steering the *Merchant Royall* in the divine course of Union. This raises the issue of parliament's own correlative duty to enfranchise the stranger in its midst. He advises the king's English subjects that their task is not to offer their service to a foreign king, but to naturalize the king's work by taking up his cause as countrymen.

Later that day, the Hays safely married in the eyes of God and the king, the assembly exchanged a wedding sermon for a Twelfth Night masque. In so doing the court transferred from ocean to forest, a move calculated to bring pleasure to a king who delighted in 'sylvan retreat'. In *Lord Hayes Masque*, Thomas Campion identifies and chastises courtly opposition to Union by way of pastoral rather than nautical narrative.[42] While the costumes, music, and stage effects all meticulously described in the Hay masque are impressively complex, its storyline is relatively simple. The figure of Night, also called Cynthia, the guardian of chastity, defends a vale where nine trees stand. During the course of the masque, Zephyr, the West Wind, Hesperus, the Evening Star, and Flora, the Queen of Flowers, eventually reconcile Cynthia to the loss of one of her virgin votaries to marriage.[43]

This is no easy task, for Cynthia is nursing a deep resentment, the reason for which is not readily apparent (except, perhaps, to the sharp-eyed). In their work of persuasion, Zephyr and Flora call on Cynthia, accompanied by a troupe of green-clad Sylvans singing 'Who is the happier of the two, a maid or wife? Which is more to be desired, Peace or Strife?'[44] Cynthia's outraged response rips wedding-lyric boilerplate

[41] *Ibid.*, 42–3. Italics are mine.
[42] Cuddy, 'Revival of entourage', 194. For pastoral as a genre of royal political instruction see Leah Marcus, 'Politics and pastoral: writing the court on the countryside', in Kevin Sharpe and Peter Lake, (eds.), *Culture and Politics in Early Modern England* (1994), 139.
[43] Thomas Campion, *A Discription of a Masque* (1607), STC 4538, sig. B3r.
[44] *Ibid.*, sig. B3v.

from its ageless, leafy setting and directs it straight to the heart of current political debate at the Jacobean court:

> Thou breathe'st sweet poison wanton Zephyrus
> But Cynthia must not be deluded thus.
> Her holy forests are by thieves profan'd
> Her virgins frighted, and lo, where they stand
> That late were Phoebus's Knights, turn'd now to trees
> By Cynthia's vengement for their injuries
> In seeking to seduce her Nymphs with love:
> Here they are fix'd and never may remove.[45]

Cynthia has turned the entire plundering retinue into trees, immobile and mute. This act, rather than the proposed marriage itself, actually constitutes the central problem of the masque. That she will have to give up her virgin to marriage is inevitable, something Cynthia herself understands. What Cynthia needs to be persuaded to relinquish is not the Nymph but the resentment which has driven her to restrain Phoebus's knights.

Cynthia gives in to the arguments of Flora, Zephyr and Hesperus with rapid grace, admitting that she does so because she is bound to submit to their overlord Phoebus, whose light outshines her own. To do so in response to their enthusiastic arguments will only redound to her credit and advantage: 'If all seem glad, why should we only low'r? Since t'express gladness we have now most power.' Indeed, her acquiescence allows her to redirect her remarkable powers, expressing them in what we might consider the theatrical counterpart to Wilkinson's rhetorical flourishes in *Merchant Royall*'s peroration. Cynthia frees the knights in a display of astonishing stage effects. A small 'engine' constructed under the stage causes the floor to drop. In groups of three, the trees sink one yard below the floor. Their branches then split open: restored to human form, courtiers step out from the treetops.[46] Music and dancing, celebrating nuptial bliss and signifying the restoration of harmony, conclude the masque.

Here the act of lyric persuasion leads to the liberation of the Sun-monarch's retinue and the consummation of a long-awaited marriage union. The transformation scene, however, directs our attention to a particular line of argument. If Cynthia's task in the masque is primarily to

---

[45] *Ibid.*, sig. B4v.
[46] Although marginal remarks in the 1607 edition of the masque indicate that the effect was actually somewhat marred by 'the simplicity, negligence or conspiracy of the painter': Campion, *Masque*, sig. C2v.

accept rather than allow the marriage of her Nymph, then the theme of
the masque turns on the process of political negotiation, not brute domination. Cynthia's report to the Sylvans of thieving, seducing knights
represents anti-Scottish sentiment in England. The knights' immobili-
sation signifies the stasis that afflicts the Union project through misunderstanding; their release in human form illustrates the transformation,
through the thawing of evil opinion, of plundering Scots into fellow
courtiers; the concluding dance enacts courtly co-operation in the king's
cause.[47]

Schooled to discern metaphoric meaning with exquisite sensitivity, a
court audience would have had no difficulties deciphering the message
of the Hay wedding. Masque and sermon both raise the issue of internal
opposition to the king's plan, flatter the court as well as the king, and call
for the court to work with the king wholeheartedly on a project of which
they were known to disapprove and on which he had already begun by
proclamation. Ultimately, however, Union's politics could not achieve the
hoped-for resolution that Union's sermons and masques, those specialists
in the strategies of paradox, could secure in words and display.

The failure of Union, however, paved the way for another course
of action, at which both texts do more than hint. Both sermon and
masque also make a case for the king's authority in matters of religion,
if we consider as additional evidence the prefatory poems Campion
included in his 1607 printed version of *Lord Hayes Masque*. One poem,
addressed to James, purports to describe a loyalty rite of the ancient,
'disunited', Scythians. Their situation requiring them to fight in alliance,
every soldier had to open his vein into a common bowl as a proof of
loyalty. That sanguinary ritual having been completed:

> They quaft to th'union, which till death should last,
> In spite of private foe, or foreign fear
> And this *blood sacrament* being known t'have past
> Their names grew dreadful to all far and near.
> O then Great monarch with how wise a care
> Do you these bloods divided mix in one,
> And with like consanguinities prepare
> The high, and everlasting Union
> Tweene Scots and English: *who can wonder then*
> *If he that marries kingdoms marries men?*[48]

[47] For another reading of the masque that concentrates on its depiction of Elizabeth I see David
Lindley, 'Campion's Lord Hay's Masque and Anglo-Scottish Union', *HLQ*, 43, 1 (1979), 1–11.
See also David Lindley, *Thomas Campion* (Leiden, 1986), 176–91.
[48] Campion, *Masque*, sig. A2r.

The reference to marrying kingdoms and men refers so precisely to Wilkinson's own words in *Merchant Royall* that it seems likely Campion consciously added rhetorical elements of the wedding sermon to enhance his own report on the Hay wedding. Whatever the reason, however, it is clear that the Scythian poem supplies a religious trope that unites the printed arguments of sermon and masque. Both authors claim that James did more than merely grace the marriage of the Hays by his presence. They employ a much stronger rhetorical strategy, figuring the king as *presiding over* the marriage in the fashion of a priest. The sacerdotal image suggested by Wilkinson's nautical topos, wherein the king can be likened to Noah, is thus strengthened in Campion's poem by associating the royal figure with 'blood sacrament'.[49]

This reading of the Hay wedding raises the question of what Union polemic was meant to accomplish. The Hay wedding texts argue for James's kingship – not of Great Britain (which, after all, he already was through self-proclamation), but of England, which required an altogether more co-operative and ineffable kind of national assent. England had to accept a union of crowns; it even had to acquiesce in its new king's proclaimed titles and prerogatives. Whether it could 'naturalize' James VI, however, would depend upon how closely it could be persuaded to 'love' its new king. And for James, this condition of love and acceptance would build upon long-standing Anglo-Scottish agreement in certain cultural essentials, defined in the king's 1604 parliamentary speech (and parroted endlessly by his Union spokesmen) as 'Language, Religion, and, similitude of manners'.[50]

True, perhaps, in the grand world of political speechery, but in the brave new world of Anglo-Scottish Calvinist consensus, Church and Kirk shared neither language – if by language we refer to common prayer – nor similitude of manners – if by manners we refer to ceremonial practice. These peculiar disparities of Anglo-Scottish Protestantism mirrored, and thus threatened to expose, the peculiar weaknesses of the English settlement itself. In the end, then, and perhaps inevitably, religion was what was at stake in the campaign of 1603–7.[51] The Union issue had the capacity to resurrect the Elizabethan struggle over the future of a Church of England 'halfly' reformed, with the Jacobean episcopate, and Archbishop Bancroft in particular, fearful that the hotter sort of English Protestants would again attempt to claim common cause with a kirk

[49] As the 'first winemaker', Noah could also function as a secularised figure for the Eucharist: Jeffrey, *Dictionary of Biblical Tradition*, 551.
[50] Sommerville, *James VI and I*, 135.   [51] Levack, *Formation*, 116.

reformed to continental specifications.[52] It would seem that, for all his public professions of the religious unity that intrinsically united his two kingdoms and argued for perfect Union, James recognized their concerns. And so, donning the language of the prayer book to vest himself and his project in liturgical imagery, the king repeatedly declared his relationship to his new subjects: not simply in the general notion of a shared Protestant communion, but also and more precisely in the English rites prescribed for that communion. Here, then, is the specific framework for the Jacobean political theology of Union as expounded on Twelfth Night 1606/7: the marriage service that united the Hays was the outward and visible sign of an ongoing and spiritual campaign.

In the summer of 1607, James's parliament finally abandoned the formal project for full political Union. But the failure of the king's ambitious plan did not put an end to the rhetoric of the Union campaign. Instead, it simply shifted to articulate another royal programme, the ongoing governance of the king's two churches. And in what might be considered the most significant campaign of this new Anglo-Scottish union project, Robert Wilkinson was once again commanded to the pulpit. It was an inspired choice. Since the Hay wedding, Wilkinson had been trading on the fame of *Merchant Royall*, pointedly referring to it in a 1607 sermon preached before Thomas Cecil, Earl of Exeter (whom he had once served as chaplain) and other county commissioners gathered at Northampton on the occasion of the Midland revolt. 'Right Honorable,' Wilkinson addressed his former employer in the preface to the print version of this sermon, 'it is not long since I came forth in a Merchant's Ship, and now it is God's providence and your good pleasure I shall publish myself in a storm.'[53]

At this time, storms also threatened the Church of England, occasioning the printing of another Wilkinson sermon. Preached at Paul's Cross and suggestively titled *Lot's Wife*, this sermon was dedicated to another patron and facilitator of the Hay wedding, Honora Denny's father, to whom Wilkinson claimed himself 'many years indebted'.[54] *Lot's Wife* appears to be a post-Gunpowder Plot sermon, in which the city of London is warned against sudden death and covert papistry.[55] This

[52] Kenneth Fincham and Peter Lake, 'The ecclesiastical policies of James I and Charles I', in Kenneth Fincham (ed.), *The Early Stuart Church* (1993), 29–30; Ferrell, *Government by Polemic*, 30.

[53] Robert Wilkinson, *A Sermon preached at North-hampton the 21st of June last past . . . upon occasion of the late rebellion and riots in those parts committed* (1607), STC 25662, sig. A3r.

[54] Robert Wilkinson, *Lots Wife* (1607), STC 25656, sig. A2r.

[55] This is the opinion of Millar MacLure, although Wilkinson's preface only implies that the sermon was preached sometime before its publication date of 1607: *The Paul's Cross Sermons* (Toronto and London, 1958), 117, 228.

reference to dangerous secret enemies sets up, in a characteristic polemical shift, a diatribe against wilier enemies openly operating in church and state: 'hypocritical' Christians who 'abuse' the church with which they have been 'blessed'.[56] Here Wilkinson shows himself once again to be a master of the 'bosom enemies' trope beloved of Jacobean conformists, but this time it has been applied to puritans (the term *hypocrite* would have tipped off an early modern audience immediately) rather than double-dealing lords.

In 1617, then, Wilkinson was called upon to bring his impeccably Calvinist-conformist credentials and his public association with James's Scottish policies to speak once again to England's continuing British Problem. The preacher, now a royal chaplain, accompanied James on his progress to Scotland, preaching at Saint Andrews on the issue of cer-emonial reform and Anglo-Scottish religious unity.[57] James's campaign to institute the Five Articles of Perth (which enjoined kneeling at com-munion and the keeping of certain holy days upon the Scots) did not play well north of the Tweed, with the reliably irascible David Calderwood going so far as to label the articles 'insolent', 'unlawful' and 'popish'.[58] The Articles were no English liturgy, however, and it would be as incor-rect to consider them a first irrevocable step towards the imposition of a prayer book on the Scots in 1638 as it would be naive to think that contemporary opinion would not have seen it that way at the time.

While Wilkinson's sermon was part of an occasional campaign to reduce the kirk to some small but significant measures of conformity, publication details raise the question of its ultimate audience. It was not printed in Edinburgh but in London, with a title that proclaimed its direct relation to the author's Hay wedding sermon: *Barwickbridge: Or, England and Scotland Coupled*. Wilkinson draws quite consciously and consistently upon *Merchant Royall* throughout *Barwickbridge*,[59] returning again and again to the issues and polemical strategies of 1603–7. It is, nonetheless, a much different piece of work than its successor, for in it the figure of the king has changed dramatically. Wilkinson's prefatory address, 'as the Babylonians said of Cyrus, The King is become a Jew, *so your Majesty at this time hath been wholly English*,'[60] documents the *ante-nati*

[56] Wilkinson, *Lot's Wife*, 53–4.

[57] Wilkinson had also served as chaplain to Prince Henry: Peter McCullough, *Sermons at Court: Politics and Religion in Elizabethan and Court Preaching* (Cambridge, 1998), 128, 189. McCullough calls Wilkinson the 'doctrinal bridge to Scots Calvinists'.

[58] David George Mullan, *Episcopacy in Scotland* (Edinburgh, 1986), 154.

[59] Although this strategy represents the market advantage in referring to one's own best-sellers, perhaps, as much as it does a dedication to thematic coherence.

[60] Robert Wilkinson, *Barwickbridge* (1617), STC 25652, sig. A3r.

naturalization of James – which in itself marks the vindication of the Union campaign.

With James refigured as an English king, the rhetorical strategies used to decry a state of internal political siege in 1607 could be redeployed with few alterations – a decade later, and against very different intestine enemies. *Barwickbridge* takes as its text Psalm 133: 1, 'Behold how good it is for brethren to dwell together in one.' Addressing a mixed congregation of Scottish and English clergy, Wilkinson admonishes those who would mistake this mutual interest for equal interest:

[H]e were a proud subject that should so equalize himself, as out of that text [2 Corinthians, chapter 11] to call the king brother, so brotherhood in the Church concludes no parity of Church functions . . .[61]

The text citation is worth noting. Chapter 11 of the second epistle to the Corinthians is Paul's declaration of equality to those he none the less calls 'superior apostles', but it begins with the following verse: 'I betrothed you to Christ to present you as a pure bride to her one husband.' Wilkinson's defence of episcopacy and the royal supremacy sets up an extended argument for the church's unity and 'purity', associating these images with the conformist practices of the Church of England:

I keep not other's vines, nor meddle with other Churches, but we of the Church of England do serve and minister to God in white . . . partly to signify the pureness and integrity which should be . . . and partly to give thanks to God and to testify our rejoicing for the peace of the Church.[62]

The preacher's thinly veiled warnings against those who would 'break the peace' of the *ecclesia* need to be read against the backdrop of his presentation of James as an English king and the clubby *we*s and *our*s with which he refers to the king's church and clergy. Wilkinson's pious declaration of his hands-off policy towards the Scottish kirk suggests that the king in fact intended to strong-arm the English church. His admonition is a reminder that the polemics of the Five Articles campaign were crafted to play as (if not more) powerfully to the less-conforming 'brethren' of the Church of England (and the bishops who loved them) as they were to instruct the David Calderwoods of James's larger religious empire.

With its polemical intent to divide and conquer in the name of moderation and unity, Wilkinson's strategy was positively Bancroftian. It hardly comes as a surprise, then, to find the preacher concluding his address to

---

[61] *Ibid.*, 15.   [62] *Ibid.*, 26.

the church where James began his overtures to the English parliament in 1604 with the words of the wedding service from the English Book of Common Prayer. 'All peace and love is founded first in religion,' Wilkinson informed the assembly at Saint Andrews, 'and if God hath coupled us, who then shall put asunder what God hath joined together?'[63]

The correct answer, I suppose, is 'Charles I'. But what is also true is something Professor Russell has often reminded us, that James bequeathed to his successor not only multiple and disparate kingdoms but also multiple and disparate churches. By polemical standards, Union boasted an excellent campaign: imaginatively voiced, sturdily constructed, powerfully supported and culturally apt. And yet neither the Union project nor its later incarnation, the Protestant Union project, was actually successful – at least not in 1607 and not in 1638. And this in itself should earn their polemics our abiding interest. The elegant defence of far-sighted but unsuccessful policy was, after all, the peculiar burden of Jacobean politics.

And of Jacobean historians, who return time and again to the historiographical drawing board to replot the course of political failure in early Stuart England. To read the texts of the Hay wedding is to be struck by the inherent instability of the opening years of a reign, and, inevitably, the importance to the historical record of historical serendipity. It seems clear that the king intended the Union project to be the basis for an irresistible introduction to his new subjects; it appears instead that the fortuitous discovery of the Gunpowder Plot did more to make James an English king.[64] But to read *Merchant Royall* and *Lord Hayes Masque* is also to recognize the staying power of words and images in any well-executed political campaign; these, not events, are the true engines of historiographical continuity. And so, as the case for Union lost its political viability, the polemics of Union became less occasional and more relevant, expressing with adaptive accuracy England and Scotland's innate but unresolved Protestant partnership.

And that paradoxical conjunction has its modern, secular counterpart in the field Professor Russell has done so much to transform. We are at a methodological crossroads in early Stuart history, divided on the issue of whether the age was characterised by conflicts powerful enough to be considered origins of civil war. It is tempting *to posit* – tracing the distance from the English hostility to James's plan to create a unified nation, on to the inter-Protestant dissension in the high ranks of the

---

[63] *Ibid.*, 39.   [64] I have argued this elsewhere: Ferrell, *Government by Polemic*, 53–8.

English church over 'Scotticising' evangelicalism, and on to the Scottish
Prayer Book revolt of 1638 – the existence of a high, or high-church,
road to civil war. But it is possible *to show* James's own abandonment of
an unpopular project, a Jacobean ecclesiastical strategy that never put
the kirk at extreme disadvantage, and a successor's ham-fisted treatment
of his inherited northern kingdom.

The analytical space created between these two methods is traversed
by historical instinct alone. The revisionist take on the Union project
stresses James's politic willingness to settle for less than his desires,
Russell himself noting that the king's abandonment of his beloved
scheme was exemplary of an lassitudinous governing strategy described
as 'let sleeping dogs lie'.[65] Other historians note a disastrous opening to
a new reign and the religious implications of an English anti-puritanism
tarred with an anti-Scottish brush, and recognize those as potentially
incendiary conditions. Both analyses are correct, for our notion of conflict in this period has changed; no longer does it carry the straightforward ideological weight of the nineteenth-century imperial project.
These days, political post-revisionism *is* religious revisionism, evidence
that an era of superb contradiction is best described by historians who
bring to their investigations a judicious mix of historiographical attitudes.
So while this essay tackles a generic collaboration – *what is the relationship
between a court sermon and a court masque in early modern England?* – and assays
a specific historical problem – *what is the political and cultural significance of the
Union campaign of 1603–7?* – it is, in the end, an *apologia* for other unions,
contemporary and academic: of the genres of masque and sermon, of
the archives of history and literature, and of the analytical impulses of
revisionism and post-revisionism.

[65] Russell, *Causes*, 44–5.

3

Capital life: members of parliament outside the House

Pauline Croft

Men gathered at Westminster for the first Jacobean parliament would be familiar with the booksellers' shops around St Paul's churchyard, one of the great intellectual attractions of the capital. In 1606 they could purchase Botero's *Treatise Concerning the Causes of the Magnificencie and Greatnes of Cities* newly translated from the Italian. Sir Robert Cotton, representing Huntingdonshire, would surely have wanted the book, for he was keenly interested in the Florentine's political ideas. Botero emphasised three conditions for urban growth. The first was 'the Residency of the Prince therein', and the second followed, since 'wheare the Prince is resident there also the Parliaments are held and the supreame place of justice is kept'. All matters of importance must have 'recourse to that place', a magnet to 'all such as aspire and thirst after offices and honors'.[1]

By the end of the sixteenth century the court rarely moved outside the Thames valley, and the main royal 'residency' was the palace of Whitehall. One of the idiosyncracies of the English capital was that its two component parts, Westminster and the City of London, were geographically and jurisdictionally separate, linked only by the Strand, a ribbon of development still with open fields north of it. Within Westminster lay Whitehall, Westminster Abbey and the older palace of Westminster itself. It no longer housed the monarch but much of the legal administration of the realm was conducted there. From time to time it was also made ready to receive a parliament.[2] By contrast, the City of London was the financial, mercantile and consumer centre of the kingdom, full of shops, taverns and merchants' warehouses, while the south bank of the Thames offered theatres, bearpits, cockfighting and brothels.

[1] Giovanni Botero, *A Treatise . . . done into English by R. Peterson* (1606). *STC*, 2nd edn, 3405. Kevin Sharpe, *Sir Robert Cotton* (Oxford, 1979) 244–5.

[2] Elizabeth Read Foster, 'Staging a Parliament in early Stuart England', in Peter Clark, A. G. R. Smith and Nicholas Tyacke (eds.), *The English Commonwealth* (Leicester, 1979) 129–46.

Men summoned to a parliament would sample the varied diversions on offer.

The establishment of the seat of medieval government at Westminster was crucial in the history of the capital. Then in the sixteenth century London became 'an engine of economic growth', a centre of conspicuous consumption and the driving force of specialisation in both agriculture and manufactures. Its food markets were expanding, the range of imported goods widened rapidly and it became an unrivalled retailing centre. However, the significance of parliamentary assemblies, as a component of that growth, has been ignored.[3] Yet between the Reading Parliament of 1453 and the Oxford Parliament of 1625, no meeting took place outside the capital, while every session except the brief one at the London Blackfriars in 1523 sat at Westminster. Botero saw the presence of the court as the main economic influence, but a parliament gave a spurt of additional stimulus, bringing extra profits to tradesmen, booksellers, innkeepers and a myriad others. At least two monarchs, Mary and James I, threatened to penalise Londoners by summoning a parliament to Oxford or York, only to find their threat empty, since no other city could provide adequate accommodation or food supplies.[4]

Conrad Russell suggested that London's unstoppable growth was a vital pre-condition conceptually, socially and logistically for the emergence of a permanent assembly in the 1690s. By contrast, Jacobean London was like modern Brighton, 'better suited to hosting conferences'.[5] However, the impact of earlier parliaments should not be underestimated, for any session brought at least a thousand people to Westminster. Over 500 men served in the Commons between 1604 and 1610, and there were around a hundred members of the Lords. Most of them would be accompanied by wives, other family members and servants, all increasing the logistical demands made by a parliament. By comparison, the Castilian Cortes after 1538 consisted merely of thirty-six men without any upper house of nobility. They were hardly noticed when they assembled in Madrid, and were too few to serve as a cultural conduit back to the cities they represented.[6] The English parliament was the largest

---

[3] F. J. Fisher, 'London as an engine of economic growth', in *Fisher, London and the English Economy 1500–1700*, eds. P. J. Corfield and N. B. Harte (1990), 185–98. Fisher's article 'The development of London as a centre of conspicuous consumption' commented only that Westminster 'was the very centre of the political map' (*ibid.*, 110).

[4] *CSPSp, 1554*, 107, 125, 133. *CSPV, 1603–1607*, 488.

[5] Conrad Russell, *Unrevolutionary England 1603–1642* (1990), xix.

[6] In 1610 there were 473 members and there had been 95 bye-elections since 1604. H. Hulme, 'Corrections and additions to the official 'Return' of Members of Parliament, 1603–1604', *BIHR*, 5 (1927–8), 96–105. Pauline Croft and I. A. A. Thompson, 'Aristocracy and representative

representative assembly in Europe, and its impact on its meeting place, on the members who came to it, and on the localities to which they returned, was proportionately great. Men who first visited the capital while serving in the Commons would be keen to return on other occasions, while those already familiar with London could more confidently offer themselves for parliamentary service. In this accelerating process, two periods stand out. Between 1601 and 1610, two parliaments met over five sessions, and between 1621 and 1629, five parliaments met over eight sessions. Such frequent summonses had not been seen since the Reformation Parliament of 1529–36, and Westminster boomed accordingly. Recognising the prospects of commercial growth, in 1609 Robert Cecil, Earl of Salisbury, built Britain's Burse, the first luxury shopping centre outside the City, on land he owned in the Strand.[7]

The impact of a parliament on the capital was only half the story. The effect on members of their metropolitan experiences was equally significant. As Russell also emphasised, a parliament was a social event, not only a point of contact between the king and his subjects but also between members, giving them 'an ideal chance to renew contact with friends or relations who happened to live in other counties' and thereby 'acquire a greater sense of England as a whole'. The insight has not been fully appreciated. The capital was an unparalleled centre for cultural, educational and recreational activities, a world apart from even the largest provincial towns such as York and Norwich. A parliament could have a major intellectual impact, not only on the member himself but also on his family and social circle.[8]

Apart from increased local status and the experience of political participation (no mean benefits in themselves), what did members gain from their stay in Westminster? As is well known, they frequently had business to transact outside the chamber, both personal and for their constituents. This could be in the law courts, or in lobbying leading patrons; many towns regarded the summons to a parliament as an opportunity to pursue multifarious local matters. The chance of specialist shopping was also appreciated. One of Rye's members in 1584–5 bought a drum for the town musters, and in 1626 the two members for Hull sought ordnance for their merchant ships, threatened by pirates.

---

government in unicameral and bicameral institutions', in H. W. Blom (ed.), *Bicameralisme* (The Hague, 1992), 63–86.

[7] Lawrence Stone, *Family and Fortune* (Oxford, 1973), 96–8.

[8] Russell, *Unrevolutionary England*, 1–11. For a survey, Paul Slack, 'Perceptions of the Metropolis in seventeenth-century England', in Peter Burke, Brian Harrison and Paul Slack (eds.), *Civil Histories: Essays presented to Sir Keith Thomas* (Oxford, 2000), 161–73.

In 1629 they lobbied for a licence for six demi-culverins for Hull's fortifications.[9]

A parliament brought scattered groups together. Four northern gentlemen, Sir John Mallory (Ripon), Sir Henry Constable (Hedon), Sir Henry Slingsby (Knaresborough) and Sir Henry Widdrington (Northumberland), met for cards and conversation in Mallory's lodgings in the Strand during the first Jacobean parliament.[10] It would have taken hours of hard riding for them to meet in the north; paradoxically, regional networks formed more easily at Westminster than at home. Similarly, residents in the capital looked forward to the influx. 'Many goode frends are come to towne this parlement', rejoiced the letter-writer John Chamberlain in April 1614.[11] The interaction between Londoners and provincials was an important aspect of a session, linking centre and locality in an exchange of news and gossip.

The publication of numerous parliamentary diaries has both enriched and complicated our understanding of debates, but few reveal much about life outside the chamber. Two sources, however, throw sustained light on the late Elizabethan and early Jacobean period. Between August 1599 and July 1605, Margaret Hoby kept the first surviving diary written by an Englishwoman. The manuscript is a fragment, and may originally have been much longer; it is conventionally pigeonholed as the spiritual exercise of 'a very private Elizabethan lady . . . a pious member of the Yorkshire gentry'.[12] Yet it throws a flood of light on the metropolitan circle of Sir Thomas Posthumous Hoby, who served in ten parliaments between 1589 and 1628. He did not sit in 1601, and his wife did not accompany him to Westminster in 1604, apparently because of ill-health. However, she described in detail their five-month visit to the capital from October 1600 to March 1601. Sir Thomas left again for London in October 1601, although not a member of the parliament then assembling. The couple travelled south in April 1603, for Queen Elizabeth's funeral (when Thomas's elder brother Edward served as a knight of the canopy), returning home in June. Although Thomas was alone at Westminster

---

[9] David Dean, 'Parliament and locality', in David Dean and Norman Jones (eds.), *The Parliaments of Elizabethan England* (Oxford, 1990) 145–6. Hull, Trinity House, LHI/1/1, 17 March 1625/6: Hull RO, January 1629, M.150 (references I owe to Simon Healy of the History of Parliament Trust).

[10] PRO, STAC 8/227/1, fo. 86.

[11] N. E. McClure (ed.), *The Letters of John Chamberlain*, 2 vols. (Philadelphia, 1939) I, 524.

[12] Joanna Moody (ed.), *The Private Life of an Elizabethan Lady: the diary of Lady Margaret Hoby 1599–1605* (Stroud, Gloucs., 1998, hereafter *Hoby*) xi, li, 226. The new edition focuses on life in Yorkshire and does not explore the Hobys' circle in London.

between March and June 1604, he and Margaret went to London again in November 1604, returning to Yorkshire in March 1605.[13]

The diary thus covers three lengthy visits to the capital between October 1600 and March 1605. Lady Hoby's utter self-absorption and constant use of the first person singular can easily mislead; on a casual reading, she travelled alone to London, received a stream of male callers, and went almost everywhere unaccompanied. This clearly was not the case. Most of her descriptions refer to the couple's shared activities, and give an excellent picture of the capital life of a parliament man at the turn of the century.

Some aspects are very familiar. Sir Thomas moved within a wide circle of men, including his lawyers, who dined and supped with him. He conducted extensive legal business, and ordered a new best suit of black satin. His wife bought two spinning wheels – easily obtainable at home – to keep herself occupied, but also made two visits to the Royal Exchange in the City, once to buy a New Year's present possibly intended for the court's annual gift-giving. She went with her mother to the new Venetian glass-houses, presumably to purchase items as well as to inspect the manufacturing process. She was given a fan, a fashionable novelty rarely needed in Yorkshire.[14]

More significant is the evidence for the Hoby circle. Thomas was the posthumous son of the Tudor diplomat Sir Thomas Hoby, while his mother Elizabeth was one of the classically educated daughters of Sir Anthony Cooke of Gidea Hall, Essex. Autocratic and intellectual, she dominated her family, and in 1574 she married John, Lord Russell, heir to the Earl of Bedford. Thereafter she was known as Lady Russell, her husband's death before his father depriving her of the title of countess. Through Elizabeth's eldest sister, Mildred Cecil Lady Burghley, Thomas was connected to both the Lord Treasurer and his younger son Robert Cecil. The Hobys were litigious; Lady Russell engaged in a notable Star Chamber case, and Thomas and Margaret Hoby brought another, arising from a deliberate attempt to disrupt their household by hostile and rumbustious northern neighbours.[15]

Lady Russell actively assisted her son's pursuit of the northern heiress Margaret Dakins Devereux, widowed for the first time in 1591. Her first

[13] *Hoby*, 118–210. P. W. Hasler (ed.), *The History of Parliament: The House of Commons 1558–1603*, 3 vols. (1981), II, 320–4.

[14] *Hoby*, 125, 130, 132, 134, 137, 139.

[15] Felicity Heal, 'Reputation and honour in court and country: Lady Elizabeth Russell and Sir Thomas Hoby', *TRHS*, 6th ser., 6 (1996) 161–78.

husband, the younger brother of the Earl of Essex, was killed on the Normandy expedition and her second, Thomas Sidney, was the brother of Sir Philip the poet and Sir Robert, future Earl of Leicester. When Sidney died in 1595, Hoby and Lady Russell successfully renewed their suit for Margaret.[16] The newly-weds lived on her estates at Hackness but they were not mere Yorkshire gentry. Both were extremely well connected, claiming cousinage with an extensive network of the Elizabethan elite.

The Hobys immediately slipped into this circle whenever they arrived in London. In 1600 they stayed initially at Sir Edward Hoby's town house in Cannon Row; they could walk from there to the law courts in Westminster Hall, and to the abbey, which they visited for worship and for viewing the monuments. Sir Edward Hoby sat in nine parliaments between 1572 and 1614, where he was far more outspoken than his brother. He was also a courtier, married to the daughter of Lord Chamberlain Hunsdon. Edward was a regular visitor to the Hobys in Westminster and his wife accompanied them to court on two occasions. The brothers must have seen the queen frequently at the opening and closing of parliaments, and on 13 November 1600 Thomas and Margaret viewed from 'a standinge' the court procession when Elizabeth returned to Whitehall. They also went to court to see the queen before returning to Yorkshire.[17]

The main family focus was Lady Russell's house in the Blackfriars, where the Hobys' wedding took place in 1596 and where they dined frequently. Lady Russell also helped them to acquire lodgings in the Strand when they moved out of Cannon Row. She retained strong court connections, not least with her nephew Robert Cecil, whom she lobbied on occasion for assistance. At the Blackfriars on 7 January 1601 the Hobys heard about 'the solemnetie at court', the New Year gift-giving between the queen and her leading courtiers and councillors, now led by Cecil. Lady Russell had just married her daughter Anne, Sir Thomas' half-sister, to Lord Herbert, heir to the Earl of Worcester, and they visited Anne's mother-in-law the countess, an additional link with high society. Lady Russell's sister Anne, another of the learned Cooke sisters and a noted patron of puritan preachers, also called on them. Widow of Sir Nicholas Bacon, Elizabeth's first Lord Keeper, she was the mother of the rising lawyer Francis Bacon, who in 1601 was sitting in his sixth parliament.[18]

---

[16] *Hoby* xix–xxviii.

[17] Hasler, *The House of Commons 1558–1603*, II, 320–3. HMC, *Salisbury*, 7, 436. *Hoby*, 124–40.

[18] *Hoby*, 120, 134, 137. HMC, *Salisbury* 9, 321; 18, 436–7. Paul Seaver, *The Puritan Lectureships* (Stanford, 1970), 25, 217, 226.

The other group close to the Hobys were the younger Cookes. 'My old aunt Cooke', as Margaret describes her, was Frances, daughter of Lord John Grey of Pirgo and first cousin to Lady Jane Grey. She was the widow of William Cooke, member of parliament and brother of Mildred Burghley, Elizabeth Hoby Russell and Anne Bacon. Sir Henry Grey, Frances's great-nephew and a gentleman pensioner at court, served in the Commons in 1601. He was married to Elizabeth Neville, daughter of another parliamentary family and another visitor to the Hobys. The Cooke clan was headed by Frances's eldest son William, who sat in parliament in 1597, 1601, 1604–10 and 1614. Clerk of liveries in the Court of Wards, a lucrative post obtained through his Cecil relatives, he was a leading resident of the parish of St Martin in the Fields. The inheritance brought by his wife, Joyce Lucy of Charlecote, also established him as a country gentleman in Warwickshire. Both were frequent visitors to the Hobys and among the group that greeted them immediately on their arrival in London. The Hobys were intensely concerned in 1603 when news came to Yorkshire of the great plague in the capital, when 'the number was taken of the Liuinge and not of the deed'. It must also have been from the interlinked family network that in May 1605 they 'hard of the Creation of Erles and Barons at London, and of the Christeninge of the King's daughter'.[19]

Thomas and Edward Hoby both lobbied Robert Cecil for valuable wardships, as did Margaret.[20] She had additional contacts, for the five Stanhope brothers who all sat in parliament under Elizabeth were her cousins. Nephews by marriage of Protector Somerset, they were members of the Edwardian Protestant circle led by William Cecil that returned to power after 1558. Sir Edward and Sir John Stanhope (Cecil's ward in 1555) served on the Council in the North, and on the northern High Commission alongside Hoby. In London Sir Edward Stanhope visited the Hobys, and in 1601 he sat prestigiously in the Commons as one of Yorkshire's knights of the shire.[21] Lady Sidney, Margaret's sister-in-law during her second marriage, welcomed them in London while her husband Robert was serving as governor of Flushing. Roland White, Sidney's steward and exceptionally well-informed correspondent during his years of absence, also called on them.[22]

[19] *Hoby*, 120, 191, 195, 216. Hasler, *The House of Commons 1558–1603*, I, 644–8; III, 222–3.
[20] HMC, *Salisbury*, 9, 180; 10, 9, 121; 11, 550; 12, 105, 517.
[21] Hasler, *The House of Commons 1558–1603*, III, 436–42. BL, Lansdowne 118, fo. 36. *Hoby*, 113, 129, 191.
[22] *Hoby*, 128. HMC, *De L'Isle and Dudley*, 2, 158, 173, 178, 181, 186.

The Hobys thus belonged to a circle with immense experience of the Elizabethan legal, administrative and parliamentary system. They must have discussed the current situation at home and abroad, quizzed Thomas about the situation in Yorkshire and speculated about the business of the next parliament. The Hobys knew they must make a good impression in the round of visiting, dining and supping. They took their own plate with them, for a handsome display in the capital would bolster Thomas's burgeoning career as a county governor in the north, where he had settled only after his marriage and faced much local dislike.[23]

The Hobys also strengthened links already formed in Yorkshire. Between 1599 and 1603 the Lord Lieutenant and President of the Council in the North was Thomas Cecil, Burghley's elder son, who inherited the title in 1598. His wife Dorothy, co-heiress of the fourth Lord Latimer, brought him Snape castle in Yorkshire, which they rebuilt, together with the money to erect a splendid Italianate villa at Wimbledon. The Hobys visited the Burghleys both at the king's manor in York and at Snape; in return the Burghleys stayed at Hackness. In Westminster, Lord and Lady Burghley were the grandest of the Hobys' friends, inviting them frequently to visit and dine in the great townhouse on the Strand that had been enlarged and adorned since William Cecil purchased it in 1561. The spacious garden created by the late Lord Treasurer was the finest in the capital. Thomas Cecil was also an experienced Commons man, serving in seven parliaments since 1563 before going to the Lords in 1601. He and Hoby were firm allies in the campaign to repress recusancy in Yorkshire.[24]

Anti-popery and positive godliness were the defining themes of the circle. At home, the Hobys regularly attended two sermons on Sundays, as well as fasts and communions, but London provided a richer diet. One of their guests was the elderly Job Throckmorton, in the 1580s the leading parliamentary orator for the Protestant cause; it is very probable that 'Mr Dr Perkins', who visited them, was the great puritan divine. The couple sometimes attended Westminster Abbey and tried out other churches including St Martin in the Fields, but Sunday afternoons were devoted to St Anne Blackfriars, close to Lady Russell's house. They went by river to the exercises led by the radical puritan lecturer Stephen Egerton, who had already been suspended twice and

---

[23] *Hoby*, 190. HMC, *Salisbury*, 7, 418; 10, 302–4.
[24] Caroline Knight, 'The Cecils at Wimbledon', in Pauline Croft (ed.), *Patronage, Culture and Power: the Early Cecils* (2001). Paula Henderson and Jill Husselby, 'Cecil House and Garden', *Country Life*, 23 March 2000, 144–5.

was under threat again in 1601. Occasionally they heard Egerton both morning and afternoon, and also attended some of his Wednesday lectures. Margaret frequently wrote up the addresses of Egerton and other London preachers in her commonplace book (which does not survive), and sent sermon notes to their own parson in Yorkshire. Lady Russell was also a great admirer of Egerton and they often dined with her before or after a sermon. On two occasions when the Hobys stayed in, through ill-health or bad weather, their friend Mr Fuller, Lord Burghley's young chaplain whom they had been invited to hear preach, visited them afterwards and relayed Egerton's lecture. The congregation reputedly contained a majority of godly women, and sometimes Lady Russell and Margaret attended on their own, but Sir Thomas was also a committed follower. In November 1601, the day after arriving home, he read his wife 'some notes of Mr Egerton's lectures', proof that when alone in London Thomas followed the same round of devotion. On Sunday 17 April 1603, when the Hobys arrived in London, they 'gott thether in time to Mr Egerton's exercises', despite their tiring five-day journey.[25]

Egerton was disciplined on 8 January 1605, as part of the drive for greater conformity to the canons of 1604. 'Mr Egerton with divers others silenced by the Bishop of London', noted Margaret. Sir Thomas after a pause for thought wrote at length to his cousin Robert Cecil, now Viscount Cranborne, carefully defending Egerton from any irregularities and acknowledging Cecil's assistance in 1601. Egerton was eventually restored in 1607.[26] The Hobys in Yorkshire felt as close in spirit to Egerton's stunned congregation as their kin who lived in Blackfriars. The silencing offended significant county interests with court contacts. The Hobys' devoted attendance, with their sermon notes attentively taken and sent on to country clergy, also reveals how the capital's puritan preachers extended their influence. In the mid sixteenth century hopes were high that reformed religion and civility would spread outwards from London.[27] Sermon-going by members of parliament and their wives assisted the transmission of godliness to the localities.

In the Commons of 1604–10 Sir Thomas Posthumous Hoby would encounter Sir Richard Paulet of Freefolk, sitting for Whitchurch (Hants).

---

[25] *Hoby*, 119–39, 173, 187, 205–6. Seaver, *The Puritan Lectureships, passim* for Egerton. R. P. Sorlien (ed.), *The Diary of John Manningham 1602–1603* (Hanover, N. H., 1976), 115, 367–8.
[26] *Hoby*, 209. Hatfield House, Cecil Papers 188/53, 28 Jan. 1604/5. I am grateful to the Marquess of Salisbury for access to the Cecil papers.
[27] Patrick Collinson and John Craig, *The Reformation in English Towns 1500–1640* (1998), 9.

His diary covers the 1610 session, and strikingly illuminates his activities both in the chamber and outside.[28] Paulet was distantly related to the marquesses of Winchester and one of a clan of members of parliament, though he could not match Hoby's circle of highly placed kin. In the Commons, however, he found himself at the epicentre of national and international events. The experiences related in Paulet's diary would widen the horizon of any provincial gentleman and inform conversations back in Hampshire for a lifetime.

Paulet's brother-in-law was the godly, wealthy Sir Henry Wallop, who sat in ten parliaments between 1597 and 1640, and Paulet's election in 1604 came when Wallop was unable to stand after being pricked sheriff of Hampshire. Paulet was active in his county, serving as a JP, collector then commissioner for the subsidy, captain of the militia, and sheriff in 1590–1. In 1604 he was accused in Star Chamber of oppressive practices as a landlord, and in May 1607 was served a subpoena from the Exchequer; he replied claiming parliamentary privilege. Paulet's local career ended in 1608 when he was dismissed from the Hampshire bench, evidence that he had abused his position, but as a member of parliament he was summoned to the fourth session on 9 February 1610.

The diary was probably intended in part as notes for the excluded Sir Henry, with whom Paulet maintained close links. The Wallops stayed in London throughout the session, and on 11 February Paulet attended sabbath morning prayer at their house. Wallop also introduced Paulet to distinguished members of the Commons. On Ascension day, they visited the sick Sir Rowland Lytton of Knebworth at his house near St Paul's. The intellectual and well-connected Lytton, whose wife was stepmother by an earlier marriage to Lady Wallop, had links with the Cecils and was knight of the shire for Hertfordshire, whose troops he had led to Tilbury in 1588. Later the same month Wallop and Paulet travelled briefly back to Hampshire, and in November Paulet escorted Lady Wallop to church.[29]

Paulet's activities outside the Commons' Chamber confirm the usual picture of members' activities. He attended both the courts of Star

---

[28] I am grateful to the Hampshire Record Office for providing a xerox of the diary from the Jervoise of Herriard MSS, and for obtaining permission to cite it. All quotations (spelling modernised) are from my transcript (hereafter *Paulet*). Dr Eric Lindquist is completing a full scholarly edition for *Parliamentary History Records*. I am also grateful to Dr Andrew Thrush of the History of Parliament Trust for access to research notes and biographies prepared on Sir Richard Paulet, Sir Henry Wallop, Sir Thomas Jervoise, Sir Nicholas Halswell, Sir Robert Halswell and Sir Robert Phelipps, allowing me to identify Paulet's circle. All references to them not otherwise footnoted are from these materials.

[29] *Paulet*, fos. 1, 10v, 14v, 31. Hasler, *The House of Commons 1558–1603*, II, 509; III, 567.

Chamber and Exchequer Chamber, and on 29 June was present at Lincoln's Inn, in the chamber of Sir James Ley, attorney of the Court of Wards, at a case involving a sister of his own ward and son-in-law Sir Thomas Jervoise. Two other relatives were also engaged in legal matters which occasionally required his help. Paulet retained Francis Stonor, an attorney, for further assistance. He was an enthusiastic shopper, buying a wide range of goods to take home including modish 'willow-coloured' stockings and children's treats. He purchased some twenty books and pamphlets, including a souvenir account of Prince Henry's installation and the printed versions of the king's speech of 21 March 1610.[30]

In Westminster terms, Paulet was a backbencher. He was named to six committees, and was prepared to give evidence against the purveyors, but there is no record of his having spoken between March 1604 and December 1610. In 1614 his sole contribution was to comment on the Lord's Day Observance Bill that the sabbath was commonly taken to mean Sunday.[31] Nevertheless, his diary shows that he paid very careful attention to bills and debates, particularly on the central issues of the Great Contract and impositions. He sat assiduously on committees, recording many of their proceedings and protocols, and also went to several conferences with the Lords. These took place outside the main chamber and in a more relaxed atmosphere. On 19 July 1610 Paulet heard the exhausted Robert Cecil, now Earl of Salisbury confess that he had forgotten the point reached in the last conference 'and desired Mr Martin to help him with his notes'. Accepting the Commons' complaints against Sir Stephen Proctor on 21 July, Salisbury described him as 'not fit ... to be a proctor to a spittle house', a pithy pun he omitted in the Lords.[32] The intimacy of conference discussions enhanced their impact on members of the lower house, who must have felt close to the inner sanctum of government.

Paulet saw the king on several occasions. They were summoned to Whitehall on 22 May, 'but no particular place named, so the house agreed to meet first in the garden'. Then they went up 'to the great chamber, where many seats were, and as soon as the room was full the king, prince [Henry] nobles and bishops came'. They saw James twice again at Whitehall, on 10 July and on 31 October, when he chastised them for their footdragging on the Contract.[33]

[30] *Paulet*, fos. 1, 1v, 19, 24, 31. Dr Lindquist's edition will also print valuable material from Paulet's accounts, which he generously made available to me.
[31] Maija Jansson (ed.), *Proceedings in Parliament 1614* (Philadelphia, 1988), 172.
[32] *Paulet*, fos. 1v, 3, 4v, 7v, 17, 26v, 28.   [33] *Paulet*, fos. 11v, 23, 29.

The proximity of the court allowed members to go there on other occasions. Paulet attended the imposing parliamentary ceremony when Prince Henry was installed as Prince of Wales on 4 June 1610, which he recorded at length, noting the presence of 'the little duke of York' and the royal ladies Princess Elizabeth and Lady Arbella Stuart. He provides the vivid detail that 'all Westminster Hall and the palace windows and leads /were/ as too full to see their coming forth as might be'.[34] The next day after dinner Paulet slipped away to the court festivities, 'walking in the garden to see those that went into the masque that night'. He returned again for the running at tilt, with the contestants in multi-coloured costumes: 'the duke of Lenox camparisons and feathers red and white ... Sir Thomas Somerset, white, yellow, green and red. Earl of Dorset, red and white. Lord North, blue and watchet'. Some made dramatic entrances in fantastical displays. 'Lord Dingle came in a cloud with envy before and his followers blackamoors. The Lord Compton came out of a beacon placed in the tiltyard'. On 5 November, the anniversary of the Gunpowder Plot, Paulet noted that 'there was that afternoon dancing before the king in the great chamber and at night a play'.[35]

Paulet never makes any criticism of James's court, but he must have known that the Contract was attempting to repair the ravages of the king's lavish spending, not least on the court Scots. He carefully noted the bills to naturalise Scotsmen, including the new favourite Sir Robert Carr. However, Carr had risen at court since the last parliamentary session, so Paulet did not know his first name and left a blank.[36]

Paulet also attended the chapel royal at Whitehall. On 1 April the sermon was followed by a communion, 'to which I went and communicated, giving for offering xii pence. There communicated divers gentlemen ... courtiers and some that I knew, as my Lord Knyvet, my Lord Stanhope, Sir Thomas Lake [the king's Latin secretary, a fellow member of the Commons] and Sir John Needham'. Then afterwards 'one came to my man to know my name, for he said he must make a bill to the king of all that received in the chapel', evidence of James's keen attention to court conformity. Paulet returned that afternoon to hear Toby Matthew, Archbishop of York, an indefatigable preacher, and took notes. The king should fear God, and must not carelessly pass over 'God's benefits and his charge. For of him to whom much is committed, much will be required'. The stern emphasis on royal duty cannot have

[34] *Paulet*, fo. 14v. Pauline Croft, 'The parliamentary installation of Henry Prince of Wales', *HR*, 65 (1992), 177–93.
[35] *Paulet*, fos. 15, 29.   [36] *Paulet*, fo. 2v.

offended, for on 22 July the archbishop preached before the king, Prince Henry and Princess Elizabeth, an indication of royal favour.[37]

Paulet also enjoyed moving in a wider social circle. On 12 February he dined with William Paulet, Lord St John, heir of the fourth Marquess of Winchester. Attending the sermon at St Peter's the Poor, he observed 'my Lord St John of Bletso, Lord Russell, Lady Cumberland and divers of the best citizens'. He maintained close relations with Lord and Lady Saye and Sele, visiting Lady Saye on the afternoon of Saturday 9 June. On Sunday he and his cousin Robert Halswell accompanied the Sayes to church, and afterwards went off to dine at their house, 'and there stayed talking until about 5 o clock and then went to my lady Marquess with my Lady Saye in her coach and so brought her home again and then came away'. 'My lady Marquess' was Lucy Cecil, a favourite niece of Lord Salisbury and the mother of Lord St John.[38] This sociable Sunday afternoon's visiting illuminates the constant informal conversations that occurred between members of the Lords and the Commons, and mirrors the relationship between Sir Thomas Posthumous Hoby and Thomas Cecil Lord Burghley.

At Westminster, country gentlemen could learn much about foreign policy. Paulet was up-to-date on French affairs, since in April his cousin Halswell returned from France, where he had been travelling with Sir Robert Phelipps, and they dined together. Halswell remained in London and the two met frequently.[39] The link explains Paulet's very full notes on 'news now of great consequence, the death and murder of a great prince, the French king' after the lower house was told on 8 May 1610 of the assassination of Henri IV. Restrictions on Catholics were increased and a night search was made of all houses and inns used by them in the capital. Paulet sat on a committee examining some London recusants who had harboured priests, when a witness incriminated 'one Mr Burd, a musician, . . . there as he thinketh at a mass'. William Byrde, composer and former organist of the chapel royal, had already published many of his compositions and psalm-settings,

---

[37] *Paulet*, fos. 6, 28.

[38] *Paulet*, fos. 1, 7v, 15. The Paulet network included Oliver St John, 3rd Baron St John of Bletso (d.1618), whose son and heir was married to the daughter of William Paulet of Ewalden and his wife Elizabeth. Richard Fiennes (*c.*1557–1613), Lord Saye and Sele, subsequently married the widowed Elizabeth Paulet as his second wife. *GEC*, 11, 335, 484–5. For Winchester's marriage to Lucy Cecil, *GEC*, 12 (2), 765–6.

[39] *Paulet*, fos. 6v, 19, 31. Paulet left Phelipps' first name blank, but Sir Robert is known to have travelled in France and Spain in 1607, 1613 and 1614–16: this must have been a visit unrecorded elsewhere. The identification is confirmed by the Somerset background of both Halswell and Sir Robert Phelipps.

so Paulet's ignorance of the name suggests an absence of musical education.[40]

The diary reveals London's extraordinary wealth of sermons, including previously unknown ones preached at Paul's Cross. Paulet belonged to a godly circle in Hampshire, and in his will, besides expressing confidence in his salvation, he left an annuity of £50 for twelve years to provide for 'a sufficient preacher to instruct the people in the knowledge of God's word and administer divine service and sacraments in my church or chapel of Freefolk'.[41] Paulet took notes on sermons – a skill redeployed in his Commons diary – and often wrote them out in full later. They may well have been rehearsed to friends on his return home, or circulated among them, as with those sent back to Yorkshire by Lady Hoby.

Paulet sought out a much wider cross-section of preaching than the Hobys. Between February and November 1610 he attended thirty-five sermons, usually two on each Sunday, including eight at St Paul's cathedral and six, possibly seven, at Paul's Cross. Paulet also attended Westminster Abbey on Saturday 24 March, James's Accession day, and on Ascension day he heard a sermon by the curate at St Clement Danes. He also went to two sermons and a reading at the Temple church, and on Shrove Tuesday joined other members of the Commons at a burial service with sermon at St Dunstan in the West. The deceased was the veteran Elizabethan parliament man Hannibal Vivian, Attorney-General of the Duchy of Cornwall, and attendance showed respect for his son Francis, who sat in 1604–10.[42] For most of these sermons Paulet gives the text and the theme, and for a handful he wrote an extensive précis.

The Jacobean bishops were prominent in London pulpits during the parliament, which required their presence in the Lords. Archbishop Matthew preached at the chapel royal, but Archbishop Bancroft was largely absent, which must reflect his failing health. His successor at Canterbury was to be George Abbot, Bishop of London, whom Paulet heard on 18 February in St Paul's. On two occasions he noted that Abbot was in church to hear other preachers, and also that Abbot preached a powder plot sermon in November. Paulet apparently sensed that Abbot was the coming man in terms of ecclesiastical promotion. However, his sermon notes are rather brief, although in St Paul's, Abbot made

[40] *Paulet*, fo. 23. Croft, 'The parliamentary installation of Henry', 187. Possibly the recusant was Byrd's second son Thomas, another musician, who lived in Drury Lane. *DNB*, 3, 575–8.

[41] *Register of Sermons Preached at Paul's Cross 1534–1642 by Millar MacLure*, revised and expanded by Peter Pauls and Jackson Campbell Boswell (Ottawa, 1989). PRO, PROB 11 / 127, fo. 366.

[42] *Paulet*, fos. 2, 3v, 8v, 10v, 29. Hasler, *The House of Commons 1558–1603*, III 559.

a pleasingly characteristic attack on 'the disobedient Jesuited papists', balanced by a side-swipe at those nonconformists who 'misliking the government of the Church of England' bred scandal and 'much schism and contention'.[43]

St Paul's, and its external pulpit Paul's Cross, were the usual places to hear visiting prelates, and Paulet heard the Bishops of Bangor, Chester, Oxford and Gloucester. From the lengthy precis of the texts and themes covered, Henry Rowlands of Bangor impressed Paulet on 25 March, with a sermon designed for outdoors but preached in the cathedral 'because the weather was too wet'. It concluded with a passionate denunciation of usury, 'taken now to be almost legitimate', as Rowlands bitterly remarked. 'It is not meet the rich borrow, for they have no need. It is not fit the poor borrow, for it will make them poorer.' This was a bold attack on modern financial practice in the heart of the City of London. Rowlands was praised in his diocese for his generous house-keeping, another indication that he was an upholder of old-fashioned values.[44]

Not all bishops were up to the standard of Rowlands. John Bridges of Oxford preached at Paul's Cross on 13 May but Paulet could make little of his efforts, only that his text out of Psalm 119 was 'divided into a complaint and a cause of complaints'. When George Lloyd of Chester preached on 20 May, Paulet wrote down the verse 'What profiteth it a man to gain the whole world and lose his own soul', but none of the exegesis. Dr John Spenser, king's chaplain, President of Corpus, Oxford, and literary executor of Richard Hooker, was also rector of St Sepulchre's, the largest parish church in the City. Paulet went to hear him at Paul's Cross on 24 June, but it was a disappointment. He only caught the text, from the first chapter of 1 Corinthians: 'he delated hereupon but I stood where I could not hear him'.[45] Paulet's experiences at Paul's Cross provide a salutary reminder that the practical problems of bad weather and inaudibility often muted the impact of preaching claimed to represent 'the popular voice of the Church of England'.[46]

Paulet's most noteworthy experience came on 10 June, when he attended St Paul's in the company of Robert Halswell and Lord and Lady Saye. The preacher turned out to be Dr Thornborough, Bishop of Bristol and Dean of York, so Paulet's party left the cathedral and went

[43] *Paulet*, fos. 2, 16v, 29. For the rise of Abbot, Kenneth Fincham, *Prelate as Pastor: the Episcopate of James I* (Oxford, 1990), 27–9.
[44] *Paulet*, fos. 3v–4v. Fincham, *Prelate as Pastor*, 73–4.
[45] *Paulet*, fos. 10, 11v, 17v. HMC, *Salisbury*, 17, 612–13.
[46] Millar MacLure, *The Paul's Cross Sermons 1534–1642* (Toronto and London, 1958), 167.

instead to a church near Leadenhall, where a more acceptable but un-named cleric discoursed on Amos chapter 6. Bishop Thornborough was a frequent dining companion of the godly Hobys, since like Sir Thomas he was an ardent enforcer of the recusancy statutes, but he was a poor preacher and a notorious pluralist. Lord Sheffield, Thomas Cecil's successor as President of the Council in the North, went so far as to describe Thornborough as an 'evil spirit'.[47] Preceded by a repu-tation like that, Thornborough's appearance in the pulpit provoked an exodus. The event put Paulet off from his usual routine of attend-ing two services each Sunday, and he spent the afternoon with the Sayes.

St Paul's dominated London sermon-going, but some parish clergy had a staunch following. Paulet went repeatedly to St Clement Danes, whose minister, Dr John Layfield, was a Cecil client, having been chap-lain to Lord Burghley (since 1605 Earl of Exeter) before receiving his benefice through the patronage of Robert Cecil. Layfield constantly em-phasised the power of scripture: 'sound and pure . . . not only directed to the whole church but to every particular member . . . a chief ground to draw us unto God'. When Layfield appeared at Paul's Cross, Paulet heard him attentively: 'I have most of his sermon written'. Paulet also went to sermons at St Giles, St Andrews Holborn, and St Katherine Cree, seeking out good preachers.[48]

Members of Stephen Egerton's congregation knew that he was con-troversial. In Paulet's account, however, there seems to be only one ser-mon that could be so described. He was away from Westminster on 11 March 1610, four weeks into the session, when Samuel Harsnett, Bishop of Chichester and a former chaplain to Salisbury, preached at Whitehall on 'Render unto Caesar the things that are Caesar's'. The sermon does not survive, so its contents are known only from its crit-ics, but in the Commons it was 'much disliked and found fault with'.[49] Members interpreted it as asserting that subsidies were not free gifts to

---

[47] *Paulet*, fo. 15. HMC, *Salisbury*, 19, 274. McClure, *The Letters of John Chamberlain*, I, 172.

[48] *Paulet*, fos. 9, 22v, 24v, 31. PRO, SP14/15/41. Hatfield House, Cecil Papers 114/73, Layfield to Cranborne.

[49] Harsnett's sermon does not appear on Dr Peter E. McCullough's exhaustive list appended on disc to *Sermons at Court: Politics and Religion in Elizabethan and Jacobean Preaching* (Cambridge, 1998), but James said that it had been preached before him: Elizabeth Read Foster, *Proceedings in Parliament 1610*, 2 vols. (New Haven and London, 1966) I, 46. The date of 11 March is fixed by the anonymous account of the king's speech, SP14/53/31, which refers to the sermon as 'on Sunday was sennight'. McCullough (disc) lists Henry Cotton, Bishop of Salisbury, as appointed to preach at court on 11 March, so Harsnett may have been a last-minute substitute who blundered into controversy.

the king, but duties the subject was obliged to render. The theme was not new, for already by 1601 high prerogative lawyers were contentiously arguing that consent to taxation was in the last resort unnecessary. Such views were equally ill received in 1610. The Commons were particularly sensitive after the debates on Dr Cowell's law-dictionary, *The Interpreter*, which espoused similar definitions of taxation. The Great Contract, presented in parliament by Harsnett's erstwhile employer the Earl of Salisbury, also focused attention on the subsidy. The king felt impelled to come to the bishop's support on 21 March, when Paulet heard him speak at Whitehall. He told the assembled members that Harsnett had said nothing but what 'every good subject and not a traitor will grant'.[50] His intervention was unsuccessful, for at the end of the session in November Harsnett and his text were still being recalled resentfully by the Commons. Years later, in 1627, just before an even more tumultuous parliamentary session, Archbishop Abbot went further, alleging that Harsnett's sermon had been burnt. Since it had been publicly praised by James, this was obviously impossible, but Abbot considered that it ought to have been burnt, and took the opportunity, while condemning the Forced Loan, of attacking the political opinions of Harsnett and other leading Arminians.[51]

Two weeks later Paulet heard the Accession day sermon at Westminster Abbey, which he attended after a morning in the House. This hitherto-unknown sermon must have been orchestrated, since it was on Harsnett's text, 'Give unto Caesar the things that are Caesar's and unto God the things that are God's'. The preacher 'showed three things specially to be due unto kings: 1) honour 2) love and 3) money and goods, as resembling the majesty of God upon earth, to whom all honour, love and free offerings do belong, which the people ought in all duty to perform unto them: and the king reciprocally to them, which is signified by his crown, sceptre of justice and sword'. Paulet gives no indication that this sermon caused offence, or disquieted him personally, and leaves the cleric's name blank.[52] One possibility would be Dr Henry Caesar, brother of the Chancellor of the Exchequer and a prebendary of Westminster, who delivered the abbey's powder plot sermon in 1610. If he preached on 24 March, it would suggest Privy Council influence, but the coincidence of Caesar's name and his text would surely not have

---

[50] *Paulet*, fo. 3. J. E. Neale, *Elizabeth I and her Parliaments 1584–1601* (1957), 415–16. Foster, *Proceedings 1610*, I, 46. J. P. Sommerville, *Royalists and Patriots: Politics and Ideology in England 1603–1640* (1999), 124, 150.

[51] Foster, *Proceedings 1610*, II, 328. *ST*, II, col. 1463.   [52] *Paulet*, fo. 3v.

gone unnoticed by Paulet.[53] There is a tantalising possibility, however, that the preacher was William Laud, already chaplain to Richard Neile, Bishop of Rochester, Clerk of the Closet, Dean of Westminster and another former chaplain of Salisbury. In September 1609 Neile selected Laud to preach before the king for the first time. He supported him for a canonry of Westminster late in 1610, and Laud became a royal chaplain in November 1611.[54] Did Neile give Laud the chance to ingratiate himself with the king on Accession day, when he reiterated not merely Harsnett's text but also James' own words to the Commons only three days earlier, on 21 March? The most surprising fact is the absence of comment on a sermon that dealt provocatively with taxation.

It is difficult to establish any theological stance from Paulet's entries. His interest in preaching and his will testify to his godly outlook. He must have had opportunities to hear Lancelot Andrewes, the most famous court preacher of the day, but there is no mention of him. At a court communion, the sermon by 'one Dr Beck', on the text 'Christ is our passover', emphasised 'that all should eat and be partakers of the sacrament, young and old, great and small . . . none must excuse himself from coming to this banquet, much less refuse . . . for if we do we deny one of the articles of the faith viz the communion of saints'.[55] This high view of the sacrament was close to Andrewes's own, but Paulet makes no comment. Nor was he obsessed by predestination, recording Rowlands at Paul's Cross depicting Christ's words to blind Bartimaeus as a picture of divine mercy, extended to all that believe and call upon Him. An evening sermon in the Temple gloried in preaching, 'no new device of Luther or Calvin but it appeared plain in Joshua's and Nehemiah's time and in the New Testament', but went on to decry 'our curiosity in these days to know God's secrets, as to know how infants and fools that cannot understand preaching may be saved, which is done by God's spirit working inwardly with their spirits'. In November 1610 Paulet went to hear both John Buckeridge, Laud's tutor, and Henry Airey, a strict Calvinist, but gives little more than their texts.[56] There is no indication here of a theologically divided church. Paulet saw the sermons he recorded as occupying common ground, and accepted a broad swathe of Jacobean divinity. He registered no fault-lines, although Harsnett's sermon and

---

[53] For Dr Caesar, L. M. Hill, *Bench and Bureaucracy: the Public Career of Sir Julius Caesar* (Cambridge, 1988), 96–7.
[54] Fincham, *Prelate as Pastor*, 42, 306. *CSPD, 1603–10*, 644.
[55] *Paulet*, fo. 6. The identity of the preacher defeated not only Paulet but also Dr McCullough (disc).
[56] *Paulet*, fos. 6, 8, 8v, 29, 31v.

its successor in Westminster Abbey were fraught with future political significance.

The Hoby and Paulet diaries reveal the broader experiences that surrounded parliamentary service. Besides frequenting the capital's law-courts and shops, Commons men moved in extended social circles, gathering information, benefiting from the fruits of others' experience and making useful contacts. The bonds between far-reaching networks of friends and kin reinforced the cohesion of the lower house, enabling them to sense horizons much wider than a single locality. The easy, sociable association with members of the Lords helped to keep both houses in tandem. The two diaries' previously unexplored evidence for the impact of metropolitan pulpits is very significant. Both Hoby and Paulet seized opportunities for sermon-attendance, and their assiduity underlines the centrality of religion to the early Stuart Commons. Paulet's record of the bishops indicates how a parliament brought extra intellectual and theological resources, not merely economic ones, to the capital. Godly members served as a conduit, transmitting London sermons back to their own parishes, including those of radicals like Egerton who were at odds with the ecclesiastical establishment. Along with Paulet's topical book-buying, this vividly exemplifies that 'consumption of culture as text' which began to expand from the capital to the provinces at the beginning of the early seventeenth century.[57]

In all these ways, links formed and strengthened at Westminster melded the Commons into something much more than an assembly of men randomly elected from across the nation. In creating this cohesion, life outside the chamber was probably as important as the debates within it. In March 1629, after another intensive period of parliamentary gatherings, the lower house rejected Charles I's order to dissolve and instead denounced innovations in both church and state. Their objective 'was the potentially revolutionary one of appealing over the king's head to the country at large'.[58] By then, a strong sense of shared experiences powerfully reinforced a new-found conviction that it was the Commons, not the king, that properly understood the concerns of 'England as a whole'.

[57] Ann Bermingham and John Brewer, *The Consumption of Culture 1600–1800: Image, Object, Text* (1995), esp. 3–5.
[58] Conrad Russell, *Parliaments and English Politics 1621–1629* (Oxford, 1979), 415.

4

The Personal Rule of James I, 1611–1620

Andrew Thrush

It is a point which deserves greater attention than it has received that from at least the end of 1610 James I detested English parliaments, and in particular the House of Commons.[1] 'Our fame and actions have been daily tossed like tennis balls amongst them,' he complained in December 1610. The Commons had 'perilled and annoyed our health, wounded our reputation, emboldened all ill-natured people, encroached upon many of our privileges, and plagued our purse with their delays'.[2] In June 1614 James told the Spanish ambassador, Sarmiento, that he envied Spain as 'the Cortes of Castile were composed of little more than thirty persons', whereas the Commons 'was made up of little less than five hundred', who lacked a head and 'voted without order, nothing being heard but cries, shouts and confusion'. He was 'astonished that the kings his predecessors had consented to such a thing'.[3] Neither these remarks, nor the comments made in December 1610, were merely momentary outbursts of anger as they have sometimes been portrayed.[4] James was bitter that his cherished plans for a formal Union between England and Scotland had been thwarted (1606–7), and he was enraged at the rejection of the Great Contract (1610). His sense of loathing was increased in 1614, when the Commons criticised royal overspending and refused to vote supply unless impositions were first abolished. Between 1610 and 1620 James regarded holding a parliament as the least attractive of his options, and aimed to rule without one for as long as possible. Indeed, several scholars have tacitly acknowledged that the avoidance of parliaments was a defining characteristic of the middle years of his reign.

---

[1] James entertained no such distaste for the Scottish Parliament, M. Lee Jr., *Great Britain's Solomon: James VI and I in His Three Kingdoms* (Urbana and Chicago, 1990), 94. All dates given in this article are according to the Julian calendar.

[2] HMC, *Salisbury*, 21, 266.

[3] S. R. Gardiner (ed.), *Narrative of the Spanish Marriage Treaty* (Camden Society, 101, 1869), 288.

[4] Conrad Russell, *The Crisis of Parliaments: English History 1509–1660* (Oxford, 1971), 283; D. Smith, *The Stuart Parliaments, 1603–1689* (1999), 103. Smith's claim that James did not aspire to personal rule is unconvincing.

A. G. R. Smith, for instance, has observed that after 1610 James 'never really recovered a spirit of goodwill' towards parliaments, while Conrad Russell has remarked that it is perhaps surprising that the years 1614–21 'have never come to be known as the "seven years of unparliamentary government"'.[5] Claims such as these echo the Assistant Clerk of the Commons, John Rushworth, who in 1659 referred to James's 'great dislike of parliaments'.[6] However, while James's detestation of parliaments has received some notice, the Jacobean Personal Rule, unlike its Caroline equivalent, has never been satisfactorily examined.[7] What strategies were adopted by James to avoid a parliament, why did these fail temporarily in 1614 and how close to collapse did they come at other times? What impact did James's Personal Rule have on his foreign policy? How widespread was the knowledge of the king's unwillingness to call a parliament and what reaction did it provoke, both in the country at large and among James's closest advisers? Finally, what parallels can be drawn between James's extra-parliamentary government and the Personal Rule of the 1630s, and what are the implications for early Stuart scholarship of thinking in terms of two periods of Personal Rule rather than one? These questions are perhaps best approached in the first instance by exploring the events of 1610–20 in some detail.

Following the collapse of the Great Contract in 1610 and the dissolution of January 1611, James appears to have concluded that he would only call another parliament if he could find no other way to make ends meet. However, since his financial situation was increasingly desperate he was soon urged to contemplate another meeting. As early as October 1611, the Berkshire gentleman Sir Henry Neville, a former member of the Commons, proposed to manage a future parliament for the king in return for appointment as Secretary of State. Neville resented having been denied office by Lord Treasurer Salisbury, whom he blamed for the failure of the Great Contract, and was supported in his ambitions by the

---

[5] A. G. R. Smith, 'Crown, parliament and finance: the Great Contract of 1610', in Peter Clark, A. G. R. Smith and Nicholas Tyacke (eds.), *The English Commonwealth 1547–1640: Essays in Politics and Society* (Leicester and New York, 1979) 126; Conrad Russell, 'Parliamentary history in perspective, 1604–1629', *Hist.*, 61 (1976), 6, n.18. See also Lee, *Great Britain's Solomon*, 93; L. Stone, *The Crisis of the Aristocracy 1558–1641* (Oxford, 1965), 103–4; R. Zaller, *The Parliament of 1621: A Study in Constitutional Conflict* (Berkeley, Los Angeles, 1971), 18; V. Treadwell, *Buckingham and Ireland 1616–1628: A Study in Anglo-Irish Politics* (Dublin, 1998), 148–9 (I owe this reference to Lloyd Bowen).

[6] J. Rushworth, *Historical Collections of Private Papers of State* (1721), I, 20.

[7] Kevin Sharpe, *The Personal Rule of Charles I* (New Haven, 1992); Esther S. Cope, *Politics without Parliaments, 1629–1640* (1987).

king's Scottish favourite, Robert Carr, Viscount Rochester.[8] As a consequence of Neville's plan, the French and Venetian ambassadors reported
that a fresh parliament was imminent.[9] Following Salisbury's death in
May 1612, the Chancellor of the Exchequer, Sir Julius Caesar, also advised a parliament, both to reduce the crown's debt of almost £500,000
and eliminate the annual shortfall between ordinary receipts and ordinary expenditure, which amounted to £160,000.[10] James was obliged to
consider this advice seriously, for despite the windfalls generated by the
recent sale of baronetcies and the privy seal loan of 1611–12, retrenchment and new cash-raising projects alone were thought unlikely to solve
his financial difficulties. Furthermore, he was unable to borrow from the
City, as he had not yet repaid the corporation a loan he had received
in April 1610.[11] In July 1612 he summoned Neville to Windsor to advise
him, again prompting rumours that a parliament would shortly meet.[12]

James was saved from having to call a parliament later that summer
by developments on the diplomatic front. In September 1612 the Duke
of Savoy, who had been negotiating for a marriage between his daughter
and Henry, Prince of Wales, offered to pay a dowry of 700,000 crowns
(£210,000).[13] Although this would eliminate less than half the royal debt,
it was a substantial sum, equivalent to three parliamentary subsidies at
the rate of 1610, and would ensure that a parliament could be avoided
for the time being. James's expectations of a large dowry were heightened in late October, when England's ambassador in Paris, Sir Thomas
Edmondes, was privately assured that France would pay 800,000 crowns
(£240,000) if Henry would marry the six-year-old Princess Christine.[14]
France was worried that a Savoyard marriage would result in her encir-
clement, as Savoy was regarded as a Spanish satellite.

Contrary to some expectations, Henry's sudden death in November 1612 increased rather than diminished James's chance of relief
through a large dowry.[15] The considerable age difference between the

---

[8] HMC, *Buccleuch*, I, 101–2.   [9] PRO, PRO 31/3/43, fos. 162v–163; *CSPV, 1610–13*, 230, 240, 276.

[10] BL, Lansdowne MS 165, fos. 211–12.

[11] R. Ashton, *The Crown and the Money Market 1603–1640* (Oxford, 1960), 118–119, 120, 157.

[12] M. Jansson (ed.), *Proceedings in Parliament 1614 (House of Commons)* (American Philosophical Society, vol. 172; Philadelphia, 1988), 238, 244; *CSPV, 1610–13*, 412; M. C. Questier (ed.), *Newsletters from the Archpresbyterate of George Birkhead* (Camden Society, 5th ser. 12, 1998), 191.

[13] *CSPV, 1610–13*, 458.   [14] PRO, SP 78/60, fos. 183–8v.

[15] N. E. McClure (ed.), *The Letters of John Chamberlain*, 2 vols. (Philadelphia, 1939), I, 391; *CSPV, 1610–13*, 452. This paragraph summarises my 'The French Marriage and the Origins of the 1614 Parliament', in S. Clucas and R. Davies (eds.), *The Crisis of 1614 and the Addled Parliament: Literary and Historical Perspectives* (Ashgate, 2002).

eighteen-year-old Henry and the young Christine had presented a serious obstacle to their union, but now that Henry was dead, James lost no time in replacing him with his second son, Prince Charles, who, at twelve, was clearly a more suitable match.[16] However, the chances of a parliament significantly improved during the course of 1613, as the Spanish faction at the French court tried to torpedo the marriage negotiations, fearing that an English alliance would strengthen the position of the Huguenots and the dissident Prince of Condé, France's heir apparent. They persuaded the regent, Marie de Medici, to offer no more than 700,000 crowns.[17] Meanwhile, James's financial situation continued to deteriorate despite strenuous efforts by the treasury commissioners.[18] By 25 November 1613 James had lost patience with the French, and ordered Edmondes to discover by 6 January 1614 at the latest how much they would eventually agree to pay.[19]

Over the next few months the prospects for a parliament improved dramatically. The reason for this lies in the hostility of most members of the Privy Council to the French negotiations and James's refusal to contemplate an alternative marriage for the prince. A majority of councillors feared that a French Match would further strengthen the position of the Scots at court, since Scotland and France were traditional allies.[20] Many of them would have preferred to match the prince with either Spain or Savoy, while a minority advocated a Protestant bride for Charles. However, James would not yet countenance a Spanish Match, having been deceived by Spain's overtures for a marriage in 1611, and there were several reasons why he would no longer consider an alliance with Savoy.[21] The supporters of a Protestant marriage were also stymied, as there were no Protestant brides available. Since James was set on a French Match, and there remained no prospect of borrowing from the City, the anti-French majority on the council urged the calling of a parliament, reasoning that if James's wants were supplied at Westminster he would have less need of a dowry. When the deadline James had set expired without word having been received from Edmondes, the anti-French councillors increased their pressure on the king, who consequently turned his thoughts to summoning a parliament.[22] Their plans were almost wrecked in mid-January, when Edmondes finally managed to extract

---

[16] BL, Stowe MS 173, fo. 205.
[17] BL, Stowe MS 174, fos. 141r–v; PRO, SP 78/61, fos. 273v, 298v, 325.
[18] For these improvements, see BL, Lansdowne MS 165, fos. 223–36.
[19] BL, Stowe MS 174, fos. 192, 194r–v.   [20] PRO, SP 94/20, fo. 242v.
[21] See my 'French Marriage' for discussion of this.   [22] HMC, *Downshire*, 4, 285.

terms from Marie. However, this last-minute breakthrough was worthless as France was now on the brink of civil war.[23] Since no agreement could be concluded while France was in turmoil, James was compelled to call a parliament.

The parliament of 1614 served merely to confirm James in his hostility towards the House of Commons. Before he had agreed to summon the assembly he had been assured by Thomas Howard, Earl of Suffolk and William Herbert, Earl of Pembroke, two of the leading councillors most opposed to a French marriage, that the Commons would supply his financial needs in return for various bills of grace.[24] However, when the parliament met, James discovered that the assurances he had been given were false, as the Commons insisted on the abolition of impositions, which were worth £70,000 per annum, before they would consider supply. Instead of a manageable Commons he faced either an acrimonious dissolution or a sizeable reduction in his ordinary income. Furthermore, as Richard Cust shows in his essay, James concluded that many members of the Lower House, especially the common lawyers, preferred to court popularity by attacking the royal prerogative, thereby threatening the fabric of the monarchy, rather than attend to his wants. Fortunately for James, the timely ending of Condé's rebellion on 5 May lessened his dependence on a parliament as it made possible a renewal of the French negotiations.[25] In early July he dissolved the assembly without having obtained a vote of supply.

Two months after the dissolution, Edmondes was sent back to Paris with instructions to conclude the marriage agreement.[26] However, the crown's needs were now so pressing – in May the royal debt stood at £680,000[27] – that James could no longer await the outcome of the French negotiations and he therefore approached the City for a loan of £100,000. His request was refused, for although he had at last repaid the loan of 1610 the crown was clearly not credit-worthy.[28] In desperation James demanded a benevolence from his wealthier subjects, which eventually yielded around £65,000. He also appointed Suffolk as Lord Treasurer, who set on foot various projects to raise new sources of revenue. Among the most important was a scheme to levy fines on all new buildings

[23] PRO, SP 78/62, fos. 13–14; BL, Stowe MS 174, fos. 226–9. For the terms obtained by Edmondes, misfiled as '1612', see PRO, SP 78/60, fos. 131–2.
[24] BL, Cotton MS, Titus F.IV, fos. 340–1.
[25] Victor-L. Tapié, *France in the Age of Louis XIII and Richelieu*, trans. and ed. D. M. Lockie (Basingstoke, 1974), 441.
[26] PRO, SP 78/62, fos. 67–71v, 92r–v.   [27] BL, Lansdowne MS 165, fo. 257.
[28] Ashton, *The Crown and the Money Market*, 120–1.

within seven miles of London contrary to a proclamation of 1603, and another which granted to the London alderman William Cockayne and his associates a monopoly to export finished cloths, a project calculated to enrich the king by £47,500 per annum.[29]

The resumption of the French marriage negotiations, the raising of a benevolence and the financial improvements pursued by Suffolk meant that James was able to postpone consideration of another parliament. However, his financial options narrowed once again in June 1615. For some time it had been apparent that the French were delaying the marriage negotiations. In December 1614 they had pleaded that the business of the estates-general kept them from treating, while in March and April 1615 Condé's absence from court was used as an excuse for inaction. However, it was probably the news relayed on 24 May by Edmondes, that the French refused to offer more than 750,000 crowns, which prompted James and the council to reconsider a parliament.[30] Several councillors declared themselves in favour, including Sir Thomas Lake, Sir Ralph Winwood and Sir Edward Coke, who argued that 'the Crowne was never maynteyned by the ordinarye but helped by parlement'.[31] However, James remained reluctant and put off a decision until after his summer progress. In the meantime, Condé once more raised rebellion in France, ending any prospect of concluding the French negotiations in the foreseeable future.[32]

One reason James was compelled to reconsider a parliament was that his alternative strategy was not yet in place. As early as June 1614 he had secretly begun to explore the possibility of a Spanish Match, and at the beginning of 1615, when it became apparent that the French were again dragging their heels, he responded to Sarmiento's renewed overtures by instructing Sir Robert Cotton to commence talks with him. These negotiations continued throughout the summer, and when Condé rebelled James ordered Cotton to draft a treaty.[33] However, James remained suspicious that Spain's offer of a larger dowry than France was willing to pay was merely intended to sabotage the French talks.[34] Moreover, he

---

[29] A. Friis, *Alderman Cockayne's Project and the Cloth Trade: The Commercial Policy of England in its Main Aspects 1603–1625* (Copenhagen, 1917), 239.

[30] PRO, SP78/62, fo. 264; BL, Stowe MS 175, fos. 284, 327v–328; SP 78/63, fos. 200–201.

[31] HEHL, EL441. For rumours that a parliament was imminent, see *CSPV, 1613–15*, 512–13; HMC, *Downshire*, 5, 281.

[32] Tapié, *France*, 441.

[33] Gardiner, *Narrative of the Spanish Marriage Treaty*, 116–17, 292; Northants. RO, Finch-Hatton MS 50, fo. 15v; Kevin Sharpe, *Sir Robert Cotton 1586–1631: History and Politics in Early Modern England* (Oxford, 1979), 131.

[34] Hubert G. R. Reade, *Sidelights on the Thirty Years War*, 3 vols. (1924), I, 215–16.

was not prepared to ask Philip III to enter into formal negotiations while still engaged with France. Consequently, in the summer of 1615 James could not yet expect to avoid a parliament by means of a Spanish dowry, although the question of a parliament and a Spanish Match were by then inextricably intertwined. The two councillors most opposed to a parliament were Suffolk and his son-in-law, the Lord Chamberlain Robert Carr, now Earl of Somerset. Suffolk had supported the demands for a parliament in 1614 in order to defeat a French marriage, but now he and Somerset feared that parliamentary supply would obviate the need for a Spanish dowry. A majority of their fellow councillors followed the same reasoning, but favoured calling a parliament since they now opposed a Spanish Match. Following the summer progress, several council meetings were held between 24 and 28 September 1615 to discuss the state of the royal finances. It was impressed upon James that retrenchment alone would not yield enough to pay off his debts, which Coke claimed, probably with some exaggeration, now stood at £700,000. In this way 'it was insinuated unto him [James] that there was no likelihood of a perfect subsistence but by relief of his people, which must be by parliament'. James was appalled, and declared that while 'he would not avoid a parliament if he might see the likelihood of comfort by it' he would 'rather suffer any extremity than have another meeting with his people and take an affront'. At the final meeting Suffolk outwardly appeared to side with the advocates of a parliament, but craftily he declared that he 'could not but move a doubt, that struck deeply with him: which was that the taking away of impositions *de facto* would not satisfy the parliament, but that the point of right would be insisted on'. Preserving the king's prerogative while satisfying the Commons would be so difficult 'that he knew not how it could be salved'. By playing on James's fear of further humiliation, Suffolk ensured that a parliament was removed from the agenda. In its place, the council turned to retrenchment, dividing itself into various sub-committees, each of which was charged with finding savings in particular government departments.[35]

Suffolk's triumph was short-lived. On 17 October 1615 Somerset was arrested on suspicion of involvement in the murder of Sir Thomas Overbury, and Suffolk and the entire Howard clan were temporarily disgraced. Consequently, on 20 October the Venetian ambassadors,

---

[35] James Spedding (ed.), *The Letters and the Life of Francis Bacon*, 7 vols. (1861–74), v, 194–207, esp. 192, 204; J. D. Alsop, 'The Privy Council debate and committees for fiscal reform, September 1615', *HR*, 68 (1995), 191–211. For the hitherto unnoticed proposals submitted on 19 October to the committee appointed to investigate the navy, see Bod. Lib., MS North, b.1.

Foscarini and Barbarigo, predicted that 'the parliament will certainly meet now, because with the fate of these persons who opposed it, all objections will disappear'.[36] On 7 November Sarmiento reported that Somerset's enemies 'are now trying to drive the King to summon a parliament, persuading him that this is the only way to remedy his necessities'.[37] At around the same time the Attorney-General, Sir Francis Bacon, prepared a paper reassuring James that, with careful handling, a future parliament would vote supply. In order to overcome the objection posed by Suffolk, Bacon advocated revising the Book of Rates and abolishing impositions, a proposal first suggested by the customs farmer Sir Lionel Cranfield.[38] By mid-December at the latest James had been won over. Barbarigo reported on 15 December that the council had issued orders to call a parliament, while on the following day Sarmiento wrote that James had declared that parliament should meet.[39] The news that a parliament was imminent was soon widespread.[40]

Yet parliament did not assemble in 1616. One explanation for this may lie in the revival of the French Match, for in December 1615 a peace conference at Loudon was established with English assistance. A few weeks before the warring parties signed a peace treaty on 23 April 1616, the Privy Council voted to resume the marriage negotiations.[41] However, it seems probable that James had already lost all faith in the French Match and that his true purpose in resuming talks was to end them.[42] Indeed, in mid-April he told Sarmiento that he hoped he might soon be free of the French talks so that he might formally open negotiations with Spain.[43] The most likely explanation for James's decision not to call a parliament lies not in the renewal of the French negotiations but in an offer made by the Dutch ambassador, Sir Noel Caron. The Dutch

[36] *CSPV, 1615–17*, 53. [37] *Archaeologia*, 41 (1867), 177.

[38] Spedding, *The Letters and the Life of Francis Bacon*, v, 176–91.

[39] *CSPV, 1615–17*, 89; Samuel R. Gardiner, *History of England from the Accession of James I to the Outbreak of the Civil War 1603–1642*, 10 vols. (New York and Bombay, 1896–1901), II, 368.

[40] M. Y. Ashcroft (ed.), *Scarborough Records 1600–1640: A Calendar* (North Yorkshire County Record Office Publications, 47, 1991), 62 (I owe this reference to Simon Healy); J. W. Horrocks (ed.), *Assembly Books of Southampton IV* (Soton Records Society, 1925), 33; HMC, *Downshire*, 5, 383, 388, 405; HEHL, Temple Correspondence, Box 4, STT 1323 (Chris Kyle transcribed this letter for me); BL, Additional MS 5,755, fo. 242; PRO, SP 46/72, fo. 147v (I owe this reference to Paul Hunneyball).

[41] HMC, *Mar and Kellie*, 74–5. For what appears to be a record of the votes cast in the council on the question of reopening the marriage negotiations, see the final folio of HEHL, EL 441.

[42] For a different view, see R. E. Schreiber, *The First Carlisle: Sir James Hay, First Earl of Carlisle, as Courtier, Diplomat and Entrepreneur 1580–1636* (Transactions of the American Philosophical Society, 74, part 7; Philadelphia, 1984), 17.

[43] BL, Additional MS 31,111, fo. 134.

had long desired to recover the Cautionary Towns of Brill and Flushing, which had been handed to England as security during the Elizabethan war with Spain. In theory these towns were a source of profit, for although their garrisons cost the exchequer £26,000 each year, their upkeep was more than covered by an annual payment of £40,000 made by the Dutch. In practice, however, James's resources were so overstretched that the Dutch subsidy was diverted to other purposes, and by the end of 1615 the garrisons had not been paid for many weeks and were close to mutiny.[44] With exquisite timing, Caron asked James in mid-December to restore the Cautionary Towns in return for settlement of the States' wartime debt. The sum owed amounted to £600,000, but the Dutch pleaded poverty and offered just £250,000 instead.[45] For the cash-strapped James this offer must have seemed like manna from heaven, and when he returned to London from Newmarket on 24 December he said no more about a parliament.[46] On 20 January – the day after Caron and two of his associates lent the king £8,000[47] – Sarmiento reported that James had finally laid aside all thoughts of summoning a parliament.[48]

Over the following few months, however, James began to doubt the wisdom of selling the Cautionary Towns. They symbolized England's commitment to the United Provinces, and to relinquish them would signal that he no longer valued the Dutch alliance. However, his debts continued to rise and by 26 April they amounted to more than £621,000.[49] The Cockayne project, which had been intended to raise additional revenue, was severely under-capitalized and had actually caused the customs receipts to fall.[50] Moreover, James would soon have to fund the establishment of a household for Prince Charles, shortly to be invested as Prince of Wales.[51] In March and early April the council debated whether to

---

[44] HMC, *Downshire*, 5, 457–8; *Letters from and to Sir Dudley Carleton, Knt. During his Embassy in Holland from January 1615 to December 1620* (London, 2nd edn, 1775), 17; M. C. Grayson, 'From protectorate to partnership: Anglo-Dutch relations, 1598–1625' (Ph.D. thesis, University of London, 1978), 168–9.

[45] *Letters from and to Carleton*, 27–8. Grayson suggests that Caron made his offer in January or February 1616, but this is incorrect: Grayson, 'From protectorate to partnership', 170.

[46] *CSPV, 1615–17*, 117.

[47] PRO, E401/1895, no fo., entry of 19 Jan. 1616; Ashton, *The Crown and the Money Market*, 22. Rumours that a parliament would meet continued into February: HMC, *Third Report*, 347 (a reference I owe to Paul Hunneyball); Horrocks, *Assembly Books of Southampton IV*, 33, n. 6.

[48] Gardiner, *History of England*, ii, 369. Gardiner's assertion that James abandoned his plan to call a parliament because he was alarmed at the anti-Spanish feeling displayed at the news that France and Spain had recently celebrated a double marriage alliance appears to be unfounded.

[49] Bod. Lib., Eng. Hist. e.30, fos. 45–6.

[50] M. Prestwich, *Cranfield, Politics and Profit under the Early Stuarts* (Oxford, 1966), 174–5.

[51] *CSPV, 1615–1617*, 192.

sell the towns, and only Pembroke, Lake and Greville were adamantly opposed.[52] James continued to hesitate, and on 19 April he again consulted his councillors, asking them 'whether this bargen bee unprofitable & dishonourable for us', as he was inclined to think it 'rather a minus mater then a supply of our estate'. He stressed that he would sell only if they could find 'noe other expedient'.[53] However, there were no realistic alternatives as James despaired of a French marriage and had no wish to call a parliament. Consequently, in May 1616 he ordered the towns to be sold.[54]

The sale of the towns produced an immediate cash windfall,[55] but James realized that without a further injection of substantial funds he could not put off a parliament indefinitely. Indeed, on 19 April 1616 he had obliquely indicated to the council that selling the towns would only enable him to avoid a parliament for about eighteen months.[56] Consequently, over the summer he formally invited Spain to enter into marriage negotiations. At first his earlier fears of Spanish insincerity appeared to be confirmed, as there was no response from Philip III, who was waiting for either a papal dispensation or the approval of Spain's leading theologians. James was offended at the apparent snub, and when Savoy occupied the duchy of Mantua and appealed to him in September for military and financial aid, he threatened to join an anti-Habsburg league and to allow Savoy to raise volunteers in England. In January 1617 he even briefly countenanced a plan whereby Sir Walter Ralegh would lead a force of privateers against the Spanish satellite state of Genoa, a proposal which delighted Savoy's ambassador.[57] However, these were empty threats, for as the Venetian secretary Lionello observed, James could only offer significant material assistance to Savoy if he called a parliament, and 'this he is unwilling to summon'.[58]

By the beginning of 1617 James's financial situation was bleak. Most of the money from the sale of the Cautionary Towns had been paid,[59] and Spain had so far failed to respond to his offer of a marriage. A

---

[52] McClure, *Chamberlain Letters*, I, 619; *CSPD, 1611–18*, 360; Grayson, 'From Protectorate to Partnership', 170.

[53] BL, Additional MS 14,027, fo. 165.   [54] *APC, 1615–1616*, 541–3; *CSPD, 1611–1618*, 368.

[55] The first instalment, of £10,000, was received on 10 June: PRO, E401/1896, no fo.

[56] BL, Additional MS 14,027, fo.165. James said that if the sale proceeded he would require 'so much to bee provided as may serve to furnish £2,000 a month till the parlement & £215,000 for the present'. The difference between the sale price (£250,000) and the immediate requirement (£215,000) was £35,000. Paid in monthly instalments of £2,000, this would all have been gone in about eighteen months.

[57] Gardiner, *History of England*, III, 51–2.   [58] *CSPV, 1615–1617*, 314–15.

[59] HMC, *Buccleuch*, I, 177.

revenue balance drawn up in September 1616 showed that over the previous year the king had spent £86,906 more than he had received.[60] Moreover, James proposed to exacerbate his financial difficulties by visiting Scotland in the following spring. In the event, the money needed to pay for the journey was found without recourse to a parliament, for in January 1617 the City finally agreed to lend James £100,000 for one year, while a further £50,000 was raised by restoring the Merchant Adventurers, who had lost their charter as a result of the Cockayne project. New sources of regular income were also found, most notably by issuing fresh grants of monopoly.[61] These and other expedients kept the wolf from the door, but as one commentator observed, they were but 'patchings and plasterings of a ruinous edifice', while Sir Thomas Edmondes complained how difficult it was to provide the king's wants without a parliament.[62]

Early in March James learned from Sarmiento, now Count of Gondomar, that Spain's theologians had approved formal negotiations for a treaty.[63] He subsequently dispatched Sir John Digby to Madrid with instructions to demand a dowry of £600,000, and to settle for no less than £500,000.[64] Like the earlier French negotiations, the Spanish marriage ultimately diminished the chances that a parliament would meet. Nevertheless, before he departed for Spain, Digby suggested to James that a parliament be held in tandem with the Spanish negotiations. He calculated that if Philip realized that James depended financially on a dowry Spain would insist on the repeal of the penal laws and toleration for Catholics, whereas if Philip believed that a parliament was imminent, he might moderate these demands, as a future House of Commons would probably be so hostile to a Spanish Match that it might actually vote a large grant just to terminate it.[65] This conversation was responsible for the rumour, current between August and October 1617, that another meeting was imminent.[66] However, although James told Digby that he favoured his proposal, he had no real intention of calling a parliament.

[60] CSPD, 1611–1618, 396.
[61] Ashton, The Crown and the Money Market, 122, 124–5; Friis, Alderman Cockayne's Project, 369; Wallace Notestein, Frances Helen Relf and Hartley Simpson (eds.), Commons' Debates in 1621, 7 vols. (New Haven, 1935), VII, 379–86. The amount raised by rechartering the old Merchant Adventurers may have been as much as £80,000: R. Brenner, Merchants and Revolution: Commercial Change, Political Conflict and London's Overseas Trades, 1530–1653 (Cambridge, 1993), 211.
[62] HMC, Downshire, 6, 128; CSPD, 1611–18, 439.   [63] Gardiner, History of England, III, 53, 58.
[64] Bod. Lib., MS Tanner 74, fo. 93.
[65] Gardiner, History of England, III, 60; PRO, SP94/23/3.
[66] CSPV, 1615–1617, 572; HMC, Downshire, 6, 262; CSPD, 1611–18, 489; M. Lee (ed.), Dudley Carleton to John Chamberlain 1603–1624: Jacobean Letters (New Brunswick, 1972), 198.

Consequently, his bargaining position was weak when Philip declared in January 1618 that he would pay the full sum of £600,000 only if the penal laws were revoked. By the time Digby returned to London in May the talks were effectively deadlocked. Although James desperately attempted to persuade the Spanish to drop their demand by reassuring them that the penalties against Catholics would be relaxed, he made little progress by the time Gondomar left for Spain in mid-July.[67]

The failure to achieve an early breakthrough in the Spanish negotiations dealt a severe blow to James's hopes. The crown's financial needs were now more urgent than ever, for between 1 October 1617 and 29 September 1618 the accumulated debt rose from £726,320 to £900,000, and there was no immediate prospect of additional borrowing as the City loan of 1617 had not been repaid.[68] Since James remained as determined as ever to avoid a parliament his only remaining choice was to fall back on retrenchment. Recent attempts to curb royal spending had been only moderately successful, as Lord Treasurer Suffolk, who had recovered favour after the fall of Somerset, was exceptionally corrupt even by early-seventeenth-century standards. Suffolk was the most enthusiastic supporter of a Spanish Match at court, and while James continued to pin his immediate hopes for relief on a Spanish dowry the Lord Treasurer's position probably remained secure. However, when these hopes evaporated in the spring of 1618, Suffolk's abuses could no longer be tolerated. Three days after Gondomar left for Spain, Suffolk was dismissed and his office placed in commission.[69] James now unleashed Sir Lionel Cranfield, who as keeper of the great wardrobe had already begun to reduce the cost of the king's household. In November 1618 the management of the navy was entrusted to a body of commissioners headed by Cranfield, who also devised new sources of revenue, most notably the pretermitted customs. James himself normally avoided administrative duties but he was now thoroughly committed to retrenchment, and threw himself into the work with such energy that Viscount Fentoun remarked that he had become his own Lord Treasurer.[70]

In the short term, the policy of retrenchment enjoyed some success: a revenue balance drawn up in October 1619 indicated that there was now

---

[67] Gardiner, *History of England*, III, 105.
[68] BL, Lansdowne MS 165, fos. 269v, 276; Ashton, *The Crown and the Money Market*, 126.
[69] Gondomar left on 16 July; Suffolk was sacked on the 19th: HMC, *Downshire*, 6, 448, 452; BL, Additional MS 34,727, fo. 31.
[70] HMC, *Mar and Kellie Supplement*, 88.

a surplus on the ordinary account of nearly £44,864, and by 25 March 1620 the accumulated debt had fallen to £712,206.[71] Nevertheless, the case for a parliament based solely upon the king's urgent financial needs remained strong. As late as January 1620 it continued to be made by Sir Julius Caesar, now Master of the Rolls, who concluded that the king had either to demand another privy seal loan or call a parliament.[72] However, it was not the state of his finances which ultimately compelled James to summon a parliament, but a foreign policy crisis arising from the activities of his son-in-law, the Calvinist Elector Palatine, Frederick V.

In mid-September 1619, James learned that, against his wishes, Frederick had accepted the offer of the Bohemian throne after the deposition of the Catholic Archduke Ferdinand, heir-apparent to the Holy Roman Emperor. Although most of the council were eager to champion Frederick's cause and desired a parliament in order to pay for a war, James was horrified, as he had worked hard to avoid another meeting with his subjects. On 12 September he declared that he was unwilling to become involved in the conflict until he knew more clearly by what right the Bohemians had deposed Ferdinand and elected Frederick, and he added that any active support for Frederick must wait until the spring, as the campaigning season had almost ended.[73] Over the following year James stubbornly resisted the pressure to call a parliament, and found alternative means to assist Frederick. He encouraged the City to lend the elector £100,000, permitted the elector's agent to levy a benevolence, and allowed volunteers to be raised in England and Scotland. In addition, a fleet of warships, mainly paid for by the maritime community, was dispatched to the Mediterranean, ostensibly for use against the Algerine corsairs but available against Spain if necessary. By the spring of 1620 at the latest, the popular expectation that the Bohemian crisis would shortly compel James to call a parliament had evaporated. However, these hopes were revived in mid-September, when news reached England that Spain had invaded Frederick's patrimony, the Rhenish Palatinate. On 30 September the council unanimously agreed that, although the king should seek a benevolence of his own in the interim, a parliament was now inescapable.[74] Nevertheless, James remained reluctant to issue the necessary writs. On 28 October Chamberlain commented that 'we are in suspence whether we shall have a parliament

---

[71] BL, Lansdowne MS 151, fo. 49; PRO, E407/78/3, no fo.
[72] BL, Additional MS 34, 324, fo. 115.
[73] BL, Egerton MS 2,593, fo. 46; Reade, *Sidelights*, I, 245.
[74] BL, Additional MS 34,324, fo. 120.

after Christmas or no', while on 3 November the Venetian ambassador observed that 'the King continues to temporize, either in the hope that the necessity will pass of itself, or at least to put off the evil day as long as possible'.[75] James prevaricated for fear that he would be unable to control the Commons if it met, for as the likelihood of a parliament grew stronger so too did the expectation that it would attack impositions and monopolies. He spent much of October trying to ensure that, if he did call a parliament, it would not prove as disastrous as his last. He turned to Bacon, now Lord Chancellor, who was instructed to consult the judges and two former Commons speakers about how best to prepare for a parliament. Bacon also drafted a proclamation for influencing the forthcoming elections and outlining the parameters of parliamentary debate.[76] Only after these foundations were laid, on the afternoon of 3 November, was a sceptical James finally won over by his council.

James's aversion to parliaments was widely known and gave rise to the fear that they would not survive. The evidence for this assertion is to be found not merely in the parliamentary record but in widely circulated treatises, newsletters and the dispatches of foreign diplomats. It can also be found in documents recording the views held by members of the Privy Council.

Under Elizabeth the Commons had taken the continued existence of parliaments for granted. However, as Pauline Croft has observed, by the end of the 1604 session its members had experienced a 'striking collapse of confidence'. By February 1606 they were discussing the fourteenth-century statutes requiring a parliament to sit at least once a year, suggesting they were already anxious about the future of parliaments.[77] This well-founded fear was fuelled by the fate of representative assemblies on the Continent and spawned the anonymous *Motives to induce an annual parliament*, an unpublished yet widely circulated tract that was probably penned sometime between January 1614 and January 1621. After tracing the history and explaining the nature of parliament, its author called for the laws requiring annual sessions to be enforced.[78] The disastrous 1614

---

[75] McClure, *Chamberlain Letters*, II, 322–3; *CSPV, 1619–21*, 472.

[76] Spedding, *The Life and Letters of Francis Bacon*, VII, 114–15; BL, Harleian MS 7,000, fo. 27; James F. Larkin and Paul L. Hughes (eds.), *Stuart Royal Proclamations, volume I: Royal Proclamations of King James I 1603–1625* (Oxford, 1973), 493–5.

[77] *CJ*, I, 271. Croft asserts that the Edwardian statutes were first mentioned in parliament in 1610: Pauline Croft, 'The debate on annual parliaments in the early seventeenth century', *Parliaments, Estates and Representation*, 16 (1996), 169.

[78] Pauline Croft, 'Annual parliaments and the long parliament', *HR*, 59 (1986), 155–71.

parliament did nothing to allay the fear that parliaments faced extinction; on the contrary, on 3 June 1614 Sir Thomas Roe vainly urged the
Commons to avert the impending dissolution, 'which was the ending, not
only of this, but of all parliaments'.[79] Following the dissolution, James
underscored Roe's prediction by demanding a benevolence. This form
of unparliamentary taxation had not been seen since 1546, and its reap-
pearance triggered a wave of protests across southern England, despite
conciliar assurances that it would not be used as a precedent.[80] The
most celebrated casualty of these protests was the Wiltshire gentleman
Oliver St John, who in April 1615 was fined £5,000 in Star Chamber for
inciting others not to pay. The severity of St John's punishment shocked
Sir Walter Ralegh, then a prisoner in the Tower, who consequently wrote
'The Prerogative of Parliaments in England proved'. This took the form
of a dialogue between two fictional characters, one a councillor who
opposed calling a parliament, and the other a magistrate who argued,
inter alia, that for kings to raise money on their own authority was dangerous, as in France this practice resulted in almost permanent civil war.
Despite the council's attempts to suppress it, Ralegh's tract enjoyed wide
circulation in manuscript form. At around the same time, a student at
Gray's Inn observed ruefully that 'some say that no parliament will be
held again in England'.[81]

James's hostility to parliaments aroused particular comment following
Frederick V's election to the Bohemian throne. Writing in December
1619, the Venetian ambassador reported that the king had no money
to fight a war, 'and detests the only proper way of obtaining any,
namely summoning parliament'. That same day, Savoy's representative
recorded that James was seeking to avoid a parliament.[82] Foreign observers were not alone in reaching this conclusion. In September 1620
John Chamberlain termed a parliament 'the last refuge if we cannot
avoid it', while in October the English ambassador to Paris, Sir Edward
Herbert, reportedly said that he did 'not think that the King will agree
to assemble a parliament on any account to obtain money'. On being
threatened with a parliament by one of the people from whom he was
extorting money, the monopolist Sir Francis Michell 'confessed he did

---

[79] Jansson, *Proceedings in Parliament 1614*, 420.
[80] R. Cust, *The Forced Loan and English Politics 1626–1628* (Oxford, 1987), 153–5.
[81] *Ibid.*, 155–6. For Ralegh's treatise, see William Oldys and Thomas Park, *The Harleian Miscellany: A Collection of Scarce, Curious and Entertaining Pamphlets and Tracts . . .*, 10 vols. (1808–13), v, 194–225. For the student's comments, see J. H. Baker, *The Legal Profession and the Common Law: Historical Essays* (London and Ronceverte, 1986), 222.
[82] *CSPV, 1619–1621*, 77; Reade, *Sidelights*, i, 256.

not expect a parliament'.[83] When James did eventually relent, the sense of relief was so general that the water-poet John Taylor composed and published 'The Subjects Joy, For the Parliament'.[84]

James's detestation of parliaments was well known to his councillors. Indeed, some of them, such as Northampton in 1614 and Suffolk in 1615, shared his view and encouraged it. Those who did favour a parliament were suspected of being too afraid of angering James to advocate one. Thus Ralegh's 'councillor' of 1615 swept aside the arguments of his interlocutor by saying that he and his colleagues

> dare not advise the king to call a parliament; for, if it should succeed ill, we, that advise, should fall into the king's disgrace. And if the king be driven to extremity, we can say to the king, that because we found it extremely unpleasing to his majesty to hear of a parliament, we thought it no good manners to make such a motion.[85]

There was undoubtedly some substance to Ralegh's claim. When the council met in mid-September 1619 to consider a response to Frederick V's acceptance of the Bohemian throne, James so overawed its members that those who came 'very well prepared to have remonstrated to his majestie, the necessitie that lay upon him to embarque himselfe into the action', and to call a parliament, discovered that 'there was left no place for their advices'.[86] James's conduct on this occasion may help to explain why, in October 1620, the Tuscan ambassador reported that 'though everyone wishes for a parliament, no-one likes to advise it'.[87] Yet James did not usually stifle debate, and had allowed the possibility of a parliament to be discussed in May 1612, February 1614, July 1615 and September 1615. In February 1614 the council were certainly nervous about recommending a parliament, but they overcame their difficulty by telling James that, while they inclined to a parliament, 'theye neyther take upon them to perswade nor diswade'.[88] In other words, they shifted the final responsibility for calling a parliament to James himself. This tactic proved effective, for James did not subsequently punish Suffolk and Pembroke for their role in advocating the disastrous parliament of 1614, but instead elevated Suffolk to the treasury.

---

[83] McClure, *Chamberlain Letters*, II, 320; *CSPV, 1619–1621*, 456; Conrad Russell, *Parliaments and English Politics 1621–1629* (Oxford, 1979), 52.

[84] Society of Antiquaries, Broadsides, no. 177. For evidence that a parliament was generally desired, see *CSPV, 1619–1621*, 433.

[85] Oldys and Park, *Harleian Miscellany*, V, 223 (and also 194).

[86] BL, Egerton MS 2,593, fo. 46.   [87] BL, Additional MS 31,112, fos. 256–7.

[88] BL, Cotton MS Titus F.IV, fo. 332r–v.

Several of James's closest advisers sought to conceal the king's hostility towards parliaments from his subjects. Shortly after the Addled Parliament, Attorney-General Bacon urged the establishment of a commission to review the Common Law, as 'it will beat down the opinion which is sometimes muttered, that his Majesty will call no more parliaments'.[89] At a council meeting held shortly after New Year 1615, Sir Thomas Lake opposed a scheme devised by the common lawyer and antiquary William Hakewill to sell the king's pardon as 'yt wyll brede an opinion the king mislykes a parliament' and 'will take awaye ordinary meanes by parliament'.[90] By 'ordinary meanes' he meant the general pardon traditionally granted at the end of a parliament as thanks for its aid and advice. Lake's objection was detailed more fully in an anonymous paper presented to the council. This declared that the pardon scheme, which had rapidly become common knowledge, 'is a thing generallie disliked, in that it is a kinde of putting of parliament out of service; for men say, there hath been tried a benevolence in steede of subsidies, and now a charter pardon instead of a parliament pardon, and so we shall have no more parliaments . . .'.[91] Hakewill's project, which its author calculated might earn the king around £400,000 each year, encountered almost unanimous opposition from the council. The Duke of Lennox, for instance, declared that 'in respect of parliament' the scheme should 'staye at this tyme', while Archbishop Abbot likened the selling of pardons to the sale of papal indulgences, a mischievous comparison which briefly earned the project's author the nickname 'Pope Hackwell'. The only councillor who looked favourably on the scheme was Edward, Lord Wotton, who despaired 'that a parliament wyll do any good'.[92] However, since Hakewill assured James that pardons had been sold for profit under Edward III, a proclamation announcing the scheme was drafted.[93] Only James's belief that the project would prove less profitable than originally suggested, rather than its unparliamentary nature, seems finally to have dissuaded him from adopting it.[94]

---

[89] Spedding, *Letters and Life of Francis Bacon*, v, 85.
[90] HEHL, EL445, undated notes by Ellesmere. The dates are suggested by Chamberlain: McLure, *Chamberlain Letters*, 1, 567–8, 581, 583, and the presence of both Winwood and Somerset at the meeting.
[91] Bod. Lib., MS Carte 121, fo. 5v.   [92] HEHL, EL445; McClure, *Chamberlain Letters*, 1, 581.
[93] Bod. Lib., MS Carte 121, fo. 1. Sir Edward Coke thought that pardons had never been sold for profit: HEHL, EL445. Hakewill may have based his scheme on the fact that Edward III issued pardons to criminals in return for military service: W. M. Ormrod, *The Reign of Edward III* (Stroud, 2000), 57.
[94] McClure, *Chamberlain Letters*, 1, 583. James briefly reconsidered the project in December 1616: Bod. Lib., MS Carte 121, fos. 3–4, 13–14v.

Perhaps the most startling evidence of the council's alarm at James's hostility towards parliaments is to be found among the notes made by Sir Julius Caesar at a council meeting on 29 September 1620. The council concluded that a war was necessary and that in previous cases monarchs had been assisted by the Commons. They then observed that the traditional grant of subsidies and fifteenths in parliament

hath nowe continued about an hundred yeres; that yet hath never bred any distast or inconvenience. The discontinuance thereof & triall of other meanes for theise 10 yeres past hath bred many privat murmurings amongst a greate number of the better sort of people.[95]

This was an astonishing statement, for by asserting that the avoidance of parliaments was both unprecedented and unpopular the council implicitly criticised the king. Moreover, it reveals that the council dated James's Personal Rule from 1610, when subsidies had last been voted, rather than 1614, when the Addled Parliament had collapsed. Given James's strenuous attempts to avoid a parliament between 1611 and 1614, this belief was unquestionably correct.

Between 1611 and 1620 James went to extraordinary lengths to avoid a parliament. Had he been solvent his task would have been simple, but since his debts continued to mount at an alarming rate he was forever engaged in the search for alternatives to parliamentary supply. As he proved reluctant before 1618 to control his overspending, and it was difficult to raise sufficient additional income, his strategy of avoidance was almost permanently close to collapse.

Before the summer of 1618 James relied heavily on windfalls to escape a parliament. Among the most significant were the privy seal loans of 1611–12, the sale of baronetcies, the benevolence of 1614 and the City loan of 1617. However, domestic windfalls alone were insufficient to stave off a parliament, and therefore James was forced to look abroad for further sums. In so doing he altered and distorted his foreign policy to a quite remarkable degree. In November 1612, for instance, he embarked upon negotiations for a Match even though Prince Charles was then only twelve and in no immediate need of a wife, while in May 1616 he sacrificed his foothold on the Continent by selling the Cautionary Towns. Indeed, until the summer of 1618 the pursuit of a dowry was an indispensable element in the strategy of avoidance. As a result, the

---

95 BL, Additional MS 34,324, fo. 119r–v.

collapse of the French marriage negotiations precipitated one parliament in 1614 and almost led to another in 1616. After the summer of 1618 the prospect of further foreign windfalls receded, as the French marriage negotiations had collapsed, the Spanish talks were deadlocked and the Cautionary Towns had been sold. Consequently, James was finally forced to embrace root and branch retrenchment. By the autumn of 1619 Cranfield's efforts had begun to achieve impressive results, and were it not for the outbreak of the Thirty Years' War James might have avoided a parliament for several more years.

Like its Caroline successor, James's Personal Rule aroused feelings of alarm and concern in the country at large and on the council. Moreover, both periods were characterised by attempts to find new sources of revenue and both were abruptly ended by war. However, Charles managed without a parliament for longer and with greater success than James. Partly for this reason, and partly because England had been down this road once before, the parliamentary backlash of 1641–2 was greater than that of 1621.

The Caroline Personal Rule almost certainly owed a great deal to its Jacobean predecessor. Charles I is sometimes depicted as a prince 'born and bred in parliaments' because he was fêted in the parliament of 1624, but as Richard Cust shows in his essay, Charles had absorbed his father's mistrust of 'popular spirits' in the Commons as early as 1621. This is hardly surprising, as his teenage years coincided with his father's desperate manoeuvrings to avoid a parliament and the débâcle of the 1614 assembly. Moreover, he cannot have failed to notice that, unlike his elder brother, his creation as Prince of Wales occurred outside parliament. As Cust also demonstrates, Charles's own brief flirtation with 'popularity' in the form of an alliance with the 'patriot' coalition in the Commons was confined to 1624 and was exceptional. On becoming king in 1625, he soon encountered serious opposition from the Commons, and by the summer of 1626 the language he used to describe the Lower House was just as intemperate as anything James had ever uttered.[96] Indeed, he was so thoroughly disillusioned with parliaments that he briefly sought to do without them. This temporary abandonment of England's representative assembly became permanent after the disastrous session of 1629, but it is now clear that this development was far from novel, for in seeking to rule without parliaments Charles did no more than follow in his father's footsteps.

---

[96] Richard Cust, 'Charles I, the Privy Council and the forced loan', *JBS*, 24, (1985), 212–13.

5

Profiting from misfortune: corruption and the Admiralty under the early Stuarts[1]

David D. Hebb

INTRODUCTION

One of the distinctive characteristics of the early Stuart period – reflecting both the growing value of seaborne trade and an increasing interest by crown and courtiers in tapping any potential source of wealth – was the exploitation of the sea, which was perceived as a vast common, as James I once put it.[2] And like the common lands of the realm, it was thought ripe for enclosure and profit. Sovereignty claims were extended, and numerous projects were put forward by inventive or industrious talents to reap profits from the sea. Some were promoted (and may actually have been) for the benefit of the commonwealth. For example, the crown fostered a project to create a national fishing fleet in imitation of the Dutch, whose numerous busses were seen as the primary cause of the commercial power and prosperity of the United Provinces.[3] While the ostensible aim of these projects was beneficial (or thought to be), the crown, Lord High Admiral and various courtiers and projectors also anticipated substantial profits.[4] Several projects promised solutions to maritime problems facing government or society. One set sought to reduce piracy, a second aimed at recovering shipwrecked goods and a third at preventing wrecks by erecting lighthouses. All were conceived as profit-making schemes, however, often with the Lord High Admiral, the Duke of Buckingham, as chief beneficiary.

---

[1] I undertook initial research for this paper as a Ph.D. student under Conrad S. R. Russell and Penelope. J. Corfield, both of whom I wish to thank for all their help over the years. An early version was given at Peter Lake's seminar in Princeton in 1996. I would also like to thank Jane Waldfogel, Peter Earle and Richard Cust for their assistance with this version.

[2] PRO, SP 14/90/136, 20 March 1617.

[3] J. R. Cramsie, 'Commercial projects and fiscal policy of James VI and I', *Hist*, 43, 2 (2000), 345–64.

[4] BL, Cotton MSS, Cleopatra, fo. 6; Sir Robert Cotton, for example, proposed farming out royal warships to merchants for private trading ventures.

PIRACY

The problem of piracy had increased in scale and consequence during the early seventeenth century, and, not surprisingly, some sought
to profit from this development.[5] Ireland featured in several schemes:
'Pirate goods and prize ships were alike laundered through the admiralty courts and marketed by merchant syndicates', as Victor Treadwell
observes.[6] And in 1624, Lord Falkland put forth a scheme proposing
to repatriate English pirates from overseas bases for resettlement and
rehabilitation in Ireland.[7] Like most such schemes, it was based on an
imperfect understanding of the problem, offered a remedy that was wildly
impractical and vastly overestimated potential profits. Falkland proposed
an amnesty 'to bring into that Kingdome all his Majestys borne subjects
with all their wealth and strengths who are Pirates residing in Argier or
any other of the Turkish ports and dominions, and so dispose of them
here' [Ireland] with their wealth as a 'tye upon their fidelityes' and means
of 'inriching' the realm. Moreover, the pirates and their ships might
be used for defence and thus keeping these 'Birds of Prey . . . [in] exercise of their vocation . . .', or so Falkland suggested. Ireland, he believed, was an attractive place to carry out this scheme because: (1) it
had suffered less from pirates than the other Stuart kingdoms (therefore
resentment would be less), (2) the land was thought better for pirates to
exercise their faculties, (3) land in Ireland was cheaper and closer to the
sea and (4) the Lord Deputy possessed 'undisputed authority to grant
pardons under the great seal' which made it easier to effect such a
policy. In case Buckingham may have wondered what was in it for him,
Falkland went on to assure that it would not be 'to my Lord Admiralls
losse' and that he 'shalbe most carefully provided for . . .' if the scheme
were approved. What Falkland had in mind, as he subsequently put it,
was, '. . . to make it worth Twenty Thousand pounds to his Highness; Ten
Thousand pounds to my Lord Admiral . . .' with another five thousand
pounds for himself and his partner.[8]

Nothing was to come of this proposal, but had it been approved it
would have ended in failure for the simple reason that by this date
there were virtually no English pirates residing in the Barbary ports.
The basis for Falkland's project was a dozen years or so out of date.
By 1624 the problem of piracy was quite different: English ships were

[5] D. D. Hebb, *Piracy and the English Government, 1616–1642* (Aldershot, 1994), 1–3.
[6] V. Treadwell, *Buckingham and Ireland 1616–28* (Dublin, 1998), 92.
[7] PRO, SP 63/228/39, fo. 131.   [8] PRO, SP 63/238/49 fo. 133.

the victims of Turkish pirates none of whom were English born.[9] Even more impractical, though more entertaining, was a proposal in 1636 to deal with one of the sad realities of piracy in the early Stuart period. Presented to Charles I as a New Year's gift, the proposal recommended 'that the whores, harlots, & idle lascivious portion of the female sect [*sic*]' should be exchanged for English male captives (taken by Turkish pirates) so that 'one harlot may redeem half a dozen captives'.[10] Unfortunately, surviving evidence does not inform us whether this was a good rate of exchange, nor is it possible to discover what Charles I thought of a proposal which valued England's mariners so cheaply and the realm's harlots so highly.[11]

SHIPWRECKS AND TENTHS

A maritime danger far more frequently encountered than piracy was shipwreck. Surviving evidence suggests that approximately 5 per cent of ships putting to sea each year wrecked, and, thus, it is not surprising that proposals were put forward to reduce losses and/or take advantage of this maritime misfortune.[12] The history of the law of wreck in this period, much like Admiralty jurisdiction, is neither clear nor free of dispute. As John Godolphin confessed in 1661, in his treatise on admiralty law, at best, all he could do was to show that definitions of jurisdiction were 'like tidal rivers with frequent flux and reflux' and that the reasoning of judgements was 'often inferential' rather than explicit.[13] Basically, though, the law of wreck at the time stated that part of the goods and cargoes of a shipwreck (usually a moiety, i.e. half the value) belonged to the crown or a delegate of the crown, chiefly the Lord High Admiral.[14] Other individuals or jurisdictions possessed rights of wreck, though many of these would be

---

[9] Hebb, *Piracy*. A few English mariners had 'turned Turk' and served on pirate vessels but they were exceptional and none were in command of pirate vessels.

[10] PRO, SP 16/311/9.

[11] PRO, SP 16/332/30, inclosure 5. One might note that in an examination of a mariner, John Dunton, he declared that the pirates especially prized English women, seven of whom were taken from his ship.

[12] D. D. Hebb, 'Shipping losses in the early modern period', unpublished paper presented to the Economic and Social History Seminar, IHR, University of London, 1992. This percentage is based on analysis of about 9,000 Spanish, Portuguese, French and English voyages.

[13] J. Godolphin, *A view of the Admiralty jurisdiction . . . whereunto is added . . . an Extract of the ancient laws of Oleron (A series or Catalogue of such as have been dignified with the Office of Lord High Admiral . . . since King John's time to the reign of King Charles the First. etc.)* (1661), preface and introduction.

[14] PRO, High Court of Admiralty (HCA) 24/91, 129, 131, 149. The salvors in this 1633 case received half.

challenged, as we shall see. The Admiral derived his right from the crown, whose rights were defined by ancient statute.[15] It seems agreed that a sunken ship (as opposed to a beached vessel) generally belonged to the crown or its delegate. For example, in 1621 a wreck near Margate was considered a valid wreck because 'yet, as six or seven tides washed over her'. Goods washed ashore, i.e. *flotsam*, were also claimed by the Lord High Admiral; the right to *jetsam* (goods deliberately thrown overboard) and *lagan* (goods sunk, but buoyed) were treated differently under law, though the Lord High Admiral might claim these as well. The position of the owner of a ship or goods lost in a wreck and the rights of salvors was also vague and fluctuated over time. As R. G. Marsden puts it, 'the view of English law was that the right to recover wrecked property depended upon the fact of a live creature escaping'.[16] For example, in 1626 the Admiralty declared a vessel at Bramston to be 'no wreck because the ships companies came ashore' while in 1637 a true wreck was declared when officials found 'no man or dog on board'. By the 1630s, it seems, salvors expected to receive half of what they brought up.[17]

Buckingham was not the first Lord High Admiral to profit from shipwreck or see that money could be made from misfortune at sea. His activity was but part of a broader movement-commencing in the late Elizabethan period and coming into full flower under James I-that was characterized by the increasing use of prerogative powers or patent rights to provide income. Although originally created to protect invention, patents or similar royal grants fairly quickly were transformed into commissions, conferring privileges, exemptions, or similar delegated exclusive powers.[18] Most of these involved the controlling or taxing of a particular trade or some industrial process, e.g. sweet wines, glass, playing cards, etc., and were used to reward courtiers for services rendered or for their 'good connections' at court.[19] However well intentioned originally, as the system developed, it became increasingly open to abuse and more

---

[15] W. Holdsworth, *A History of English Law* (1938), x, 388–9; the key statute is 17 Edward II 1324, and for the powers of the Lord High Admiral, see PRO, HCA 30/1036.

[16] R. G. Marsden, *Select Pleas in the Court of Admiralty* (Seldon Society, vols. 6 and 11, 1892–7), 6, xxxiv–xl.

[17] See footnote 14 above.

[18] G. D. Duncan, 'Monopolies under Elizabeth I, 1558–85', Ph.D. thesis, University of Cambridge (1977); R. Cizden, 'Monopolies in England 1603–30', M.Litt. thesis, University of Oxford (1984); S. Adams, 'The Patronage of the court in Elizabethan politics of the 1590s in perspective', in J. Guy, ed., *The reign of Elizabeth I, Court and Culture in the Last Decade* (Cambridge, 1995), 39–40; L. L. Peck, *Court Patronage and Corruption in Early Stuart England* (1990).

[19] B. E. Supple, *Commercial Crisis and Change in England, 1600–1642* (1959), 230.

and more an appendage of political patronage, until it degenerated, to quote one historian, into 'mere licensed freebooting'.[20]

The Cinque Ports were one of the first to use a clause of their charter to assert a right to wrecks, though whether this right extended as far as they claimed, including the whole of the Goodwin Sands, is questionable. Other ports followed suit and many lords of the manor also claimed a right to wrecks along the shores of their manors. At this distance in time it is difficult to ascertain the validity of many of these claims. The crown had delegated some rights, but, as it would argue in the 1630s, these rights were by no means as extensive as recipients claimed, either in terms of geography or what might be recovered without giving the Lord High Admiral his moiety.[21] The Admiralty argued that many of these claims or grants were invalid or temporary and that the crown could withdraw them at will. Whatever the truth, the right to wrecks was valuable. It was clearly in the interest of the Admiralty and crown to exercise the right to wreck exclusively and view delegations of its power as limited or invalid.

If Buckingham was not the first to seek profit from wrecks, his admiralty can be distinguished by the thoroughness and ruthlessness with which he exploited this source of profits. Unlike the illustrious Lord Howard of Effingham, Buckingham had no naval experience or interest, but the income or potential profits and powers of the Lord High Admiral were sufficient for him to want the office. At first Buckingham held it jointly with Nottingham, but after a year he bought sole right to the office for £3,000 down and a pension £1,000 per annum (paid for by the king), a fraction of the income (or potential income) of the office. Recently Buckingham has been presented as a king's man who came to the Admiralty with the zeal and purpose of a reformer. Buckingham is portrayed as 'a new broom' wishing to 'sweep away the accumulated abuses of the Navy'.[22] While Buckingham may have been intent upon sweeping away corruption, his tenure suggests he equally interested in sweeping every possible profit of office into his own purse.

[20] S. R. Gardiner, *History of England from the Accession of James I to the Outbreak of the Civil War, 1603–1642*, 10 vols. (1895–9), III, 73, 76, 204; Supple, *Commercial Crisis*, 230; R. Zaller, *The Parliament of 1621: A Study in Constitutional Conflict* (Berkeley, 1971) for discussions of monopoly, patents and their abuse.
[21] PRO, SP 14/110/61. For instance, Sir John Killigrew, a lord of a Cornish manor, admitted in a private letter to appropriating a valuable wreck that rightly should have gone to the Admiralty.
[22] R. Lockyer, *Buckingham, the Life and Political Career of George Villiers, First Duke of Buckingham* (1981), 48–51.

The two interests could easily exist side by side. The pre-Buckingham Admiralty was undoubtedly riddled with corruption, and the reforms of Buckingham's commissioners did much to reduce the flow of Admiralty funds to the pockets of low-level officials, but the new efficiency also served to increase the amounts available to the Lord High Admiral.

The potential benefits of office were sufficient to attract most men and a certain lure for a man like Buckingham. The long-drawn-out maritime war against Hapsburg Spain and Portugal resulted in new power and, especially, new wealth accruing to the office of Lord High Admiral. Naval expenditure grew as dockyards were erected and staffed, ships built and manned and provisions bought, etc. Greater spending gave the Admiral more patronage and opportunity to reap the rewards of office. A less obvious but no less valuable perquisite was the Lord Admiral's 'Tenth', i.e. the right to claim 10 per cent of value of all enemy ships and cargoes captured or 'made prize' during war. For a prize to be legal, it had to be declared in the Admiralty Court. The Admiral's Tenth came free and clear for all expenses since they were paid by ship owners prosecuting a prize cause in the Admiral's Court. As a result of the war against Spain and Portugal, this perquisite came to be of enormous value, as can be seen from the work of K. R. Andrews, who provides some prize money figures.[23] The prize ship *San Felipe*, for instance, taken in 1587, had a cargo valued at over £100,000, while the Portuguese carrack *Madre de Deus*, captured off the Azores in 1592, was worth at least £140,000, and another great carrack, the *São Vallentim*, taken just before the war ended, was of similar value.[24] Andrews found hard evidence for the three years following the Armada when approximately 300 enemy ships worth £400,000 were made prize. During the entire war about 1,000 enemy ships were taken which, extrapolating from known values, would mean that prize goods came to over £1,300,000. The Lord High Admiral thus received during the war years £130,000 in Prize Tenths – all legal income and acquired at no personal cost or effort – a perquisite that made the office of Lord High Admiral highly desirable.

Buckingham's term at the Admiralty is characterised by a general extension of the rights, and more particularly by a ruthless new attempt to exploit systematically any source of income perceived as falling within the Admiralty's grasp. His 'fertile brain teemed with projects by which

[23] K. R. Andrews, *Elizabethan Privateering: Privateering during the Spanish War 1585–1603* (Cambridge, 1964), *passim*, provides a wealth of information on prize values.

[24] However, looting by privateers in the case of the *Madre de Deus* meant that not all of the value reached the Admiral's Court.

his own purse was to be replenished' as S. R. Gardiner observed.[25] Unfortunately for Buckingham the great bounty of Prize Tenths would elude him for several years since England was at peace when he took possession of the office. The wars with Spain and France in the mid 1620s would, however, eventually bring in about £90,000 in Tenths to the Lord High Admiral.[26] And in asserting prize claims he was not shy. When the East India Company seized a Portuguese carrack in Asian waters worth £100,000, Buckingham, with support from the king, threatened to take it all if he did not get his cut; the company's ships were prevented from sailing until the directors agreed to pay up, handing over £20,000 in the end.[27] The early years of peace during Buckingham's tenure (and the dearth of prize money), however, may have encouraged him to develop novel sources of income using Admiralty powers. One of the first sources that captured his interest was profiting from ships that wrecked in English waters.

Buckingham's interest in wrecks was evident from the first; the form of his patent of office (drafted specifically at his instigation) included novel phrases granting authority over wrecks, which, as the leading authority on the Admiralty observed, 'were wholly unfounded in law'.[28] The zeal with which the Lord High Admiral went after wrecks was also unheralded. When, for example, the Lord Admiral learned that two recent marine casualties were not considered by his own court to be valid wrecks, he sought a legal opinion on whether he might appeal against his own court to procure the profits of these wrecks. During his tenure at the Admiralty, virtually anything lost in English waters or shores was laid claim to by the duke, and he asserted claim to all wrecks in the Narrow Seas, which by early Stuart definition stretched to the shores of France. Agents of the Lord High Admiral scoured the coasts and offshore shoals asserting the Lord Admiral's right whenever a wreck was reported. For example, on 2 December 1619, it was reported by William Ward to Lord Zouch that 'Ramsgate men saved a ship on the Goodwin Sands . . . [but] Captain Turner [Buckingham's agent] has gone along the coast bidding people retain all things saved for the Lord Admiral.'[29] Ward wished to have Buckingham's man committed to Dover Castle; however, Zouch

---

[25] Gardiner, *History of England*, IV, 1–55.
[26] J. C. Appleby, 'English privateering during the Spanish and French wars, 1625–30', Ph.D. thesis, University of Hull (1983).
[27] Gardiner, *History of England*, V, 238; BL, India Office Library, Court Minutes, VI, 24, 466–555.
[28] Marsden, *Select Pleas in the Court of Admiralty*, ii, xviii.
[29] PRO, SP 14/111/57 and Inclosure.

was more prudent, being reluctant to cross the Lord High Admiral when the lure of sunken treasure had fastened upon the duke's mind.[30]

Buckingham's interest in wrecks was active in another sense, for he did not simply wait to assert a claim after salvors had started working. He hired divers to recover the goods from wrecks, bringing in Jacob Jonson, a professional from the Netherlands, to work on wrecks. For years Jonson worked for the Admiralty salvaging valuable wrecks along the south coast of England, eventually operating as far as Castlehaven in Ireland, where he worked the wreck of a rich Spanish prize captured by the Dutch. And when it came to salvage, Buckingham did not want just some wrecks but rather sought a monopoly. The duke recognised that each wreck was but a component part of a regular trade that passed along the English coasts; over time, wrecks would occur up and down the coasts. Getting an exclusive right to wrecks along the entire coastline would result in substantial profits year in and year out. The volume of seaborne trade had increased greatly in the previous decades so that many more ships were wrecking, which made an exclusive right to wrecks worth more. Moreover, the amount of precious metals, especially Spanish silver, being shipped had grown enormously in the late sixteenth and early seventeenth century, and therefore wrecks were likely to be worth more. Some sense of the profits available from wrecks and the amounts of bullion being shipped can be derived from the following examples. In December 1619, merchant strangers were sentenced before the Star Chamber for exporting gold to a total of 140,000 pounds sterling.[31] A few months later, Sir John Killigrew provided evidence that ships valued at £100,000 had been wrecked on the Lizard in recent years.[32] About the same time, an East India Company ship, worth £16,000, was lost between Gravesend and London.[33] In 1627, two Dutch East Indiamen wrecked on the Needles; and 17,000 pieces of eight and several wedges of silver were recovered from one, half of which went to the Admiralty.[34]

How much the Lord High Admiral actually profited from wrecks has not been fully documented; however, a surviving Vice-Admiral's account

---

[30] J. Conrad, *Nostromo*, Penguin edition (New York, 1960), 367, 'There is something about a treasure that fastens upon men's minds.'

[31] PRO, SP 14/111/66. In the same month, two Dutch ships had been cast away on the Goodwin Sands, one with £8,000 on board.

[32] PRO, SP 14/112/90.   [33] PRO, SP 14/113/32.

[34] PRO, SP 16/142/6, 18, 22; J. R. Bruin, F. Gaastra and I. R. Schoffer, *Dutch Asiatic Shipping*, 2 vols. (The Hague, 1979), II, 58; P. Marsden, *Ships and Shipwrecks* (1997); *International Journal of Nautical Archaeology*, 10/3 (1981), 266. Recoveries were from the *Kampen* only, those from the *Vliegende Draak* are unknown.

shows why Buckingham was so interested in claiming an exclusive right
to wrecks. Between 1628 and 1633, Sir James Bagg, the Vice-Admiral
of Cornwall, reported that he had collected £29,253 from the sea.[35] In
another account, Sir John Hippesley provided the duke with £30,000
in a year.[36] And after Buckingham's death, the Admiralty commissioners estimated that Buckingham had derived from his Admiralty rights
£30,000 or £40,000 per annum – a sum that, as Secretary Nicholas put
it, 'is more than a song to part with'.[37]

Buckingham's quest for an exclusive right to wrecks began only a few
months after becoming Lord Admiral. His first target was the Cinque
Ports, the strongest and richest jurisdiction claiming a right to wrecks. By
December 1619, when the Lord Warden was informed that the Lord
Admiral was claiming all wrecks in the jurisdiction of the Cinque Ports,
Zouch wrote directly to Buckingham asking him to stop until he heard
what could be said on the other side. Buckingham did not mask his intention, replying on 7 December 1619 that he 'Considers that he has a
right, as Lord Admiral, to all wrecks floating on the Narrow Seas . . .'[38]
Whether orchestrated by Buckingham or encouraged by the scent of
blood, others began to attack the Cinque Ports' right. Zouch was informed by one of his deputies of a new shipwreck on the Goodwin Sands
that had been seized by inferior gentry who felt emboldened 'since publication of the Admiral's warrant'.[39] A few months later, Buckingham
wrote to Zouch again, and though his words dripped with sympathy,
his intent remained unchanged. The Lord High Admiral wrote that he
was sorry that his actions 'should give his Lordship so much trouble',
but never mind, he was looking into it and hoped the 'harmless contention will soon come to a good conclusion'.[40] The 'good conclusion'
Buckingham had in mind soon became apparent: if the Lord Admiral could not easily break the Cinque Ports charter, or at least that
part covering a right to wrecks, Zouch would simply have to be persuaded to sell his right to wrecks to Buckingham, which he did for
the not inconsiderable sum of £1,000 down payment and £500 per
annum.[41]

[35] PRO, SP 16/256/21.
[36] PRO, SP 16/19/17; SP 16/539/17; also, see R. G. Marsden, 'Admiralty Droits', *Law Quarterly Review*, October 1899, 539.
[37] PRO, SP 16/539/17.
[38] PRO, SP 15/111/61, SP 15/111/57 I and SP 15/111/65 provide the details of this dispute.
[39] PRO, SP 14/111/64 I.   [40] PRO, SP 14/112/73. 7 February 1620.
[41] Gardiner, *History of England*, VI, 100; included in the impeachment charges against Buckingham was his acquisition of offices and rights.

LIGHTHOUSES

If there is something terribly logical in the way Buckingham moved
from profiting from the occasional wreck to getting a virtual monopoly
to exploit all wrecks in English waters, then the way he moved to take full
advantage of misfortune of the sea is even more impressive. Profitable
as wrecks might be, such income still depended upon chance: storms,
the occasional negligence of mariners, etc. Thus, short of employing
'wreckers', the Lord High Admiral remained dependent on the chance
of ships wrecking. Moreover, any profits from wrecks depended upon
successful salvage of a wreck, always an uncertain prospect. There was,
however, another way of tapping potential profits of maritime misfortune.
Again Buckingham was not the first to see the opportunity, though he was
not backward when given a chance. Credit for spotting the opportunity,
however, must go to other, politically less powerful, though none the less
greedy courtiers and projectors.

   Although at one time it was believed medieval monks and hermits kept
lights to help mariners navigate safely, this now seems myth. However, by
the mid sixteenth century some lights had been erected to guide ships into
harbour, and proposals were made occasionally to put up larger seamarks
or lights, but usually nothing permanent resulted. The mariners' guild,
Trinity House, gained a right to erect lights by the Seamarks Act of 1566,
but did nothing for some time, chiefly because guild members would
have had to pay for any lights or marks. Not until the middle of the
reign of Elizabeth I, however, was a 'lighthouse' established, when a
fire was placed in the tower of Tynemouth Castle, thereby technically
qualifying it as England's first lighthouse. But the Tynemouth light, and
some later imitators, were more in the way of being harbour lights than
real, purpose-built lighthouses set up to warn passing ships of danger.

   The late Tudor period did see at least one proposal for a proper
lighthouse. In 1580, Gawen Smith proposed erecting a lighthouse on the
Goodwin Sands. He claimed his light would rise 20 to 30 feet above the
high-water mark and be visible for 20 to 30 miles at sea. This project
came to nothing, probably because the Privy Council were suspicious
of its practicality or wary of opposition from merchants and shippers,
since the scheme was dependent upon charging passing ships between
9 and 10 pence a ton. As G. G. Harris, the historian of Trinity House,
has remarked, it was a characteristic element of the Elizabethan period
for promoters to advance projects 'ostensibly for the public benefit [but
which were] in reality intended for private gain. Lighthouses did not

escape their attention'.[42] That Smith's motive was primarily pecuniary is suggested by another project which he pushed at the same time: in this he proposed to maintain a ship near the Goodwin Sands, to go to the rescue of shipwrecked sailors, charging a 'savior fee', duly graduated according to status or station of the life being saved. Two other lighthouse projects were projected in the late Tudor period. In 1585, a lighthouse at Winterton, in Norfolk was put forward, but nothing came of it after Walsingham made a note to consult local gentry in order to learn what maritime and port interests thought.[43] Also, in 1594, Sir Martin Frobisher proposed the establishment of a light at Spurn Head, but nothing came of this either, perhaps because Frobisher died shortly thereafter.[44]

Two lighthouses, one at Dungeness in Kent and the other at Winterton, Norfolk, mark a true beginning of interest in projects of this type. The history of the Dungeness project is archetypal, and is worth recalling, for it sheds light on the way social connections and political influence were used to procure delegations of crown rights. The project began legitimately when the Reverend John Allen, Burgess of Rye, proposed a lighthouse near Dungeness Point, east of the town. Then, a customs officer, William Bullock, became involved (probably for less altruistic reasons), but lacking sufficient influence he was compelled to turn to William Bing, who used his connections to approach a more political figure, William Lamplaugh, a Clerk of the Kitchen and kinsman of the Earl of Arundel. Success was more likely to come, Lamplaugh suggested, if they channelled the project through Sir Edward Howard, nephew of the Earl of Nottingham, the Lord Admiral. On 31 May 1615, the Privy Council took up Howard's petition, and, after a delay of three months, granted Howard his wish.

However, all did not go smoothly for the projectors. In January 1616, Lord Zouch solicited the views of Cinque Port residents and passed on their objections.[45] Not everybody, it now appeared, was in favour of a light, or at least willing to accept an imposition of fees to pay for the light. A charge of 1 penny per ton (borne equally by ship owners and merchants) was intended, with this rate being applied to inward-bound vessels only. The patent, however, as procured by Sir Edward Howard, managed to get the rate effectively doubled by having the fee apply to

[42] G. G. Harris, *Trinity House of Deptford* (1969), 181. This fine work along with his transcriptions in *Trinity House Transactions, 1609–25* (1983) are a prime source for maritime history.
[43] PRO, SP 12/146/97.
[44] Harris, *Transactions*, 33, 35. His son, Peter Frobisher tried to revive the scheme in 1618.
[45] HMC, Rye MSS, XIII, pt 4, 50.

both inward and outward voyages.[46] This doubling of the rate may be easily explained, for one half of the profits were now to go to Howard with Lamplaugh and Bullock getting but a quarter each. Bullock may have profited more for a relation of his, Hugh Bullock, actually managed the building of the lighthouse. Like proverbial thieves falling out over the loot, the Dungeness triumvirate soon fell to fighting amongst themselves. First in 1620, following the death of Sir Edward Howard, his brother and executor sold Howard's share to Bullock who, with a controlling interest, then set out to gain total possession of the lighthouse and its profits. Lamplaugh (and later his widow) fought off the takeover for some time, but by 1635 Bullock was in complete control. Bullock certainly thought it was worth the fight, though the level of profits anticipated by the original patentees never lived up to expectations. The merchants never did pay their share and for over twenty years, the ship owners protested – petitioning Trinity House, the Lord High Admiral, the Lord Treasurer, parliament and the king to get rid of this levy.

The foremost consequence of this first lighthouse project was not navigational, but rather the encouragement it gave other speculators to seek similar bounties by way of royal licence.[47] The next project was at Winterton, where the offshore sands presented some danger, especially for ships engaged in the growing coal trade between Newcastle and London (which may have been the real attraction). As early as 1606 some seamen had petitioned the Privy Council for the establishment of seamarks, buoys and beacons in the area. The petition did not succeed, apparently because local and commercial interests opposed paying a fee of 1 shilling towards the cost of the light there. With the example of Dungeness at hand, however, a projector, William Welwood, took up the cause. He was a writer on maritime matters and may have used his knowledge and skills to make a case for the project. However, with no influential political figure greasing the way, his project soon languished. Others, however, saw the potential and had the political clout or cunning to push the project through. Chief among these was John (later Sir John) Meldrum, typical of the parasitic sort of figure increasingly found on the fringes of the court of James I.[48] He relied upon a schoolboy connection with Sir William Alexander (later Earl of Stirling and Master of Requests)

---

[46] BL, India Office Library, Court Minute Books, vol. 4, 121, and Harris, *Transactions*, 149–50.

[47] Harris, *Trinity House*, 187–92 supports this conclusion and also makes the point that this effectively broke any monopoly rights the guild may have entertained in this area.

[48] Meldrum had done some soldiering, become involved in a colonizing scheme in Ireland and managed to procure through Alexander a grant for fines and forfeitures.

to further his interests. The two conspired to use Alexander's father-in-law, Sir William Erskine, to front the application for the lighthouse grant. Alexander later revealed that Erskine was used because he was owed something for his services and the crown might feel obliged to pay him off. The necessity of obtaining political influence to procure a lighthouse patent can be seen from the financial arrangements agreed. Nothing was put down in writing at the time, but, as we learn from a Chancery case after the parties had fallen out, Alexander was to get half the profits for using his connections at court.

Early on the trio ran into serious opposition, for Trinity House managed to persuade the Privy Council to approve their request to build a lighthouse at Winterton and collect tolls at a rate of 6 pence for ships of less than 100 tons and 8 pence for vessels of greater tonnage. Fishing boats were to pay 1 shilling a season. Moreover, Trinity House had also procured from the Privy Council a declaration that they 'shoulde only and solely have the erectinge and disposinge' of all seamarks and signs within the realm.[49] The Privy Council may have been responding to pressure brought by Trinity House, which was seeking to establish or defend a perceived monopoly. The council may also have wanted to nip in the bud a growing competition for lighthouse rights. Despite the council's declaration, Meldrum and partners were not finished; Alexander, after all, had the king's ear and knew how to play his master. A question was raised whether because of the Act of 1566 (and a later grant of 1594 to Trinity House) the king no longer had the power to make grants in this area. Even if James recognized this as bait, he could not leave it alone and allow a precedent limiting his prerogative power. James responded by calling for a legal opinion on the matter and personally gave instructions to the Attorney-General as to how he wanted it considered.[50] Sir Francis Bacon produced his report on 15 March 1617.[51] At first it seemed Bacon upheld Trinity House's claim to sole rights in the control of lights and seamarks, but then undercut it by declaring that their proposal to erect a lighthouse, etc., could only be done 'without laying any imposition or taxe' upon any of his Majesty's subjects or others as a means of defraying costs. Bacon had delivered the worst of both worlds. All of Trinity House's revenues were now in jeopardy and James was dissatisfied – to put it mildly – so much so that the king demanded another opinion.

---

[49] Harris, *Trinity House*, 187–92.

[50] Harris, *Transactions*, 28, instructions from Secretary of State Sir Ralph Winwood to Attorney-General Sir Francis Bacon, 28 February 1617.

[51] *Act of the Privy Council, of England 1616–17* (1929), 204–5; by then Bacon was Lord Keeper.

The new Attorney-General, Sir Henry Yelverton, could see what the king wanted and replied in June with a subtle and largely satisfactory opinion. In his opinion a general right of Trinity House was recognised, but then he went on to declare that this by no means could 'inhibit the crown' or exclude the king from granting rights to build lighthouses where Trinity House had none.[52] On 31 July, Bacon received his new instructions to see whether the Privy Council could find any grounds for objecting to the king granting Erskine the right to a lighthouse at Winterton. By now Bacon could see what James wanted, and no legal impediment was found; on 28 November 1617 consent was given for a lighthouse at Winterton.

Meldrum and partners were not home and dry, though, for they didn't have the actual patent in hand. Protests continued, especially against the payment of fees, and an enquiry was held at Norwich where numerous objections were voiced. Meldrum soon approached Sir Henry Helmes to see about obtaining the patent, but his request was met with virtual blackmail: Helmes threatened to arrange to cut the Great Seale (thereby making any patent invalid) unless he received a payment. Eventually the patent in the name of Erskine and Meldrum was handed over, which gave them the right to build a lighthouse and, more importantly, to collect 1 penny per ton on both inward and outward voyages. Trinity House continued to raise objections, which by August 1618, had become sufficiently noticeable for Chamberlain to be found berating the imposition of fees and its effect on coal prices.[53] Discontent over the exorbitant fees grew. Newcastle ship owners petitioned and threatened to cease trading in consequence. In October, the Privy Council responded by holding an enquiry.[54] As well as the patentees, customs officials were called to testify. The latter stated that the levy would bring in £1,050 per annum while annual costs were only £378. The patentees claimed to have spent £2,100, but in the Commons debates in 1621 it was suggested that something like £400–600 was probably spent on the lighthouse itself, leaving the remaining £1,500–1,700 available for gifts, bribes and legal charges.[55] The Privy Council responded by suspending all fees and recommending arbitration. The patentees replied by appealing to the king, who favoured enforcement of the patent, and the collection of fees resumed despite the protests of the Lord Mayor of London.

[52] Harris, *Transactions*, 29 contains a copy of Yelverton's report.
[53] N. E. McLure (ed.), *The Letters of John Chamberlain*, 2 vols. (Philadelphia, 1939), II, 168.
[54] APC, 1618–19, 272, 275, 341.   [55] *House of Commons Journals, 1547–1628–29*, 529–83.

The reason for such perseverance on the part of the patentees can be seen from the profits available. Trinity House provided the following figures for the Winterton Lighthouse for the period 26 March 1629–25 March 1634:

1629–30	*1630–1*	*1631–2*	*1632–3*	*1633–4*
£852:0:4	£1,021:6:4	£941:12:9	£1,214:0:9	£1,093:1:5

Gross receipts for five years = £5, 122.1.7, collection fees: = £968.14.2, and an additional £160 was spent on maintenance and service. Total operating expenses = £1, 128.14.2. Thus, net profit for the five years came to £3,993.7.5 or about £798.13.6 a year.[56]

Given such profits, it is little wonder others sought similar concessions from the crown. Sir John Killigrew was one of the first and most hopeful proposing to erect a lighthouse at Lizard.[57] According to Killigrew, merchants had lost £100,000 in ships and cargoes there in the previous ten years.[58] In light of the opposition to the fees associated with Dungeness and Winterton lighthouses, Killigrew proceeded cautiously. Through the offices of Thomas Locke he was taken to court to see Sir Christopher Perkins, who agreed to assist. However, Perkins soon advised him that he should pursue the matter by stealth and proceed 'by way of a voluntary contribution'. If Killigrew were to request powers to levy or impose fees 'it would have had verie hard passage'. Better, Perkins assured his client, to first obtain a patent to erect the lighthouse, and then, after it had been operating for some time, he should seek some contributions and procure certificates from seafaring men as to its contribution to safety, following which 'it will . . . be easy to obtain an imposition . . .', or so Perkins assured him.[59] Killigrew followed the strategy and succeeded in getting a patent, despite some initial opposition from Trinity House. Only the Lord High Admiral seemed to hesitate, perhaps a sign that Buckingham was thinking of extending his authority to cover lighthouses as well.[60] But, as might be expected, voluntary contributions did not come rolling in nor were seafarers all that ready to proclaim that the lighthouse contributed to safety. Officers of Weymouth and Melcombe Regis reported that 'experienced mariners of town declare that the light at Lizard Point [is] needless, and rather, dangerous than profitable; in hazy weather it cannot be seen, and in clear weather the land can be seen, but it may

[56] Harris, *Transactions*, 140–1.
[57] PRO, SP 14/109/42. His campaign began in May 1619.
[58] PRO, SP 14/112/90.   [59] PRO, SP 14/109/42.   [60] PRO, SP 14/109/160.

help conduct enemies and pirates to the coast'.[61] And, on 28 October, while the council was looking into the matter of whether fees should be imposed, the officers of the customs of Poole wrote that 'The "discreetest and most capable shipmasters" declare the Lizard lighthouse to be rather burdensome then commodious, the Lizard being so well known. Have received 21s 4d for it since Midsummer, chiefly Newfoundland fishermen who paid with much grudging.'[62] By the 20 January 1620, Killigrew was hoping to get a new patent to compel contributions; it was in Buckingham's hands, he informed Sir Dudley Carleton, and not only that, Secretary Naunton was assisting him.[63]

Despite all these friends at court, Killigrew's project did not prosper. In February 1620, Killigrew wrote again to Carleton hoping the English ambassador might be able to persuade Dutch merchants to contribute.[64] On the surface it seemed a good idea to get Dutch support for they – as much as anyone, perhaps more than the English – would benefit from a lighthouse on the Lizard. Killigrew claimed they would be 'able to gain their ports . . . not have to stand at sea; or run into English ports; [and thus be] saved from frequent shipwreck'.[65] In any case, the prospects of getting an imposition put on English merchants and ship owners was fading through the continued opposition of shipping interests, speaking through Trinity House.[66] As a measure of his desperation, Killigrew now offered Carleton half of all profits if he could get the Dutch to pay up. Carleton had come to believe that hard-headed Dutch merchants would never pay a set tonnage fee or accept an imposition, such as Killigrew wished, so he tried to persuade them to make a contribution in the form of a gift or mere bounty. This, he suggested, would overcome their fear of compulsion and make them feel in control. In response the Dutch suggested rather vaguely that they might be willing to consider a contribution, but it seems more likely that they were just delaying or being polite, for not a guilder was ever forthcoming.

Killigrew had spent £500 on the lighthouse but had received no return for his money. He began to despair of ever obtaining impositions and claimed it cost him 10 shillings on a stormy night just to keep light glowing. He was getting ever more desperate and coming to believe his failure

[61] PRO, SP 14/153/07.   [62] PRO, SP 14/153/104.   [63] PRO, SP 14/112/27.

[64] PRO, SP 14/41/113. Since at least May 1619 Carleton had been involved to some extent.

[65] PRO, SP 14/112/45. Trinity House also thought the lighthouse was very unnecessary since most ships entered the Channel by day, it was claimed.

[66] PRO, SP 14/150/1. Trinity House calculated the proposed tax would yield Killigrew about £400 per annum.

was due almost entirely to the Dutch.[67] By August 1621, he was facing ruin and fixating more and more on the Dutch. Much of the trouble, Killigrew pleaded, grew out of his case being left to Moy Lambert, a well-known figure in Dutch maritime circles. Killigrew claimed that Lambert had a personal grudge against him. In anger, he wrote to Carleton, threatening that 'I will send his [Lambert's] whoor from Falmouth to Rotterdam to his wyffe who I hope will pull his eys out for the preceedings here'.[68]

Whilst his efforts in the United Provinces were getting nowhere, Killigrew's pleadings at home were beginning to pay off. In December 1622, another patent was granted to Killigrew and his brother-in-law, Robert Mynne, but this one provided for the imposition of a half pence per ton on passing ships, shared equally by ship owners and merchants. Fishermen were exempt. Soon, however, a chorus of protest drowned out Killigrew's joy, and the Privy Council took up the matter and ordered the suspension of the impositions. This was too much for Killigrew. The light was extinguished; in actual fact, it had been lighted only sporadically after the first, hopeful year.

In retrospect, it is clear that Killigrew was doomed to failure. Without an involuntary levy (enforceable by the state) his basic patent was worthless. Contrary to what some modern economists seem to believe, *pace*, R. H. Coase, the lighthouses of the English past were not commercial propositions functioning as truly private enterprises.[69] Merchants and ship owners would not pay for the service willingly: only the state with its coercive powers could compel payment. Without state power, a private enterprise lighthouse could not operate profitably. Killigrew's project illustrates this all too clearly. Additionally, the timing of his venture could not have been worse. Just when he approached the crown, opposition was growing against patents, especially those imposing taxes for private gain. And not only ship owners or merchants were against his project, even the residents of the Lizard were opposed. As Killigrew observed, 'most houses on the Lizard are built of ships' timbers from wrecks' and consequently a lighthouse on the Lizard would deprive local people of an occasional windfall.[70]

---

[67] PRO, SP 14/112/11. Killigrew to Carleton.   [68] PRO, SP 14/112/45.

[69] D. D. Hebb and J. Waldfogel, 'The lighthouse in history and economics', presented at the Allied Social Sciences Association meeting, Chicago, January 1998. This study shows that, although ostensibly for the public good, most lighthouses were of doubtful utility, e.g., the incidence of shipwreck is no greater in the years when the Eddystone lighthouse was not operating.

[70] PRO, SP 14/115/3. 4 May 1620.

Killigrew's plan of tapping Dutch commerce was an alluring one, especially given the opposition in England to his proposal. The Dutch had
no standing before the Privy Council; they could not thunder in parliament against undesirable and unnecessary levies or elect MPs to present
their case. Buckingham was one who appreciated this, and though he
may have harboured thoughts of obtaining lighthouse rights and dues
for the whole of England, he could see that this was becoming politically
impossible. The lucrative potential of lighthouses had not passed his notice, however, nor that Dutch financial support should be procured. The
Goodwin Sands was seen as the perfect place to put a lighthouse to tap
the Dutch trade.[71] We learn from a petition by John Hardy that he and
a Mr Duffield spent three years with the duke in hope of being employed
in the project of erecting a light on the Goodwin Sands.

Sir John Coke was instructed to get the Dutch Ambassador to
England, Sir Noel Carron, to persuade his government to back
Buckingham's lighthouse scheme. Since the Dutch suffered much for
want of a lighthouse on Goodwin Sands, Coke believed, they would naturally offer to contribute liberally to the project. Once more, the English
ambassador, Sir Dudley Carleton, was brought in to press the case in the
Netherlands. He was ordered to inform the States General that the Lord
High Admiral was graciously offering to erect and maintain the light
on the Goodwin Sands, and that, as the chief beneficiaries, they should
contribute 'either by a tonnage on all ships passing that way, or by an
annual payment in gross'. Additionally, Carleton was told that the terms
of the levy or payment should be 'made certain as possible' – a reflection,
perhaps, of how the Dutch had used the vagueness of Killigrew's proposal to evade any firm commitments.[72] But once more, even when the
lighthouse projector was the mighty Duke of Buckingham, Lord High
Admiral of England, and the king's favourite, the Dutch were not willing
to enrich an English projector, especially when the lighthouse seemed of
questionable benefit.

Parliamentarians also increasingly began to take a dim view of forcing ship owners and merchants to enrich powerful courtiers or their
friends. Impositions for lighthouses were high among the grievances
raised in the Commons during the Parliament of 1621.[73] John Angel,
MP for Rye, called for transfer of Dungeness light to Rye's control, and

[71] PRO, SP 14/31/43, SP 14/155/28, 48; SP 14/184/61. Also, Marsden, *Select Pleas*, introduction.
     Buckingham's project is much like Gawen Smith's.
[72] PRO, SP 14/155/28. 9 December 1623.
[73] PRO, SP 16/155/53. Meldrum's patent was 6 in a list of 13.

another MP, Robert Snelling, who represented Ipswich, tried to have the lighthouse patents declared void.[74] In condemning the Winterton light, he said that the charge was 'exceedingly great'. The Chancellor added, however, that in taking away single monopolies (like those for the Dungeness and Winterton lighthouses), there was a greater danger in creating a general monopoly of the sort Trinity House was seeking, and Sir Edward Sackville agreed, noting that granting exclusive power to any party, like Trinity House, would mean that there would be 'no lights, but where they will, and when they will'.[75] It was also generally agreed that, though Trinity House might not be as greedy as some of the worst private projectors, this organisation had done little or nothing with its existing rights and was even thought negligent by some.[76] Another MP, Sir Thomas Roe, known for his soundness and moderation, also spoke against a continuance of the Dungeness lighthouse patent, and went on to submit a report which concluded that such lighthouse projects should not be tolerated, declaring that 'Sir Edward Howard's debt [should] not to be paid by the Commonwealth'. Surprisingly, given his reputation, Sir Edward Coke's contribution was rather muted. He counselled caution until the views of the Lord High Admiral were known. He went on to express doubt on the Winterton and Dungeness patents believing them invalid because the patentees had no special skills; however, he believed that those of Trinity House were generally valid, but that the guild had been remiss in carrying out their duties and needed supervision. Soon thereafter he reported back that Buckingham had said he would consent to any provision the House should make for the 'Good of the Commonwealth' and that thanks should thus be given to the duke and the king.[77] Although both the Dungeness and Winterton patents (and Trinity House's attempt to extend its powers) were condemned in the bill subsequently drawn up and passed within the week, the patentees were saved when the House was adjourned. When called into session again, in November, lighthouses were again on the agenda but the parliament was prorogued after a few weeks before condemnation of the lighthouse patents would have effect. Even so, the iniquity of the projects was recognised, and after the end of the parliament, the king felt compelled to declare that existing lighthouse patents would be allowed to stand – but only if their charges were found not to be excessive – otherwise the patents would be declared null and void (but with full compensation to the patentees).

[74] *CJ*, 529–46.   [75] *CJ*, 529.   [76] *CJ*, 546.   [77] *CJ*, 599.

In the 1624 parliament the Committee on Grievances took up the issue of lighthouses and concluded that matters had 'grown worse since the last Parliament'. New complaints were made about the Lizard lighthouse, suggesting either that the project was still going or that its revival was feared. But once again, though a bill was prepared and progressing smoothly through the Commons, parliament was prorogued abruptly before it could become law.

If the merchant and shipping community had hoped for redress with the succession of Charles I, they were in for bitter disappointment. The new king continued the old ways, and Buckingham kept his hold on the Admiralty. The enormous profits from 'Tenths' that came with the wars against France and Spain may have satisfied the duke, though they were to cause resentment. One of the charges brought against Buckingham when he was impeached in 1626 was the size of his income and his concentration of offices and powers, specifically his Admiralty with Cinque Port rights.[78] The death of Buckingham did not improve matters, however; Charles put the Admiralty in commission but kept the rights of wreck and profits of the Admiralty for himself.[79] If anything, royal control led to Admiralty powers being exploited even more rigorously, as Hugh Dade informed Secretary Nicholas: 'He goes nowhere on the coast of Suffolk about his business . . . but he is informed that his Majesty has granted all Admiralty jurisdiction and wrecks in that coast to the Queen, which terrifies . . . Begs show Queen for how her rights extend and bridle.'[80] It was not simply that the crown was more vigorous in exploiting existing rights; a broad programme was initiated to concentrate and extend the crown powers in this area. In 1631, a leading Admiralty official, Sir Henry Martin, drew up a plan to recover 'decayed' royalties and rights of wreck from lords of the manor, etc.[81] Another piece of the programme was a special commission set up in 1633 to settle disputes between the Common Law and the Admiralty, which, in many instances, resulted in the Admiralty's hand being strengthened. Plans were also drawn up to call in all charters and grants as a prelude to reducing or rejecting local claims. The notes of Secretary Nicholas reveal plans for exclusive control over all salvage.[82] And enforcement of

---

[78] Gardiner, *History of England*, VI, 100–105.

[79] The next Lord High Admiral, James, Duke of York, was not granted the right to wreck in his patent.

[80] PRO, SP 16/346/37. Dade to Nicholas, 1636.   [81] PRO, SP 16/208/fos. 564–80.

[82] PRO, SP 16/322/17. It was proposed that all salvage should be strictly confined to officers of the Admiralty and they be responsible to his Majesty in their accounts.

the crown's claims over wrecks was undertaken with a new energy.[83] All those thought to be infringing upon the Admiralty's rights were to be sent to the Star Chamber. This extension of crown power naturally only served to increase resentment and distrust. Nicholas's man, Francis Barrat, advised that 'the rabble of these sea-borders' (as he called the locals) would 'rather trust God with their souls than the Admiral with their goods'.[84] There would be no amelioration before the outbreak of the Great Rebellion, and indeed it would only be in the Restoration that the High Court of Admiralty would be bridled and the money-spinning powers of the Lord High Admiral circumscribed.

CONCLUSION

The exploitation of the sea for profit by the crown, the Lord High Admiral and political fixers at court was a distinctive feature of the period, and the cases presented above stand as a dark counter to the picture of a reforming duke or paternal monarchy. 'Extortion' is perhaps the best word to describe them. The greed and rapaciousness of Buckingham cannot be explained away, and yet it would be wrong to attribute these developments simply as the work of an 'evil counsellor'. The sleaziness of official life with court officers and ambassadors all looking for their cut, so evident in the lighthouse cases, was an essential, cancerous feature of crown finance and politics under the early Stuarts. Rarely was the king or the Lord High Admiral first in finding some new way to profit from maritime misfortune, though a desire for money soon brought their involvement. This account also may serve to illustrate the aggressive intrusion of the Stuart government into the lives and liberties of its subjects. Government was concerned chiefly to siphon off profits rather than make the commonwealth prosper, and the whispers of special interests were listened to more intently than pleadings like that made by the Mayor of Rye, who remarked (apropos the Dungeness lighthouse) that 'being a public benefit it should be in public [rather] than private hands'.[85]

---

[83] PRO, SP 16/341/14 and SP 16/345/94, e.g. the disputes between Boston and also the Earl of Northumberland with the crown.
[84] PRO, SP 16/322/17.
[85] PRO, SP 14/160/60. Mayor of Rye to Lord Zouch on 10 March 1624.

6

Negotiating grace

Cynthia Herrup

'The most important symbolism of a parliament,' according to Conrad Russell, 'was that of unity.'[1] By suggesting the importance of symbols, Russell implies that what mattered to contemporaries was not only what parliaments actually did, but also what they could be seen to have done. Thus, as he has argued, the 1620s were difficult years for parliaments because the appearance of unity became more difficult to maintain when external pressures cast doubt on parliaments' abilities to realise their traditional responsibilities: supply, counsel and legislation.

Parliaments displayed their unity in many ways, and historians (not least Russell himself) have productively analysed what members said to one another, wrote in their diaries and correspondence and had said or written about them by outside observers. To these sources, scholars have added the more formal information disseminated in set speeches, statutes and taxation records. The essay below looks at the symbolism of unity from yet another source: general pardons. These pardons were issued routinely at the end of most parliaments. As acts of both royal prerogative and parliamentary consent, they were physical evidence of parliamentary unity. By the 1620s, the delivery of such pardons was also, at least for some members, a tangible demonstration to their countrymen that the time in Westminster had been well spent. But like other parliamentary business, general pardons were a more complicated business under the early Stuarts than they had been under other monarchs. Fewer of the parliaments of James I and Charles I passed parliamentary pardons, and fewer of those that did pass them did so without extended negotiations.[2]

---

[1] Conrad Russell, 'The nature of a parliament in early Stuart England', 11, repr. in Russell, *Unrevolutionary England 1603–1642* (Oxford, 1990). After this essay went to press, I discovered an important work by M. A. R. Graves and C. R. Kyle, '"The Kinges most excellent majestie oute of his gracious disposicion": the evolution of grace bills in English parliaments 1547–1642', *Parliaments, Estates and Representation*, 18 (1998), 31–51. From a different starting point Graves and Kyle have reached some of the conclusions discussed below. I am sorry not to have had time to absorb their work more fully.

[2] Because the pardons discussed below did not apply to Scotland, I have referred throughout this essay to James I rather than to James VI/I.

Parliamentary pardons were symbols of unity, but their production under the early Stuarts exposed potentially dangerous constitutional as well as political and personal fault-lines. In his provocative recent book, *State Formation in Early Modern England*, Michael Braddick argues for closer scholarly attention to the ways in which different elements of governance gained and lost legitimacy.[3] This essay is also an attempt to accept that challenge.

THE RISE OF PARLIAMENTARY PARDONS

The prerogative to issue pardons was among the most ancient and unlimited of royal powers. The idea that a sovereign could excuse punishment dated back to Rome and was part of the English royal tradition from at least the tenth century. Kings were to forgive where justice was deserved but would be detrimental; a king's power to pardon the condemned was intended to remind subjects of the unearned blessing of God's compassion. The prerogative was a responsibility 'solely and inseparable to the person of the king', perhaps the most personal of all prerogatives.[4] Fittingly, then, there were few restrictions on the royal pardon. The most absolute limitation was that monarchs could only forgive things in which they had an 'interest'. Pardoning was a power to be used for the good of the commonwealth, never against the good of an individual. Kings could not deprive subjects of private satisfaction; they could not, for example, protect killers from appeals of felony, deprive informers of their spoils, or pardon common nuisances.[5]

Parliaments would seem to have little place in the exercise of such a power, yet from the fourteenth century on, parliaments had played a repeated role in its application. In the reigns of Edward III and Richard II, parliaments passed legislation intended to narrow the opportunities for corruption in the soliciting of pardons. Monarchs could not be forced to obey these guidelines, but the legislation made popular expectations of the process clearer.[6] In the early seventeenth century, members of parliaments complained about specific pardons, but they could not force a monarch's hand any better than had their predecessors. Parliament's most effective influence on pardoning was through its

---

[3] M. J. Braddick, *State Formation in Early Modern England, c.1550–1700* (Cambridge, 2000).

[4] BL, Stowe MS 561, fo. 28v for the quote, but the sentiment is conventional.

[5] Sir Edward Coke, *3rd Part of the Institutes of the Laws of England*, 4 parts (4th edn, 1669), ch. 105. and Giles Jacob, *New-Law Dictionary* (1750), 'pardon'.

[6] *SR*, 1, 2. Legislation could be bypassed by including what was called a *non obstante* clause in a pardon's charter. The clause translated roughly to: 'any act statute ordinance cause matter or thing whatsoever to the contrary thereof in any wise notwithstanding'.

endorsements of general pardons. Unlike special pardons, which answered particular petitions, general pardons were broadly framed acts of grace available to anyone who fell within their purview. Direct access to the king (or access to someone who had access to the king) was unnecessary; general pardons could be purchased directly from the office of the Lord Chancellor. Since they were more available and more affordable than special pardons, not surprisingly, general pardons were extremely popular. So many individuals took advantage of the coronation pardon granted by Henry VIII that the names filled four patent rolls. Although James I had issued an exceptionally generous and exceptionally popular pardon in 1624, several thousand subjects still sought out the coronation pardon offered by Charles I just two years later.[7]

Monarchs issued general pardons when, where and as they chose. The oldest tradition was the coronation pardon, but general pardons also marked dynastic occasions such as births and provided indemnity after wars or rebellions. The specific contents of each pardon was different, but the scope was always broad: most forgave all save the worst of felonies, suits already in process and transgressions that closely touched the finances of the crown.[8] The customary instrument for such grace was a royal proclamation, but in 1377, for reasons that remain unclear, Edward III celebrated his royal jubilee by issuing a general pardon with the 'assent' of parliament. Its preamble offers no explanation of this, no grant of particular authority to the assembled parliament, and no acknowledgment that this process differed from the one used fourteen years earlier in celebration of the king's fiftieth birthday. The pardon's alleged inspiration was Edward's 'great compassion' towards his subjects and his sorrow at their losses in 'evil years' of wars, diseases and crop failures; he issued it, the preamble said, to inspire subjects to 'thereby have the greater courage to do well hereafter'. The pardon was conventional in everything but the way that it was issued. The change from proclamation to parliament, however, meant that what had previously belonged solely to the king was for the first time published as a parliamentary statute.[9]

Whatever Edward III's intention, from 1377 on, two distinct sorts of general pardons existed: those issued by monarchs autonomously as proclamations and those issued by kings in parliament. Kings and queens

[7] H. Maxwell-Lyte, *Notes on the Historical Uses of the Great Seal* (1926), 215; PRO, E315/1660.

[8] See, for example, Paul Hughes and J. F. Larkin (eds.), *Tudor Royal Proclamations* (New Haven, 1969), 394 (Mary), 452 (Elizabeth). The later coronation pardons are not in print, but two examples among many can be found at BL, Additional Charters 74, 209 (1604); 73, 987 (1626). For parliamentary pardons, see below.

[9] 50 Edward III c.3; cf. T. F. Tout, *Chapters in the Administrative History of the Middle Ages*, 6 vols. (Manchester, 1928), III, 318.

took advantage of both instruments, but over time the terms of the two diverged. The older type, what, for the sake of clarity, I will call *pardons of grace*, originated in a sovereign's 'special grace', 'certain knowledge' and 'will'. It usually contained little or no preamble and excepted relatively few categories. A *parliamentary pardon* was usually wordier and narrower: a preamble explained in detail what had moved the sovereign to grace and extensive exceptions were routinely included to reassure subjects that the pardon would enhance not detract from the country's peace.[10] Many preambles and exceptions followed their predecessors closely, but even these contained details and a tone reflecting immediate circumstances.[11] Because parliamentary pardons listed exclusions rather than inclusions, the scope of any one is hard to assess, but the parliamentary pardon of 7 Henry VIII c.11, excluding all felonies except minor larcenies, became the standard text concerning capital crimes. The situation with less serious offences was more fluid, but parliamentary pardons routinely disallowed any act whose fine provided the government or its agents with a steady income.[12]

Edward III had used a parliament to publicise a pardon inspired by the conventional opportunity of his jubilee; in the early modern era, the conclusion of a parliament was itself an occasion celebrated with a pardon. Many late medieval parliaments had concluded with pardons, and although these often warned that it would be foolhardy to assume that there would be regular parliamentary pardons, the Tudors did routinise the practice. As the preamble to 7 Henry VIII c.11 explained, pardons were not intended 'by often forgiveness and remission to give audacity to offenders upon hope of impunity, but that his great bounteousness of benefit be a preemptory monition to his subjects . . .' That said, Henry VIII granted parliamentary pardons about every six years throughout his reign; Elizabeth I about every four years during hers.[13]

By 1603, both the process and the substance of these pardons were standard. After discussion with king and council, the Attorney-General would produce a draft pardon based on earlier examples for the king's approval.[14] As parliament drew to a close (indeed, sometimes as a signal

[10] Contemporaries used the term general pardon less specifically; for them, it might mean pardons of grace and parliamentary pardons, parliamentary pardons alone, or even any exceptionally generous special pardon.

[11] Compare, for example, 7 Henry VIII c.11 with 5 Elizabeth I c.30.

[12] *SR* includes the final texts of the parliamentary pardons; the originals, few of which contain emendations, are in the House of Lords Record Office, series OA.

[13] Edward VI was equally generous; the exception among the Tudors was Mary I. Her parliaments issued no pardons, but since her brief reign included not one, but two, coronation pardons, that may explain the lapse.

[14] See, for example, *APC, 1621–23*, 98, 101–2 (1621); *APC, 1623–25*, 205–6 (1624).

that a dissolution was imminent), the document, engrossed and endorsed
with the sign manual, was sent from Whitehall to Westminster (usually
to the House of Lords). In contrast to other proposed statutes, a parliamentary pardon was intended to receive a single reading in each House
and was allegedly not open to discussion. After both Houses consented
to the text, during the closing ceremonies of the session, representatives
thanked the monarch for his or her generosity. The sovereign's consent
was added to theirs, and the pardon appeared in the official records as
that parliament's final public act.[15]

Over the sixteenth century, parliamentary pardons became not just
more frequent, but also procedurally more accessible than pardons of
grace. Starting with 21 Henry VIII c.1, parliamentary pardons carried no
fees except for the one paid to the recording clerk. To take advantage of
Elizabeth I's coronation pardon, for example, cost the taker a 'customary'
26s 8d (still a bargain compared to the cost of a special pardon), but
any of her parliamentary pardons could be had for 1s or less.[16] The
frequency and the complexity of parliamentary pardons, moreover, inspired a body of case law about their application; by mid-century the
judicial consensus was that, barring specific circumstances, one did not
need to plead a parliamentary pardon in order to take advantage of it.[17]
When the Stuarts arrived in England, then, they inherited (in addition
to older sorts of special pardons and pardons of grace) the practice of
issuing statutory pardons. Reinforcing parliament's public participation
in exercises of even this most personal of royal prerogatives, parliamentary pardons were symbols of unity. They also provided frequent and
predictable respites from many of the realm's most irritating laws.

The factual narrative of James I, Charles I, their respective parliaments and their parliamentary pardons deviates significantly from Tudor
practice. James and Charles each granted coronation pardons, but James
I followed his with only three parliamentary pardons (1606, 1610 and
1624) in five parliaments, and Charles I with no parliamentary pardons
at all. James I was responsible for both one of the longest periods in
memory without a general pardon (1610–24) and one of the most generous pardons offered in the early modern era (21 James I c.35). Typically,

[15] HLRO, Braye MS 65, 6, 8; Elizabeth Read Foster, *The House of Lords* (Chapel Hill, 1986), 52,
83, 198–9. With minor variations, Tudor process was the same: see M. A. R. Graves, *The Tudor
Parliaments: Crown, Lord and Commons 1485–1603* (1985), 152; S. Lehmberg, *The Later Parliaments of
Henry VIII 1536–1547* (Cambridge, 1977), 118–19; G. R. Elton, *The Parliament of England 1558–1581*
(Cambridge, 1986), 45–6 for examples.
[16] Hughes and Larkin, *Tudor Proclamations*, 452; *SR*, 4, pt 2, *passim*.
[17] William Lambard, *Eirenarcha* (1619), 559–60; Coke, *Institutes*, III, 234; Jacob, *New-Law Dictionary*.
However, if a pardon excepted individuals by name (and many did), it was necessary to plead
that you were not among the excepted persons.

his heir was more consistent: he issued only one pardon of grace after his coronation, to celebrate the 1630 birth of the Prince of Wales. Charles I's reign had fewer general pardons than any reign since Edward II's. Michael Graves calls the passing of pardons in the Tudor parliaments 'mere formalities'; early Stuart parliaments were less quiescent.[18] They were the first parliaments we know of that repeatedly tried to negotiate the contents of their pardons – the first to ask for and see a pardon's heads well before its formal presentation (1621 and 1624); the first to prefer to recess with no pardon rather than to approve one not to their liking (1628 and 1629).

The years between 1603 and 1642 contain enough oddities concerning parliamentary pardons to sustain a commentary in which arguments about the status and content of parliamentary pardons meld seamlessly into broader and more familiar conflicts over finance, religion and prerogative in the reigns of the first Stuarts. Negotiations about pardons often became part of larger parliamentary discussions.[19] In the parliaments of 1614, 1626 and 1629, the pardons fell hostage in part to arguments over the king's supply; in 1621 and 1628, to disagreements about the king's prerogatives; in 1626 and 1628 (as well as in 1641), to fears over the king's desire to protect his councillors. No one issue stymied any pardon, any more than a single issue explained a contentious parliament or a decision to dissolve a parliament. By 1643, however, it had been thirteen years since the last pardon of grace and nearly twenty years since the last parliamentary pardon. Yet, as Russell has always reminded us, what looks like coherent narrative can easily turn out to be an illusion built of our own expectations. The failure of proposed parliamentary pardons is less a tale of contending special interests than it is a story about agreements and ambiguities. To understand that, we need briefly to explore first why people appreciated parliamentary pardons.

PARDONS AND REGULATORY STATUTES

The increase in parliamentary pardons under the Tudors reflected the increasing frequency of parliaments, and, it has long been thought, the deepening financial demands of governance. Because early modern

---

[18] Graves, *The Tudor Parliaments*, 86; on the pardon in 1630, see BL, Additional MS 35, 331, fos. 38–38v; BL, Egerton MS 784, 155–6. Cf Graves and Kyle, 'The Kings most excellent majestie'.

[19] The point of ongoing tension pardons seem not to have touched is popery. Whether because the fines were too lucrative or because the reaction to concessions allegedly promised to foreign monarchs was too strong, parliamentary pardons in this period never excused the laws against recusants.

monarchs had growing expenses and shrinking revenues, they relied more heavily than their predecessors had upon parliamentary grants of subsidy. Therefore, the logic runs, they were also more inclined than their predecessors to satisfy co-operative parliaments with grants of mercy. S. E. Lehmberg considers financial support from parliaments to have become the rationale for parliamentary pardons as early as the 1530s. Geoffrey Elton notes that when supply had been asked for and granted, such pardons 'always' passed the Houses. In his study of the later Elizabethan parliaments, David Dean amalgamates pardon and supply into a single chapter and concludes that by the 1580s, the pardon was 'probably seen as a sort of quid pro quo for the subsidy'.[20]

Yet I would suggest that in this case as in others, we have assumed the critical role of subsidies without fully considering their limitations. The frustrations of subsidy finance are too well known to need repetition; however much parliaments might offer, problems of assessment and collection produced a decreasing return throughout this period, a result perhaps too paltry to tempt a monarch on these grounds alone to offer a parliamentary pardon. And parliamentary pardons themselves cost the sovereign money; by forgiving financial penalties without charging high fees, kings who issued such pardons further reduced their own revenues (particularly when the generated income went not to the crown but to licensed agents). The more popular the pardon, the less money likely to reach the Exchequer or to be available for petitioners. Sir Robert Heath claimed that the pardon proposed in 1621 would have cost the government the equivalent of three subsidies; after three subsidies that same year, King James told the Commons that he would offer no pardon until he knew what they would offer him 'lest otherwise we give back the double or triple of that we are to receive . . .' Except in times of war, the preambles to parliamentary pardons are as apt to mention the 'great increase of treasure' that mercy will deny the sovereign as to express thanks for any offsetting support. The rhetorical value of emphasising royal sacrifice is unmistakable, but it was generally accepted that parliamentary pardons lost rather than raised money for the crown.[21]

---

[20] Lehmberg, *Later Parliaments*, 118–19; Elton, *Parliament of England*, 5; David Dean, *Law-making and Society in Elizabethan England: the Parliament of England 1584–1601* (Cambridge, 1996) ch. 2, 34.

[21] Elizabeth Read Foster, 'Staging a parliament', in Peter Clark, Alan G. R. Smith and Nicholas Tyacke (eds.), *The English Commonwealth 1547–1640* (New York, 1979), 143; James VI/I, 'His Majesty's declaration', in Johann Sommerville (ed.), *James VI/I: political writings* (Cambridge, 1994), 251 ff; see also the preambles to 21 James I c.35; 32 Henry VIII c.49; 7 Edward VI c.14; 8 Elizabeth I c.29.

The fiscal profit in pardons, as councillors and projectors knew, would have come from replacing virtually free parliamentary pardons with ones available for higher, yet (theoretically) manageable prices. Schemes about how to do this surfaced repeatedly in the early seventeenth century and received serious consideration. The best-documented plan originated with William Hakewill, a respected legal antiquary and member of parliament, who early in 1615 suggested selling general pardons without parliamentary authority for £5 each; he estimated a potential profit of roughly £400,000. Even those chary of his predictions thought that such pardons could earn the monarch £100,000 or more.[22] If monarchs preferred parliamentary pardons to pardons of grace, financial need alone is an unlikely explanation.

More important than what parliamentary pardons earned for the crown, perhaps, was what they spared the subject. Whereas most medieval parliaments passed fewer than a dozen statutes, Tudor parliaments commonly endorsed twice that many or more pieces of legislation. Some of these acts concerned felonies, but more addressed the quotidian tensions of communal (and particularly economic) life and concerned transgressions that carried financial rather than corporal penalties. The Tudor parliaments oversaw an unprecedented rise in what Hayward Townshend in 1601 called 'penal and entrapping laws'. More than 100 penal statutes were in force early in the reign of James I, and the result was that more people, and especially more of the 'middling' and 'better' sorts, found themselves (whether intentionally or not) acting against the law.[23] Although neither of the early Stuart kings seemed keen to add significantly to this body of statutes, their governments were very interested in enforcing what had already been enacted, and in giving renewed authority to the collection of old debts and lapsed ancient obligations. Parliamentary pardons, which routinely spared more statutory offences than they did Common-Law felonies, assured periodic relief from these economic burdens.

[22] On Hakewill's scheme pro and con: HEHL, Ellesmere MS 445; Bod. Lib., Carte MS 121, fos. 1–20; N. E. McClure (ed.), *The letters of John Chamberlain*, 2 vols. (Philadelphia, 1939), I, 567–8, 581, 587. On other schemes: Frederick Dietz, *English Public Finance 1558–1641* (New York, 1932), 145, 234; BL, Additional MS 34, 324, fos. 69–74; BL, Harleian MS 389, fo. 199; PRO, C115/n6, 8711.

[23] Townshend as quoted in M. W. Beresford, 'The common informer, the penal statutes and economic regulation', *EHR*, 2nd ser., 10 (1957–8), 223 of 221–37. Elton, *Parliament of England*, 385–8 and Dean, *Law-making*, 291–4 list the Elizabethan contribution to this corpus. For their impact, see, for example, C. J. Kitching, 'The quest for concealed lands in the reign of Elizabeth I', *TRHS*, 5th ser. (1974), 63–78; D. R. Liddington, 'Parliament and the enforcement of the penal statutes: the history of the act "in restraint of common promoters"', *PH*, 8, pt 2 (1989), 309–28.

These sorts of pardons seem to have been understood differently than pardons forgiving petty thefts or felonies; parliamentary pardons, as a member of the House of Commons put it in 1610, were those 'whereof honest men that are yielders of the subsidy may have some benefit and not offenders only'. One of the alleged advantages of Hakewill's pardon-selling scheme was that 'honest men' were its intended market: the plan 'would bring ease and quiet no less to the better sort', to men 'burdened with old debts', and to those suffering 'the vexation of inferior officers'.[24] Members of parliament were particularly keen that parliamentary pardons forgive fines for problems linked to property such as alienating land without royal licence, concealed wardships, debts or wastes. The fact that the only men whom all elements of the early Stuart parliaments agreed to exclude by name from parliamentary pardons (Sir Stephen Proctor and Sir Giles Mompesson) had built their fortunes on the enforcement of these and similar penalties was not coincidence. Nor was it accidental that parliamentary pardons foundered in 1621 in part over how much old debt should be forgiven; in 1628 and 1629 (in addition to the king's desire to protect his favourites) over the king's unwillingness to forgive either penalties or feudal obligations that produced large revenues. When James I presented the 1624 parliament with a pardon that was exceptionally generous in forgiving such obligations, the members are reported to have cried 'Vive le Roy' as a single voice.[25]

The importance of the growing number of penal statutes and of continued enforcement of older financial obligations in parliamentary pardons is obvious from the pardons themselves. The preambles of both successful pardons and those that died before passage insist that the presence of so many laws invariably bred disobedience. From the 1550s on, the preambles discuss the problem in similar terms: having opened with a reprise of royal responsibilities and an acknowledgement of the public's affection, each laments the failure of the nation's statutes to bring either order or clarity to daily life. While the tone evokes a disappointed parent trying to reinstil discipline in his or her unruly children, the words acknowledge that in the current situation, as one Henrician preamble said, 'even the repentant can not be delivered if His Majesty shall suffer the weight and burden of justice to remain upon their shoulders'.

---

[24] Elizabeth Read Foster (ed.), *Proceedings in Parliament 1610*, 2 vols. (New Haven, 1966), II, 144; Bod. Lib., Carte MS 121, fos. 13–13v, 15.

[25] *CJ*, I, 713 for the report, 575–6, 592, 690 for the concerns. The 1624 Parliament made significant progress (much of it by building on proposals presented to its predecessor) in reforming the operation of penal statutes.

An Elizabethan prologue talks about 'the danger of diverse penalties and forfeitures'; a Jacobean one regrets the 'manifold inconveniences' that such laws bring to great numbers of people. Having recognised the subjects' dilemma, the text invariably turns back to the sovereign. Because the monarch is merciful, he or she prefers for the moment to instruct his or her people rather than to profit by their weaknesses. Hence, 'moved by Almighty God', the typical preamble concludes, the monarch offers a parliamentary pardon.[26]

COMMON GROUND

Men in Westminster and Whitehall worked from a shared understanding of the breadth and limits of parliamentary pardons. The granting of parliamentary pardons had distinct advantages. The most powerful restriction on the royal pardon (the restriction to matters of the king's 'interest') was elusive, since the boundary between the king's interest and the interest of the community was never clear nor stable. Judges established this boundary case by case, but as the number of statutory transgressions and the government's reliance on informers and revenue farmers grew, the safest way to pardon offences created by parliament may well have seemed a pardon that was itself a sort of statute.

Passing pardons in parliament seemed to suit popular expectations as well. The effect of a generous pardon from the king in parliament, Sir John Mallory assured the Earl of Salisbury in 1610, would '[be] great satisfaction, soon bring our business to a period and make us welcome home to our poor neighbours'. Sir Thomas Wentworth argued in both 1621 and 1625 that subjects would be more forthcoming if, as soon as possible, members could carry home 'a free and princely pardon . . .' What the common sort wanted from parliaments, Wentworth believed, was 'a good pardon, some beneficial laws, and ease and discharge of their grievances and pressures'.

When asked to consider the sale of general pardons, the king's councillors recognised these expectations and worried about the impact of seeming to bypass parliaments. 'It is a kind of putting a parliament out of service, for men say there has been tried a benevolence instead of subsidies & now a charter pardon instead of a parliament pardon . . .', one sceptic wrote. Even proponents of the project recognized the problem;

---

[26] Quotations from 7 Edward VI c.14; 5 Elizabeth I c.30; 21 James c.35. See also the draft preambles in HLRO, Parchment Collection 179/2 (1628); 180/1 (1641); Bod. Lib., Carte MS 121, fos. 1–1v, 3.

if they implemented Hakewill's project, advisers hoped to avoid criticism by exploiting the king's imminent trip to Scotland. Rather than a
usurpation of parliaments or a money-making enterprise, the pardons
could be presented as evidence of the king's desire that his absence cause
no inconvenience for his subjects.[27]

A shared sense of what parliamentary pardons should look like com-
plemented the consensus about the needs that pardons served. King,
council and members of parliament favoured history (factual and embroidered) as the surest guide. Hakewill's project was risky in part because
it appeared to have no precedent in England at least 'since the Conquest'.
'I fear this is the first,' one adviser wrote and 'that which is strange had
needs be good in these distracting times.' Another councillor thought
that there was a precedent: since 1616 marked James I's fiftieth year
as a king, Edward III's jubilee pardon could be used as the exemplar.
That recent pardons had been too severely 'pruned and pared', a third
thought, might offset this project's newness. Other advisers were less
concerned that the project had no history than that it would suggest the
wrong history. Selling pardons, they argued, could evoke 'the inprosper-
ous example in the indulgences in the Church of Rome'. Chamberlain's
dubbing of the project's author 'pope' Hakewill shows how close to the
surface such comparisons could be.[28]

History's most powerful lesson, however, was that past parliamentary
pardons had been better pardons. Members of parliament in particular looked fondly backwards to past generosities. The pardons of 50
Edward III, 5 Elizabeth I and 13 Elizabeth I were the nostalgic standards.
In 1610, the Commons heard a complaint that more recent 'pardons
were cut so short as no man almost could receive benefit by them'. In
1621 Hakewill asked for a committee to consider why 'pardons of late
times have been shortened', and Wentworth wanted to be sure that the
king knew how 'the grace of pardons have declined ever since 5 or 13
Elizabeth I'. Sir Edward Coke concluded that so many exceptions had
become standard in parliamentary pardons that they were in fact of
little benefit.[29] However accurate these conclusions, they clearly set a
threshold for the pardons of contemporary monarchs.

---

[27] Foster, *Proceedings in Parliament 1610*, II, 32–3; J. P. Cooper (ed.) *Wentworth Papers 1597–1628*, ed.
(Camden Society, 4th ser., 1973) 167, 238; Bod. Lib., Carte MS 121, fos. 7–7v, 13v.
[28] Bod. Lib., Carte MS 121, fos. 7, 13, 15; McClure, *Letters of Chamberlain*, I, 581.
[29] Foster, *Proceedings in Parliament 1610*, II, 142–4; eds. Wallace Notestein, Francis Helen Relf, and
Hartley Simpson (eds.), *Commons Debates in 1621*, 7 vols. (New Haven, 1935), II, 332–3, 339;
CJ, I, 592; see also BL, Harleian MS 390, fo. 416.

General agreement existed among the ruling classes that the best pardons were those that were traditional in content and that brought ease to the country. Parliamentary pardons could fill the need, but only if the king and Houses could agree. Unfortunately, arguments about the contents of specific parliamentary pardons easily escalated into more diffuse objections, because whatever the consensus about their contents, confusion existed about the nature of these pardons. What parliamentary pardons actually were – royal or parliamentary, gift or exchange – was never uncontested. The acceptance of specific parliamentary pardons could not escape from questions about the general status of parliamentary pardons because in the end, parliamentary pardons were about money and authority, not subsidy money necessarily, but the money that pardons cost, the money that they forgave, and the money that they earned. Who controlled the process that determined each of these decisions? Over the decade of the 1620s, the strikingly different attitudes of James I and Charles I towards the history and nature of these pardons added considerably to the perplexity.

UNSTEADY GROUND

However firmly pardons of every sort were royal and recognized as such, the practical history of parliamentary pardons suggests something constitutionally more complex. Like the category 'king in parliament', which both joined the monarch to and separated him or her from Westminster (since kings were theoretically part of parliaments the phrase was at the very least redundant), the notion of a parliamentary pardon was a contradiction left undefined by contemporaries. Issuing a general pardon with the members' endorsement flattered everyone involved. For Lords and Commons, it made a show of their importance and their encouragement of royal grace. For the monarch, it marked the conclusion of a parliament as a public moment of unity, bounteousness and thanksgiving.

Yet what exactly were these pardons? Using recognisable (albeit abbreviated) statutory forms intimated that parliamentary pardons were statutes as well as proclamations; pairing subsidies and pardons implied (without specifics) some sort of synergetic relationship between the two. Parliamentary pardons worked best when consensus about their contents allowed them to remain productively ambiguous; their value fell when disagreements exposed their hybrid constitutional position and their connection to already contentious matters of advice and counsel. Could members convened to give advice be barred from advising on pardons?

Could sovereigns blessed with the power to offer mercy be told how to wield that power? Parliaments had an undoubted right to discuss bills that were brought before them, but were parliamentary pardons bills?

On the one hand, late medieval monarchs had sometimes said that they proffered parliamentary pardons at 'the instance and prayer of the said Commons'. Coke found this fitting since, he said, it was the Commons who 'know best where the shoe wrings them and wherein and how they are to be eased'. Procedural commentators admitted that despite the prohibition on debating parliamentary pardons, 'yet upon reading of it [the pardon] sometimes exceptions are taken in that it is not so favourable as in former times'.[30] The pardons were read to the assembled members as bills were, passed between the Houses, and subjected to votes. Like bills, they began with explanatory preambles; like bills, they were highly specific and complex and had limited power unless renewed. Pardons became acts as other acts did, in the formal ceremonies concluding parliaments. Although they arrived in parliament already endorsed by the sign manual, parliamentary pardons received a second consent from the monarch after the Houses had approved them. The pardons appeared with other acts in print and routinely contained the phrase 'enacted by the authority of this present parliament' or its close equivalent.

On the other hand, since the authority to issue pardons belonged solely to monarchs, all of the legislative forms might be seen as superficial trappings. Parliamentary pardons were business that only monarchs could begin or complete, and pardon preambles always voiced royal rather than solely parliamentary concerns. If the physical presentation to the Houses of the pardons already engrossed and signed was not signal enough that Whitehall expected consent not counsel, parliaments' own procedures underlined it. The pardons bypassed the stages in which debate on bills normally occurred. Pardons appeared last in the list of successfully concluded public business; that marked them as both a part of and apart from a parliament's other statutes. And as Elton has pointed out, giving the royal assent to parliamentary pardons was somewhat nonsensical, since in effect, the sovereign was accepting a bill that was a free gift of his or her own grace.[31]

The timing of these pardons within parliaments allowed a second ambiguity: what was the relationship between grants of royal mercy and grants of parliamentary supply? The arrival of the pardon at the end

---

[30] 1 Henry IV c.20; Coke, *Institutes*, 240; BL, Harleian MS 1012, fo. 1v.
[31] Elton, *Parliament of England*, 130. See also Hayward Townshend, *Historical Collections of an Exact Account of the Proceedings of the Four Last Parliaments of Queen Elizabeth* (1680), 13, 44, 49.

rather than at the beginning of sessions may have been an attempt to prevent debate (although given the frequency with which rumours about the pardon leaked from the Privy Council, one could argue that an earlier presentation might have restrained discussion rather than encouraged it), but it permitted the conclusion that the pardon was a response to financial help. The closing ceremonies reinforced the impression by setting the pardon and the grant of subsidy together yet apart from other business, emphasising their shared peculiarity of being both acts of parliament and gifts from one segment of parliament to another.

The preambles to parliamentary pardons in some ways supported what the order of business suggested about pardons as expressions of thankfulness for money. Most referred to 'correspondence[s] of gratitude' or to recent 'manifest declarations' of the subjects' love. Sir Francis Nethersole explained parliamentary pardons to Elizabeth of Bohemia as 'a matter of grace the kings of this realm use to grant to the people as thanks for their subsidy'.[32] In 1621, Sir Nathaniel Rich claimed that when past monarchs had refused to show parliaments drafts of proposed pardons, members had withheld supply. He was wrong, but his confusion was understandable. James I spoke of 'retributing' subsidies with mercy and John Rushworth predicted that since the 1621 meeting ended without a pardon, the lack of such 'retribution' would be high on the next parliament's list of grievances. As Lord Chancellor Coventry said in opening the parliament of 1628, 'aids granted by parliaments be commonly accompanied with wholesome laws, gracious pardons and the like'.[33]

Yet Whitehall also insisted that while pardons and subsidies were, as Randolph Crew noted, usually 'sisters', the connection was not organic. In 1610, James I specifically insisted that his grace was not dependent on parliamentary funding. At least one of the king's councillors believed that pardons preceded subsidies in parliamentary ritual specifically to prevent anyone concluding that the one drew too closely upon the other. Another adviser contended that although 'pardons in parliament are not otherwise granted but so as to be coupled with a subsidy', both subsidies and pardons were 'most graceful, when each are free and without reciprocal contract'. Members in Westminster did not necessarily dispute that ideal. Wentworth, for one, worried about the subsidy becoming a form of 'merchandise'. And Coke, who championed parliaments' rights

---

[32] 21 Henry VIII c.1; see also 18 Elizabeth I c.24; PRO, SP16/108/52 cited in eds. Mary Frear Keeler, Maija Jannson Cole and William R. Bidwell (eds.), *Proceedings in Parliament 1628*, 6 vols. (New Haven, 1977) VI, 199.

[33] Notestein, Relf and Simpson, *Commons Debates in 1621*, II, 409; James VI/I, 'His Majesty's declaration', in Sommerville, *Political writings of James VI/I*, 264; John Rushworth, *Historical Collections* (1669), pt 1, 115; Keeler, Cole and Bidwell *Proceedings in Parliament 1628*, II, 6.

to contest any individual case of pardon, recognised that if the Houses established that the subsidy was provisional upon the pardon, the king could say that the pardon was provisional upon the subsidy; the result, he concluded, 'would derogate from our free gift'.[34]

So the parliamentary pardon was a tangle of possibilities: was it a peculiar sort of proclamation or was it a peculiar sort of statute? If it was the former, then why have the Houses consent to it; if it was the latter, then on what grounds could one refuse to let the Houses discuss it? Was the relationship of pardon to subsidy a traditional, but not invariable conjunction of gifts, or a more integral reciprocity? If the two grants were coincidental, why allow the peculiarities of timing? If the subsidy inspired the pardon, why respond with what was effectively a remission of some of the revenue about to be collected?

These idiosyncrasies were most visible when arguments arose about the contents of a specific parliamentary pardon. The ramifications of such discussions depended on the responses of the monarch. James I, despite the grandiosity of his rhetoric, was exceptionally attentive to complaints about parliamentary pardons and exceptionally co-operative in his replies. At the behest of the Commons, he allowed the Attorney-General to amend the 1610 pardon to exclude Sir Stephen Proctor. In 1621, he offered to let a pardon pass without a completed grant of the subsidy. In 1624, clearly having in mind the failures of 1621, he had the Lord Keeper open parliament by assuring the members that as 32 Henry VIII was remembered as the learned parliament, 39 Elizabeth I as the devout parliament and 19 James I as the gracious parliament, the current meeting would be the bountiful parliament in honour of 'that large pardon you expect this time'. Not only did James make good that expectation, he allowed the Attorney-General to share a detailed outline of the heads of the proposed pardon with the Commons well before the session ended.[35]

In contrast, Charles I had no interest in negotiating either the terms or the processes of grace with his parliaments. He was more concerned with preserving what his father's Archbishop of Canterbury, George Abbott, had called 'the dutiful awe of the people to the king'. Attentive to history, he was unwilling to allow his father's exceptional generosity

---

[34] Notestein, Relf and Simpson, *Commons Debates in 1621*, II, 163–5, 409; James VI/I, 'Speech in parliament, 1610', in Sommerville, *Political writings of James VI/I*, 194; Bod. Lib., Carte MS 121, fos. 7, 13.

[35] Foster, *The House of Lords*, 198–9; James VI/I 'His Majesty's declaration', 264; John Hacket, *Scrinia Reserata* (1693), 177–9.

to become precedent. Yet his father's flexibility could not be undone; as members of parliament argued, 1624 was history, too. In 1628, when suspicion over whom the king might pardon became an issue, the process surrounding the act of pardon became the grounds of conflict. Individual members of parliament wanted to see the proposed pardon (or at least its outline) before it was engrossed. Sir Walter Earle said that showing the proposed heads of the pardon to the Commons was an 'ancient custom'. Coke claimed (not quite accurately) that he had done this when he was Attorney-General, that James I's later legal officers had as well, and that 'if he [the king] will have our consent to have it enacted the heads must be brought to us'. The old king's behaviour in 1624 was repeatedly the point of reference.[36]

Charles's own reading of history led him to argue that what was being asked was decidedly not what he understood 'to be the course of the house'. He may have been correct, but his view was not persuasive, even after the Attorney-General offered to show an annotated version of 21 James I c.35 informally to any member of the 1628 parliament who requested it. Instead, the Commons took the unprecedented step when the pardon came of sending it to committee for discussion and amendment. The committee, chaired by John Selden, vetted the 1628 text line by line against the model of 1624 and found it wanting. The proposed pardon was less generous than 21 James I c.35, but since that was the broadest parliamentary pardon in more than fifty years, that was not surprising. The members complained and Charles dissolved parliament without agreement on the pardon. 'Too large to the faultiest, too straight to the more innocent, and so it lies dead,' was the verdict of newsletter writer Joseph Mead. When a new parliament met in 1629, the king tried to use the promise of a generous pardon 'to bring them all within a circle of love and clemency'. The Lords agreed, but the Commons (according allegedly to Bishop John Williams) refused even to consider it.[37]

Parliamentary pardons were not inherently controversial. Like all pardons, they were a conjurer's trick, obscuring legal problems that they had no capacity to reform.[38] Yet these pardons became a site of conflict

---

[36] HEHL, Ellesmere MS 445; *CJ*, 1, 690; BL, Harleian MS 390, fos. 364, 366; Keeler, Cole and Bidwell, *Proceedings in Parliament 1628*, IV, 281, 294–5, 297–8, 331–4.

[37] *CJ*, 1, 912–19; HLRO, Parchment 179/2; Keeler, Cole and Bidwell, *Proceedings in Parliament 1628*, IV, 331, 468; Hacket, *Scrinia Reserata*, pt 2, 83.

[38] I hope to expand this point in a larger project for which this essay is a preliminary exercise.

in the 1620s because they could change the landscape of so many more important issues: finance, precedent and the need for wise counsel. Such conflicts were not easily resolved because parliamentary pardons, unlike pardons rooted solely in royal grace, were constitutionally peculiar. As a manifestation of prerogative presented to the Houses for consent, parliamentary pardons were both royal and statutory. As a manifestation of grace presented at the same time as a subsidy, they were both gift and trade. Unexamined, these ambiguities were harmless, but when discussed, they left parliamentary pardons hostage to unanswerable questions.

All of the elements of the ruling elite in England in the 1620s agreed that the demands of penal laws, feudal remnants and property transfers could be oppressive. All agreed that good parliamentary pardons brought popular approbation to both kings and parliaments and that parliaments without pardons could bring popular disdain. All agreed that honour and history, 'the honor of the custom of the realm', should be the touchstones of parliamentary pardons.[39] But putting custom into practice meant defining what that custom was. In such circumstances, the monarch's temperament was critical. James I was amenable to making 'custom' a negotiated process; Charles I was not. The problem was not that king and parliament had different values, but that they had differences over how to apply the values which they shared. When it came to parliamentary pardons, the unity they represented was a critical, but fragile symbol.

[39] Bod. Lib., Carte MS 121, fo. 7.

Religion

7

The pastoral tightrope: a puritan pedagogue in Jacobean London

J. F. Merritt

I

Scholars working on the activities of pastors and their congregations in early modern England are currently confronted with an increasingly divergent historiography. One of the most contested issues has been the relationship between doctrine and pastoral activity. In particular, to what extent did clergy think it necessary or even desirable to avoid doctrinal issues in a pastoral context? Was a simple moral code and basic credal information the only message that ministers ultimately expected to convey to their flocks in practice? Were puritan ministers – doctrinally demanding and naturally keen to appeal to the godly minority within their congregation – fundamentally unwilling to address the local community as a whole? Conversely, one might ask whether pastorally sensitive clergy necessarily met this challenge by deciding to jettison the teaching of the intellectually demanding and pastorally divisive doctrine of predestination. More broadly, can we in fact really hope to re-create the pastoral goals and practical activity of university-trained ministers in the post-Reformation church?[1]

The difficulty in answering these questions partly derives from historians' use of evidence. If we have tended to assume a stark dichotomy between the worlds of university and parish, between the history of doctrine and social history, then this is partly because historians themselves tend to prefer the study of either one or the other. But the concentration on only one type of source material inevitably colours the way that its broader significance is portrayed. In this way, for example, controversial

[1] K. Parker and E. Carlson, *'Practical Divinity'. The Works and Life of Revd Richard Greenham* (Aldershot, 1998); I. Green, *The Christian's ABC* (Oxford, 1995); idem, *Print and Protestantism in Early Modern England* (Oxford, 2000); C. Marsh, *Popular Religion in Sixteenth Century England* (Basingstoke, 1998). These questions have been most recently addressed in P. Lake, *The Boxmaker's Revenge* (Manchester, 2001) and C. Haigh, 'The taming of the Reformation: preachers, pastors and parishioners in Elizabethan and early Stuart England', *Hist*, 85 (October, 2000).

divinity on the one hand, or those works written for a popular audience on the other, are often studied in isolation from one another, with relatively little attempt to bring them together. Such a division of labour is, of course, natural given the volume and complexity of religious source materials available. Nevertheless, such an approach can contribute to an artificial divide; one that assumes that the authors of controversial divinity on the one hand, and of pastoral manuals on the other, *necessarily* compartmentalised their lives in such a way, dividing their doctrinal writings and their pastoral activities.

The present article seeks to bridge this gap and to avoid this compartmentalisation by focusing on a single minister, his career in relation to both university debates and parochial religion, his full body of publications across the divides of genre, and the social context in which he operated. The fruits of this approach suggest that we must be wary of presupposing a sharp discontinuity between the worlds of university and parish religion.

The particular divine selected for study is one Robert Hill. Hill's career and surviving writings make him particularly apt for such an investigation, partly because his prolific publications enable us to document his ideas throughout the whole course of his career. As he was the author of a best-selling popular guide to Christian living, this also allows us to contextualise such a work among the full range of his other publications. Finally, Hill's close involvement in the predestinarian disputes in Cambridge in the 1590s also makes him an appropriate vehicle for investigating how far such university debates truly had any impact on the later pastoral careers and teaching of those ministers who lived through them.

We should begin with Hill's background, which reveals very clear puritan credentials. Despite humble origins in the Derbyshire town of Ashbourne, 'that poore and untaught towne', as he later described it, Robert Hill came as an undergraduate to Christ's College, Cambridge. Like many others who attended Christ's, he was strongly inspired by the teaching there of the famous puritan divine William Perkins. After obtaining his first degrees, Hill then moved in 1589 to St John's College, where the atmosphere nurtured by the Master, William Whitaker, meant that Hill found himself among a cohort of godly young men granted fellowships in the early 1590s. These included several who would later become notable puritan figures, such as William Crashawe and Abdias Ashton.[2] As a fellow of St John's, Hill was immediately pitched into the religious controversies that shook the college and the university

[2] *New DNB* (forthcoming), s.n. Robert Hill; PRO, Prob. 11/142/87; P. Lake, *Moderate Puritans and the Elizabethan Church* (Cambridge, 1983), 116–17, 169–71.

more generally. In these he seems happy to have assumed a very public role. In 1589, he joined the campaign orchestrated by the notorious puritan Henry Alvey (soon to be President of St John's) in favour of the imprisoned separatist Francis Johnson. With others of his college, Hill marched through the streets of Cambridge to force an appeal and signed a petition on Johnson's behalf – one of only eleven St John's men to do so.[3] Similarly, in 1595, Hill signed another very public petition against the Arminian William Barrett, once again in the company of Alvey and others of St John's. The same year, a disputed election for the mastership of the college found Hill among those writing to Lord Burghley in support of candidates who included Alvey, and complaining that they had been maligned as 'puritani'. Around this time, Hill also launched a direct attack on the Arminian sympathiser and future Regius Professor, John Overall, condemning his teaching on predestination in a letter of complaint to the Bishop of London, an incident to which we shall return.[4]

Other more personal links sustained Hill's ties to puritan Cambridge throughout his life. One was marriage to a daughter of Henry Alvey. Although the date of this marriage remains uncertain, at the end of his life Hill still found a place in his 1623 will for the elderly Alvey.[5] More generally, it is clear that it was Hill's beliefs and his personal ties to leading Cambridge puritans that first led him into print. In this regard, the most important influence in Hill's life was undoubtedly that other great puritan figure of Elizabethan Cambridge, whom we have mentioned earlier, William Perkins. Hill was a dedicated disciple of Perkins, whose works he translated and edited, and whose memory he constantly sought to keep alive. Hill never lost an opportunity to celebrate Perkins's life and writings. He was happy to reminisce about the great man from his own personal experience and it is from Hill that we learn that Perkins had only the use of his left hand. Many divines in the years after Perkins's death sought to gain some reflected glory from editing his works (and the whole posthumous Perkins industry is an important area of historical study in its own right) but there is no doubt that Hill's devotion was genuine.[6]

3 H. C. Porter, *Reformation and Reaction in Tudor Cambridge* (Cambridge, 1958), 188–9; Lake, *Moderate Puritans*, 191, 194, 197–9.
4 Porter, *Reformation and Reaction*, 346; T. Baker, *History of St John's College*, ed. J. E. B. Mayor, 2 vols. (Cambridge, 1869) II, 607.
5 PRO, Prob. 11/142/87. Hill bequeathed £10 and a sugar loaf to his father-in-law, 'Mr Henry Alvey of Cambridge'. For Alvey's activities in Cambridge, see Porter, *Reformation and Reaction*, 187–203, 206; but cf. Lake's evaluation, *Moderate Puritans*, 197–9.
6 See for example, W. Perkins, *Lectures Upon the Three First Chapters of the Revelation*, ed. R. Hill, (1604), 'Epistle dedicatorie', sig. 3, Av–A3v; which contains a dedication to the Montagu family, and makes much play of their shared knowledge of Perkins when students at Christ's College. R. Hill, *The Pathway to Prayer and Pietie* (1613), 'A consolatorie epistle against all crosses', 239 notes Perkins's

Hill's personal admiration for Perkins was combined with an fervent advocacy of his ideas, most especially of Perkins's uncompromising views on the doctrine of predestination. Indeed, it was Hill, at the author's own request, who translated Perkins's classic exposition of predestination, *A Golden Chaine*, into English in 1591.[7] Ten years later, Hill produced another tract, entitled *Life Everlasting*, in which he presented an unflinchingly severe doctrine of predestination mostly based on the writings of Zanchius of Heidelberg, which one modern commentator has described as a densely scholastic work filled with 'abstruse metaphysical speculations'.[8]

It would be wrong, however, to suggest that Hill remained entirely confined to the world of Cambridge colleges. The 1590s also saw the development of his first links with godly laity. In Norwich, Hill appears to have been one of the assistant preachers appointed by the lay feoffees of the famous puritan parish of St Andrew's, and Hill certainly received the patronage of godly members of the city's aldermanic elite.[9] He also sought to encourage members of the gentry who might promote a godly agenda through parliamentary legislation. By the end of the decade Hill used the dedication of his works to urge Sir Peter Fretchville (knight of the shire for Hill's own county of Derbyshire) to 'speake for such good things, as may further Religion' in the coming parliament of 1601.[10]

II

At first sight, then, Hill looks like a typical puritan divine. We would presumably expect him to follow a suitably godly career, thundering the

---

disability, adding 'yet [he] hath done more good by his one hand, in this Church, then the most have done by both theirs'. Porter, *Reformation and Reaction*, 264–8; I. Breward (ed.), *The Work of William Perkins* (Appleford, Berks., 1970), introduction, 103. For the career of another Perkins editor, see J. Eales, 'Thomas Pierson and the transmission of the moderate puritan tradition', *Midland History*, 11 (1995).

7 W. Perkins, *A Combat Betweene Christ and the Divell Displayed* (1606), 'The Epistle Dedicatorie'. This posthumously published work contains a dedication composed by Hill dated 1604, followed by another by Thomas Pierson, dated 1606. W. Perkins, *A Golden Chaine*, ed. R. Hill (1612), sig. 3r.

8 R. Hill, *Life Everlasting: or the True Knowledge of One Jehovah, Three Elohim, and Jesus Immanuel: Collected out of the Best Modern Divines* (Cambridge, 1601). D. D. Wallace, *Puritans and Predestination* (Chapel Hill, N.C., 1982), 59, 61.

9 In T. Newhouse, *A Learned and Fruitful Sermon Preached in Christs Church Norwich*, ed. R. Hill (1612), Hill dedicates the work to Thomas Layer, a mayor and JP of Norwich and he discusses other of his Norwich patrons, including mayor Francis Rugg. For Layer and Rugg, see B. Cozens-Hardy and E. A. Kent, *The Mayors of Norwich 1403 to 1835* (Norwich, 1938), 61–2, 64. No relevant parish records survive for St Andrew's for this period., but I would like to thank Matthew Reynolds for discussing the Norwich religious context in Hill's time.

10 Hill, *Life Everlasting*, 690, preface.

doctrine of predestination from the pulpit and dividing his parishioners into sheep and goats. He would be largely cut off from the broad mass of his parishioners, preoccupied with the debates of predestinarian theology and the needs of a small, godly elite.

Yet further examination reveals that Hill was anything but a detached academic. On the contrary, his greatest claim to fame perhaps lies in his extraordinary skills as a religious populariser. In 1596, he published *The Contents of Scripture* – effectively an abridgement and explication of the Bible, 'whereby the yong beginner might get entrance into reading, & the old reader be readied in remembring'. Against those who might consider such a work to be presumptuous, or even an example of 'dumbing down' (in modern parlance), Hill robustly defended the need for such aids, which, he maintained, would ultimately lead the reader to move on to the Bible itself.[11] Such an approach was characteristic of Hill, who specialised throughout his career in translating, popularising and making accessible to a lay audience the theological writings of other divines, especially the works of the most prominent foreign reformed theologians. He translated extended works of theology, but also borrowed written prayers, striking images or snippets of pastoral advice from continental divines and inserted them (with appropriate acknowledgement) into his own works.

But if the *Contents of Scripture* was published during Hill's time in Cambridge, his most popular work emerged after he moved to the capital. About 1602, Hill obtained a lectureship at the fashionable parish of St Martin in the Fields, a position he held for the next eleven years.[12] It was for this parish that he composed a catechetical work that went through no less than eight editions and was even translated into Dutch. This was originally published in 1606 under the title *Christs Prayer Expounded, a Christian directed, and a Communicant prepared*, but it was greatly expanded in 1609 under what became its familiar title, *The Pathway to Prayer and Pietie*. These later editions broadened the scope of the work, including new material, such as 'A Direction to Christian Life' and 'An Instruction to Die Well'. This largely catechetical work vividly reveals the extent of Hill's pastoral abilities and concerns. The *Pathway* is distinguished by its crystal-clear form of exposition, its striking use of homely similes, and its willingness to tackle difficult pastoral issues and awkward questions. Above all, it was *not* just a handbook for the zealous

---

[11] R. Hill, *The Contents of Scripture* (1596), sig. A5v–A8.

[12] R. Hill, *Pathway to Prayer and Pietie* (1609), epistle dedicatory. In this dedication, which is dated 1608, Hill refers to having been lecturer at St Martin's for six years.

godly.[13] For example, Hill assumes that his readers will be subject to many petty foibles and he addresses these pragmatically and encouragingly, rather than raging against the weakness of the average parishioner. In his directions concerning sermons, for example, Hill provides no fewer than twelve reasons why people sleep at sermons, including 'the heat of the Ayre, where many are together', 'the cares of this World', 'sorrow' and the 'neglect of such as sit by us, who suffer us to sleep'. Accordingly, Hill offers twelve practical remedies, which include eating sparingly beforehand, standing to keep oneself awake, considering 'that I would be offended if any slept, whilest I talked unto them', and also (rather pathetically) the reflection 'that by it I discourage the Minister'. For those that remain awake, they are counselled 'I must not be wearie, if the Sermon be long' and that 'I must write the Sermon if I can'.[14]

While Hill's work has sometimes been mentioned in the same breath as Arthur Dent's *The Plain Mans Path-Way to Heaven*, they are, in fact, very different works. Dent's is a literary, Renaissance dialogue. The focus is a well-meaning but ignorant person, who is chastised, threatened and bullied into a sense of his own damnation, and the work contains a very detailed discussion of the doctrine of predestination.[15] By contrast, Hill's *Pathway* is simpler – we are not following the progress of an imaginary discussion in which one individual is led to salvation. The *Pathway* is easier to dip into, its information arranged into clear, self-contained sections, while large portions give practical advice in the form of simple questions and numbered answers, often consisting of only a single sentence.[16] There are are only a handful of explicit references to the doctrine of predestination; rather, the focus is on answering the needs of those trying to live a Christian life in an urban environment. Hill dedicates the work to his parishioners in St Martin in the Fields, and he tells us that it was 'penned at the first for the benefit of this

---

[13] This fullest version of this work is most easily consulted in a facsimile of the 1613 edition printed as part of the series *The English Experience*, no. 744 (Amsterdam, 1975). I have generally used the 1613 edition of this work, unless dating is a particular issue. C. W. Schoneveld, *Intertraffic of the Mind* (Leiden, 1983), 209.

[14] Hill, *Pathway* (1613), 103, 105–7.

[15] A. Dent, *Plain Mans Pathway to Heaven* (1601). A useful discussion of the work is E. K. Hudson, 'The *Plaine Mans* Pastor: Arthur Dent and the cultivation of popular piety in early seventeenth century England', *Albion*, 25, 1 (Spring 1993).

[16] See also the table of questions, following the 'Preface', which directs readers to relevant pages, *Pathway* (1613). Note that the first section, 'Christs prayer expounded', uses the fiction of two speakers, 'Euchedidacalus', a teacher of prayer, and 'Phileuches', a lover of prayer. Hill makes very little of this device, however, and the rest of the volume reverts to simple question-and-answer format. There are also a range of prayers for various occasions.

Parish'.[17] A later addition to the *Pathway* finds Hill commending what he calls 'these treatises', hoping that his St Martin's parishioners 'will be as readie to reade them, as you have beene willing to heare them', raising the possibility that parts of the work derived from sermons preached by Hill, which he later adapted to a question-and-answer format. Many of its exchanges seem to derive from his own practical experience, and it is possible that Hill (although only a lecturer in the parish) may have undertaken catechising and possibly even given spiritual advice.[18]

If Hill's work was aimed at a broadly based, and not necessarily godly, readership, then this was only appropriate. The parish of St Martin's, in particular, was certainly not a godly commonwealth. It was a large, socially complex parish in Westminster, its burgeoning population made up of people from many social levels, from a substantial contingent of courtiers and government bureaucrats, through to prosperous craftsmen and victuallers, servants, and poor immigrants from the countryside.[19] Hill's catechism addressed itself to various portions of this society: to masters and servants, to sick people worried about consulting Catholic doctors, through to men and women tempted to separatism who feared kneeling at communion.[20] The fear and social division generated by poor immigrants into the capital – a particular concern in Westminster – also makes Hill's comments on the proper attitude towards the poor all the more striking. A vigorous social discipline characterised the government of Westminster parishes such as St Martin's, yet Hill reined in the tendency to equate poverty with sinfulness, warning that one should not 'contemn such as are in povertie' and urging 'that I give not to the poore with reproaching them'.[21]

In his discussion of dying, Hill has much to say about the plague. Here it is worth noting that Hill had first-hand experience of the devastating

---

[17] Hill, *Christs Prayer* (1606), 'Epistle dedicatorie'; Hill, *Pathway* (1610), 'Epistle dedicatorie'.

[18] Hill, *Pathway* (1613), 'The preface of prayer'. Hill also speaks of his ' ministrie' at St Martin's, and elsewhere seems to expect that lecturers might sometimes expect to fill a pastoral role beyond preaching. He notes that those overwhelmed by fears of damnation might confess their sins 'to my godly Minister *or* to such Preacher of Gods word, as is able to comfort me' in regard of his knowledge or ability to preserve secrecy, 'Christs prayer', *Pathway* (1613), 56 (italics mine).

[19] The religious and social complexion of St Martin's parish is discussed more fully in J. F. Merritt, *The Social World of Early Modern Westminster: Abbey, Court and Community, 1525–1640* (Manchester, forthcoming), ch. 9. The urban focus of Hill's *Pathway* is noted in P. Seaver, 'The puritan work ethic revisited', *JBS*, 19 (1980), 48–9. Hill, *Christs Prayer* (1606), 'Epistle dedicatorie'; *Pathway* (1610), 'Epistle dedicatorie'.

[20] Hill, *Pathway* (1613), 'A direction to die well', 137–8, 'A communicant instructed', 30–33.

[21] Hill, *Pathway* (1613), 'Christs prayer expounded', 42, 'A direction to live well', 81.

plague epidemic of 1603 shortly after first coming to St Martin's. He seems to have stayed in the parish throughout the outbreak, living in the house of one of its vestrymen.[22] In what is an unusual discussion of such issues, Hill explains why those infected should not expect to call for a minister, why they must obey the plague regulations (Westminster's were a model for the country), and discusses the extent of one's obligations to others – including attending their deathbed or providing a funeral. Hill explains why good people die of the plague while others are not infected, and he even offers twelve points of comfort for those suffering from the disease. These include the practical observation that it is a short sickness and more tolerable than 'the French disease', that victims will still have their sense and memories at their death, 'that many Noble personages, Godly Preachers, Expert Physitians, Skilfull Lawyers, and most Christian people have died of it', and that if you happen to recover 'you are like to bee after far more healthfull'.[23] Once again, for those who feared they might not die a 'good' death, he ultimately concluded 'we must iudge men by their life, and not iudge any by their death'.[24] Again, there is an engaged, practical tone to Hill's work, realistic about people's fears and the devastating effects of disease; this is no sharply prescriptive piece of puritan raillery.

The specific religious context in which Hill operated during the early Jacobean period is also relevant here. We know that Hill, unlike some parish lecturers, lived in his parish, and his involvement there appears to have been extensive.[25] And even if St Martin's parish was far removed from the godly commonwealths of East Anglian market towns, it did possess its active godly element. It was a parish which funded its own lecturer, and its vestry, in the years following Hill's appointment, embarked on an ambitious campaign to promote regular catechising and attendance at communion, while providing a constant stream of support for poor 'godly' ministers.[26] The lay enthusiasm of St Martin's vestry may have been a mainstay to Hill, but he was clearly aware of the dangers of the more radical Protestant ideas that were endemic in the capital

---

[22] W. Perkins *Lectures Upon . . . Revelation*, ed. R. Hill, 'Epistle dedicatorie', sig. A4.

[23] Hill, *Pathway* (1613), 'A direction to die well', 140–7.   [24] *Ibid.*, p. 122.

[25] E.g. WCA, F2, vol. 1, fos. 84, 114, 147, 161–2.

[26] WCA, F2001, fo. 56; F2, vol. 1, fos. 132, 181. See also, Merritt, *Social World*, ch. 9. Hill remarks on his having lived and preached among St Martin's parishioners: 'you have I confesse knowne my conversation, bin acquainted with my ministrie, countenanced me in my calling, maintained me in health, comforted me in sickness, & afforded unto me much more kindnesse then can be quited by this paper present', *Christs Prayer* (1606), 'The epistle'. From 1607 Hill also held the tiny living of St Margaret Moses, but while he preached there conscientiously his meagre income did not enable him to make it his place of residence. *Pathway* (1613), 'epistle dedicatorie'.

in this period. Indeed, in the different editions of the *Pathway* published between 1606 and 1613, he expanded sections directed to those who had been 'tempted' to leave the established church – a combination of pleading and argument that obviously came from the heart.[27] In addition, Hill added a completely separate section defending set forms of prayer, based on part of a treatise by the London minister 'H.H.' (presumably the respected puritan Henry Holland).[28] By 1610, Hill was convinced of the need to restrain more committed Protestants, given the dangers of Brownism and anti-nomianism. In a visitation sermon preached that year to the clergy of Middlesex (which included parishes such as St Martin's, in the 'suburbs' of London) he emphasised the need for faith to be combined with prudence, and warned that 'faith without wisedome makes a skismaticall auditorie.' At the same time, he chastised 'our raw yong ministers nowadaies, who like greene wood give much smoake and little heat'. His particular concern seems to have been unwary ministers from parishes in the penumbra of London, whom he reminded gravely: 'It is not a reed but a mallet that must knock downe an heretick.'[29]

III

At this point, it would be tempting to present Hill as a puritan firebrand of the 1590s going soft, and shedding the abstract doctrinal preoccupations of his university days. The pastoral needs and simple realities of the metropolis (one might suggest) forced such a natural pedagogue into adopting the mannerisms of a sensitive, conforming 'Anglican' minister, rejecting divisive and arcane predestinarian ideas in order to deal with the practical needs of parishioners. This process would seem to be capped appropriately by Hill's appointment to the prosperous City living of St Bartholomew Exchange in 1613. Shortly thereafter, Hill organised the building of a comfortable parsonage house complete with tapestries and book-lined study.[30]

[27] Hill, *Christs Prayer* (1606), 1, 66; *Pathway* (1610), 1, 76–7. The latter sections focused especially on Brownists, a number of whom had recently come before the local Middlesex sessions, see W. Le Hardy (ed.), *Calendar of Middlesex Sessions* (n.d.) VI, 54, 155.

[28] *Pathway* (1609). The section follows 'A communicant prepared'. Henry Holland regularly published under the initials 'H.H.'. Hill notes that he has converted Holland's treatise into a question-and-answer format 'by mutuall conference'.

[29] Gonville and Caius College, Cambridge, MS 256/693, sermon 23, dated 20 September 1610, described as preached by Dr Hill in St Clement Danes at a visitation, before the Bishop of London.

[30] *New DNB* (forthcoming), s.n. Robert Hill; For an inventory of possessions in St Bartholomews's vicarage during Hill's time, see E. Freshfield (ed.), *The Vestry Minute Books of the Parish of St Bartholomew Exchange* (1890), 79.

But in fact I would argue that Hill's career teaches us nothing of the sort. The disjunction between Hill's doctrinally focused Cambridge days and his London career is something of an illusion. To begin with, as we have seen, his pastoral and pedagogical interests clearly predated his London lectureship. If anything, Hill was inspired by the example of William Perkins, who attempted to bridge the gap between university theology and popular audiences through his immensely popular lectures at St Andrew's church in Cambridge. Perkins was the ultimate populariser, as ready to preach to poor prisoners as to prosperous townsfolk and godly members of the university.[31] In addition to Perkins's formidable talents as a preacher, Hill himself commended 'an excellent gift he had to define properly, devide exactly, dispute subtilly, answer directly, speak pithily, and write judicially'.[32] In this Hill was a worthy pupil and he was deeply interested in exploring a whole range of pedagogical techniques to get his message across (including, as we have seen, abridgements of the Bible). But he was adamant that the tenets of true doctrine should not be compromised in the process.

We can see this conviction – that doctrinal truth must not be diluted in the pastoral context – as a point of principle from Hill's early days in Cambridge. This message emerges more clearly if we return to an episode mentioned earlier: Hill's confrontation with John Overall. This clash is often dated by historians to the period around 1600, when the Regius Professor Overall was enmeshed in a series of doctrinal disputes with the College Heads. But in fact there is clear evidence to date it to the period 1595–6, at the height of the controversies over William Barrett and the formulation of the Lambeth Articles.[33] This redating may even suggest that it was Hill who was behind the first public clashes involving Overall, and who may have prompted Whitgift's comment that he had heard that 'Mr Overall is somewhat fractious'.[34] At the heart of the quarrel with Overall was Hill's conviction that the doctrine

---

[31] Breward, 'Introduction', *The Works of William Perkins*, 9–10; Porter, *Reformation and Reaction*, 267–9.

[32] Perkins, *Lectures Upon . . . Revelation*, 'Epistle dedicatorie', sig. A3v.

[33] Lake, *Moderate Puritans*, 201–42; Porter, *Reformation and Reaction*, 344–7, 364–75, 378–9. The account of the dispute makes it clear when the incident took place when Overall himself was vicar of Epping. Overall held the living only briefly, from 1593 until 1596, the year that he was appointed Regius Professor of Divinity. He was succeeded at Epping by Roger Dodd, vicar from 1596 to 1607: *VCH, Essex*, 5, 133; R. Newcourt, *Repertorium Ecclesiasticum Parochiale Londinense*, 2 vols. (1708–10), II, 248. The dating can be narrowed down even more precisely, since in his report on the Epping incident to the Bishop of London, Hill identifies himself as a bachelor of divinity, a degree which he received in 1595 (*Alumni Cantabrig.*, s.n. Hill). Cf. Porter, *Reformation and Reaction*, 397, 407.

[34] The comment was made when Overall was being considered for the Regius Professorship of Divinity, Porter, *Reformation and Reaction*, 375.

of predestination should not in any way be watered down or passed over when preaching to a lay congregation. Sometime around 1595, when Overall was vicar of Epping, he discovered that members of his Epping congregation had become panic-stricken over the question of their salvation and convinced that Christ had not died for them. In response, Overall had reassured them by preaching a sermon in which he emphasised that Christ died for all and not just for the elect, and that reprobation was only for sin. Hill, rather mysteriously, seems to have been present at the sermon, and in a letter to the Bishop of London he reported Overall's words. Hill condemned all the points made in Overall's sermon, and particularly denied that Christ died for all men. Here he explicitly rejected the idea that predestinarian doctrine should be softened in order to reassure a worried congregation.[35] There can be few more obvious examples of the Cambridge disputes of the 1590s spilling directly into parish life, with both Hill (the translator of *A Golden Chaine* and petitioner against William Barrett) and Overall (later Regius Professor under fire from the college heads for his views on predestination) continuing this battle in an Essex parish.

We know little of what followed from this clash, although Hill may have emerged rather battered – it is possible that he withdrew from Cambridge into the country.[36] Nevertheless, by 1601, Hill published *Life Everlasting*, in which he once again insisted that the doctrine of predestination must be 'preached publikely to the people', against those who suggested that it should 'only bee handled in schooles among the learned'.[37] Hill does write in characteristically emollient vein that people have been so preoccupied with disputations that they are neglecting the heart of religion. But when he complains that 'we are so disputing predestination' he concludes not with 'rather than following a godly life' but with the danger 'that we forget that there is predestination'.[38]

The next year, Hill moved to St Martin's, where there is good reason to think that his puritan reputation was known. The move certainly did not mean turning his back on Cambridge and the concerns that had occupied him there. Indeed Hill hung on to his Cambridge fellowship

---

[35] CUL, MS Gg/1/29, fos. 119r–122v.

[36] In October 1596, Hill dedicated *The Contents of Scripture* to the ancient Marian exile, Sir William FitzWilliam, thanking him for having 'maintained me liberally in your family' and dating the work from FitzWilliam's residence at Park Hall, Essex. Park Hall was very close to Epping, but the significance of this is not clear. In 1601, Hill mentions having lived in the 'country' for the past few years: *Life Everlasting*, 'Preface to the Reader'.

[37] Hill, *Life Everlasting*, 639.

[38] The 'Preface to the Reader' continues, 'Read this treatise with sobrietie, and read not so much to know, as to acknowledge the truth'. See *ibid.*, 639–44 more generally.

for seven years after taking up the lectureship at St Martin's.[39] It seems
unlikely that Hill abandoned his belief in doctrinally informed preaching
precisely at the moment when he became a parish lecturer. But perhaps
ten years of preaching in the capital altered his views? Once again, the
evidence is unequivocal. In 1612, Hill reaffirmed his commitment to
Perkins's *A Golden Chaine*, which he had so painstakingly translated more
than twenty years before. He did this in a fascinating way – by transforming the entire text into the form of a catechism. Instead of one
continuous text, the reader now found a series of questions, answered
in Perkins's own words. By turning it into a dialogue, Hill hoped to
'give much light unto it & cause it to bee read with greater delight',
since 'variety of one meat diversly dressed delighteth the appetite, and
commendeth the cooke'.[40] As Hill commented on this mode of presentation, 'I have experience what profit is in this course by some labours
of mine owne in this kinde'.[41] The volume is a monument to the central
place that Hill felt this work deserved in Christian teaching, and yet it
is worth remembering that in the same year, Hill was working on the
fifth edition of the *Pathway*, and had only just given his visitation sermon
warning about faith without prudence. Clearly, for Hill at least, there
was no incompatibility here.

Hill did admit the difficulty of the *Golden Chaine* as a book, and hoped
that his efforts might make it more accessible. In the preface to this new
version, he particularly condemned those who thought the doctrine of
predestination was 'either unnecessary to be learned, or at the least in
the last place'. Equally, he chastised those who complained that 'predestination is a doctrine too high for their learning: Election, a matter they
think least of'.[42] As ever, Hill had an accessible image to hand: 'For may

---

[39] Hill's tenure as fellow at St John's, from 1588/9 to 1609, can be traced through the payment of his
stipend in the college's rental books. The first and last entries are St John's College, Cambridge,
Rentals 1575–99, fo. 263v and Rentals 1600–1619, fo. 214. As late as 1607, Hill still identi-
fied himself in published work as a fellow of St John's. It seems quite likely that the vicar of
St Martin's, Dr Thomas Montfort, knew of his confrontation with Overall. Hill noted that he
preached 'by the assignment' of Dr Montfort, who was also a prebendary of St Paul's, where
Overall was Dean, see Hill, *Pathway* (1610), preface. For more on Montfort, see Merritt, *Social
World*, ch. 9.

[40] Perkins, *A golden chaine* (1612), 'The epistle dedicatorie'.

[41] *Ibid.*, sig. 3r. This final comment may refer to the *Pathway*'s origin in sermons. As we have seen,
Hill had also converted a treatise on set prayer by Henry Holland into a question-and-answer
form as part of the *Pathway*.

[42] *Ibid.*, 'The preface to the reader'. Hill also complained of the ultimate frivolousness of those who
failed to avail themselves of the doctrine: 'many are naked, but Christs garment will not fit them;
it is either too long, or too short; too streight, or too wide; too hote or too cold; too light or too
heavie, or somewhat is in it that they will not weare it'.

not a sonne of man know whether he be of his fathers family, and may not the sonnes of God know, whether they belong to the household of God? Yes surely.' Passing over the doctrine was simply not an option for Hill. That being said, Hill did decide to add a comforting appendix to Perkins's text, entitled 'An Excellent Treatise of comforting such, as are troubled about their Predestination'. But needless to say, this treatise was a translation, not of some work by Overall, but of the most hard-line Calvinist of them all, Theodore Beza.[43]

For Hill, then, the effective teaching of the doctrine of predestination was as important to him in 1612, after ten years as a London lecturer, as it had been at any time in his career – and he was willing to say so publicly. Hill might chide young ministers for not keeping an eye on religious extremism, but he was not backing away from the teaching of hard-line Calvinism.

So what does this mean for how we 'read' a catechism such as Hill's *Pathway*? Surely it means that we cannot read the *Pathway*, which avoids detailed discussion of predestination, as encapsulating the essence of Christian teaching as Hill saw it, or as an exhaustive guide to what the parishioners of St Martin's heard whenever Hill gave a sermon or catechised parishioners. That is not to say, however, that the *Pathway* was incompatible with a strong belief in predestination. Indeed, if one studies the text carefully, related issues do emerge – such as a discussion of whether God was the author of sin – and here Hill employs a series of characteristically down-to-earth comparisons, including a rider spurring a lame horse and carrion smelling under the sun's rays.[44] Later editions of the *Pathway*, which included 'A direction to die well', also sometimes let slip the predestinarian assumptions that underlie the practical advice. Among consolations for the dying, Hill counsels them to remember that 'As in Adam all men die, so in Christ shall all (that is, all the elect, whereof I am one,) so, I say, in Christ shall all be made alive'.[45] The key here may be that Hill simply felt that preaching and catechising *in person* were betters means of teaching predestination in its more detailed aspects than in a book of general instruction such as the *Pathway*. Elsewhere, Hill insisted that it was preaching which alone was the ordinary means of salvation.[46]

Moreover, there are also hints of a more exclusive view of the Christian community in the *Pathway*. It is possible to glimpse a thread running

---

[43] *Ibid.*, 'The preface to the reader', 563–75.
[44] *Pathway* (1613), 'Christs Prayer expounded', 80–1.   [45] *Ibid.*, 'Direction to die well', 160.
[46] Newhouse, *A Learned and Fruitful Sermon*, ed. R. Hill, epistle dedicatory.

through the work of guidance that is aimed more specifically at the godly portion of the congregation, easily missed amid the wealth of general practical advice, but clear enough to the godly reader. Most remarkable are Hill's comments on the Lord's Prayer. The very first interpretation which Hill provides for the start of the petition 'Give us this day our daily bread' is that the words 'give us' (rather than 'give me') are intended to teach us 'to pray especially for the prosperity of the godly'. It is remarkable that Hill's mentor Perkins makes no attempt in his own exposition of these words to restrict them to the godly.[47] This is also true of Hill's interpretation of 'lead us not into temptation', which contains a discussion of 'why are the godly led into temptation?'. 'Forgive us our trespasses' also prompts, among other considerations, the thought that 'I must labour to bee in the number of those (us) who may sue for pardon.'[48] There are other occasions too, where Hill seems to have a godly audience in mind. The addition of a separate defence of set or read forms of prayer presupposes some advanced Protestant sensibilities, and his exhortation not to be solemn in manner when one should be cheerful seeks to curb excesses which contemporaries easily caricatured as puritan.[49] But elsewhere the language is more neutral or ambiguous. When Hill instructs parishioners that before taking communion they must be sure to be in charity with their 'brethren', this term could refer to the general congregation as well as holding the more exclusive sense used by puritans – again the different readers could perhaps make their own reading.[50] Ultimately, Hill offers a vision of the community which recognises the godly without severing them from their neighbours. Most notable here, and emblematic of Hill's whole approach, is his advice on charitable giving: 'that especially I must give to the godly'.[51] It is worth emphasising that here, as elsewhere, Hill specifies 'especially' and not 'only' the godly. Similarly, advice on how to behave on Sundays instructs readers to visit 'any' who are 'comfortless', but also urges that 'I must bee carefull to provide something, which I may distribute to the necessitie of the Saints'.[52] Here was a vision of the local community that did not seek simply to divide it. After all, every member of the community might have the potential to join the godly.

[47] Hill, *Pathway* (1613), 'Christs prayer', 42; W. Perkins, *An Exposition of the Lords Prayer* (1595), 40. This interpretation is not among the standard views summarised in Green, *The Christian's ABC*, 487, 494–5.

[48] Hill, *Pathway* (1613), 'Christs prayer', 74, 54.   [49] *Ibid.*, 'A direction to live well', 76.

[50] *Ibid.*, 'A Communicant instructed', 27. See also *ibid.*, 'Christs prayer expounded', 39.

[51] *Ibid.*, 'A direction to live well', 81.   [52] *Ibid.*, 'A direction to live well', 86.

IV

Where does this leave us? It leaves us, I think, with Hill on a tightrope, juggling exclusive and inclusive views of the Christian community. This was of course a tightrope that was walked in different ways by all puritan pastors. But not all chose to tackle it the same way. Hill's approach might be contrasted with that of his famous contemporary, the notorious nonconformist Samuel Hieron. One of Hieron's surviving sermons provides an indication of how he approached his ministry. Here he explains that it is the use of preaching to work a kind of separation among men. Before the godly preacher begins his work, all the congregation is generally comprehended under the name of 'Christian', and all are of one mind regarding religion. But after the preaching of the true word of God, differences emerge, and the true identities of the godly and ungodly become apparent. And if we believe Richard Quick's life of Hieron, we can see that Hieron's sermon paraphrased above was no mere rhetorical flourish. Indeed, on his deathbed Hieron reportedly confessed tearfully 'that in publick I have bin somewhat full in reproof, in admonition, in Instruction'. Small wonder, perhaps, that the minister who succeeded Hieron reported that Hieron's efforts had fallen on stony ground, resulting in only two converts in his Devon congregation (for all his enthusiastic following among the local gentry).[53]

It would be wrong, however, to imply that Hill believed his own pastoral approach to be fundamentally different to that of Hieron. In fact, Hill was a great admirer of Hieron, and his last published work (in 1620) was a posthumous edition of Hieron's works, complete with a flattering biography of a man whom he had known since the 1590s.[54] It is in the pages of this very same edition that we can read the text of the divisive sermon summarised above, and this in a volume where, as Hill declared, the reader 'may easily see that it was not he [Hieron] that spake, but the holy Ghost speaking in him'.[55] Right at the very end of his life, Hill

---

[53] *The Workes of Mr Samuel Hieron* (1620), 'The discoverie of hypocrisie', 238. Dr Williams Library, MS 38.34: Richard Quick, 'Sacrae Icones', 51–99. The controversies surrounding Hieron's funeral sermon *The Worldling's Downefall* (1618 edn), sig. A2–A4v also vividly demonstrate his problematical relations with his flock. I am grateful to Dr Peter Marshall for drawing this sermon to my attention.

[54] *The Workes of Mr Samuel Hieron* (1620), ii, 'To the reader'. The publication history of Hieron's collected sermons is confusing: the copy I have used is CUL, E.9.21.

[55] *Ibid.*, p. 238. Hieron was not the only divisive puritan with whom Hill would appear to have enjoyed amicable relations. In his will, Hill appointed as the executor of his library his neighbouring minister George Walker (like him an ex-fellow of St John's), whose heresy-hunting had stirred up angry confrontation among London puritans: PRO, Prob 11/1422/87; Lake, *Boxmaker's Revenge*, 221–46.

still clearly believed that he and Hieron were ultimately on the same side.

For all his reverence for Hieron, however, we can assume that Hill wanted to avoid the divisiveness which Hieron proclaimed on a parish level. We should not simply assume a sort of guilt by association. Moreover, unlike Hieron – but very much like his mentor Perkins – Hill generally avoided any direct involvement with politics, or outward non-conformity, and managed comprehensively to side-step issues of clerical conformity and church government. This was not always easy. Hill's own devotion to the translation of reformed contintental divines may have inadvertently led him into hot water. An anonymous radical puritan tract published in the Netherlands in 1618 (but possibly written some years earlier) maintained that Hill's 1606 translation of the *Institutions of Christian religion* by Gulielmus Bucanus had been interfered with at the press. In place of Bucanus's discussion of church government (which necessarily promoted Presbyterianism), a 'discourse of Bishops governement [was] put into the roome thereof; both without Doctor Hils knowledge'. It is impossible to know for certain whether Hill was indeed ignorant of the substitution, rather than carrying it out himself. The Stationers' Company registers record that, very unusually, the book had been licensed personally by Bishop Richard Vaughan, a man revered by Hill as one of his patrons.[56] It is certainly possible that it was Vaughan who intervened to save Hill from the imputation of Presbyterian sympathies, and it may be this event to which Hill alludes in a curious passage in the *Pathway* in which he refers to 'my late exile . . . [when] I had beene undone, if others had not sought to undoe me'.[57] Hill praised Vaughan after the bishop's early death as 'an ornament to our Church in which he was a preaching Bishop' and 'a most watchfull and temperate Governour', noting 'the encouragements I had from him in my ministrie'.[58] Clearly, Hill would have been happy with an episcopate staffed by evangelical, pastorally minded men such as Vaughan. He was also prepared to defend

---

[56] Anon., *A True, Modest & Just Defence of the Petition for Reformation Exhibited to the Kings Maiestie* (Leiden, 1618), 'To the reader', sig. a2v. On the publication of this work see K. L. Sprunger, *Trumpets from the Tower* (Leiden, 1994), 139–40, 214. I would like to thank Dr Anthony Milton for this reference. See G. Bucanus, *Institutions of Christian Religion* (1606), ed. R. Hill, which was dedicated to the young Earls of Essex and Salisbury. The translation argues that there ought to be degrees among ministers (p. 500), that there has always been imparity in holy orders (p. 561), and that the bishop and governors of the Church should have the power of excommunication (p. 593) – all of which are obviously not in the original text by Bucanus. E. Arber (ed.), *A Transcript of the Register of the Stationers Company*, 5 vols. (1875–94), III, 316.

[57] Hill, *Pathway* (1613), 'A preface of prayer'.   [58] Hill, *Christs Prayer Expounded* (1607), dedication.

disputed ceremonies, albeit in a robustly Reformed way. In the *Pathway* he provided reasons for kneeling at communion, although his emphasis was on the peace of the church, and he more happily cited similar usage within the church of Bohemia, one of the foreign Reformed churches.[59] Nor did Hill demonstrate any particular aversion to forms of church decoration: as rector of St Bartholemew Exchange he was happy to register his acceptance of a cloth embroidered with 'IHS' donated by a parishioner, even if by the 1640s the parish later condemned it as idolatrous.[60]

Nevertheless, while Hill may have flinched from Hieron's divisiveness and active nonconformity, he was still anxious in his pastoral ministry to resist any of the doctrinal compromises which might make the Christian message more appealing, but ultimately (in his eyes) erroneous. Hill seems to demonstrate that a moderate puritan *could* compromise, and *could* be flexible to the pastoral needs of his community, without doing it in a manner which required any *doctrinal* modification. And he could also do so without failing to acknowledge the distinctive role of the godly. It is perhaps fair to suggest that personality also played a role here – with Hill ever the gentle persuader in the pastoral context, even if with a core of steel.

There are other aspects of Hill's career that invite further exploration. One basic point that underlies his and so many other clerical careers of this period is the fact that his 'tightrope' was always a financial one. Until his appointment to the living of St Bartholemew Exchange, when he was in his late forties, Hill's life was always financially precarious. From the 1590s onwards, he was at the mercy of lay patronage, as part-time chaplain, tutor and lecturer. Hill felt the vulnerability of his position keenly – as he explained rather painfully to the parishioners at St Martin's: 'Now though I cannot say to you, as Paul did to the Corinthians, I am yours to live and die with you: (for no Minister can say it, who dependeth upon voluntarie contribution) yet this I will say, and say for ever, I am yours to live, and pray for you'.[61] This lack of financial security may also have had an important impact on the pattern of Hill's publications. Hill is not the only author whose flow of publications slowed to a trickle when

[59] Hill, *Pathway* (1613), 'A communicant instructed', 30–3.
[60] Guildhall Library, MS 4384/1, fo. 287; MS 4383/1, fo. 175; MS 4384/2, fo. 1. See further discussion in J. F. Merritt, 'Puritans, Laudians, and the phenomenon of church-building in Jacobean London', *HJ*, 41/4 (1998), 957–8.
[61] Hill, *Pathway* (1609), preface (dated 1608).

he finally gained the financial security that he craved.[62] The nature, timing and quality of the printed publications by Hill and other pastors that survive may often reflect their changing personal circumstances as well as their pastoral initiatives. Learned theological tomes might best impress a potential lay patron, but catechetical works and pastoral manuals could also reassure godly patrons of the pastoral commitment of the petitioner, as well as putting these abilities on public display to the widest possible audience.

Hill also provides us with an example of a puritan clergyman who was used to living in situations in which the laity played a significant role in church affairs, but who generally seems to have been able to find a workable *modus vivendi* with flock and vestry. He did this, moreover, without using his pulpit to attack the government, or to exhort magistrates towards the imposition of draconian social discipline. It is interesting to note what happened to his successors. In his lectureship at St Martin's, he was later succeeded by the notorious John Everard who, while clearly enjoying support among the vestrymen, used the pulpit first to make a series of attacks on the Spanish Match, and then a series of increasingly heterodox sermons.[63] At St Bartholomew Exchange, Hill's successor found himself consistently at odds with the powerful vestry over jurisdiction and finance in a way that Hill never was.[64] Perhaps, then, there is a need for historians to find room for emollient, unifying, pastorally sensitive puritan clergymen such as Hill in their picture of the religious life of London – alongside the more famous cantankerous, divisive and controversial figures – as long as this can be achieved without sacrificing our sense of the vigorously puritanical core of Hill's ministry.

When reviewing Hill's complete writings and career, it could be suggested, of course, that he wrote two kinds of divinity – the *Pathway* for a general congregation, and versions of *A Golden Chaine* for the puritans in his flock. But this seems too neat a division of genres, and misses both the pastoral and pedagogical inspiration that informs both works. To imply that Hill was just a 'parish minister' or 'pastor', serving his flock with a simple, consensual Christian message, and avoiding all those

---

[62] Hill might usefully be compared with another editor of Perkins's work, Thomas Tuke. Tuke published frequently – and on a large range of topics – before his appointment to the living of St Olave Jewry, but thereafter he virtually ceased publication: *New DNB* (forthcoming), s.n. Thomas Tuke.

[63] WCA, F2, I, fo. 71; F2, II, fos. 356, 402; J. Everard, *Some Gospel Treasures Unopened* (1653), sig. a2v–a3r; Merritt, *Social World*, ch. 9.

[64] Freshfield, *Vestry Minute Books*, 88, 90, 98, 99. The reluctance of members of the congregation to kneel at communion was noted in 1631 and 1633: *ibid.*, xvii.

troublesome and misleading doctrinal issues, is to make a nonsense of what Hill was trying to do. We cannot know how successful Hill was as a lecturer and pastor. Even Hill told his St Martin's parishioners in typically self-deprecating fashion that he had enjoyed the love and largess of '*many of* you (for what lecturer for ten yeares together can please al [?])'.[65] What is clear, however, is that Hill made a very determined effort to communicate directly and flexibly with his parishioners without denying the existence of a godly elite, and without sacrificing the doctrinal principles that he had learned at the feet of William Perkins, or alienating his urban audience. In his own mind, at least, he had negotiated the tightrope successfully.

---

[65] Hill, *Pathway* (1613), Preface (italics mine).

8

The creation of Laudianism: a new approach

Anthony Milton

The policies implemented by Archbishop Laud during the Personal Rule of Charles I continue to attract scholarly attention, as historians puzzle to explain why these policies created quite so much hostility. It has been suggested more recently that the Laudian policies were not necessarily as innovative as their opponents claimed, that individual elements of their policies can be found to have precedents stretching well back into the Jacobean period, and even earlier. What is distinctive about the 1630s, it has been argued, is both the systematic way in which ceremonial and disciplinary policies were enforced, but also in particular the rationale with which these policies were imposed, the ideological background which infused with more alarming significance what were forms of church decoration and outward worship which were not in themselves unprecedented or inherently objectionable.[1]

But what then was this crucial ideological context of Laudianism, and where should we look for it? In my own work, and that of a number of other historians, the answer has been to look at the writings of those who were at the heart of the so-called 'Durham House Group' – the court-centred group of divines, closely bound by personal links, who manifestly considered themselves to be an embattled minority, involved in a struggle for survival with a Calvinist establishment who were dangerously indulgent towards puritan activities and doctrines. And indeed, when we examine in detail the work of divines such as Laud himself, and Richard Montagu, John Cosin and others, we can find evidence of ecclesiological and doctrinal assumptions which are very different from those of their contemporaries, and which delineate a distinctive view of the

I wish to acknowledge my great debt to the Earl Russell for the invaluable encouragement and advice with which he greeted my first faltering attempts to study Laudianism, and his kind support ever since.

[1] J. F. Merritt, 'Puritans, Laudians and the phenomenon of church-building in Jacobean London, *HJ*, 41/4 (1998); P. Lake, *The Boxmaker's Revenge* (Manchester, 2001), ch. 11, esp. 304.

world, in which particular ideas of the nature of the Church of England, its succession, and its relationship with the Church of Rome and reformed Protestantism are very prominent. That is certainly what I have argued elsewhere, and it makes perfect sense to depict the 1630s as a time when this particular court faction of divines, who identified themselves and were identified by their opponents as an alienated and distinctive group, gained sufficient influence to dictate the implementation of a series of divisive ecclesiastical policies.[2]

But while we may be able to reconstruct the world-view which made this particular clerical faction wish to implement the ecclesiastical policies of the 1630s, it is more difficult to reconstruct precisely how people at the time were meant to understand the rationale behind these policies. For with only minor exceptions, this clerical court faction actually had very little to say in justification of their policies. Apart from William Laud's speech at the censure of Burton, Bastwick and Prynne, and Francis White's treatises in defence of the Book of Sports, one cannot find a single prominent Laudian bishop writing defences of the policies being implemented, and it is not until the 1650s that we find any systematic justifications of the historical and doctrinal basis of the religious policies of the Personal Rule.

The preconceptions and the world-view of the formulators of these Laudian policies can be reconstructed, then, but the answer to the question of how these policies were presented to, and understood by, contemporaries on the ground is less clear. Where did the ideological cutting edge to the Laudian policies come from? What justifications and explanations of these policies were available to people at the time, and how were they generated? The sources for answering these questions are not weighty theological treatises, but rather a whole series of minor works composed in defence of the policies of the 1630s – pamphlets, sermons, mini-treatises – written by a series of minor and often rather obscure authors, not always very comprehensive in their coverage of the relevant issues, and not produced in a very systematic way.[3] They are not ideal

---

[2] A. Milton, *Catholic and Reformed* (Cambridge, 1995); N. Tyacke, *Anti-Calvinists* (Oxford, 1987); K. Fincham, 'Introduction', in Fincham (ed.), *The Early Stuart Church* (1993), 1–22.

[3] This being said, there is however a suggestive grouping of sermons and other works published in support of the policies around 1636–7. 1636 saw the publication of visitation sermons delivered in 1635 and 1636 by Edward Boughen, John Featley, Jasper Fisher, John Pocklington, William Quelch and Alexander Read, and sermons and controversial works by John Browning, Peter Hausted, Peter Heylyn, Christopher Dow and Edmund Reeve. 1637 saw the publication of 1636 visitation sermons by Samuel Hoard and Richard Tedder, other sermons by Thomas Lawrence, Humphrey Sydenham, Anthony Sparrow, William Watts and John Yates, and further

sources, but they were the places that contemporaries went to for explanation of the policies being carried out, and several of the authors clearly
gained preferment on the basis of their publications.

But how should we study these writings? One approach is to gather all
these disparate materials together and to see what pattern of beliefs and
preoccupations emerges, to sift out the inconsistencies, and to construct
a sort of 'ideal type' of Laudianism. This, of course, is the approach
adopted by Professor Lake in his celebrated and now seminal study of
'The Laudian Style'. The result is a subtle, sophisticated and insightful
analysis which is by far the best account of Laudian ideology that we
have. It is a necessary beginning. But this 'ideal type' methodology does
run the risk, as Professor Lake notes, that differences of emphasis and
opinion between different writers are glossed over, and that therefore
the overall coherence of the position may be exaggerated (given that
some authors might only have agreed with parts of the world-view thus
constructed). The differing motivation behind individual authors, and
the effect that this might have on what they wrote, is also inevitably
neglected.[4] It is for these reasons that Professor Lake emphasises that his
'ideal type' is not a listing of Laudian ideas, or a stable doctrinal position,
but rather a distinctive style, tone and aesthetic which contemporaries
perceived as coherent, and which had a formidable resonance among
both friends and enemies of the movement.

But now that that style has been so successfully delineated, it is perhaps time for the second stage – to look more searchingly at the different authors from whom the 'ideal type' has been constructed. Such a
study may also help us to answer the question of where these ideas were
coming from. Did these pamphlet apologists emerge from a distinctive
background? In other words, were there massed ranks of 'Laudians' out
there, adherents to these ideas, waiting to emerge, and finally finding

---

controversial works by Heylyn, Dow, Pocklington and Gilbert Ironside. It is also notable that a
remarkable number of Laudian works were published by the London stationer John Clark, although it is not yet clear how far this is evidence of an orchestrated campaign. Clark's involvement
is also noted in an unpublished paper by Arnold Hunt, 'Defining orthodoxy in the early Stuart
church'.

[4] P. Lake, 'The Laudian style', in Fincham, *Early Stuart Church*, 161–85, at 162–4. It should be
emphasised that the problems with the methodology of the approach described above are most
clearly laid out and explained by Peter Lake himself. What is suggested here is a supplementary
approach, not an alternative one, and certainly not one that is intended in any way to negate
his findings. In another article – 'The Laudians and the argument from authority' in B. Y.
Kunze and D. D. Brautigam (eds.), *Court, Country and Culture* (Rochester, 1992) – Professor Lake
emphasises some of the differences in emphasis and polemical tactics within the Laudian position.
My intention here is to suggest that some of these inconsistencies may derive from the personal
and polemical background from which the writings emerged.

their distinctive voice? How can we identify such 'Laudians' – that is, at what point do people stop being common-or-garden conforming and possibly anti-puritan divines and become 'Laudians' instead? And if even these apologists did not share many of the opinions of the 'ideal type', what does this tell us about the nature and coherence of 'Laudianism'?

I

In this article, I would like to focus on the man who might legitimately be described as the chief ideologue of the Laudian movement: Peter Heylyn. He was by far the most prolific defender of Laudian policies, writing two books in support of the altar policy, a defence of the Book of Sports, and a more general defence of Personal Rule policies against the assaults of Henry Burton. All of these defences, moreover, were written with the blessing of the government, and became *de facto* the official explanations and defences of Laudian policies.

When we study Heylyn's career, however, it becomes increasingly difficult to identify him as a natural spokesman for Laudianism. For example, it is far from easy to discern a great deal of pietistic ceremonialism in Heylyn's early works. Rather, his first poetical and prose works composed in his late teens and early twenties breathe more the spirit of John Marston's satire-ridden Inns of Court, or the bickering senior common rooms of Oxford colleges, rather than Lancelot Andrewes's incense-filled chapels. Like many churchmen of the period, Heylyn aspired to be a poet, but while he read and admired writers such as Spenser and Drayton, Heylyn's favourite writer of all, who finds his way into poems addressed to his alma mater, to his friends, to his enemies, and even to Prince Charles, was the Roman satirist Martial. While he regularly quoted bits of Martial in his other poems, Heylyn also tried his hand at translating some of Martial's epigrams himself, and headed unerringly for the most lewd and tasteless.[5] It is Martial's sardonic humour (and sometimes rather crude eroticism) that shines through much of Heylyn's early writing.

When not writing poetry, Heylyn's great intellectual passion was not theology, but rather political geography. His fame was initially established by his *Microcosmos*, 'a Little Description of the Great World' – an enormously successful work which went through eight editions before the Civil War, growing hugely in size and altering perceptibly in argument in

---

[5] Peter Heylyn, *Microcosmos* (Oxford, 1625), 475. For his devotion to Martial, see BL, Additional MS 46885A, fos. 7r–v, 18v; W. Braekman, 'Peter Heylyn's holograph collection of poems', *Studia Germanica Gardensia*, 13 (1971–2), 135–7; Magdalen College, Oxford, MS 224.

the process. It is in the *Microcosmos* that we find Heylyn's first reflections on religious and political topics, and immediately we find surprises. In the first edition, published in 1621 when he was still only twenty-one years of age, Heylyn displayed strongly pro-Palatine sentiments at a politically sensitive time. Initially, when his geographical guide reached the Palatinate and Bohemia, Heylyn warily commented: 'I say nothing of the deplored estate of this country, holding it more fit for my prayers, then for my penne'. This was not a promise that Heylyn kept to, however, as later on his sentiments got the better of him as he praised 'the sacred person of this Frederick', whom he believed had been prophesied to bring ruin upon the papacy. The better to effect his predestined role, Heylyn beseeched 'the God of battles, and Lord of hosts, to blesse his Troopes with the trophies of victory, that hee may tread upon the necke of the Romish Adder, and outstare the Antichristian Basiliscke, till his enemies are made his footstoole' – apparently an allusion to a famous woodcut in Foxe's *Book of Martyrs*.[6]

Microcosmos reveals not merely a Palatine patriot, but also one with apparently mainstream Jacobean Calvinist sympathies. Over the course of the work, Heylyn heaps praise on the French anti-Arminian divine Pierre du Moulin, applauds Hus, Wyclif and Jerome of Prague, and writes approvingly of iconoclasm in Berne.[7] He displays a fervent anti-Catholicism, strongly affirming that Rome is Babylon and the Pope Antichrist, accepts the truth of the story of Pope Joan, and packs his narrative with racy accounts of the sexual misdeeds of monks and nuns.[8] His expressed opposition to foreign Presbyterianism does not prevent him from applauding without qualification the writings of William Fulke and Thomas Cartwright against the Rhemish New Testament. His historical list of the 'Worthiest English Scholars' includes only three divines who lived after John Jewel, and these are the famous puritan figures John Rainolds, Laurence Humphrey and William Whitaker (with no mention of Richard Hooker).[9] He gives an especially warm and positive reading of the medieval heretics the Albigensians, and presents an account of the succession of the Protestant church which gives pride of place to the Albigensians as the hidden congregation of true believers. In Heylyn's own words: 'If now the Papists aske mee where was our Church before the time of Luther; I answere that here it was: that here God was worshipped

---

[6] Peter Heylyn, *Microcosmos* (1621), pp. 154, 166 The woodcut is in John Foxe, *Actes and Monuments* (1583), p. 205. I am very grateful to Tom Freeman for drawing this allusion to my attention.
[7] Heylyn, *Microcosmos* (1625), 100, 280, 295, 473, 474.   [8] *Ibid.*, 176–7, 181–2, 196–8.
[9] *Ibid.*, 118. The 1621 edition only lists Humphrey: Rainolds is added in the 1625 edition (p. 474) and Whitaker in the 1627 edition (p. 472).

according to the manner by himselfe prescribed, and by the reformed Churches followed. Here I say were those few Israelites hidden, who had not bowed their knees unto Baal.'[10] These are not the opinions that we would expect to hear from a Laudian divine – and if it might be objected that this is to adopt too narrow a view of Laudianism, this is certainly how Heylyn himself in effect defined it in the 1630s. His writings composed during the Personal Rule refute as puritanical virtually all of the points that have just been described.[11] Of course, other prominent figures in the Laudian movement, such as Lancelot Andrewes, Richard Neile and even Laud himself, may have departed from earlier Calvinist views, but none seem to have undergone so swift and complete an ideological conversion as Heylyn.[12]

If we were looking into Heylyn's early background, not for incipient Laudianism, but for the origins of a Calvinist word-view, we would not need to look very far. His kinsman was the famous puritan sheriff of London and member of the Feoffees for Impropriations, Rowland Heylyn; his schoolmaster in Burford held on to a living in the Cromwellian church; he studied at Magdalen College, Oxford where one of his tutors was the 'verie zealous and pragmaticall Puritan' Walter Newberry; and he received early patronage from the puritanically inclined Earl of Danby, and support from the Calvinist dean of Winchester John Young.[13] Indeed, Heylyn's apparent connections with the Inns of Court and avowed early friendship with the anti-Arminian Nathaniel Carpenter, his dedicated reading of, and esteem for, the works of Spenser and Drayton, and his admiring account of the exploits of the Earl of Essex, might all hint that Heylyn's place was among the Jacobean Spenserians described in the work of Professor Norbrook.[14] That being said, Heylyn was not a man whose convictions were ever likely to lead him into conflict

[10] Heylyn, *Microcosmos* (1625), 110. In the 1636 edition this is significantly reworded to read 'our Faith before the time of Luther': *Microcosmos* (7th edn, Oxford, 1636), 113.

[11] E.g. Peter Heylyn, *A Briefe and Moderate Answer* (1637), 71–2, 125, 127–9, 156–7; idem, *The History of the Sabbath* (1636), II, 188. Heylyn's account of his clash with Prideaux in 1627 (see his *Examen Historicum* (1659), II, appendix) implies that he there refuted the position on the Albigensian succession that he had expounded in his *Microcosmos* published just two years before, and which was reprinted in 1627, the very year of his confrontation.

[12] N. Tyacke, 'Archbishop Laud' in Fincham, *Early Stuart Church*, 58; idem, *Anti-Calvinists*, 110–12; idem, 'Lancelot Andrewes and the Myth of Anglicanism' in P. Lake and M. Questier (eds.), *Conformity and Orthodoxy in the English Church, c.1560–1660* (Woodbridge, 2000).

[13] Peter Heylyn, *Memorial of Bishop Waynflete*, ed. J. R. Bloxam (The Caxton Society, 1851), xii; idem, *Ecclesia Restaurata; or The History of the Reformation of the Church of England* 2 vols. (Cambridge, 1849), I, pp. xxxiv, xxxviii, xlvi–li, lxvii–viii; idem, *The Parable of the Tares* (1659), epistle dedicatory; idem, *Ecclesia Vindicata* (1657), epistle dedicatory.

[14] Heylyn, *The History of the Sabbath*, I, 45; Heylyn, *Microcosmos* (1625), 394, 475; D. Norbrook, *Poetry and Politics in the English Renaissance* (1984).

with the crown in practice. The example of John Taylor the Water Poet reminds us that a partisan support for the Palatinate in the early 1620s was quite compatible with a fiercely loyal royalism in the 1640s.[15] But more simply, Heylyn was manifestly on the look-out for royal patronage from a very early age. Indeed, the first two editions of the *Microcosmos* were dedicated to Prince Charles, and in each case Heylyn secured their formal presentation at court. In between, for all his support for the Palatine cause, he also wrote verses applauding Charles' Spanish adventure in 1623.[16]

Nevertheless, there is a stark disparity between the religious views expounded by Heylyn in the 1620s and 1630s. We can explain this in a variety of ways – as a maturing of religious views, or an empathic response to the new religious trends of the 1630s, or a more vehement style of anti-puritanism prompted by his involvement in a bizarre Star Chamber case in 1628 when he supplied his friend William Phipps with information concerning a plot by local puritans in Lechlade to deprive him first of his living, and then of his life.[17] But Heylyn himself has provided us with sufficient information to explain the change. In a later work he explains quite explicitly that before the late 1620s he had not 'fastned my relations upon any one man, in order to my future preferment in Church or State', but by 1629 he had begun 'to apply my self to the Lord Bishop of London [Laud]'.[18] The pretext may have been provided by Heylyn's public clash with Laud's enemy in Oxford, the Regius Professor John Prideaux, which brought Heylyn to Laud's attention, although it may have been their shared suffering of the gibe of 'papist' in the Oxford schools that brought them together rather than any immediate ideological sympathy.[19] It is small wonder, though, that late in life, Heylyn found himself most often accused not of popery, or even of royalism, but of time-serving.[20]

---

[15] B. Capp, *The World of John Taylor the Water-poet, 1578–1653* (Oxford, 1994).

[16] Heylyn, *Ecclesia Restaurata*, I, xlii, xlvi–li; BL, Additional MS 46885A, fo. 18r.

[17] Heylyn, *Memorial*, xix; PRO, SP 16/159/28.

[18] Peter Heylyn, *A Survey of the Estate of France* (1656), sigs. a1v–a2r.

[19] Peter Heylyn, *Cyprianus Anglicus* (1667), 175–6. Heylyn's account of the ideological basis of his clash with Prideaux over the succession of the church is seriously misleading: see my discussion in *Catholic and Reformed*, 303–5, 310 and above, n. 11. The most likely explanation is that Heylyn's cocksure delivery made Prideaux feel that he was being publicly mocked (not an unusual phenomenon), and that misunderstanding and personal animosity produced an exchange which Heylyn found it profitable to gloss as an ideological conflict. Laud's own clashes over the succession of the English church display a more obvious and consistent ideological agenda: Heylyn, *Cyprianus*, 53–4; William Laud, *The Works of William Laud*, eds. W. Scott and J. Bliss, 7 vols. (Oxford, 1847–60), III, 145.

[20] See Heylyn's attempts to deny the charge that he was best-suited to describe the world in his cosmographical writing because all his life he had loved the world so much: Peter Heylyn, *Extraneus Valupans* (1656), 50–1.

Heylyn appears to have sought to gain Laud's support, and his own promotion, by seeking out puritan conspiracies. He seized on the opportunity of his trip to the Channel Islands in 1629 with his patron the Earl of Danby to blow the whistle on Guernsey Presbyterianism in a lengthy report which he sent on to Laud (its tone implies that it was unsolicited, but the fact that Heylyn was appointed a royal chaplain extraordinary in February 1629 immediately prior to his departure, and had apparently already made Laud's acquaintance the year before, makes some prior collusion with Laud likely). Heylyn's report was presumably written without the support of his supposed patron Danby, the Governor of Guernsey, who in fact would present Laud with a series of arguments *against* the mooted policy of reducing the island's form of church government to the English model. Heylyn was then very consciously switching patrons when he urged Laud 'to make use of that favour which most worthily you have attained to with his Majesty' to return the island of Guernsey to episcopal discipline, and pleaded that he would be happy if 'in this, or in any other your Lordships counsels for the Churches peace, I may be worthy of imployment.'[21] His search for public employment under Laud continued in 1630, when he prompted the government's attack upon the Feoffees for Impropriations in a very public and highly provocative sermon in Oxford, a copy of which he sent, bound in vellum, to Laud. Announcing a Presbyterian conspiracy against the state in the most inflammatory language, Heylyn once again demonstrated his ability to discern puritan subversion where others had not thought to find it.[22]

Not all of Heylyn's attempts at promotion involved attacking puritans. He shrewdly assessed the king's interests, and brought his historical and polemical skills to bear in writing a *History of St George* with an eye to the King's particular and well-known enthusiasm for the Order of the Garter.[23] Recently, historians have noted how in the 1630s Spenserian notions of chivalric culture mutated from praise for the

---

[21] *CSPD Addenda: 1625–1649*, 556; Heylyn, *Survey*, 412, 422; PRO, LC 5/132, 87, 165, 166.

[22] Magdalen College, Oxford, MS 312, esp. 39–41; Heylyn, *Cyprianus*, 210–12; G. E. Gorman, 'A Laudian attempt to "tune the pulpit": Peter Heylyn and his sermon against the Feoffees for the Purchase of Impropriations', *Journal of Religious History*, 8 (1974–5); William Prynne, *Canterburies Doome* (1646), 386. Heylyn's knowledge of, and hostility towards, the Feoffees may in part have stemmed from the active role played in the organisation by his rich relative Rowland Heylyn. The fact that Rowland Heylyn had drawn up his will in the previous September, in which the puritan dignitary had dispensed his considerable fortune among every conceivable relative and godly cause, but had left nothing to the son of his first cousin once removed, Peter Heylyn, may be mere coincidence: we cannot be sure that Peter knew of the contents of the will, which was not proved until 1632 (PRO, PROB. 11/161, fos. 179r–181r).

[23] It is worth noting that it was Laud who presented the work to the king, though, and this as early as 1631 – important evidence of their alliance before the beginning of Laud's archiepiscopate (Heylyn, *Memorial*, xx–xxi).

military advancement of European Protestantism into a 'sacralised loyalty' to an imperial monarch. In the move from Heylyn's *Microcosmos* to his *History of St George*, we can perhaps see this transformation within the career of a single individual.[24]

The first tasks which Heylyn performed for the government, before the defences of Laudian policies which made him famous, were concerned with attacking the regime's opponents, often by highly unscrupulous means. In 1632 he was charged in the king's name with reviewing Prynne's *Histriomastix*. Heylyn came up in record time with a vicious critique which secured Prynne's prosecution for sedition. Prynne later complained with some justice of how Heylyn had maliciously selected 'scattered fragments or dimidiated sentences' from the book, 'annexing such horrid, seditious, disloyall, false glosses, applicacions, construccions and inferences, as none but heads intoxicated with malice, disloyalty, and private revenge could every fancye.'[25] These were skills that would soon be further in evidence. In the previous year, Heylyn had been placed in a prebendal stall in Westminster Abbey, clearly with the intention that he should dig up information on Laud's opponent, the dean John Williams. Within seven months he was already offering information against Williams to Secretary Coke which he had wheedled out of the civil lawyer William Spicer. Two years later he again played a prominent role in the drawing up of thirty-six articles of complaint against the dean by the prebendaries. At the hearing of the commission into the grievances in February 1636, Williams commented prophetically 'If your Lordships will hear that young fellow prate, he will presently persuade you that I am no Dean of Westminster'. Just a matter of months after this hearing, Heylyn embarked on a pamphlet battle with Williams over the government's altar policy, in the course of which he composed what were the principal defences of this Laudian policy.[26]

Heylyn also levelled his guns at Laud's opponent and his own nemesis, the Oxford Regius Professor of Divinity John Prideaux, accusing him of heterodoxy after an acrimonious clash at the Act in 1633, and the following year mischievously publishing in translation an earlier lecture that Prideaux had given on sabbatarianism. Heylyn supplied his own

[24] J. S. A. Adamson, 'Chivalry and political culture in Caroline England', in K. Sharpe and P. Lake (eds.), *Culture and Politics in Early Stuart England* (1994), 161–96, esp. 174–5; Norbrook, *Poetry and Politics*, 240–1.
[25] S. R. Gardiner (ed.), *Documents relating to the proceedings against William Prynne in 1634 and 1637*, (Camden Society, n.s. 18, 1877), 32.
[26] See my 'Canon Fire: Peter Heylyn at Westminster', in C. S. Knighton and R. Mortimer (eds.), *Westminster Abbey Reformed: Nine Studies, 1540–1642* (forthcoming, 2002).

preface to the work, and presented the lecture as if it defended the newly reissued Book of Sports.[27] His own substantial defence of the Book of Sports – a *History of the Sabbath* – was submitted to the press the following year, to be followed by a general defence of the policies of the Personal Rule in 1637.

In career terms, these various pieces of hatchet-work and polemical writing paid major dividends. In January 1630 Heylyn was appointed a royal chaplain in ordinary, and a few months after his sermon against the Feoffees he was granted a prebendal stall at Westminster and the living of Hemingford Abbots. Further crown appointments followed like clockwork after the completion of each polemical task. Hardly a single piece that Heylyn published after 1630 was not specifically commissioned by the government.

When we read Heylyn's 'Laudian' works in the context of his earlier writing and his career as a hit-man, several points leap out. Firstly, all the elements from his earlier imitations of Martial are apparent in his polemical works. Heylyn was a master of the art of invective, and a highly accomplished polemicist. Williams and Burton in particular were subjected to withering sarcasm. There is also precious little theology in these writings, and given what we have seen of Heylyn's early career we should hardly expect any. Wherever possible, Heylyn prefers to adopt the stance of the historian or political geographer, and he constantly endeavours to link religious voluntarism to political sedition. Most of all, his work breathes the spirit of the journeyman polemicist. At least to begin with, it seems reasonable to assume that Heylyn was not drawing upon his own deeply felt convictions when writing defences of the policies of the Personal Rule. He was generating the ideas to fit what he took the policies to be, formulating the arguments and evidence to support the position with which he had been presented. Often in the process he was giving an ideological thrust to what might have been a temporary policy manoeuvre, radicalising the policies themselves, and accentuating the divisive manner in which they were implemented and interpreted.

This would help to explain the fact that, when we read through Heylyn's polemical treatises of the 1630s, there is an unmistakeable air of over-kill. Heylyn was the first to invoke the example of the chapel royal as requiring the movement of altars to the east end, or to claim the authority of the king's ruling in the St Gregory's case as a virtual act of

---

[27] Laud, *Works*, v, 87–91; A. Milton, 'Licensing, censorship and religious orthodoxy in early Stuart England', *HJ*, 41 (1998), 648. Heylyn later denied that he was the informer against Prideaux: Heylyn, *Examen Historicum*, II, appendix.

state, followed by a host of subsequent writers in both cases. His anti-sabbatarian tracts were a great deal more extreme in argument (and more cavalier in their use of facts) than were those of other government apologists. Indeed, divines writing in support of the Laudian reforms such as Joseph Mede and even John Cosin privately criticised Heylyn's works.[28]

Heylyn's ideas came from a variety of sources: we can find echoes of earlier authors, and the established anti-puritan tradition certainly supplied some ready associations of puritanism with Judaism and populist sedition which could help to drive his arguments forward. But Heylyn's originality stemmed partly from his ingenious deployment of historical materials and earlier documents in support of his arguments, and also from his readiness in the heat of the debate to go beyond accepted boundaries. Thus, to defend the Book of Sports, he not only maintained the lawfulness of recreations on the Lord's day, but created a whole falsified history of Sunday-worship in England, condemned even the use of the term 'sabbath' and associated even the use of the word 'sabbath' with puritanism. Not only was Sunday not the Jewish sabbath, but the church still had the authority to change the day of worship to any other day of the week if it so desired. The need to refute Williams led him into detailed arguments defending the use of the terms 'altar' and 'sacrifice' – when Williams cited the Second Edwardian Prayer Book against him, Heylyn responded with the simple expedient of disowning the whole book as the product of Calvin's malign influence. When Williams referred to episcopacy as 'apostolic', Heylyn declared that even this was dangerously puritanical, because it implied that episcopacy wasn't simply *jure divino*. If Williams sneered at a passing reference to the new 'piety of these times', then it must be maintained that the government had indeed embarked upon novel and important policies, and that churches were now being 'more beautified and adorned than ever since the Reformation'. If Burton complained at the alteration of the passage in the Fast Book that had referred to how Roman Catholics' 'religion is rebellion', then he must be answered by a vindication of Catholic loyalty and a frank assertion that 'the Puritan religion is rebellion, and their faith faction' just as much as that of Rome.[29]

[28] J. Mede, *The Works of . . . Joseph Mede* (1664), 1028, 1036, 1041; J. Sansom (ed.), *The Works of . . . John Cosin*, 5 vols. (Oxford, 1843–55), IV, 451–61. On Mede's position see A. Milton, 'The Laudians and the Church of Rome c.1625–1640', University of Cambridge Ph.D. thesis (1989), 10, 29 n. 59.
[29] Heylyn, *The History of the Sabbath*, II, 63–4, 95, 181–2, 250, 262; idem, *Antidotum Lincolniense* (1637), II, 84–6, 110–31; III, 7–8; idem, *A Briefe and Moderate Answer*, 155–7.

To conclude, Heylyn was not a long-time ardent ceremonialist finding his voice for the first time in the 1630s, but nor was he a mere mouthpiece for his masters. In the cases of the Channel Islands and the Feoffees for Impropriations, he actually initiated government policies by identifying puritan potential where it had not before been discerned, and when he mounted attacks on the regime's established opponents – Prynne, Burton and Williams – he defined government policies in more radical terms, and raised the political and ideological stakes by the extremism which he imputed to the regime's opponents, and the ideological agenda which he glossed onto the government's own policies.

II

Heylyn may have been exceptional in the degree to which he was a polemicist whose earlier published views were barren of any obvious Laudian sentiment (although that is not to say that Heylyn was simply insincere: what he clearly relished was working to a patron's brief, and seeing how far he could exceed his expectations, and after a while he seems to have convinced himself of the verity of his arguments). But even if Heylyn is unusual, when it comes to explaining the timing and nature of his entry into Laudian debate, there are some suggestive echoes in the case of another notorious apologist for Laudian policies, John Pocklington. Unlike Heylyn, Pocklington had Laudian 'form' stretching back to the mid-Jacobean period, and earlier associations with Samuel Harsnet, among others.[30] But his publishing career, and thus his career as a 'public Laudian', was intimately bound up with his relations with Laud's *bête noire* John Williams, Bishop of Lincoln. Williams was still acting as Pocklington's patron in 1631, writing to Laud on his behalf and recommending him for a royal chaplaincy. The fall of his patron Williams, however, seems to have been the cue for Pocklington's rise. His notorious pamphlets on the sabbath and the altar were published in 1636 and 1637 respectively, and the latter work in particular was a very public attack on Williams. In this book, entitled *Altare Christianum*, Pocklington claimed that he was not aware of the identity of the authors of the tracts written anonymously by Williams and Heylyn, and 'my speech therefore must

---

[30] CUL, MS VC Ct I.8, fos. 255–8; MS Mm/1/46, 387–8; BL, Add. MS 39948, fo. 184. Pocklington certainly harboured high ambitions: he had stood in for Harsnet as Master of Pembroke College in the 1610s, and the title page of his *Sunday no Sabbath* still has him identifying himself as 'late fellow and President of Pembroke and Sidney'.

needs be innocent, and my personall reflections none at all' – a comment that must have prompted some hollow laughs in Lincoln diocese. All the more so as Pocklington was at the same time anxiously seeking to secure the conviction of Williams's chaplain John Hacket for speaking slightingly of Heylyn's work in a sermon.[31]

After these publications, and his informing against Hacket, the rewards came thick and fast for Pocklington. He was appointed a royal chaplain in ordinary within three months of his defence of the altar policy being entered at the press, and was given a prebendal stall at Windsor two years later – and this for a man turning sixty who had hitherto failed to get any effective promotion at court, despite attempts stretching back to 1617.[32] Pocklington's tracts are not the purely intellectual exercise in polemic that we find in Heylyn – he has distinctive views about the nature and worship of the early medieval church which we can find hints of earlier in his career.[33] But it was Laud's infamous feud with Williams which provided the opportunity, rationale and occasion for these curious and provocative views to be expressed in print. Without it, Pocklington's chosen medium for disseminating his views would apparently have been a weekly lecture in early medieval church history which in 1632 he was proposing to found in Sidney Sussex College, Cambridge (the list of topics which Pocklington proposed for this lecture survive, and they clearly indicate some of the preoccupations which found expression in his pamphlets).[34] The public encounter with Williams, however, helped to shape the ways in which these ideas were expressed, partly because Pocklington lifted material from Heylyn, but also because he projected his own radical gloss very specifically on to the ecclesiastical policies of the regime.[35]

This should also perhaps prompt us to restore the Williams/Laud clash once again to the centre of the religious politics of the 1630s. It has been embarrassing for church historians that in the main pamphlet controversy concerning the restoration of altars the anti-Laudian side was represented by a bishop whose chapel was one of the most lavishly

---

[31] LPL, MS 1030/6, 53, 58, 65; John Pocklington, *Altare Christianum* (1637), 'To the Christian reader'. Hacket claimed that Pocklington and Williams had already fallen out 'because he [Pocklington] was a Tell-tale, and made needless Complaints against his Brethren' (John Hacket, *Scrinia Reserata* (1693), II, 110).

[32] PRO, LC 5/134, 180, 412; *DNB*.

[33] CUL, MS VC Ct I.8, fos. 255–8; MS Mm/1/46, 387–8.

[34] Sidney Sussex College, Cambridge, Muniments Box 1. I would like to thank Dr Nicholas Rogers, the college archivist, for bringing these papers to my attention.

[35] E.g. Pocklington, *Altare Christianum*, 82, 146.

adorned outside the chapel royal itself.[36] But the shape of the pamphlet controversy suggests that it was in some sense merely a bolt-on to the existing personal quarrel between the two bishops, an artificially manufactured ideological clash, with the rationale supplied by polemicists vying for Laud's support, and knowing precisely whom Laud wanted to target. And given that it was Williams rather than Prynne or Henry Burton who was Laud's preferred target, the fact that in many ways Williams occupied a moderate, even conservative, position explains precisely why Heylyn and Pocklington had to adopt such a radical and divisive stance (with which, of course, they managed to brand the whole Laudian movement). Similarly, Clive Holmes has demonstrated in a fascinating (and currently unpublished) paper that there were a number of individuals based around the Lincoln chapter in the 1620s whose grubby personal and domestic clashes with Williams acquired a political and ideological dimension, with the bishop's enemies suddenly (and somewhat incongruously) transformed into Laudian zealots, and themselves the targets of choice for parliamentary attacks on 'Arminianism' and 'popery'.[37] Certainly, it is notable that it was Pocklington who was singled out for the most draconian attacks in the Long Parliament: his *Altare Christianum* and *Sunday No Sabbath* were ordered to be burnt, and the licenser of the *Altare*, William Bray, forced to preach a recantation sermon simply for his involvement in the book's publication. The House of Lords also directed that Pocklington be deprived of all his ecclesiastical livings, disabled from ever holding any place in the church, and be forbidden from ever coming within the verge of the court again. All of this unparalleled assault (and no other Laudian divine suffered any such penalties) was conducted by the House of Lords – in which Williams, of course, sat. Just ten days later, Pocklington's diocesan colleague Hugh Reeve, also a previous client of Williams, was condemned by the same House for teaching transubstantiation. Both the public expression of Laudianism and the most public parliamentary assaults upon it are thus inextricably linked with the picaresque career of John Williams.[38]

---

[36] See the description of Williams's chapel at Buckden in Anthony Cade, *A Sermon Necessarie for These Times* (Cambridge, 1639), sig. ¶ 2r–v. This is a 1634 visitation sermon, dedicated to Williams. The agenda behind the writing and publication of this work is not straightforward: I hope to discuss it in more detail elsewhere.

[37] Clive Holmes, 'High law and low life: the case of John Pridgeon', paper delivered at a day-seminar in honour of Dr Brian Quintrell, University of Liverpool, 25 November 2000.

[38] LJ IV, 161, 163, 168, 170, 180, 183, 219; William Bray, *A Sermon of the Blessed Sacrament* (1641). Note Williams's defence of Reeve in 1631: LPL, MS 1030/4. I am very grateful to the Earl Russell for first drawing my attention to the prosecution of Reeve many years ago.

Other advocates and apologists of the policies of the 1630s seem to
have arisen from different backgrounds. In many cases, one can trace earlier clashes with godly elements (for example, Christopher Dow),[39] or a
taste for elaborate ceremonial, or a dislike of Calvinism. However, it must
be stressed that in many other cases one can find earlier links to godly patrons or puritan religious networks, or earlier expressions of violently anti-
Arminian sentiments, in the examples of divines such as Samuel Hoard,
Thomas Lawrence, Fulke Robartes, Walter Balcanquahall or Humphrey
Sydenham.[40] Sydenham published very clearly anti-Arminian sermons
in the 1620s, but strongly ceremonialist sermons in the 1630s.[41] It has
been suggested that Sydenham may represent the survival of an old-style
Whitgiftian form of Calvinist anti-puritanism (and it is certainly true that
anti-puritanism is one of the threads that links his writings in the 1620s
and 1630s).[42] But Sydenham's collection of sermons published in 1637
could just as easily be seen as a determined attempt to embrace what
'Laudianism' seemed to be about. Certainly, it is difficult to imagine
Whitgift bandying about a term like 'sacred sensualitie', and moreover,
Sydenham's sermons carry a grovelling dedication to Laud.[43] Many
things may be happening here, and it would be wrong to suggest merely
that cynical opportunism was at work. This group of what one might call
'Laudian converts' is an important and complex one which requires more

[39] Lake, *The Boxmaker's Revenge*, 277. As well as writing pamphlets in defence of Laudian policies,
Dow was an energetic enforcer of Laudianism in the 1630s: A. Fletcher, *A County Community in
Peace and War: Sussex 1600–1660* (1975), 76, 78–9, 87, 90, 131.

[40] Hoard was a chaplain of that famous patron of the godly the Earl of Warwick, and a recent
supporter of the puritan Thomas Hooker; Thomas Lawrence was a chaplain to the Earl of
Pembroke; Fulke Robarts had earlier in his career enjoyed close links with godly preachers in
Norwich; and Walter Balcanquahall had been a delegate to the Synod of Dort: see Samuel Hoard,
The Soules Miserie (1636), epistle dedicatory; *DNB*; Tyacke, *Anti-Calvinists*, 189n, 191; K. Fincham,
'Episcopal government 1603–1640' in idem, *Early Stuart Church*, 90.

[41] Humphrey Sydenham, *Five Sermons Preached upon Severall Occasions* (1627); idem, *Sermons uppon
Solemne Occasions* (1637). For violently anti-Arminian passages in the 1627 collection see pp. 37,
53–4, 64, 66, 67, 69; for passages lauding elaborate church decoration and ritual, and praise for
the 'new life' given to ceremonies by the current regime in the 1637 collection, see pp. 14–32,
269–70.

[42] P. Lake, 'Serving God and the times: the Calvinist conformity of Robert Sanderson', *JBS*, 27
(1988), 116, n. 61.

[43] Sydenham, *Sermons uppon Solemne Occasions*, epistle dedicatory, 28. It may be noteworthy that
Sydenham's collection published in 1627 includes a sermon preached in Oxford in February
1626 (originally intended for the 1625 parliament) which complained of corrupt forms of ecclesiastical promotion, and lamented (presumably with some self-reference) how learned divines
in the universities 'lie mouldring for non-employment, and dashed for slownesse of promotion'
and doomed to 'spin out the remainder of their age in a discontented contemplation of their
misfortunes' (*Five Sermons*, 154–5). It is an intriguing thought that Heylyn, very soon to make his
own audacious bid for Laud's patronage, may have been in the audience at St Mary's.

extended analysis elsewhere. The main point for our present purposes, however, is that this clutch of minor writers who supported Laudian policies in print came from an extremely diverse range of ideological backgrounds and influences, and that few had emerged publicly as ardent ceremonialists before the 1630s. This was not a faction tightly bound by common ideas and patronage finding its voice for the first time, and Heylyn was not alone in performing a rapid somersault in his views to embrace what he perceived to be the Laudian agenda.

Nevertheless, it was the public meaning of Laudianism that was being shaped by these divines, and whatever their precise opinions, they were formulating particular explanations of government policy, and often in the process creating much more radical views of what was intended. Peter Lake has subtly charted the interplay of 'minimum' and 'maximum' positions in Laudian thought, and has noted an increasing radicalization of the Laudian position in the 1630s.[44] It may well be that it was the mechanics of Laudian polemic and its production which was creating a form of *functional* radicalization. That is, once Heylyn and Pocklington had made their own pitch, others had to match it or beat it to gain the same applause. At this point it may also be helpful to consider an analogy from more recent times. In his work on Adolf Hitler, Ian Kershaw has emphasised the importance of the phenomenon dubbed by a contemporary as 'working towards the Führer' – the process whereby subordinates sought to craft initiatives and arguments to suit the vague and broadly defined principles expounded by Hitler, and in the process often came up with much more extreme and radicalised policies.[45] Now Laud was much more of an administrator than was Hitler, but in *ideological* terms, we can perhaps detect a process in the 1630s of what one might call 'working towards the archbishop'. Laud was clearly frightened of puritans and wanted more diligently observed ceremonial, and this was enough to encourage opportunists to thrust puritan plots and ceremonial initiatives under his nose on a regular basis. But Laud publicly provided little compelling religious rationale for his policies, even if his prejudices and preferences were clear. It was for others to provide the intellectual rationale for his and Charles's policies, and this they did, in the process generating substantially more radical justifications. The result was a process of functional radicalization which often left the bishops themselves far behind, culminating in such bizarre texts as the *De Templis*,

[44] Lake, 'The Laudians', esp. 169–70.   [45] I. Kershaw, *Hitler 1889–1936: Hubris* (1998), 530.

and a host of very curious and crypto-Catholic positions defended in the universities.[46]

To get a sense of this process, we need only look at the policy of railing in altars. Laud in his speech at the censure of Burton, Bastwick and Prynne defended it purely on the grounds of preventing profanation, as did the 1640 Canons.[47] In John Pocklington's *Altare Christianum*, however, it is repeatedly explained that the intention is to keep the table from all manner of profanation 'and to preserve it entire and apart for priests to officiate in'. The 'Governors of the Church' (Pocklington declared) have railed in altars 'to strike the minds of all beholders with some reverence and respect to keepe their true distance, and to make a difference between place and place, person and person, holy and profane', restoring the ancient 'Sacrarium' which 'none might approach, but the Priests themselves'. Other writers increasingly copied this justification of the policy.[48] And thus Bishop Wren found himself having to insist in his defence in 1641 that he had never suggested that the railing of communion tables was anything more than an attempt to prevent their profanation – he had certainly never insisted that only priests should be allowed to go inside them. In this case, at least, Wren was being tried by Pocklington's pamphlet. Similarly, Wren insisted that he had never called the communion table an altar in his published articles (and Laud too was very sparing in his use of the terms 'altar' and 'sacrifice'), yet the term is everywhere in Laudian polemic, with the words of Hebrews 13:10 (we have an altar) repeated as a divine injunction (and clearly so used by parish ministers, too, including the vicar of Grantham). The particular irony here is that in much of the rest of his defence Wren clearly had a copy of Heylyn's *Coale from the Altar* as his guide.[49]

This disjunction between policy-maker and apologist is curious,[50] but does not make the Laudian polemic irrelevant – it is manifestly the case

[46] R. T., *De Templis* (1638); D. Hoyle, 'A Commons investigation of Arminianism and popery in Cambridge on the eve of the civil war', *HJ*, 29 (1986); Milton, *Catholic and Reformed*, 72–7.

[47] William Laud, *A Speech at the Censure* (1637), 52; G. Bray (ed.), *The Anglican Canons 1529–1947* (Church of England Record Society 6, 1998), 570.

[48] Pocklington, *Altare Christianum*, 62, 67, 146.

[49] Christopher Wren, *Parentalia* (1750), 75, 76–7. Compare the use of the Latin translation of the Prayer Book and the case of St Gregory's in *ibid.*, 75–6 with Peter Heylyn, *A Coale from the altar*, (3rd impression, 1637), 23, 63–6. On the use of Hebrews 13:10, see e.g. *ibid.*, 32–3, 73; Robert Shelford, *Five Pious and Learned Discourses* (Cambridge, 1635), 19; John Swan, *Profanomastix* (1639), 34, 35; John Yates, *A Treatise of the Honor of Gods House* (1637), p. 62.

[50] Part of the intention behind the 1640 Canons' words on the topic of altar rails may have been a desire to fix the policy with a more practical justification in order to discourage the glosses provided by writers like Pocklington – I owe this suggestion to Dr Ken Fincham.

that Pocklington, Heylyn and the rest received constant preferment for their pains. It is true that Laud always did his best to keep them at arm's length, and indeed went to extraordinary lengths to avoid even mentioning Heylyn by name, but there is also no evidence that he sought to dissuade Heylyn from his tasks, or that he urged him to moderate his style. Richard Montagu complained in the 1620s how Bishop John Buckeridge, a member of the Durham House group who gave their qualified support to Montagu's work, was 'ever wont to hold the reyns hard that I went not to[o] quicke', but it is difficult to detect the same restraining policy at work in the 1630s (although Laud did seek to moderate overtly anti-Calvinist behaviour in the University of Oxford, where as chancellor he could be more directly accused of involvement).[51] Laud's *Speech at the censure of Burton, Bastwick and Prynne* was entered in the Stationer's Register on the very same day as Heylyn's own more inflammatory *Briefe and Moderate Answer* to Burton's charges, and the two works were clearly intended to be read in tandem (although Heylyn's work had in fact been completed several months earlier, and was clearly used as a source by Laud).[52] Laud must have known that he was playing with fire by encouraging such unscrupulous extremists, and he seems always to have nursed the hope that when the inquest came (as he knew it must) he could dissociate himself from them. Certainly, at his trial Laud tried (in deeply unconvincing fashion) to disclaim all direct responsibility for the advancement of Heylyn and Pocklington.[53] The archbishop may have hoped that he could thereby let his clerical rottweilers run the risks for him, and then later watch them become the scapegoats for the more abrasive style of the Personal Rule. But it is a moot point who was exploiting whom. Heylyn was certainly exploiting the polarised religious policies of the 1630s, and was indeed partly helping to create such a lucrative polarisation. The preoccupations of Charles and Laud were clear for all to see, and it was relatively simple for an ambitious clergyman to court their support by

[51] G. Ornsby (ed.), *The Correspondence of John Cosin* (Surtees Society, 52, 55, 1868–72), I, 66. For Laud in Oxford, see e.g. *Works*, V, 15–16, 186, 206, 268.

[52] Laud, *Speech*, 73; Heylyn, *Cyprianus*, 332.

[53] Laud, *Works*, IV, 294, 296. Laud's claim that Heylyn was advanced by Danby is highly dubious for the period after 1629: Heylyn himself later claimed that it was Laud who had secured him a royal chaplaincy in 1630 (Heylyn, *Survey*, preface, sig. a2r), and that he assisted Laud at the consecration of St Katherine Cree church in January 1631 (Heylyn, *Cyprianus*, 213). Laud's promotion of Pocklington can be documented directly, despite his claim that he did not know who had recommended him to be made a royal chaplain 'nor is there any proof offered that I did it' (*Works*, IV, 296; VII, 598–9). On Laud's patronage more generally, see Milton, 'The Laudians', 7–8; K. Fincham, 'William Laud and the Exercise of Caroline Ecclesiastical Patronage', *JEH*, 51 (2000), 69–93.

playing on their fears (and thereby perhaps increasing their paranoia). When minor divines pontificated in provocative tones about what the religious intentions of the government were, they were not necessarily going to be the ones to suffer when the worried backlash came.

Moreover, it must be emphasised again that, even if they were not formulating policy, there was a real sense in which it was writers such as Heylyn and the rest who were ultimately the ones spelling out the actual meaning and nature of Laudian policy. In this sense, 'Laudianism' as an ideology was partly a creation of these polemicists. But the point here is not just that the rationale of the Laudian movement was in a sense artificially created (and again it must be stressed that I am not denying that the creators and enforcers of the policy, the Durham House Group, did have their own distinctive and sincerely held world-view which informed their actions). Rather, the broader point is that 'Laudianism' itself had an unstable quality – the explanations and defences of Laudian policies were constantly on the move, as were their exponents, adjusting and developing their ideas. And here Peter Lake's caveats are entirely correct: the body of 'Laudian' texts *are* incoherent and inconsistent.[54] There *are* some remarkable overlaps and echoes in this body of writings, it is true.[55] But generally there is a marked degree of inconsistency. We may classify the tracts as 'Laudian' for their readiness to defend the policies being pursued in the 1630s, and their repetition of some standard tropes about ceremonies and puritans – but when we tie them down to specific issues, we often find the different writers remarkably at variance, often directly contradicting each other on points of detail and interpretation. For example, while Giles Widdowes's anti-puritan tracts anticipated by several years the Laudian stress on the importance of ceremonial reverence (and were certainly consulted by Heylyn), his strongly sabbatarian opinions set him at odds with much later Laudian writings. Edmund Reeve in his *Communion Book Catechisme* (1636) betrayed many Laudian sentiments, but approved of altars standing north and south, and his ideas also went against the Laudian policy on the sabbath.[56] Reeve lavished praise on

[54] Lake, 'The Laudian style', 162–3.
[55] These often seem to derive from the fact that the authors were using the same patristic source or Old Testament example. Some of the overlaps are also simply the result of authors copying each other. Thus, Pocklington's model of the ancient subdivision of churches was taken up by Thomas Lawrence and Fulke Robarts: Pocklington, *Sunday no Sabbath* (1636), 27–8; idem, *Altare Christianum*, 62–5; Thomas Lawrence, *A Sermon Preached before the Kings Majesty* (1637), 9; Fulke Robarts, *God's Holy House and Service* (1639), 41.
[56] Giles Widdowes, *The Schismaticall Puritan* (Oxford, 1630), sigs. C1r–v, F2v; Edmund Reeve, *Communion Book Catechisme* (1636), 137, 189. It is in writings on the sabbath in particular that we find the most chaotic disagreements on the Laudian side – see e.g. Richard Bernard, *A Threefold Treatise*

the books of homilies as constituting a crucial doctrinal resource of the Church of England, whereas several other Laudian divines sought to dismiss them because of their value to those promoting sabbatarianism or opposing church decoration.[57] Where divines like Heylyn praised the First Edwardian Prayer Book, John Browning (author of a collection of tracts entitled *Concerning Publike-Prayer, and the Fasts of the Church*) expressed a very low opinion of it.[58] Where Edward Boughen maintained in a visitation sermon of 1635 that doctrine and ceremony were intimately linked, Samuel Hoard in a sermon *The Churches Authority Asserted* delivered at Laud's visitation in 1637 denied that there was any link at all.[59]

It has been argued that the Laudian position itself contained some inherent ambiguities, tensions and potential inconsistencies, especially when it came to the question of the precise authorities according to which the disputed policies and ceremonies were to be obeyed.[60] But incoherence and inconsistencies may also derive from the peculiarly un-stable nature of Laudian 'orthodoxy' and the apparently uncoordinated manner of its creation. The extremely varied provenance of these writ-ings is doubtless important here. Some of them are officially sponsored pamphlets; others are blind bids for patronage from clerics venturing into print for the first time. Some of them are sermons given at the vis-itations of Laudian bishops. Others represent the settling of old scores with puritan opponents. A few may represent the first teetering steps into ceremonialist discourse by individuals used to more godly topics. In the case of some authors like Joseph Mede and Robert Sanderson, they may be deliberate attempts to tone down the level of the debate being em-braced by extremists like Heylyn and Pocklington.[61] Other works may perhaps be explained by the controversial divine Peter Hausted's frank admission in his case that he was publishing his collection of ten sermons 'in order to feel the Pulse of the Times' for his own more unconventional brand of ceremonialist writings. Hausted's work reflects the emergence of a new brand of radical and provocative ceremonialism in the univer-sities, ready to push to the absolute limit the boundaries of Protestant

of the Sabbath (1641), 113–14. Ken Parker notes the incoherence of the Laudian position: K. L. Parker, *The English Sabbath* (Cambridge, 1988), 202–6.

[57] Reeve, *Communion Book Catechisme*, sigs. C1 r–v, D4r, pp. 115–16; Milton, *Catholic and Reformed*, 332.

[58] P. Heylyn, *Antidotum Lincolniense*, I, 110–26; John Browning, *Concerning Publike-Prayer, and the Fasts of the Church* (1636), 185.

[59] Edward Boughen, *Two Sermons* (1635), I, 4; Samuel Hoard, *The Churches Authority Asserted* (1637), 31.

[60] Lake, 'The Laudians', *passim*.

[61] Robert Sanderson, 'A sovereign antidote against sabbatarian errours' (1636) in *The Works of Robert Sanderson D.D.*, ed. W. Jacobson, v, 5–16; Mede, *Works*, 1,028, 1,036, 1,041.

orthodoxy.[62] But amid such incoherence, the question of what counted as true 'Laudianism' was a moot point.

There is also an even more fundamental sense in which the nature of 'Laudianism' was unstable, and that lies in the fact that the meaning of 'Laudianism' in the local context was shaped by the individual minister on the ground, who sought to explain to his flock in either a positive or a negative way why the altar was being moved, or recreations allowed on the sabbath, or preaching restricted. The pamphlets and sermons printed with apparent government approval might provide some ideas, but the ultimate gloss came from the minister himself. And in the accusations against scandalous ministers in the early 1640s we can perhaps find some of the evidence for what followed from this interpretative blank cheque that local ministers were handed. When we look at reports that Francis Wright said 'that he did conceive that ther was moore than a sacramentall presence of Christs bodie' on the altar to which he worshipped, or Gawin Nash accused of bowing towards the consecrated elements and preaching 'that Christ was corporally present in the sacrament: that he was soe humble as to dwell under a crumme of bread', or Dr Clarke calling the wine sacred wine after the end of communion, or Michael Barnes justifying the Roman Catholics' practice of having images in churches, and a host of other examples, we may be seeing a number of things.[63] These may represent untruthful attacks on anti-parliamentary clerics, as some have argued. But the charges may also often represent either bewildered misunderstanding on the congregation's part, or some very incautious language from ministers. The clergymen may have been either groping in vain for explanations and justifications of Laudian policies, or they may have been fired with enthusiasm from their reading either of Heylyn or (as seems increasingly common) the writings of Chrysostom or, even more, some rather literal readings of the Old Testament.[64] And

[62] For other Cambridge examples see above, n. 46. For Oxford examples, see the manuscript sermons of William Page (Bodl. Lib., Barlow MS 54, fos. 29–36), John Potinger (Bodl. Lib., Rawlinson MS E.21 (h), fos. 196–209), and Edmund Diggle (Bodl. Lib., MS Eng. th. e. 173, fos. 5–19).

[63] W. Notestein (ed.), *The Journal of Sir Simonds D'Ewes from the Beginning of the Long Parliament* (New Haven, 1923), 82, 248, 261; John White, *The First Century of Scandalous, Malignant Priests* (1643), 26; L. B. Larking (ed.), *Proceedings in Kent* (Camden Society 80, 1862), 191.

[64] An interesting example of a local clergyman in the 1630s carefully noting and evaluating the pamphlet controversy concerning canonical ceremonies is the copy of the 1604 canons annotated by William Sterne, rector of Glooston. These annotations are currently the subject of important research by Andrew Cambers at the University of York. I am grateful to Mr Cambers for showing me his unpublished paper on Sterne, 'Reading and religious politics: revisiting the Canons of 1604 in the 1630s'.

when we look at the response to Laudianism, we need to bear in mind these multiple, radicalising and uncontrollable glosses, combined with extraordinarily powerful rumours of the popish proclivities of Laud and his associates, which made people perceive dangerous innovation and popery in policies which involved nothing of the sort.[65]

Even more fundamentally, perhaps, we may need to cease regarding 'Laudianism' merely as *either* the ideas of a small faction of divisive courtiers who dragged the country behind them briefly, and then went to earth again (although, just to stress again, I am not denying that there was indeed such a group), *or* the product of a whole class of hidden 'Laudians' suddenly jumping out of the woodwork with a complete ideology. Rather, the suggestion here is that we need to see Laudianism as a *process* – a process through which English Protestants singly and collectively moved. The incoherence of the body of texts defending Laudian policies is in this sense particularly significant. Of course, for *anti*-Laudian writers this was not the point: there was some polemical mileage to be gained in stressing their opponents' intellectual incoherence, but the basic thrust of anti-Laudian writings was to find a coherent and dangerous 'party' position, to find the 'ideal type'. And in this search for an 'ideal type', just as in contemporary attacks on Roman Catholicism, the most radical and outspoken authors were of course deemed to be the most honest and representative.[66]

But if we think of Laudianism in terms of a process through which people moved, then we may also need to think again about the nature of events after 1640. Perhaps these events should not be seen simply as those experienced by a country united in its rejection of a small group of people called Laudians, and falling out over what to replace them with (although this is not to deny that there was such a minority group which lost power in 1640). Rather, we may also need to think of them as events occurring in a country which was trying to wipe out its own recent past, with people seeking to redefine themselves, and to negotiate their ways out of a process in which they had been to varying degrees engaged. For as it was a process, Laudianism was a process and an experience (as I hope to argue elsewhere) from which many people emerged out on the other side, transformed into more tactful forms of conformist, or even rediscovering godly roots once more. And for these people, the more that

---

[65] E.g. PRO, SP 16/453/96, 454/42, 456/36, 459/69. I hope to deal with the importance of rumours in the religious politics of the period in more detail elsewhere.
[66] Milton, *Catholic and Reformed*, 236–7.

Laudianism could be branded as the distinctive work of a tiny minority, the more they could refashion and validate their own position. When Lord Falkland urged parliament in 1641 to distinguish between 'those who have beene carried away with the streame, and those that have been the streame that carry'd them', he was making a valid distinction, but his confidence that such a distinction could be made was also an ideological, even a polemical, position.[67] Some were very happy to be carried along by the stream, but prompt to jump out of it when they saw the waterfall coming. The Laudian experiment was one in which a wide range of people were happy to be creatively involved, but which few were ready to own after the calling of the Long Parliament.[68]

---

[67] Lord Falkland, *A Speech to the House of Commons concerning Episcopacy* (1641), 11.

[68] Thus, by 1641 even John Pocklington was trying to dissociate himself from the movement, complaining to parliament that his books had been published without his 'procurement, motion or knowledge', and that he only 'composed them for his own satisfaction': Prynne, *Canterburies Doome*, 358.

9

Provincial preaching and allegiance in the First English Civil War, 1640–6

Jacqueline Eales

'[I]f the pulpits teach not obedience (which will never be if Presbyterian government be absolutely established) the king will have but small comfort of the militia' – Charles I to Henrietta Maria, Newcastle, 30 November 1646.[1]

Charles I's letter to his queen, written after his defeat in the First Civil War, succinctly expresses the relationship between religion and politics in early modern England. If the established church reflected and reinforced royal power, then any assault on the church hierarchy, such as that posed by Presbyterianism, would also undermine the crown. At the heart of the attack on the bishops by the Presbyterian clergy and their independent allies lay the argument that there was no divine right for episcopacy, which was a human invention. This was seen as a potentially explosive doctrine by the Stuart kings, who feared that it could be turned against monarchy itself. At the very least the public examination of the nature of divine right, of the origins of ecclesiastical and political power and of the extent of obedience could lead to attempts to limit the royal prerogative.

In the 1640s such a debate was carried into the English provinces partly through the means of preaching which, in a society where illiteracy was widespread, was able to reach audiences that printed works could not necessarily reach. The opinions of the clergy were regarded as highly influential and preaching was seen as such a powerful medium that a Canterbury alderman could claim that in 1633, after hearing a sermon in the cathedral in favour of the newly installed altar, 'I went away with my haire on end and came no more to the Cathedrall in eight yeares after'.[2] In the 1640s royalist preachers sought to emphasise that resistance to the king was rebellion against God's ordinances, while parliamentarian

---

[1] J. Bruce (ed.), *Charles I in 1646: Letters of King Charles the First to Queen Henrietta Maria*, (Camden Society, 63, 1856), 79. I first noticed the significance of this quotation during a weekly undergraduate tutorial with Conrad Russell in the autumn of 1972.
[2] R. Culmer, *Cathedrall Newes from Canterbury* (1644), 9.

preachers sought to justify armed resistance. The debate about resistance took place within the wider context of parliamentarian fears that the king was in the grips of a Catholic plot to introduce tyranny and subvert the true faith, which royalists countered by stressing the dangers posed by parliament to the social hierarchy and to the stable government of both state and church. Rival preaching campaigns not only helped to politicise and shape public opinion in the early 1640s, but most crucially they also helped to break down the barriers to civil war.

Conrad Russell has identified religious division as one of the key causes of the Civil War, along with the British dimension and the financial problems of the ancien regime.[3] Yet, although early modern sermons have become an increasingly important area of study, historians have given little attention to the effects of provincial Civil War preaching campaigns on public opinion.[4] In contrast, the sermons preached between November 1640 and April 1653 to the Long Parliament have been the subject of numerous studies.[5] This can be explained partly by accessibility, since 250 of the 350 or so parliamentary sermons have survived in print, whereas the vast majority of sermons preached in the provinces have left no record.[6] The centralisation of the printing trade in the capital meant that relatively few sermons preached outside London were published, although a number of royalist sermons were printed at York and Oxford. There are some other notable exceptions, such as the sermons preached at the parliamentarian stronghold of Great Yarmouth by John Brinsley, the Presbyterian, and William Bridge, an independent preacher newly returned from the Netherlands. Brinsley published a number of his sermons, in which he called for church reformation and endorsed the authority of the Westminster Assembly of Divines convened in order to formulate reforms. He also preached in favour of the Covenant of 1643, which endorsed uniformity of religion

---

3 See in particular Conrad Russell, *The Causes of the English Civil War* (Oxford, 1990); *Unrevolutionary England, 1603–1642* (1990) and *The Fall of the British Monarchies, 1637–1642* (Oxford, 1991).

4 For early modern preaching see L. Ferrell, *Government by Polemic: James I, the King's Preachers and the Rhetoric of Conformity, 1603–1625* (Stanford, 1998), P. McCullough, *Sermons at Court: Politics and Religion in Elizabethan and Jacobean Preaching* (Cambridge, 1998), L. Ferrell and P. McCullough (eds.), *The English Sermon Revised: Religion, Literature and History, 1600–1750* (Manchester, 2000) and W. Sheils, 'Provincial preaching on the eve of the Civil War: some West Riding fast sermons', in A. Fletcher and P. Roberts (eds.), *Religion, Culture and Society in Early Modern Britain* (Cambridge, 1994).

5 See, for example, H. Trevor-Roper, 'The fast sermons of the Long Parliament', in H. Trevor-Roper (ed.), *Religion, Reformation and Social Change* (1972); J. Wilson, *Pulpit in Parliament: Puritanism during the English Civil Wars, 1640–1648* (Princeton, 1969); T. Liu, *Discord in Zion: The Puritan Divines and the Puritan Revolution, 1640–1660* (The Hague, 1973); S. Baskerville, *Not Peace but a Sword: The Political Theology of the English Civil Revolution* (1993).

6 Wilson, *Pulpit in Parliament*, 7–11.

in the three kingdoms and preached against separation into gathered churches.[7] The central thrust of Bridge's printed works, discussed below, was the justification of resistance against the king. There are also sermon notes and other manuscript descriptions, which can extend our knowledge of provincial preaching and, even where the text of a sermon has not survived, evidence about the conditions in which it was preached can still be highly revealing. All of these sources must, of course, be analysed with care, since a preacher might modify his address according to his audience, printed versions of sermons might differ from the original spoken text, while sermon notes and other accounts could come from either sympathetic or hostile witnesses. Moreover, the impact of a sermon heard from the pulpit was very different from that read as a printed text.[8]

With these caveats in mind, this essay will consider not only the influence of the Long Parliament sermons in the localities, but also the range of preaching available outside the capital. This will demonstrate the importance of preaching in transmitting debates about the nature of political and religious authority and what constituted rebellion into the parishes. Recent research has emphasised the influential role played by the circulation of news on public opinion in the early Stuart period.[9] The clergy clearly had a substantial role in this process, not only through their preaching, but also by being required to read royal proclamations and other declarations from king and parliament from their pulpits.[10] The clergy were also directed to tender a series of parliamentarian oaths including the Protestation and the Covenant to all of their adult male parishioners. Thus, the parish church and its congregation acted as a focal point for public declarations of allegiance throughout the 1640s and the sermons that were preached there undoubtedly had a significant impact on that allegiance. If we are to look anywhere for the motivation

---

[7] See for example, J. Brinsley, *Church Reformation, Tenderly Handled in Foure Sermons* (1643); *The Saints Solemne Covenant with Their God* (1644); *The Sacred and Sovereign Church Remedie* (1645); and *The Araignment of the Present Schism of New Separation in Old England* (1646).

[8] On this point see J. Rigney, ' "To lye upon a Stationers stall, like a coarse piece of flesh in a shambles": the sermon, print and the English Civil War', in Ferrell and McCullough, *The English Sermon Revised*, 188–207.

[9] R. Cust, 'News and politics in early seventeenth-century England', *P & P*, 112 (1986); J. Raymond, *The Invention of the Newspaper: English Newsbooks, 1641–1649* (Oxford, 1996); and J. Raymond (ed.), *News, Newspapers, and Society in Early Modern Britain* (1999).

[10] For an extremely cogent discussion of the relationship betwen preaching and the 'public sphere' in the post-Restoration period see T. Claydon, 'The sermon, the 'public sphere' and the political culture of late seventeenth-century England', in Ferrell and McCullough, *The English Sermon Revised*.

that led to popular support for king or parliament, we should perhaps start with provincial preaching.

As the First Civil War progressed, the pulpit became increasingly contested territory and the questions of who should preach and what they should say turned some pulpits into battlegrounds. At the end of July 1642, when Matthew Clarke rose to preach in the parish church at Leominster in Herefordshire he found his path to the pulpit blocked by thirteen armed local royalist volunteers, including a chandler, a carpenter, a mason and a tanner, who threatened to cudgel him to the ground.[11] The conditions of civil war also encouraged the emergence of a wide spectrum of preaching. In 1646 the Presbyterian minister Thomas Edwards complained in his catalogue of current heresies, *Gangraena*, that 'Sectaries, or Dissenters from what's setled by the civill Sanction, do come into publike Churches, causing tumults and riots, and by violence put by the Ministers from preaching, pulling them out of their Pulpits, abusing them grossly, and preach openly with all kinds of reproaches against the established Religion'.[12] By the time that Charles I had been defeated in 1646, the Presbyterian supporters of parliament like Edwards found themselves ranged against not only the royalist clergy, but also against independent and lay preachers, who demanded greater religious freedom and opposed parliament's plans for a national church.[13]

It should not be forgotten, however, that despite the demands of the Reformation, many parishes still lacked frequent preaching, for example, Pennard in Glamorgan, where the parishioners claimed in 1642 never to have had more than four sermons a year.[14] Thus, a central focus for parliament's church reforms was to provide a preaching parish ministry by ejecting slack preachers from their livings. Yet sermons, where they did take place, gathered people from all social strata to hear current issues being analysed publicly. In a society in which orality was a central means of disseminating information, preaching not only conveyed news about the conflict to congregations, but given sufficient spin could also inflame passions and reinforce commitment to one side or the other. Preaching also provoked direct action on the part of a congregation, who might deliberately attend in order to prevent a sermon being preached by a man they disliked, or alternatively they might respond to a sermon

---

[11] BL, Additional MS 70106, Relation of Matthew Clarke, 31 July 1642.
[12] T. Edwards, *The Third Part of Gangraena* (1646), 268.
[13] For the disputations that took place between these groups see A. Hughes, 'The pulpit guarded: confrontations between orthodox and radicals in revolutionary England', in A. Laurence, W. Owens and S. Sim (eds.), *John Bunyan and His England, 1628–88* (1990).
[14] *CJ*, 2, 55.

from a sympathetic preacher. Thus, in December 1643, when one of the prebendaries at Canterbury preached in the aftermath of the official iconoclasm in the cathedral against the 'rifling and pillaging [of] churches', his sermon provoked a minor 'mutiny' against the parliamentarian regime in the city.[15] The publication of some sermons also gave their arguments a considerable afterlife, as John Brinsley emphasised in the preface to a sermon preached at the monthly fast in December 1642, when he wrote 'that what was then transient in the Eare, may now be Permanent to the Eye'.[16]

As members of a national profession, the clergy were perhaps less inclined than other social groups to view the events of the Civil War solely from a regional perspective and the evidence demonstrates that in certain pulpits the themes handled at Westminster were being actively addressed in provincial sermons. It has, for example, been widely argued that the parliamentarians were cautious about putting the case for principled resistance to royal power.[17] In fact this issue was tackled by the parliamentary preachers from an early stage through the issue of idolatry. The argument that an idolatrous ruler could be overthrown was a commonplace of English resistance literature written during Mary Tudor's reign by men such as John Ponet and Christopher Goodman. In the 1640s the treatment of this subject carried a radical political edge when it was aimed at the religious practices condoned by the king and the bishops in the 1630s, including the introduction of the railed altar and of images in parish churches, which seemed to some to herald a return to Catholic practices. The entrenched fear of Catholicism as a persecuting and tyrannical faith, which promoted superstition and idolatry, helps to explain our Canterbury alderman's horror in 1633 at hearing a sermon in favour of altars.[18] The issue of idolatry became a frequent theme of sermons to parliament and both of the sermons preached to the Commons on 17 November 1640, Elizabeth's accession day, tackled the issue of idolatry and described it as a national sin. Cornelius Burgess dwelt on the Old Testament story of Queen Maacha, who was deposed by her son Asa, because 'she had made an idol in a grove'. Not only did this story raise the issue of resistance, but it also had particular

[15] Culmer, *Cathedrall Newes*, 12.

[16] J. Brinsley, *A Parlie with the Sword about a Cessation* (1642), A2r; see also *Church Reformation* and *Sacred and Sovereign*.

[17] Russell, *Causes of the English Civil War*, 132–6; see in response J. Sommerville, *Royalists and Patriots: Politics and Ideology in England, 1603–1642* (Harlow, 1999), 250–4.

[18] P. Lake, 'Anti-Popery: The Structure of a Prejudice', in R. Cust and A. Hughes (eds.), *Conflict in Early Stuart England: Studies in Religion and Politics, 1603–1642* (Harlow, 1989).

resonances in 1640, when the religious practices of the Catholic queen, Henrietta Maria, had already come under criticism. In his afternoon sermon Stephen Marshall similarly argued that the English nation had deserted the Lord by, amongst other things, the introduction of idolatrous practices.[19]

The publication of these sermons meant that they could be widely read and copies of both of them survive, for example, in the library of Henry Oxinden of Barham, in Kent. Although Oxinden was not such a systematic collector or annotator as the famed iconclast William Dowsing, he nevertheless collected printed sermons preached in London and in the provinces during the 1640s.[20] Once war broke out, the issue of resistance was tackled more directly by parliamentarian preachers. In 1642, in a sermon to the volunteers from Norwich and Great Yarmouth, William Bridge developed the familiar parliamentarian argument that the king had two bodies, a personal one and a legal one, and that the war was not against the king's person, but was an act of self-defence. Bridge thus argued that 'there is much difference between taking up of Armes against the Kings Person, and taking up of Arms for the defence of the Kingdom, without the Kings command' and he went on to blame the king's evil counsellors for this necessity. In two tracts written in 1642 and 1643, in answer to Henry Ferne's anti-resistance works against parliament, Bridge elaborated on his views. He argued that parliament was one of the higher powers to which obedience was due, that self-preservation from foreign invasion and 'popish rebellion' was sufficient cause for war and that the command of parliament was sufficient authority. He took a contractual and anti-patriarchal view of political society, arguing that 'the prince hath no more power than what is communicated to him from the communitie' and defining arbitrary power as that of 'a father in his family'. In the printed preface to another sermon preached to the Commons in February 1643 Bridge argued that kings were bound by

---

[19] C. Burgess, *The First Sermon Preached to the Honourable House of Commons* (1641), 11–12; S. Marshall, *A Sermon Preached before the Honourable House of Commons* (1641), 40. The relationship between idolatry and resistance is discussed more fully in J. Eales, 'Iconoclasm, iconography and the altar in the English Civil War', in D. Wood (ed.), *The Church and the Arts* (Oxford, 1992), 313–27.

[20] Oxinden owned at least 15 per cent of the printed sermons delivered to the Long Parliament. He may originally have owned more, but his library, which is now part of the Elham parish library at Canterbury Cathedral Library, has suffered a number of depletions. I am grateful to the librarian, Sheila Hingley, for her advice on this collection. He also owned copies of most of the sermons preached at York, Oxford and Great Yarmouth, which are discussed below. For Dowsing see J. Morrill, 'William Dowsing, the bureaucratic puritan', in J. Morrill, P. Slack and D. Woolf (eds.), *Public Duty and Private Conscience in Seventeenth-Century England* (Oxford, 1993).

human laws and that to argue that resistance could only be defensive was 'non-sense, for so a man may be resisting ever, and never'.[21]

In addressing the Kent county committee at Knole in 1644, Joseph Boden was similarly unequivocal in endorsing an offensive war against 'the brats of Babylon', whom he defined as 'the Prelates, Papists and Atheists, with all the frie of Antichristian factors and panders'. His arguments that the royalists had promoted superstition and idolatry served to reinforce the legitimacy of parliament's resistance and he cast Charles I as 'one of those tenne, of whom we read, Revel. 17. 12. that . . . shall give their power and strength to the Beast'. By arguing that the royalists were fighting against 'our King and Generall Christ', Boden could label them as the traitors and rebels, and went so far as to argue that 'the people of God have a commission not only for a defensive, but an offensive Militia, and Posture of Warre'. He continued 'I know many have taken great paines, and to good purpose, to prove it lawfull, in the present cause of God, the kingdome and parliament to take up and make use of Armes, in defence of Religion, the Church, and the truths of God therein'. Boden acknowledged that some men might claim to be too frightened of death to take up arms, but he reassured them that blood thus shed shall be 'precious in the sight of the Lord' and that other worthy men had already sacrificed their lives in the cause of God, 'witnesse our Brook, our Hampden, and others'. He also pursued his arguments from the national to the county arena and emphasised that providentially God had defended Kent from invasion by 'cruell and blood-thirstie men'.[22]

Preachers in both camps used arguments of providentialism to argue that God was on their side, but also warned against complacency in relying on God's support to win. The war was seen by clergy on both sides as a national judgement for forsaking God's path and military setbacks were interpreted as further scourges to be endured before victory could be attained. Yet even the victors would have to eliminate personal sins and humble themselves before the Lord. Thus, at Great Yarmouth, Brinsley argued that the sword that had been unleashed by civil war was sent by God and only when the 'crying sinnes of the Land be taken away by a Nationall Reformation' would the sword be sheathed.[23] It was only

---

[21] W. Bridge, *A Sermon Preached unto the Voluntiers of the City of Norwich* . . . (1642), 17; *The Wounded Conscience Cured, the Weak One Strengthened and the Doubting Satisfied* (1642), 2; *The Truth of the Times Vindicated Whereby the Lawfulnesse of Parliamentary Proceedings in Taking up of Arms is Justified* (1643), A2v, 14, 51; and *Joabs Counsell and King Davids Seasonable Hearing It* (1643), A3r.

[22] J. Boden, *An Alarme Beat Up in Sion* (1644), 15–6, 29–31, 12.

[23] Brinsley, *Parlie with the Sword*, 27.

after the royalist defeat at Naseby that parliamentarian preachers allowed
themselves to claim imminent victory. In a sermon preached at Lancaster
to the county committee on 18 December 1645, Nathaniel Barnet asked
whether their opponents would continue to fight 'against God now his
hand is lift up against' them. Similarly, in a sermon preached during the
recruiter elections at Bristol on 28 February 1646, the army chaplain,
Samuel Kem, referred to God's glory 'in the midst of us', which he linked
to the 'clear routing' of the enemy at Naseby.[24]

The direct participation of preachers in Civil War politics can be
traced back to 1640, when there are accounts of clerical involvement in
parliamentary electioneering in some areas. Henry Neville, for example,
blamed his defeat in the Essex county elections to the Short Parliament
on the preaching of Stephen Marshall and other clients of the Earl of
Warwick.[25] These ministers would soon become closely associated with
the reform programme of the Long Parliament and Marshall was one
of the key preachers to parliament at fasts and on days of thanksgiving.
Initially these occasions were arranged on an *ad hoc* basis, but in January
1642 following pressure from parliament, a royal proclamation instigated
a regular fast accompanied by prayer and sermons on the last Wednesday
of every month, which was to be observed in all 'cathedrall, collegiate,
and parish churches and chappels' in England and Wales.[26] Members
of the House of Commons kept the monthly fast until 1649, when it
was discontinued, ostensibly because it had become ritualised, although
the opportunity such gatherings provided for royalist intrigue should not
be overlooked. This commitment to the parliamentarian monthly fast
was mirrored in numerous communities outside London as well. Ralph
Josselin, minister of Earls Colne in Essex, for example, preached sermons
lasting up to three hours on most monthly fast days between February
1642 and February 1649.[27]

The importance placed on politically correct preaching was reflected
in the successive purges of the ministry undertaken by parliament
throughout the 1640s. As early as December 1640 a select committee
of the Commons chaired by the MP for Kent, Sir Edward Dering,
was named with powers to consider ways of replacing 'scandalous
ministers'. Simultaneously the Commons called for its members to supply

[24] N. Barnett, *God Lift up Hand for Lancashire* (1646), 44–5; S. Kem, *The King of Kings His Privie Marks* (1646), 31.
[25] PRO, SP 16/449/48.
[26] *A Proclamation for a Generall Fast throughout this Realm of England*, 8 January 1641/2.
[27] C. Durston, '"For the better humiliation of the people": public days of fasting and thanksgiving during the English Revolution', *SC*, 7 (1992), 138–9.

information about the state of preaching in their counties and why 'there is such a want of preaching ministers'.[28] The resulting complaints about negligent, immoral and 'ceremonious' clergy were used to eject them from their livings. The details of the first hundred clerics whose benefices were thus sequestered were published in 1643 under the title *The First Century of Scandalous, Malignant Priests* by John White, who replaced Dering as chairman of the committee. The cases came from areas which at that date were under parliamentarian control and the majority were from Essex, Suffolk and Kent. Many of the allegedly 'malignant' priests were accused of preaching or speaking out against parliament, such as William Graunt, vicar of Isleworth in Middlesex, who 'hath often preached against the present defensive warre, averring the same to be against the Kings Person and wishing their hands might rot off, that should be lift up therein'.[29] Some of these clerics had read the declarations and proclamations from the king from their pulpits, but had refused to read parliamentary ordinances. Yet others were accused of neglecting their cures and rarely or never preaching at all, while some were accused of aggressively adopting the Laudian innovations of the 1630s particularly the railed altar, which according to puritan and other critics was synonymous with Catholic practices.[30]

Once parliament had won the First Civil War in 1646, it was able to extend the policy of sequestration into the counties which had previously been under royalist control and almost 3,000 clerical ejections took place in the 1640s and 1650s.[31] The rate of ejections was also speeded up as local committees took over the work from the committee at Westminster.[32] The evidence from these cases against the 'malignant clergy' show that the parliamentarians greatly feared that royalist preaching would damage support for their cause. Similarly, the royalist camp acknowledged the powerful role played by parliamentarian preaching in strengthening resistance to the crown. In October 1643 Charles I abolished the Wednesday fast, because the prayers and sermons of many 'seditious lecturers' had been used to 'stir up and continue the rebellion raised against us'. Instead, he ordered that an alternative fast should be held on

---

[28] *CJ*, 2, 54.   [29] John White, *The First Century of Scandalous, Malignant Priests* (1643), p. 16.
[30] Eales, 'Iconoclasm'.
[31] I. Green, 'The persecution of "scandalous" and "malignant" parish clergy during the English Civil War', *EHR*, 94 (1979), 507–51.
[32] C. Holmes (ed.), *The Suffolk Committees for Scandalous Ministers, 1644–1646*, Suffolk Records Society, 13, (Ipswich, 1970), 23–4; J. Sharpe, 'Scandalous and malignant priests in Essex; the impact of grassroots puritanism', in C. Jones, M. Newitt and S. Roberts (eds.), *Politics and People in Revolutionary England* (Oxford, 1986), 269–70.

the second Friday of every month starting in November.[33] This rival fast was observed at the royalist headquarters in Oxford and a number of the sermons preached there to the court and to the members of the Oxford parliament, which opened in February 1644, were published. Amongst the preachers on these occasions were James Ussher, Bishop of Armagh, Walter Curle, Bishop of Winchester, Henry Hammond and Thomas Fuller. Ussher, for example, preached on the classic anti-resistance text Romans 13:1 and 2.[34] Ussher was adamant that violent or defensive resistance to the king was illegitimate, but his tone was moderate and he recognised that some men could not yield in their consciences to the king's command. In such a case, he argued, a Christian man only had recourse to 'sollicite, beseech, [and] earnestly pray for the reversing of the Decree'.[35]

Oxford also provided a safe refuge for royalist ministers such as Paul Gosnald, rector of Bradfield St Clare in Suffolk, who was accused locally of preaching that 'they weare all traitors that tooke up armes against the king'. Following the royalist defeat at Marston Moor in July 1644, Gosnald preached before the Oxford parliament in August on the text of Psalm 122:6. 'pray for the peace of Jerusalem'. In his sermon he hawkishly urged his auditors not only to pray but also to 'fight and pay for the peace of Jerusalem'. Quoting I Samuel 15:23, he likened rebellion to the sin of witchcraft and characterised the parliamentarians as men driven by the devil, a motif which would appear regularly in other royalist sermons.[36] Other royalist preachers at Oxford, such as Griffith Williams, Bishop of Ossory, and George Wilde, used the pulpit to urge their auditors not to make peace at the expense of the church.[37]

In the early stages of the conflict the king could also rely on the cathedrals to act as bastions for the royal cause. In York, for example, where the king rallied his forces in the summer of 1642, a variety of royalist preaching could be heard in the minster. This was in contrast to the sermons of the local puritan clergy, who preached in and around York in support of parliament in March to July 1642. In November 1642 Robert Mossom, an army chaplain, preached two sermons in the minster

[33] Durston, 'For the Better Humiliation of the People', 133.
[34] 'Let every soule be subiect to the higher powers: for there is no power but of God. Whosoever resisteth the power, resisteth the ordinance of God.'
[35] J. Ussher, *The Soveraignes Power and the Subjects Duty* (1644), 20, 27, 29.
[36] Holmes, *The Suffolk Committees for Scandalous Ministers*, 28–9; P. Gosnold, *A Sermon Preached at the Publique Fast the Ninth day of Aug. 1644* (Oxford, 1644).
[37] G. Browell, 'The politics of providentialism in England, c. 1640–1660' Ph.D. Thesis, University of Kent, 2000, 58.

about the duty of the subject and the unlawfulness of rebellion. He drew on traditional theories of patriarchy and just war in order to illustrate his text taken from Proverbs 30:31: 'And a King, against whom there is no rising up'. Like Gosnald, Mossom linked civil war with 'Satan's Kingdome'. He emphasised that even if the king was seduced by evil counsellors or commanded something evil, his subjects could not oppose him with 'Force and Armes', their only recourse was prayers and tears. The king's power he argued came from above, from God, and God would punish an evil king with 'his own hand'.[38]

After the royalist defeat at Marston Moor and the establishment of a parliamentarian garrison in York, the tenor of preaching in the minster inevitably changed. On 20 September 1644 the puritan John Shaw preached in the minster before Ferdinando, Lord Fairfax, the English and Scottish commissioners and the county committee for Yorkshire, when they and 'divers knights, gentlemen and citizens' took the Covenant. This was exactly a year after the Covenant had been taken by members of parliament at Westminster and this highly public occasion was clearly aimed at bringing the Yorkshire elite into line. Shaw warned against complacency following the parliamentarian victory at Marston Moor and argued that further religious reform was still necessary. He cited the now familiar story of Asa's deposition of Queen Maacha to argue that only after the removal of her idols was 'quietnesse and peace setled in the Land'. Shaw's sermon was aimed at answering objections to taking the Covenant and to proving that the power of bishops came not from divine right, but from human command 'at most'. He also emphasised the doctrine of the king's two bodies, arguing that the king's commands are either 'personall or legall' and described parliament as the 'highest Court', which executed the king's legal commands, even when he was not himself present.[39] In the following year the city corporation appointed four pro-parliament preachers, Thomas Calvert, Edward Bowles, Nathanial Rathband and Theodore Herring, to preach both in the minster and in the city churches of York.[40] In other dioceses the cathedral clergy were also gradually replaced by parliament with puritan preachers, who were more reliable in the 'common cause'.

Apart from the cathedrals there were a number of other high-profile venues for provincial preachers in the period. The assizes similarly

---

[38] R. Mossom, *The King and His Throne* (1643), passim.

[39] J. Shaw, *Brittains Remembrancer: Or the Nationall Covenant* (1644), *passim*.

[40] C. Cross, 'From the Reformation to the Restoration', in G. Aylmer and R. Cant (eds.), *A History of York Minster* (1977), 214.

provided a public forum, in which a variety of preaching might be heard in the counties, but this showcase was closed down when the traditional judicial circuits were postponed and abandoned during the period of civil warfare.[41] Instead, sermons were probably routinely addressed to the members of the county committees, who took over local administration in the areas held by Parliament. Once war broke out there were sermons to strengthen the resolve of army recruits, and army chaplains would become some of the most outspoken preachers on both sides. In particular, Thomas Edwards associated the spread of independency with the preaching of chaplains in the New Model Army.

William Bridge's sermon to the parliamentarian volunteers in Norfolk gives an insight into the arguments used to persuade men to overcome their natural distaste for civil war in 1642. Bridge urged them to behave valiantly in defence of the Protestant religion against the 'malignant Jesuiticall party' and to avoid the pillaging, plundering, capture and murder of 'your people' by the enemy. He encouraged them by asserting that 'your cause is good, your enemies weak, your victory certain, your service honourable, safe, warrantable'.[42] The survival of a series of letters written by Nehemiah Wharton, a London apprentice and parliamentarian volunteer, in the two months before the battle of Edgehill, give a valuable insight into the effects of preaching felt by an individual soldier. As he and his company marched from London through the Midlands to Worcester, he recorded the impact of sermons from Christopher Love, John and Obadiah Sedgewick, Stephen Marshall, Samuel Kem and others. There was a clear correlation between the delivery of a sermon and incidents of iconoclasm by the soldiers in local churches. In mid August as they marched westwards out of London, Christopher Love delivered a 'famous sermon', following which the soldiers burnt the altar rails from churches in Chiswick and Uxbridge.[43] Yet, in striking contrast to contemporary opinions about the power of preaching, a recent survey has argued that the influence of preachers on the soldiery was limited and even marginal.[44] These findings raise parallel questions about the nature and impact of preaching and of clerical influence in the provinces, which as we have seen so far there has been little attempt to assess.

---

[41] See, for example, J. Reading, *A Sermon Delivered at Maidston in Kent at the Assizes there Held Aug. 23 1641* (1641).

[42] Bridge, *A Sermon Preached unto the Voluntiers*, 12, 18.   [43] PRO, SP16/491/119.

[44] B. Donagan, 'Did ministers matter? War and religion in England, 1642–1649', *JBS*, 33 (1994), 119–56. For the army chaplains more generally see also A. Laurence, *Parliamentary Army Chaplains, 1642–1651* (Woodbridge, 1990).

A notable exception is William Sheils's survey of the sermons preached in nine pulpits in York and the West Riding in the critical months just before the outbreak of warfare. His work is based on the notes taken by an anonymous scribe of forty-four sermons delivered by puritan preachers in response to the king's proclamation for monthly fast sermons in 1642. These preachers made it clear that responsibility for the coming crisis lay with the king and his advisers and not with the parliament, although they did not directly raise the issue of armed resistance.[45] Nevertheless, as Dr Sheils argues, these clerics prepared their congregations for the onset of civil war. He goes on to note that the evidence of these sermons demonstrates that 'the religious issues were those most forcibly placed before the people' and that the conviction shown by committed parliamentarians was 'the result of such preaching'.[46] His findings coincide with Conrad Russell's observation that social and economic accounts, which ignore the preaching available in men's home parishes, 'tells us nothing about their likely allegiance in the civil war'.[47]

In order to illustrate the context of provincial preaching in the period leading to the king's defeat in 1646, it will be instructive to compare evidence from two contrasting areas of the country, namely Herefordshire, which was largely under royalist control until late in 1645, and Kent, where parliament maintained control from the summer of 1642. In 1641 the Herefordshire godly characterised the county as a dark corner of the land and it was certainly an area of 'slow Reformation' where there was still a sizeable Catholic population. The puritans were an isolated minority clustered in the extreme north-west of the county and godly preaching was a recent import with roots no further back than the reign of James I.[48] Kent offers a striking contrast, since it was a county where a 'fast Reformation' had undoubtedly taken place in the mid sixteenth century and where there was a long-standing tradition of puritan and even lay preaching by both men and women, dating back to Elizabeth's reign. In Kent strong pockets of puritanism were to be found in parishes in the environs of London, in the Weald and in the towns including Maidstone, Ashford, Canterbury, Sandwich and Dover.[49] As Russell points out, three Kent towns with long-standing traditions of puritanism – Ashford, Canterbury and Cranbrook – were among twenty-two towns or parishes

[45] Sheils, 'Provincial preaching on the eve of the Civil War'.

[46] *Ibid.*, 311.   [47] Russell, *Causes of the English Civil War*, 2.

[48] T. S. Smith, 'Herefordshire Catholics and the rites of passage, 1560–1640', *Transactions of the Woolhope Naturalists Field Club*, 42 (1978).

[49] R. Acheson, 'The development of religious separatism in the diocese of Canterbury, 1590–1660', Ph.D. Thesis, University of Kent, 1983.

nationally which also provided parliamentarian volunteers before war was declared.[50] There was thus a clear correlation between preaching and Civil War allegiance in these communities, which is apparent elsewhere.

Herefordshire and Kent are also both counties where there are rare survivals of the information collected by MPs about the state of preaching in their counties in the winter of 1640–1. This material provides an insight into the different traditions of preaching that had grown up in the two counties by that time. In Herefordshire this information was collected by the local puritan circle for their county MP and leading lay patron, Sir Robert Harley, a member of the committee for scandalous ministers. This Herefordshire group overwhelmingly supported a Presbyterian church settlement and would later form the core of the parliamentarian party in the county.[51] The survey of preaching was co-ordinated by Harley's rector at Brampton, Stanley Gower, who argued that out of 170 ministers in nearly 200 parishes there were 'but 20 constant and conscionable preachers', although he feared that this was more than in the whole of Wales. The remaining 150 ministers were described as absentees, 'noe preacher' or men who seldom preached. They were not all necessarily the 'dumb dogs' of puritan propaganda, but they certainly would not have conformed to the puritan ideal. Gower singled out six of his fellow puritans as the only 'constant and conscionable' preachers in the county. A few other ministers earned the accolade of a 'good preacher' or a 'constant preacher'.[52] The isolation felt by the puritans in Herefordshire is underscored by the fact that within two years most of the leading puritan clergy had fled the county. John Tombes of Leominster left for Gloucester and then Bristol, while John Yates of Leintwardine and William Lowe of Aston sought the safety of London, where they were soon joined by Gower and John Greene of Pencombe, who had been nominated as the county's representatives to the Westminster Assembly of Divines.[53]

In his survey Gower blamed the bishops and the cathedral clergy for the lack of adequate preaching in the county. He attacked the bishops for ordaining insufficient men and for restraining lecturers from preaching in a Calvinist strain 'against arminianism, of predestination, faith, effectual vocacon, regeneration etc'. The cathedral clergy in Hereford

---

[50] Russell, *Causes of the English Civil War*, 21–2.
[51] For a fuller discussion of the role of the Harleys in fostering puritanism in Herefordshire see J. Eales, *Puritans and Roundheads: The Harley of Brampton Bryan and the Outbreak of the English Civil War* (Cambridge, 1990).
[52] Corpus Christi College, Oxford, Ms 206.   [53] Eales, *Puritans and Roundheads*, 152.

preached rarely, he argued, while 'putting down' all sermons in the city on the sabbath 'to bring men to the cathedral'.[54] The lack of a tradition of puritan preaching in Hereford and in most of the county provides the context for the hostile reception of parliamentarian preachers there during the crisis of 1642.

The rivalry between the Herefordshire puritans and the cathedral clergy intensified in the spring and summer of 1642, when the two groups embarked on conflicting preaching campaigns. Between April and June 1642 the monthly fast was the occasion for a sequence of royalist sermons in the cathedral, which scandalised the local godly network and provoked them into an alarmed exchange of letters and sermon notes. Admittedly, the surviving accounts of the royalist sermons were circulated by the parliamentarians, but they are nevertheless valuable, because they emphasise the key points of contention between the two parties. In particular, the puritans felt that they were being isolated and stigmatised as rebels against religion and the social order, because of their support for parliament. A local puritan layman thus complained to Harley that the royalist preachers aimed to work 'a hatred in the harts of the people against the parliament and all good ministers & people, calling them schismatick and other reproachful nicknames'.[55]

Unlike the parliamentarian preachers in Yorkshire investigated by Dr Sheils, the Hereford cathedral clergy were on the offensive. On Wednesday 27 April 1642 Henry Rogers preached a highly political sermon on the text 2 Samuel 15:23, describing the revolt of Absalom against his father, King David. The sermon raised the twin spectres of heresy and mob rule in order to gain sympathy for the royal cause. London was according to Rogers a centre of religious sects, of anabaptists, separatists and others, where the 'base rabble rout' prescribed government to the parliament and made 'laws of their owne'. Yet he was confident that, just as Zadok the priest and the Levites had sided with David, so 'all the Lord's priests and prophets in this kingdome are with our Charles, in their hearts and affecttions and their purses and persons'. He also inveighed against Korah, Dathan and Abiram, who had revolted against the priestly and political power of Aaron and Moses. Rogers concluded by reminding his auditors of the constitutional role of parliament by stating that the 'senate was never above the Emperor but subordinate to him' and finished with God's injunction 'touch not myne annoynted'.[56]

---

[54] Corpus Christi College, Oxford, Ms 206, fos. 9r–11r.
[55] BL, Additional MS 70004, fo. 265r.   [56] BL, Additional MS 70003, fos. 237r–238r.

Rogers's sermon dealt with two important Old Testament narratives, which would become central to the royalist position in the 1640s, the story of Absalom's revolt and the rebellions of the Exodus. The directions for the royalist fast issued in 1643 specifically stipulated that the subject of the morning lesson should be either Absalom's rebellion or the revolt of Korah, Dathan and Abiram and these themes were frequently used by royalist preachers in other regions.[57] Rogers also returned to the charge of rebellion in a sermon preached on 1 July when he reputedly described Sir John Hotham as a traitor for refusing the king entry to Hull. At the same time the dean of the cathedral, Jonathan Brown, was reported by a local puritan as having preached a 'very pestilent' sermon against London and the parliament.[58] This may have been the dean's fast sermon preached on 29 June and heard by the royalist gentleman Sir Humphrey Mildmay, who in contrast described Brown as preaching 'learnedly'.[59]

When the parliamentarians tried to set up their own lecture in Hereford they found it difficult to find a parish to accept them, and when they preached they were threatened with violence. When John Yates started a sermon in Hereford at the end of June 1642 many of the congregation assembled in the churchyard where they cried 'roundheads' and some of them threatened to stone him.[60] John Tombes's pulpit in Leominster was the target of another disturbance at the end of July, but he had already become the first parliamentarian preacher to flee the county. By early 1643 Tombes was settled in Bristol, driven there he claimed in fear of his life.[61] The migration of the partisan clergy is a notable feature of the Civil War period, for without the ties of kinship and landed property that bound the gentry to their localities, many clerics left their cures for safer livings or to serve as army chaplains. The royalist clergy might congregate in York or in Oxford, as we have seen, while the parliamentarians were drawn to the safety of London and the southeast. So great were their numbers that Samuel Torshell, who had left the Cheshire parish of Bunbury for London late in 1642 to 'seek refuge in these more safe coverts', wrote a defence of their actions in the following year entitled *A Case of Conscience Concerning Flying in Times of Trouble*.[62]

---

[57] Durston, 'For the Better Humiliation of the People', 136.
[58] BL, Additional MS 70004, fo. 265r.
[59] P. Ralph (ed.), *Sir Humphrey Mildmay: Royalist Gentleman* (New Brunswick, 1947), 168.
[60] BL, Additional MS 70004, fos. 3v–4v, 265r.
[61] BL, Additional MS 70106, letter from Tombes, 5 August 1642; J. Tombes, *Jehovah Jireh* (1643).
[62] S. Torshell, *A Helpe to Christian Fellowship* (1644) foreword.

Although the leading parliamentarian clergy gradually left Herefordshire, the royalists were not able to preach unhindered. Parliamentarian
forces under the command of the Earl of Stamford entered Hereford in
the first week of October 1642, where their chaplain John Sedgewick
delivered two sabbath sermons, which 'much affected' the local inhabitants, because 'they neiver heard the like before'. Such a reaction is
understandable given the lack of a tradition of puritan preaching in
the city.[63] Stamford withdrew from Hereford at the end of November,
but the parliamentarian garrison set up at the Harley family home at
Brampton Bryan survived as an isolated enclave until 1644, when it sur-
rendered to the royalists. The prisoners taken from Brampton were then
interrogated by a royalist army chaplain, Edward Symmons, who attempted to prove their disloyalty to the crown. Their answers are highly
relevant to this present discussion, because their resolve to fight against
the king had been reinforced by the preaching of parliamentarian ministers and by fear of a Catholic plot. The prisoners thus claimed to
have been persuaded to fight against 'Antichrist and popery' by the
command of parliament and the example of 'all godly and powerfull
ministers, leading, encouraging and stirring them up thereunto'. In particular, they singled out a sermon by Stephen Marshall, a copy of which
they had at Brampton, as particularly influential.[64] This was Marshall's
famous parliamentary fast sermon of 23 February 1642, which took as
its text Judges 5:23: 'curse ye Meroz'. The immediate context of the
sermon was the Irish rebellion, but as political events shifted in the spring
and summer of 1642, the application of Marshall's words to the split in
England became ever more apparent. Marshall cried down the neuters,
who like the Meroz would not further the cause of God, the 'Lord acknowledges no neuters . . . it is Christs rule, he that is not with me is
against me'.[65]

It was not until December 1645 that parliament gained permanent
control of Hereford. In 1646 the parliamentarian county committee,
which had been largely unable to function since its appointment in April
1643, ejected at least fifteen local clerics including Henry Rogers, John
Coke, the son of the Bishop of Hereford, and Thomas Swift, grandfather
of the satirist. More ejections were to follow in the later 1640s and 1650s.[66]
In a plan similar to that introduced at York, a parliamentary ordinance

[63] PRO, SP16/492/32; *LJ*, V, 453.
[64] E. Symmons, *Scripture Vindicated* (1644), Preface to the Readers.
[65] S. Marshall, *Meroz Cursed* (1641 Old Style), 22–3.
[66] A. G. Matthews, *Walker Revised* (Oxford, 1988), 209–28.

provided for six ministers approved by the Westminster Assembly to preach in the cathedral and other churches in Hereford and county. According to Calamy, these preachers ordained many ministers for England and Wales and 'stemm'd the tide against the sectaries of those times' until 1660, when they were in turn ejected at the Restoration.[67]

Although Calamy thought that the Presbyterian clergy were finally able to dominate in Herefordshire, the same cannot be said in Kent, where a variety of preaching had already sprung up by 1640. The importance placed on securing the support of preachers in a county so close to parliament's headquarters is reflected in the high number of clerical ejections in Kent, which ran above the national average between 1642 and 1660 when some 233 benefices and canonries were sequestrated or forcibly vacated from a total of 450.[68] Concerns about preaching very similar to those expressed by the puritans in Herefordshire were raised in petitions from Kent and from Canterbury, which were presented in the Commons by Sir Edward Dering in January 1641.[69] As MP for the county Dering also received petitions and letters from individual ministers and parishes in Kent, which demonstrate that even a century after the Henrician Reformation there were places where parishioners felt that through the inadequacy of clerical wages, non-residency or other neglect they were denied the 'settled ministry' and regular preaching which they desired. These papers also demonstrate a strong and widely dispersed puritan influence in the county.

Dering's papers also show that sermons in favour of railed altars or against parliament's Scots allies were regarded as particularly contentious in the county before the outbreak of civil war. Twenty-two parishioners complained that their curate, Thomas Vaughan of Chatham, had preached that the Scots were 'daring rebels' whose religion 'is nothing but rebellion', while three parishioners complained that Edward Wallis, minister of Tudley and Capel, had railed against the Scots 'in his pulpit and out of his pulpit' calling them 'dogs and divells' and saying that 'if ever Scote goe to heaven, the divell will goe toe'. Wallis was later ejected from his living in 1643 for his involvement in the Kent rising against parliament along with four other Kent clerics.

The hostilities which developed between the puritans and their critics in Kent in the 1630s are well illustrated by the case of Robert Barrell,

---

[67] A. G. Matthews, *Calamy Revised* (Oxford, 1988), 215, 329, 399, 504.
[68] Green, 'The Persecution of "Scandalous" and "Malignant" Parish Clergy', 522–3; A. Everitt, *The Community of Kent and the Great Rebellion, 1640–1660* (Leicester, 1966), 299.
[69] L. Larking (ed.), *Proceedings, Principally in the County of Kent*, (Camden Society, 80, 1862) 26–38.

perpetual curate of Maidstone, who was involved in long-running disputes with the town council over tithes and fees. In May 1641 the puritan
elite of Maidstone seized the opportunity to petition parliament against
him.[70] Fifty-three parishioners, including the mayor, Martin Jeffery,
accused Barrell of preaching once every four or five weeks and using
his sermons to strike at 'sincerity and forwardnesse in profession, under
the names of faction, schisme and singularity'. He had also 'rebuked'
Thomas Wilson, the puritan minister of nearby Otham, for preaching twice on the sabbath, which Barrell described as 'but prating and
babling'. Barrell's lack of preaching had led, the petitioners believed, to a
reign of 'ignorance, lewdness and disobedience' in the town, which they
noted had 6,000 inhabitants, but only one parish church. In response the
Commons ordered on 12 February 1642 that Wilson should be made
town lecturer in Maidstone.[71]

The complaints against Barrell were renewed when he preached a
provocative assize sermon at Maidstone on 24 July 1642. This was the
occasion of a major power struggle between parliamentarians and royalists and was attended by a group of seventeen MPs with Kent seats or
connections in order to prevent the spread of 'rumours to the scandal
of Parliament'. They were unable to obtain permission to address the
court, but in response to their presence a group of royalists drew up
a petition to the king and an address to parliament. Barrell used this
public rift to preach against parliament and the Scots and in favour of
the commission of array. Complaints about the sermon were heard by
the House of Commons and in 1643 Barrell's curacy was sequestered
and in 1644 he was replaced by Wilson.[72]

A similar struggle for control of the pulpit was being waged at the
same time in Canterbury, where the tensions that developed between the
cathedral clergy and local puritan ministers were revealed by Richard
Culmer. Culmer's *Cathedrall Newes from Canterbury* (1644) was written as a
justification of his own acts of iconoclasm in the cathedral in the previous
year and it is a well-known source of information about iconoclasm and
religious conflict. Yet it also contains important evidence about reactions to royalist preaching, which have previously been largely ignored.
Culmer thus complained that for many years cathedral sermons had

[70] Larking, *Proceedings*, 227, 149, 183, 190, 202–5. For Wallis see Matthews, *Walker Revised*, 227.
[71] *CJ*, 2, 427.
[72] The power struggle at the assizes are discussed more fully in J. Eales, 'Kent and the English Civil
Wars, 1640–1660', in F. Lansberry (ed.), *Government and Politics in Kent, 1640–1914* (Woodbridge,
2001).

been aimed against godliness and religion in order to advance 'popery, prelacy, superstition, prophanenesse etc'. He cited a number of sermons including one preached on 23 November 1639, in which the preacher affirmed diocesan bishops to be *jure divino* and Presbyterian government to be 'a Gemmy, a toy, or Gu-gaw' and inveighed against the Scots, saying 'a nation at enmity with my king, a nation at enmity with my God'.[73] By the time that Culmer's book was published, the deputy-lieutenants of Kent had already complained to parliament in October 1643 about the preaching of the cathedral clergy. On receiving their letter the Commons had ordered the mayors and corporations of both Canterbury and Rochester to list the names of 'well affected... and orthodox' ministers in order to replace the prebends and preachers in the cathedrals. In March 1644 the dean and chapter at Canterbury were sequestrated and in October Culmer was chosen as one of the six cathedral preachers in place of the recently deceased William Dunkin.[74]

In *Cathedrall Newes* Culmer characterised the cathedral clergy at Canterbury as promoters of royal absolutism and also gave details about their more recent sermons, such as that by Thomas Paske, in which he declared that 'all were revolted from the King, and must come as Benhadad's servants did with ropes about their necks', which had also been reported to the Commons in January 1642. Culmer cited another sermon by John Jeffrys, who preached before the king in March 1642 when he was accompanying the queen to Dover, that Presbyterian government came from 'Corah, Dathan and Abiram'. Culmer also accused Humphrey Peake of preaching on 5 November 1642 that there was now 'in this land a conspiracy against the king to take away his life' and comparing the conspirators to Korah, Dathan and Abiram. Peake also allegedly preached that those who died fighting against the king at Edgehill were the children of the Devil and that their blood was on their own hands. Peake was imprisoned following this sermon and sent for as a deliquent by the Commons. Culmer concluded that if all cathedral sermons were extant 'all England would see... how little our laws and liberties are beholding to tyrannical prelacie and Cathedrals'.[75]

Although Culmer was enraged by royalist preaching in 1644, he was soon to encounter enmity from other quarters and he later believed that

[73] Culmer, *Cathedrall Newes*, 8–9.
[74] *CJ*, 3, 299, 359; *LJ*, 7, 10; P. Collinson, 'The Protestant cathedral, 1541–1660', in P. Collinson, N. Ramsay and M. Sparks (eds.), *A History of Canterbury Cathedral* (1995), 200.
[75] Culmer, *Cathedrall Newes*, 10–12; W. H. Coates, A. S. Steele and V. F. Snow (eds.), *The Private Journals of the Long Parliament 3 January to 5 March 1642* (1982), 222–3; *CJ*, 2, 841.

his ministry in East Kent in the second half of the 1640s and 1650s was opposed by a combination of royalists, religious sectaries and Levellers.[76] In 1646 Thomas Edwards also complained in *Gangraena* about the spread of separatism in Kent. Edwards accused the independents of spreading numerous heresies and he was particulary incensed that they used their pulpits to preach against Presbyterianism.[77] There was clearly considerable support for the religious sects in Kent and the royalist Kentish Petition of March 1642 thus specifically called for provision against 'schismatical and seditious sermons and pamphlets' and a law to be made against laymen for daring to exercise the 'Holy Function of the Ministry'.[78] In the previous year two conforming ministers of Wealden parishes, Robert Abbott at Cranbrook and James Wilcock at Goudhurst, had been opposed by large groups of independents amongst their congregations, who had separated into gathered churches.

Wilcock found that his preaching was smeared by them and his own curate, Edward Bright, as 'odious, blasphemous, popish and superstitious', because he preached in favour of the prayer book, the surplice, the use of the cross in baptism, kneeling and bowing during divine service. Wilcock believed that Bright's followers were 'Mechaniques only, ignorant and unlearned Tradesmen, Women and Children', whereas he was supported by the 'Gentlemen and Schollers' in the parish. In 1641 and 1642 Wilcock published seven of his sermons, in which he described the separatists as heretics and rebels against royal power. However, his insistence on the common ground between the English church and Rome, and that Catholics were the more noble adversaries than separatists, because they were open about their accusations, did not help his position.[79] Wilcock was apprehended by parliamentarian troops whilst preaching in 1642 and was confronted by Colonel Robert Gibbons, who declared 'Sirrah! you that stand prating there, come down, or I will shoot you down!'[80] Wilcock's dramatic removal may well have persuaded Abbot to leave Cranbrook for the living at Southwick in Hampshire under the patronage of Lady Honoria Norton.[81]

[76] R. Culmer (the younger), *A Parish Looking-Glasse for Persecutors of Ministers*, (1657), 21.
[77] T. Edwards, *The Second Part of Gangraena* (1646), 105–6, 150, 163–4, 175–6.
[78] *The Petition of the Gentry, Ministers, and Commonalty of Kent. Agreed upon at the Generall Assizes … March 28. 1642* (London 1642).
[79] James Wilcock, *A Challenge Sent to Master E. B. A Semi-Separatist* (1641), 14; *Six Sermons Lately Preached in the Parish Church of Goudhurst in* Kent (1641); and *The English Protestants Apology* (1642).
[80] J. Kemble (ed.), *Certaine Considerations Upon the Government of England by Sir Roger Twysden*, (Camden Society, 45, 1849), lxxxi.
[81] Matthews, *Walker Revised*, 209.

There is also evidence of considerable rivalry between the Presbyterian and independent groups in Kent towns such as Dover and Sandwich. In July 1642 John Durant had been appointed as lecturer in St Peter's Sandwich by the Commons, where Thomas Edwards alleged as many as 200–300 people would gather to hear him preach in private. In 1644 at Dover in Kent, John Vincent, the lecturer appointed by parliament, was opposed by local sectaries, who engaged in a 'hurliburly made in St James church' against him and 'persecuted him otherwise'.[82] By 1646 Durant and John Davis had been accepted as pastors of the congregational churches in Canterbury and Dover respectively and Samuel Fisher, a former army chaplain and later Quaker convert, had also established a following as a baptist peacher at Lydd. The more militant attitude displayed by the independents was summed up by Edwards when he claimed that Durant had prayed in Sandwich two or three times that 'the King might be brought up in chains to the Parliament'.[83] Amongst Edwards's other targets in Kent were John Saltmarsh, a Yorkshire independent who had been made rector of Brasted in Kent in 1644. Edwards accused Saltmarsh of covering up the preaching of one of his followers, a female lay preacher, who met other women in order to preach and expound biblical texts to them.[84] The strength of these gathered churches in Kent may well have persuaded the county committee not to press ahead with parliament's plans to introduce a Presbyterian system in Kent in 1646. These brief surveys of Herefordshire and Kent illustrate the central role played by preaching in the development of Civil War parties in the counties. In Herefordshire, where puritan preachers were a distinct minority, support for parliament was highly restricted and there was considerable enthusiasm for the royalist cause. In Kent, where puritan preaching had deeper and more diverse roots, support for parliament was consequently both stronger and more widely distributed.

As civil war became imminent, many of the cathedral and parish clergy throughout the English counties were actively engaged in preaching about the central issues of Civil War debate and they were naturally inclined to seek national solutions to these issues. Their sermons appealed not only to the 'Gentlemen and Schollers', whom Wilcock claimed as his supporters, but also to the 'mechanics and weavers', women, boys and

---

[82] *CJ*, 2, 671; Edwards, *The Second Part of Gangraena*, 175–6; Culmer (the younger), *A Parish Looking-Glasse*, 3.

[83] Edwards, *The Second Part of Gangraena*, 175; for Durant and Davis see Matthews, *Calamy Revised*, 158–9, 17; for Fisher see *DNB*.

[84] Edwards, *The Second Part of Gangraena*, 105–6,

children, whom he regarded as his enemies. Sermons were also one of the key ways in which information about the war and the issues surrounding it were conveyed into the provinces, along with the more general circulation of news both in print and by word of mouth. Some of the clergy undoubtedly argued for peace and reconciliation, but others helped to prepare their congregations for the breakdown of social ties, the violence and bloodshed, which were an inevitable part of civil war. The parliamentarian preachers in particular were concerned to demonstrate that the war was legitimate and to encourage men to fight for the parliamentarian cause. Preaching campaigns also helped to maintain high levels of religious and political tension in both urban and rural communities. As we have seen, sermons could also be the occasions for localised confrontations between the two sides. Above all, preaching helped to break down the reluctance both sides felt to embarking on civil warfare.

The reactions of contemporaries to hearing or reading sermons clearly emphasises the importance of preaching as a factor in sustaining Civil War allegiances throughout the First Civil War. Thus the parliamentarian supporters at Brampton Bryan claimed to be heavily influenced by 'godly ministers' and by the preaching of Stephen Marshall in particular. Similarly, Nehemiah Wharton described the preaching of army chaplains as highly influential. On hearing Obadiah Sedgewick preach at Worcester on the fast day in September 1642, Wharton concluded that 'his doctrine wrought wonderfully upon many of us, and doubtless hath fitted many of us for death, which we all shortly expect'.[85] Sermons, with their ultimate focus on the life of the soul after death, were able to reconcile current issues of political and religious principle with the promise of eternal salvation for those who stood up for God's cause. No other form of contemporary political discourse could make the same claim nor went so far in overcoming the individual's natural inhibitions for civil war.

[85] PRO, SP16/492/28.

Popularity

The people's love: the Duke of Buckingham and popularity

Thomas Cogswell

Early in the 1630s, the spectre of the Duke of Buckingham began troubling the sleep of Mr Towson. These visitations were not polite social calls, for Charles I's murdered favourite repeatedly delivered the same message. So insistent were these dreams that in 1634, Buckingham's old retainers arranged an audience with the duke's young son. Then through this spirit medium, Buckingham advised his heir 'how he should carry himselfe to regayne the People's love and wynne the Parliament'.[1]

Buckingham's advice seems improbable. The impressive and rapidly expanding body of work on European 'minister-favourites' has illuminated much about how these early modern phenomena manoeuvered at court, but none of it suggests that popularity was high on any favourite's list of priorities. Buckingham does not seem a logical exception to this general rule. Between a flamboyant lifestyle and a lengthy list of amours, which may have included James I, Buckingham would have been a public relations nightmare in puritan England. He could, moreover, have done little to correct the situation; as he confessed to the 1625 parliament, he had no illusions about 'my own weakness', possessing 'neither rhetoric not art'. Nor would he let others help him overcome these defects. While the Elizabethan Earl of Essex was fond of issuing public explanations, Buckingham was not. Indeed, when someone offered to draft one, the duke 'refused with a pretty kinde of thankfull scorn, saying that he would trust his own good intentions which God knew'. Even when accused of poisoning James I, he still refused, since 'he saw no fruit of Apologies but the multiplying of discourse'. Such an Olympian attitude to public relations, Sir Henry Wotton noted, went with being a royal favourite who knew all too well 'that naturall Incompatibility, which in the experience of

---

[1] BL, Harleian MS 7056, fo. 34v.

all Ages hath been noted between the Vulgar and the Soveraign Favour'.[2] In short, popularity, like the relief of La Rochelle and the maintenance of a dignified lifestyle, seems well beyond Buckingham's powers.

Yet in this regard, as in so much else about this protean figure, it is rash to underestimate the duke. Plainly at the end of his life, Buckingham was a serious public relations liability, whom some reviled as the 'Duke of Fuckingham'. Yet a few years earlier, the populace had lionised him as 'St George on horseback'. Furthermore, the careful calibration of his popular standing at any given moment can obscure a more important point. Once he shifted from favourite to public minister in 1624, Buckingham became obsessed with his public image. Wotton's recollection notwithstanding, his thoughts rarely wandered far from improving it, and in light of his periodic triumphs, his professed lack of 'rhetoric and art' should best be ascribed to polite modesty. His constant pursuit of popularity is even more fascinating, given its comparative novelty. Monarchs periodically attempted to woo the public, and the Tudors proved particularly adept at political theatre. Yet such grandstanding was much more unusual from a favourite. Wotton rightly argued that the Elizabethan Earl of Essex was the prototype for Buckingham. Both men were fond of sprawling their figures across canvases and of hearing scholars and clerics praise their genius and piety; both were given to flamboyant gestures; and both courted popularity. Yet the contrasts are equally striking. Essex never occupied centre stage in the parliament-house, a venue where Buckingham regularly performed. Likewise, when Essex attempted to launch a publicity campaign to celebrate his triumph at Cadiz, the Privy Council scuttled the idea; Buckingham had fewer restraints in this regard, or indeed in any others. In short, while Buckingham ultimately failed as a statesman, his public relations efforts are well worth attention, for he was able to develop a series of political experiments, which had fascinated Essex a generation earlier.

This essay examines Buckingham's attitude to the public, and it analyses the various means by which he attempted to fashion popular opinion. In the end, it will become plain that the only thing odd about the 1634 scene was Mr Towson's involvement: Buckingham on his own had long brooded over how best 'to regayne the People's love and wynne the Parliament'.

---

[2] M. Jansson and W. Bidwell (eds.), *Proceedings in Parliament 1625*, (New Haven, 1987) 433–4; Henry Wotton, *Reliquiae Wottonianae* (1651, ESTC R109190), 25, 92. See also J. H. Elliott and L. W. B. Brockliss (eds.), *The World of the Favorite*, (New Haven, 1999).

I

Conspicuous consumption was far from the only concern of a Jacobean favorite, who soon acquired a host of decidedly unglamorous duties. Favourites resolved squabbles among feuding courtiers; they relayed diplomatic overtures; and above all else, they screened the suitors who thronged about the king. Admittedly their duties allowed them to assist friends, but generally only after dribbling favours across a broad range of courtiers. Their prominence moreover was profoundly site-specific. Within the court, these favourites occupied centre stage; outside of it, they hovered with the supporting cast in the wings. Quite simply, a ruler as experienced and as loquacious as James I had no need for help with the public. Amid these duties, a favourite had to find time for his education, a task which James personally took in hand. The gregarious old man enjoyed instructing a succession of young men in the finer points of statecraft and theology. The last of these was George Villiers, who rocketed from obscurity in Leicestershire to the peerage, swiftly reaching his apogee as Duke of Buckingham. His ascent corresponding with the outbreak of the Thirty Years War, young George's tutorials included extended digressions on the dangers of popularity and on the necessity of preserving the *arcana imperii*.[3]

Once war erupted, James sought a diplomatic solution and a Spanish bride for Prince Charles. Yet a growing number of his subjects regarded this policy as a Habsburg ploy to forestall English intervention overseas and to subvert the Church of England at home. Ministers warned that if England did not assist their continental brethren, then 'the Curse of Meroz may light upon us' by which 'we and ours may be destroyed'. Pundits meanwhile mocked James's Great Britain, which was 'a great deal less than Little England was wont to be'. Such pointed criticism brought back potent memories of James's struggle for control of the kirk and Scotland. In 1598, he had cautioned his heir against 'some fierie spirited men in the ministerie', who 'begouth to fantasie to themselves a Democraticke forme of government'. From these revelries, it was only a short step to naming themselves 'tribuni plebis; and so in a popular government by leading the people by the nose, to beare the sway of all the rule'. In due course, James established control, but the fear of

---

[3] Roger Lockyer, *Buckingham* (1981), 28–9 and 38–40; I. A. A. Thompson, 'The institutional background to the rise of the minister-favorite', in Elliott and Brockliss, *The World of the Favorite*, 13–25. See also Neil Cuddy, 'The Revival of the Entourage', in D. Starkey (ed.), *The English Court* (1987), 172–225.

another Calvinistic challenge never left him. In 1616, he again warned against the 'new Puritanicall straines, that makes all things popular' and against ambitious gentlemen who 'cannot be content with the present forme of Government but must have a kind of libertie in the people, and must be gracious Lords, and Redeemers of their libertie'. Spotting these rebels was easy enough, given their fondness for giving 'a snatch against a Monarchie, through their Puritanicall itching after Popularitie'. Consequently, when a crisis developed after 1618, James reverted to this well-established mode of thought. In 1620, for instance, he issued a public reminder: since 'matters of state . . . are no Theames, or subjects fit for vulgar persons or common meetings', everyone, 'from the highest to the lowest', should 'take heede, how they intermeddle by Penne, or Speech, with causes of State, and secrets of Empire, either at home, or abroad'.[4]

These restrictions also applied to parliament-men, and in 1621, when they urged James to end the Spanish Match, his response verged on the Pavlovian. As parliament-men shaded into 'the Puritan Ministers in Scotland', who brought 'all kinde of causes within the compasse of theire iurisdiction', James perceived his bugbears, 'some Tribunitiall Orators', eager to 'usurpe upon Our Prerogative Royall and meddle with things farre above your reach'. Unfortunately, his resolute response led first to a parliamentary confrontation and then a rancorous dissolution. In the resulting crisis, opponents and defenders of James's policy quarrelled in manuscript and in print. Once Charles and Buckingham rode into Spain disguised as Jack and Tom Smith, James himself entered the fray, imploring his subjects to 'remitt the Care to Royall Pan / of Jacke his sonne and Tom his man'.[5]

Buckingham learned his lesson well, but the king's policy about popularity, while clear and concise, was nonetheless awkward. At the best of times, the public responded coolly to a *privado* who necessarily did nothing to restrain James's financial and moral exuberance. Yet as the crisis intensified, Buckingham's public image deteriorated, and when critics chided James, they excoriated the favourite and his family as crypto-Catholic hispanophiles and moral degenerates. Amid the shower of abuse, the recollection of Bacon's earlier advice only made him more uneasy; he

[4] Thomas Gataker, *A Sparke toward the Kindling of Sorrow* (1621, ESTC 102988), 37–8; W. Scott (arr.), *Somers Tracts . . .*, 13 vols. (1809–15), II, 473; J. P. Sommerville (ed.), *The Political Writings of James I* (Cambridge, 1994), 26, 219, 222; P. L. Hughes and J. F. Larkin (eds.), *Stuart Proclamations*, 2 vols. (Oxford, 1973–83), I, 496. See also T. Cogswell, 'England and the Spanish Match', in R. Cust and A. Hughes (eds.), *Conflict in Early Stuart England* (Harlow, 1989), 107–133.

[5] Sommerville, *Political Writings of James I*, 255–7, 259; J. Craigie (ed.), *The Poems of King James VI* (Edinburgh, 1958), 192–3.

might at any time 'be offered as a sacrifice to appease the multitude'. His unpopularity was equally apparent in the parliament-house. The 1621 session had scarcely begun before Buckingham was struggling to elude an anti-corruption dragnet, which netted comparative small fry like Sir Giles Mompesson before entangling Buckingham's sibling and ultimately the favourite himself. Before evading this potential disaster, another loomed with an investigation of the Irish revenues, from which Buckingham had handsomely profited. Meanwhile, unflattering comments rained down; the intent of Sir Hamon L'Estrange's exhortation, 'away with Achitopells', was just as plain as Sir Henry Yelverton's comparison of Buckingham to Edward II's notorious favourite, Sir Hugh Despencer. Buckingham eventually revealed that he was 'parliament-proof', but only after enduring constant reminders of his unpopularity.[6]

This painful experience underscored the lot of a Jacobean favourite. These 'mushrooms' were unnatural creations, and once outside of the court hot-house where they had been bred, they rapidly languished. This stark fact made it appropriate that in Buckingham's first eight years at James's side, his finest performance before a large audience came in 1621. He appeared, not in the Palace of Westminster in his parliament robes, but at his country house dressed as a gypsy. Courtiers in similarly absurd garb then praised him as that 'Glory of ours, and grace of all the earth'. They celebrated neither his wisdom nor his virtue, but simply

> How well your figure doth become your birth,
> As if your form and fortune equal stood.

For his part, Buckingham leapt about, extolling 'James the Just', who achieved his ends 'By peace, and not by human slaughter'. The highlight came went he addressed his master, asking:

> May your goodness ever find
> In me, whom you have made, a mind
> As thankfull as your own is large.[7]

International peace and personal pleasure have rarely sounded better together. Yet with his outgoing manner and growing command of issues,

---

[6] 'Advice to Buckingham', in James Spedding *et al.* (eds.), *The Works of Francis Bacon* (1874), VI, 14; Wallace Notestein (ed.), *Commons Debates 1621* (New Haven, 1935) V, 272; VI, 395. See also Victor Treadwell, *Buckingham and Ireland, 1616–1628* (Dublin, 1998), 148–85.

[7] Ben Jonson, *The Gypsies Metamorphosed*, in Stephen Orgel, *The Complete Masques of Ben Jonson* (New Haven, 1969), 330, 370. For a penetrating analysis of the play as 'a reassuring display of submission', see Martin Butler, '"We are One Mans All": Jonson's *Gypsies Metamorphosed*', *Yearbook of English Studies*, 21 (1991), 253–73.

the favourite was eager for a more substantial role. James, however, was not. Consequently he had his handsome gypsy prance about him on two other occasions.

II

There was another kind of favourite, which the Earl of Essex had been perfecting when Elizabeth brought him up short. Patron of the godly and Protestant champion, Essex had enjoyed such popularity that Elizabeth became apprehensive. By 1596, Francis Bacon was recommending a dangerous balancing act: while the earl publicly courted popular favour, he also had 'to take all occasions, to the Queen, to speak against popularity and popular causes vehemently; and to tax it in all others'. These details could hardly have eluded Buckingham, surrounded as he was with Essex protégés from his father-in-law, the Earl of Rutland, to his clients, Lord Brooke, Sir John Coke, Sir Robert Naunton and Bacon himself. These memories became critically important in 1623 as Buckingham assumed a leading role in Prince Charles's 'new romance'.[8] What began in February 1623 as a lark with two friends riding out of the country in false beards ended a year later with Buckingham standing up before the parliament-men.

The disintegration of the Spanish Match precipitated Buckingham's metamorphosis from court favourite to chief minister. While James clung to diplomatic solutions, no matter how humiliating, Charles and the duke organised a broad 'patriot' coalition with influential but hitherto awkward peers and parliament-men. They then hoped to persuade a majority to vote a generous supply, which in turn would satisfy James's objections. While sympathetic surrogates could shepherd along the doubtful, they were hopeless at critical moments which demanded a firm lead from the top. James, however, was psychologically unable to handle this part, and Charles's speech impediment limited him to a supporting role. Bacon, meanwhile was urging the duke forward: since 'in the opinion of the people you are green,' he urged him to 'fix and bind in the reputation what you have gained' and to perform 'some remarkable thing ... whereby the world might have taken notice'.[9] To break this impasse, Buckingham stood up before parliament on 24 February 1624.

[8] Spedding et al., Works of Francis Bacon, IX, 44. See also Paul Hammer, The Polarisation of Elizabethan Politics: the Political Career of Robert Devereux, and Earl of Essex, 1585–1597 (Cambridge, 1999).
[9] Spedding et al., Works of Francis Bacon, XIV, 444–5, 447. See also T. Cogswell, The Blessed Revolution: English Politics and the Coming of War, 1621–1624 (Cambridge, 1989), 57–134.

The duke conceded 'how unusuall it was for him to speake in so great and iudicious an Auditory'. In fact, not only had no other Jacobean favourite delivered such an address, but many backwoodsmen had never even heard the celebrated favourite's voice. He ensured that his listeners paid careful attention. With the outbreak of war, many contemporaries had become news junkies. It was a frustrating addiction; while diplomats and couriers regularly hurried across the realm, they could only guess at the contents of the dispatches.[10] On 24 February, however, Buckingham ushered the parliament-men into the *arcana imperii*, presenting not just glosses, but actual texts. Not surprisingly, while his listeners' hands were weary from transcribing such a long address, the atmosphere in the room was euphoric.

Most common assumptions, the duke announced, were incorrect, especially about himself. Although long scorned as a Habsburg stooge, he had in fact been a double agent eager to ferret out secret Spanish designs, and after many adventures, he at last reported success: Charles now plainly 'saw his Fathers Negotiations plainely deluded, Matters of Religion gained uppon and extorted, [and] his Sister's Case more and more desperate'. Even more astonishing revelations followed. Against relentless pressure to convert, Buckingham 'shewed himselfe resolute', and his obstinacy flummoxed the Spanish bishops who thought James had 'graunted as much in effect as a Tolleration'. Charles responded by denouncing them as 'Beastes and Blinde and could not read their own language', much less Latin. Buckingham offered a cooler explanation; James had simply granted 'a temporary Suspension of Penall Lawes', not a formal toleration which would require the 'Consent of Parliament'. Therefore, 'if his Highnesse had bin of my Lord Bishopps opinion that these Conveniences had mounted to a Tolleration, he had never accepted of these articles to have gayned any alliance in the universall World'. When Gondomar himself insisted that James *had* agreed to a toleration, Buckingham delivered the lie direct; 'he had bin acquainted with the Treaty from the beginning and yet never heard word fall to that purpose'. This exchange, which the Spaniards took 'very offensively', forced a radical reassessment of their opinion of Buckingham. Although the favourite had seemed a Catholic, just 'like his kindred', these adroit diplomats concluded that they themselves had been duped; Buckingham

[10] HEHL, HM 807, fo. 2. See R. Cust, 'News and politics in early seventeenth century England, *P&P*, 101 (1986), 60–90; for an alternate view, I. Atherton '"The itch grown a disease": manuscript transmission of news in the seventeenth century', in J. Raymond (ed.), *News, Newspapers and Society in Early Modern Britain* (London, 1999), 38–65.

was in fact 'a most obstinate, perverse and refractory Puritan'. The favourite's emergence as a Protestant champion begged a vital question – who was responsible for nearly tucking Charles into bed with the Infanta? Thoughtfully, the favourite fingered the Earl of Bristol, the ambassador in Madrid, as the Spanish mole within the English negotiating team.[11]

In the end, Buckingham modestly insisted that 'if the bringing us from Darkness to light did deserve any thankes, wee owe it and must wholly ascribe it to the Prince'. But the audience could not help applauding the favourite's *tour de force* performance. 'There have ben,' one observer noted, 'such things discovered and delivered that passed in Spaine which never came hitherto to any mens knowledge out of that sanctuarie.' Buckingham's liberality with documents seduced even the wariest parliament-man, for 'in every pointe, to cleere himselfe from slander and partiallity, he shewes all such letters as had passed betweene his Maiestie and the Kinge of Spaine'. For the first time in his career, Buckingham was 'infinitely applauded', and his address quickly became a *de rigueur* item for separate collections. He found himself 'the Darling of the Multitude', while the parliament-men 'would scarce be contained from acknowledging him the Preserver of the Nation'.[12] If anyone had overlooked his performance, the Spanish ambassadors promptly highlighted it by demanding that Buckingham deserved the axe for slander. One parliament-man responded that the Spaniards 'were loathe that any honest Lord's head should stand on his shoulders'; a second hoped to see '1000 of their heads on the ground and his [Buckingham's] to stand'; and a third proclaimed that 'never any man deserved better of his King and country'. In short order, Buckingham found himself lauded as 'the Princes and peoples Favourite'.[13] The lavish praise for the 'peoples Favourite' continued for months. On 3 March, he returned to the parliamentary centre stage to outline Spanish plans to dominate the entire continent; on 15 March, he publicly softened the king's more

---

[11] HEHL, HM 897, fos. 4v, 7–7v, 9v.

[12] *Ibid.*, fo. 12; BL, Trumbull MSS VII/150 and 151, Beaulieu to Trumbull, 27 Feb and 5 March 1624; Trumbull MSS XLVIII/114, Castle to [same], 28 Feb 1624; Arthur Wilson, *The History of Great Britain* (1652, ESTC 38664), 264. On the circulation of the narration, see Bedfordshire and Luton Archives and Records Service, St John of Bletsoe MSS J 1272–3; Hampshire RO, Jervoise MSS, O6 unfoliated; Centre for Kentish Studies, Knatchbull MSS U951/O10/11; Chester RO, Davenport Commonplace Book, CR 63/2/19, fos. 37–9. In light of the BL's ongoing reorganisation of the Trumbull MSS, all references to these items refer to the old cataloguing system.

[13] Samuel Clarke, *The Lives of Thirty-Two English Divines* (1677), 98; Houghton Library, English MS 980, 35; Lockyer, 181–2.

awkward demands; and on 17 April, he described the first steps towards military intervention. By then, he had warmed to the new role as he badgered James for permission to present yet more secret dispatches to the Commons. All of this only confirmed his new status; 'whereas he was before a Favourite to the King, he is now', James Howell observed, 'a Favourite to Parliament, People and City'.[14]

Contemporaries soon learned of Buckingham's stunning transformation. They read tracts in which celebrated controversialists like John Reynolds praised ' the thrice Noble Duke' and Thomas Scott exclaimed, 'God will blesse thee and establish thy house forever.' They sang ballads heralding the duke as someone who 'hath done more / Then twenty favorites have done before'. They pressed into the Globe to see Middleton's dramatisation of Buckingham's narration. And they delighted in prints which displayed the duke triumphant over 'Briberie' and 'Faction'. 'The eyes of this people', a contemporary observed at the end of the session, 'could not be more fixed on a Meteor then they have been upon the motions of the Duke.'[15] Without any doubt, this was the zenith of Buckingham's career.

III

A year later Buckingham again stood before parliament recalling the 'honor and happiness' which he had received when 'I had the honor to be applauded by you'. Since he had 'the same heart to speak with and the same cause to speak in and the same persons to speak unto, I have no doubt of the same success and approbation'. Yet this time the outcome was different, and only a hasty dissolution saved the duke from censure. As the attacks increased in 1626, the duke was perplexed. 'How well', he told his fellow peers, 'I stood in their opinions not long since your Lordships know, and what I have done since to lose their opinions I protest I know not.' Charles was equally baffled, given that in 1624 'there was nobody in so great favor with you as this man whom you seem now to persecute'.[16] Yet the explanation for his sudden unpopularity,

---

[14] NLS, Denmilne MSS 33.1, no. 62; James Howell, *Familiar Letters* (1890), 213; Cogswell, *The Blessed Revolution*, 181, 198, 242–5.

[15] [John Reynolds], *Votivae Angliae* (Utrecht, 1624, ESTC 117031), [sig. *Iiv]; [Thomas Scott], *Vox Dei*, reprinted in *Vox Populi Vox Dei Vox Regis* (n.p., [1624], ESTC 116997), 74; Beinecke Lib, Osborn b197, 225; BL, Trumbull MSS, XVIII/122, Castle to Trumbull, 11 June 1624. See also T. Cogswell, 'Thomas Middleton and the court, 1624: *A Game at Chess* in context,' *HLQ*, 48 (1984), 273–88.

[16] Jansson and Bidwell, *Proceedings in Parliament 1625*, 434–5; M. Jansson and W. Bidwell (eds.), *Proceedings in Parliament 1626*, 4 vols. (New Haven, 1991) II, 395.

while involved, is quite comprehensible. The thunderous applause in 1624 could not drown out discordant noises, the loudest of which came from Whitehall. Although the ensuing incident only fleetingly occupied the public and failed to dislodge Buckingham, it nevertheless proved a grave crisis which significantly altered his relations with James I and the public.

By April 1624, the tide was fast running out on pro-Spaniards at court. Lord Treasurer Middlesex was up on corruption charges; Bristol was entangled in treason allegations; and the Spanish ambassadors could not break Buckingham's hold over James. Yet this moment of apparent triumph left the duke highly vulnerable, for as Buckingham performed the impossible and mastered parliament, James's misgivings became increasingly obvious. Consequently in April, when the Spanish envoys secured a private audience, they knew precisely how to gain the old monarch's attention. The favourite's clients allegedly kept James 'closed up'. Meanwhile, Buckingham 'had reconciled himself to all the popular men of the state ... whom he met at Suppers and Ordinaries to strengthen his popularity'. To them, he 'hath oftentimes brag'd openly in Parliament, that had made the King yield to this and that'. Hence a 'triumviri' actually ruled the kingdom, 'whereof Buckingham was the first and chiefest, the Prince second, and the King the last'. Soon there would be little room for James unless he could break free 'from this Captivity' and punish 'so dangerous and ungrateful an affecter of greatnesse and popularity, as the Duke was'. This analysis reduced James to mumbling that 'he could not believe yet that he affected popularity to his disadvantage'; after all, Buckingham 'was not popular'.[17] The duke, in response, protested his innocence before collapsing into bed for several crucial weeks. Having discredited him, the duke's opponents then sought to replace him as they paraded Mr Brett, Middlesex's comely young brother-in-law, before James. The fate of the kingdom – and the favourite – then wavered in the balance.

The crisis soon subsided. Both the prince and the parliament-men defended Buckingham, while the old king and his ailing favourite were eventually reconciled. The Spanish ambassadors, having blotted their diplomatic copybook, abandoned their clients and left town. Yet the heavy casualties notwithstanding, the counter-attack had one lasting consequence; it prompted James to reassert himself. For the preceding six

[17] *Cabala* (1654, ESTC 21971), 91–2. See also Robert Ruigh, *The Parliament of 1624* (Cambridge, Mass., 1971), 257–302.

months, James had largely ceded authority to his son and favourite; after the Spanish accusations, he insisted on having the last word. A private letter from Buckingham during his convalescence to James illustrated the new arrangement. First, the favourite praised the king for having 'no consete of my popularitie'; 'otherwis,' he asked, 'whie should you thus studie to indere me with the upper and loer howse of parlement and so consequentlie with your whole kingdome'. The entire situation shifted when the duke advanced an unusual definition of popularity: 'were not onelie all your people but all the world besids sett together on one side, and you alone on the other, I should to obey and please you displeas nay dispise all them, and this shalbe ever my popularitie'.[18] Such compliant language renders more comprehensible James's decision to set his face against Mr Brett and the Habsburg envoys.

The duke shortly returned to classic form, immersing himself in a host of delicate high-level negotiations. Yet James, having secured Buckingham's obedience, repeatedly exercised *his* prerogative, and these object lessons, which Buckingham often found exceedingly frustrating, only ended as the king finally lost consciousness in March 1625. James blocked efforts to purge Spanish sympathisers; he scuttled Buckingham's plans to set out a massive fleet; he volunteered English vessels to help Louis XIII repress the French Protestants; and his scrupulous politeness actually improved Anglo–Spanish relations over the winter of 1624–5. Count Mansfelt's multi-national expedition was the centrepiece of the duke's new bellicose policy, but James lumbered it with so many peculiar restrictions that the force quickly consumed 15,000 men, £200,000 and all hope of even modest success. Finally, although Buckingham had initially pressed for a French Match, James insisted on concluding it even after the French price soared to levels which were domestically disastrous. Thus, a few weeks before James's death, the Bohemian ambassador was astonished to find Buckingham concluding an agreement with earnest pleas 'de ne parler des affaires avec Sa Majeste'. Plainly, the duke's bravado notwithstanding, 'il faut que l'on se conforme a l'honneur et a la volonte du Roi'.[19]

This situation left Buckingham in a profoundly awkward position, for in the last year of James's life, his actual authority was less than it appeared to be. Thus, many in 1625 held him wholly responsible for a host of questionable decisions ranging from the loan ships, the perilous state of

---

[18] NLS, Denmilne MSS 33.1.7, no. 88.
[19] J. J. von Rusdorff, *Memoires et négociations secrètes* (Leipzig, 1789) I, 531, 485. I will develop the importance of this struggle between James and Buckingham elsewhere.

the fleet and Mansfelt's expedition to the French Match, the Catholic toleration and the Arminian revival. This is not to suggest that Buckingham
was blameless in these affairs; rather it simply points out a bitter irony
about popularity. Thanks to his ability to manoeuvre James out of the
Spanish labyrinth, Buckingham enjoyed unprecedented popularity in
1624. But his triumph later made it impossible for him to disassociate
himself from James's string of final decisions. During his impeachment,
the duke bitterly lamented to the Earl of Clare that 'other mens action
were made his, and muche putt upon his score, when others were pec-
cant'. Clare's reply could serve as an epithet for all senior administrators
as well as for Buckingham: 'those that had power to do, were allways
thought to do what was done, were it good or bad'.[20]

IV

After the 1625 parliament, criticism of Buckingham mounted as the
public added the débâcles at Cadiz and Re, together with the Forced
Loan, to his score. At the same time, some of the duke's protégés urged
him to abandon the pursuit of popularity in favour of experiments in
prerogative taxation. These 'new counsels' tantalised Buckingham, but
never completely persuaded him. Notwithstanding successes like the
Forced Loan, the fact remained that it was impossible to imagine an
honourable end to the war effort without at least grudging popular and
parliamentary support. Therefore, he repeatedly strove to recover the
halcyon world when he had been 'the Favourite of God, his King, Prince
and Countrey'.[21]

   Given the extraordinary response to his Spanish narration,
Buckingham logically saw the path back to public favour through public addresses, and in 1625–6 he delivered three major and dozens of
minor speeches. Although in Clarendon's opinion hardly 'any great
Scholar', Buckingham was 'well Letter'd . . . in a naturall and proper
Dialect', and this characteristic was apparent in these speeches. No one
except Buckingham would have attempted to forestall impeachment by
genially insisting, 'Gentlemen, it is no time to pick quarrels one with another. We have enemies enough abroad.' Furthermore, since his liberality

---

[20] P. R. Seddon (ed.), *Letters of Holles 1587–1637*, 3 vols. (Thoroton Society Record Series, xxxi, xxxv, xxxvi, 1975–86), II, 330.
[21] George Marcelline, *Epithalamium Gallo-Britannicum* (1625 ESTC S111979), 39. On the 'new coun-sels', see R. Cust, *The Forced Loan and English Politics, 1626–1628* (Oxford, 1987), 27–36.

with the secrets of state helped explain his 1624 triumph, he was equally generous in his later outings. Indeed, his preferred genre was strategic *tours d'horizon*. In March 1626, for instance, he handled the dynamics of Dutch, Danish and Imperial politics, a disruptive French ambassador, coastal freebooters, both Mansfelt's and Wimbledon's expeditions as well as the recent Huguenot peace. Likewise, far from dismissing criticism, he carefully itemized the charges before refuting them. The one new element in his later addresses was an increasingly pathetic willingness to do whatever might bring back the balmy days of 1624. In 1625, he assured the parliament-men, 'I have not had a thought not an action but what might tend to the advancement of the business and to please your desires.' In March 1626, he was still eager to find a way that 'may repossess me of that I have accounted one of my greatest losses: their good opinions'. In April, he volunteered information which, 'he hopes might acquit and restore him to your good opinions'. In June, his answer to formal impeachment charges still included the declaration that 'it has been my study to keep a good correspondency between the King and his people'. Hence 'it remains in your hands to make me happy or not'.[22]

The duke was destined to be unhappy, and after the 1626 parliament, he abandoned any further grand addresses as the swift pace of events invariably overwhelmed his oratory. Any positive benefit from his 1625 address vanished amid a furore over a released Jesuit. His initial refutation of charges in March 1626 had no impact since almost daily 'new busines came in against the duke', and the most damaging of information came from Bristol, who offered a stunning alternative version of events in Madrid. Far from the stout Protestant champion, the duke in 1623 had allegedly shopped the prince and his faith to the Spaniards. By the time he answered these charges in June, the Commons had abandoned attempting to assign legal guilt; instead, its members just denounced him as 'so averse to the good and tranquillity of the church and state that we verily believe him to be an enemy to both'.[23] Therefore, however much the duke enjoyed a large audience, his grand addresses were no longer effective.

This decision did not signal his acceptance of unpopularity; it simply marked a shifting emphasis from speechifying to print and manuscript.

---

[22] Earl of Clarendon, *The Character of Robert Earl of Essex . . . and George Duke of Buckingham* (1706, ESTC T53988), 30; Jansson and Bidwell, *Proceedings in Parliament 1625*, 435; *Proceedings in Parliament 1626*, II, 405, 409; III, 58; I, 565.

[23] NLW, MS 9061 E/1402; Jansson and Bidwell, *Proceedings in Parliament 1626*, III, 440–1.

Welcome support came from the literary circle around Bishop Corbet, which kept up a steady counter-battery fire on the pot-poets vilifying the duke in popular doggerels. Likewise, the duke's entourage effectively used the burgeoning manuscript market to answer Dr Eglisham's lurid account of James's death. He had less luck with print culture. Thomas Scott, who had proven so useful in 1624, was murdered in 1626. Some whispered that the duke had ordered the assassination in order to forestall a literary attack on him, but Scott's last work proven a mundane, albeit uplifting, sermon on perseverance. Middleton soon joined Scott in the grave without penning a sequel to his 1624 sensation, *A Game at Chess*. The duke had no problem getting John Reynolds, another of the 1624 controversialists, to write a stirring pro-war tract for the 1628 parliament. Unfortunately the result proved unprintable, when Reynolds called for the eradication of the Arminian faction. Catholic intellectuals of course offered unwavering support, but in 1627, Edmund Bolton doubtless did nothing to increase Buckingham's following by dedicating a strident defense of Nero to the favourite.[24]

In short, while Buckingham's advocates defended him in both print and manuscript, none ever managed to seize popular attention. At the same time, the regime had successfully launched a formidable preaching campaign in aid of the Forced Loan.[25] These developments, together with a growing sense of desperation, prompted the duke to attempt one of the great novelties in early modern public relations. In 1627, he decided to stage-manage a military campaign with himself cast as the valiant warlord.

V

The continental crisis spawned the first corantos, which had by 1621 spread to London. Whitehall, although profoundly ambivalent, eventually permitted a private consortium to issue a newsbook, provided it contained no domestic coverage. But some within Whitehall wanted to exploit, not curb, these early periodicals. Early in the 1620s, Sir Thomas

[24] J. A. W. Bennett and H. R. Trevor-Roper (eds.), *The Poems of Richard Corbett* (Oxford, 1955); Folger Shakespeare Library, V.a. 402, fos. 68v–70; Thomas Scott, *Josephs Flight Out of Aegypt* (Amsterdam, 1635 ESTC S96179); John Reynolds, 'Regalytie and obedyence'. BL Add. MS 24,201, fo. 26; Philonactophil [Edmund Bolton], *Nero Caesar, or Monarchie Depraved* (1627, ESTC S107107).
[25] Cust, *The Forced Loan*, 62–5. On the duke's efforts to defend himself, see Cogswell, 'Underground verse and the transformation of early Stuart political culture', in S. Amussen and M. Kishlansky (eds.), *Political Culture and Cultural Politics in Early Modern England* (Manchester, 1995), 277–300.

Wilson proposed a government-friendly coranto 'to raise the spirrits of the People and to quieten ther conceipts and understanding'. Across the continent 'the ploughman and artisan can talke of thes matters and make both benefitt and recreation by knowing them'; hence Whitehall was foolish to ignore the possibilities of news-sheets. Therefore, Wilson would create 'a reddy way wherby to disperse into all the veynes of the whole body of a state such matter as may best temper it and be made agreeable to the disposition of the head or the principall members'. Consequently the regime would have

a way that when ther shalbe any revolt or back slyding in matter of religion or obedience (which commonly growes upon rumors amongst the vulgar) to drawe them in by the same lynes that drew them out by spreading amongst them such reportes as may best [be] made for that matter to which we wold have them drawne.[26]

Unfortunately, Wilson's proposal fell foul of James's opposition to any popular interest in politics. Yet by early 1627, Buckingham's desperation drove him to revive Wilson's plan.

Raison d'état might well have persuaded Charles I to wink while Louis XIII broke the autonomous Huguenot community. After all, the sooner Louis established control at home, the sooner he could intervene in the anti-Habsburg struggle abroad. Yet the domestic cost of such a policy was too grim to contemplate. In 1626, Charles had sworn to protect the Huguenots after English loan ships had unexpectedly weakened them in the previous year. Indifference to La Rochelle's fate therefore would have utterly discredited the Caroline regime. Alternatively, military intervention on behalf of the Huguenots allowed Buckingham to pose as a Protestant champion and possibly to regain his lost popularity. Consequently, in late June 1627, Buckingham led 7,000 English troops ashore at the Ile de Re a few miles from La Rochelle.[27] There, he took extraordinary steps to maximise the political advantage of this action.

Once ashore, Buckingham issued *A Manifestation* declaring 'the intent of these Armes is no other but onely for the good of the Churches, which ... he [Charles] findes himselfe obliged before God and men to protect and succour'. After the Huguenots were secure, then 'these Drummes beating, these displayed Ensignes shalbe shut up again, and

---

[26] PRO, SP 14/124/113.
[27] S. L. Adams, 'The road to La Rochelle', *Huguenot Society Proceedings* (1975); T. Cogswell, 'Prelude to Re: the Anglo-French struggle over La Rochelle, *Hist.*, 62 (1986), 1–21.

all this noyse of Warre shall remaine in night and silence'. In addition
to this melodramatic opening, the duke sought to thrust the expedition
into public view. First, a bouncy song compared the duke to Edward III
and Henry V before wondering if it 'may bee his chance to conquer
all France' and so 'through the world be renowned'. For the higher end
of the literary market, there was Michael Drayton's cheerfully franco-
phobic *The Battaile of Agincourt*; the mere report that 'the English Armies
are return'd againe', the poet argued, would make the French confess
that 'Our conquered Fathers . . . / Quake in their Graves to feele them
landed here.' Then a broadside, replete with Buckingham in the guise
of a heroic knight, carefully listed the ships, the regiments and the com-
manders. The curious could also buy a map of the island, depicting the
Citadel where Buckingham had bottled up a French garrison. Finally,
Buckingham asked for the realm's prayers as well as its attention. For
several months, congregations prayed for God 'to goe forth with our
Armie' and 'to bring safety to this Kingdome, strength and comfort to
Religion, and victory and reputation to our Countrey'.[28] The contrast
with earlier expeditions was startling. When Mansfelt and Wimbleton
had earlier led nearly 30,000 men out of the country, a nearly complete
official silence engulfed them. In the summer of 1627, however, everyone including Wilson's 'ploughman and artisan' was urged to regard the
expedition, to pray for the men and to follow their exploits on a map.

   This effort, while impressive, did nothing to address the serious issue
of motivation, for the duke's *Manifestation* left unanswered precisely why
in the middle of a Spanish war Buckingham opened another front in
France. To correct this omission, Secretary Coke produced a brilliant
popular account of the expedition's diplomatic background. At first,
Charles approved it for publication, but almost immediately he asked the
council to ratify his action. In the end, the councillors declined publishing
a tract designed simply for 'the satisfaction of the people and foren states,
who happily wil bee as sufficiently satisfied with the successe of the action,
as they can bee with woords'.[29] Yet the government's position must be
clearly understood; while it was averse to an public explanation of the

---

[28] *A Manifestation, or Remonstrance* (1627, ESTC 119127), 6, 8, 9; 'A Song', in F. W. Fairholt (ed.),
   Poems and Songs Relating to . . . Buckingham (1850), 13–4; *A Catalogue of all the Kings Ships* (1627 ESTC
   247465); *A True and Perfect Description of . . . the Isle of Ree* (1627, ESTC S3372); *A Prayer to be used . . .
   as long as His Maiesties Navie and forces are abroade* ([1627], ESTC S122717). See also T. Cogswell,
   'The path to Elizium "lately discovered": Drayton and the early Stuart court', *HLQ*, 54 (1991),
   210 *et seq.*
[29] PRO, SP 16/72/48. See also Cogswell, 'The politics of propaganda: Charles I and the people in
   the 1620s', *JBS*, 29 (1990), 187–215.

expedition's motives, it was quite willing to approve rousing accounts of the expedition's progress.

By 1627, Nathaniel Butter and Nicholas Bourne had established a successful partnership, bringing out two or three issues of *Mercurius Britanicus* each month. To the delight of many at court, Ben Jonson and other authors mocked these early newsbooks. Yet with its French invasion, the government decided to imitate Butter and Bourne. Once on the island, Buckingham's protégés like Henry De Vic, Robert Mason, Richard Graham, Richard Oliver and Thomas Fotherly began sending back detailed dispatches. It is now unclear whether the authors realised that they were writing copy, but their colleagues in Whitehall, most notably Edward Nicholas, were certainly eager to put a positive spin on the expedition.[30] In August, visitors in Thomas Walkley's shop spotted a highly unusual item – *A Iournall* 'Published by Authoritie' offering the public 'all the Proceedings of the Duke of Buckingham his Grace, in the Isle of Ree'. Such was the demand that it went into a second edition. Hard on the heels of this sensation came *A Continued Iournall of All the Proceedings of the Duke of Buckingham . . . until this 17. Of August*. Butter and Bourne cannot have been pleased; it boasted a variant on their title, *The Continuation of Our Weekly Newes,* and it borrowed their practice of placing a date on the title page to distinguish between issues. The government had effectively cloned their product.

The reportage presented an engaging picture of the troops and their general 'In Whom are combined Religion, Fortitude and Clemencie'. When the initial landing had met unexpectedly stiff French resistance, Buckingham had stiffened the troops by landing in the midst of a wavering regiment. In subsequent weeks, his diligence was as apparent as his valour. When the army moved, Buckingham marched 'in the foremost companies', and when it dined, the men ate well, thanks to his care that 'there was no want of any thing'. Likewise the general sought no personal exemption after he decided not to billet the army in the town of St Martins, lest it offend the inhabitants; therefore, as the soldiers settled down for the rainy night outdoors, they saw that Buckingham 'lay amongst them in the open Field, with no other bedding, save one cloake under his head, and another upon him'. Such leadership 'did so animate the Souldiers that I have hard many of the Souldiers wish that the French would stand one Encounter, that they might shew their love

---

[30] PRO, SP 16/73/102 and 16/75/16. See also Joad Raymond, *The Invention of the Newspaper* (Oxford, 1996), 1–19; Joseph Frank, *The Beginning of the English Newspaper* (Cambridge, 1961), 1–18; and Folke Dahl, *A Bibliography of English Corantos and Periodical Newsbooks 1620–1642* (1952).

unto theire Generall'. Until then, the men merely 'thanked God with a loude voyce that they had such a worthy Lord Generall'.[31]

Having pioneered this market, Butter and Bourne were understandably loathe to yield to a newcomer, no matter how well connected. Thus, by 1 August, *Mercurius Britanicus* began reporting on the expedition. The coverage was generally cursory and anodyne, offering late-breaking details like the interception of a French resupply effort or a thwarted assassination of Buckingham. Such a complex story did not readily fit in the coranto format, and for this reason, a week after the *Iournal* had caused a sensation, they followed with their own, *A True and Exact Relation of the most remarkable passages . . . in the Ile of Ree*. Given its upbeat tone, the tract cannot have seriously displeased the duke's handlers. 'My Lord Duke', it noted, 'hath gained a great deale of honour in this imployment', and he 'is loved and admired of all men for so many great and excellent parts'. Meanwhile, his men had invested the Citadel so tightly that 'a dogge cannot come into it'. Yet amid the buoyant news were unsettling notes. In spite of protestations that Buckingham had come to assist La Rochelle, the *Relation* let slip the embarrassing news that formally the Rochelois 'have not as yet made any open declarations' welcoming the duke. In addition, Butter and Bourne issued contradictory statements about the Citadel. In the *Relation*, the stubborn French defence was pronounced 'troublesone, and not onely hindered our designes, but maketh them likewise more difficult to effect.' Yet on 17 August, the *Mercurius* blandly announced that the Citadel 'is yielded up to the Duke his Grace'.[32] Coranto-makers famously reversed themselves in a few sentences, but with a topic this important, the regime would have appreciated if Butter and Bourne had got it right or, in the case of La Rochelle's allegiance, not mentioned it at all. In 1938, Laurence Hanson, a bibliographer, noted a series of newsbooks covering the Ré expedition and then wondered aloud if they might be related to 'a tightening of censorship'. Butter and Bourne would have gladly confirmed Hanson's suspicion.

In early August, the Privy Council confined Butter to a few days in the Gatehouse, and when he failed to absorb that object lesson, Secretary Conway intervened a month later. The editors were well aware of

---

[31] *A Iournall of All the Proceedings* (1627, ESTC S101789), 6–7; *A Continuued Iournal . . . until this 17 of August* (1627, ESTC S111523), 10–11. For the second edition of the *Iournal*, see ESTC S125564.

[32] *The Continuation of Our Weekely Newes*, 17 August (ESTC S101789), 5–6; *A True and Exact Relation of the most remarkable passages . . . in the Ile of Ree* (1627, ESTC S4441), 10–12; Laurence Hanson, 'English Newsbooks, 1620–1641', *The Library*, 4th series, 18 (1938), 374.

'his Maiesties dislike of the Libertie taken in printinge of weekly couran-
toes and pamphletts of newes without anie rule or warrant', and to
forestall any problems, Conway's servant was to approve each issue in
advance. Their excitement, however, led the editors to overlook this
restriction with the result that 'some things have ben lately published
for which his Maiestie hath iust cause of offense'. Therefore, Conway
warned the Stationers' Company that, although Butter served as a senior official that year, it had to have a closer eye on the newsbooks, lest
the government imposed further restrictions on printing. The full weight
of the government having landed, Dr Mede predicted that 'Currantes
wilbe scarce hereafter; for there hath a check bin given the Printers'. In
the event, the subsequent newsbooks were very cautious. The 3 October
issue, for example, contained a brief report that 'Our army are in very
good estate, being well provided of all necessities.' Beyond that, the
editors gave the island a wide berth. Yet when the government publishing operation expanded its remit to cover an Anglo–French naval
action off the Dutch coast and borrowed the title of Butter and Bourne's
suppressed newsbook – *A True and Most Exact Relation* – the editors could
not resist a dig at 'another unknowne Mercurie sprung up within these
few dayes'. Faithful readers of the *Mercurius* were urged to examine their
rival 'and compare him with the continuation of our weekly Newes'.[33]

Having silenced any unauthorised voices, Mr Walkley's operation 'by
Authoritie' cornered the popular demand for news, which it then milked
with four additional issues of the *Continued Iournall*. The results were predictable: the island was 'very rich'; 'the Country people' held a weekly
market selling 'Butter, Cheese and Fish'; and the troops 'have plenty of all
Provision'. The men themselves were in excellent physical condition, save
for excessive 'eating of Grapes and drinking of Wine, which agrees not
with English bodies as well as beere'. They 'are reputed as daring men as
any in the World', men who thought 'no labour too difficult, nor danger
too perillous, where the honour of their Countrey and their proper duty is
engaged.' Their high spirits only matched 'the Example of their Generall,
who cherisheth the valiant, incourageth the wavering, and punisheth
(though mildely) the slothfull and unactive Souldier'. He personally

33 *APC*, XLII/470; Trumbull MSS Misc XVIII/82, Conway to Master Warden *et al.*, 5 Sept 1627;
BL, Harleian MS 390, fo. 292; *The Continuation . . . to the 3 of October* (1627, ESTC S123702), [1], 7.
See also *A True and Most Exact Relation of the taking of . . . the Saint Espirit* (1627, ESTC S2936); and
D. F. MacKenzie, *Master Wardens and Liverymen of the Stationers' Company* (typescript deposited at
the Huntington Library).

'comforts them in their evening duties, and by visiting and relieving the
sicke and wounded, obligeth the hearts of his Soldiers unto him'. This
report, the editor conceded, might trouble some at home who 'either
affected to the French, or disaffected to his Excellencie' have 'made the
Siedge the subiect of their iests and table talke'. Against these 'malevolent'
spirits, the editor called for 'serene and more impartiall iudgements' to
consider the expedition, which was 'honorable, profitable and feasable,
being grounded upon the necessities of Policie and Religion'.[34]

Among contemporary letter-writers the impact of this PR campaign
was unmistakable. The careful assessment of the latest news was a passion with Dr Mede, and before he gave credence to a bleak report of
conditions on Ré, he noted 'the new Journall, published by authoritie,
October 2 telles it otherwise'. Equally popular was Mr Walkley's map; it
turned up at the dinner party in rural Suffolk where Rev. Rous wheeled
it out to silence a critic of the duke, and in Westminster, the Earl of
Clare pored over it with Buckingham's protégés. Yet arguably the greatest impact can be seen in the way in which the government spin found
unconscious echoes. In Oxford, Mr Crosfield noted the initial success
of the duke, 'a man in whome are combined Religion, fortitude and
Clemency', and in London, Clare found himself noting that the English
blockade of the Citadel was so tight 'a mouse can not creepe in'. The
steady drip of good news made even professional critics of the duke waver.
Scepticism, for instance, was Clare's first response to 'the Dukes hazan-
nas' which 'fill court and cuntry'. Nevertheless 'the gazetts and ballets'
soon prompted him to ponder whether with 'the first frutes of tollerable
success . . . the wynd [had] altered'. Hence Buckingham's brother was
only somewhat exaggerating when he told the duke in September that
'in every good mouth both here and in the neighbouring partes about
us, you are lauded as much as formerlie dispraysed'.[35] Needless to say,
much of the credit for this attitudinal shift can be traced to the sheets
coming off Mr Walkley's press.

Regrettably, total victory on the propaganda front could not guarantee even a draw on the battlefield. It is now easy to spot the uneasy
fit between reportage and reality. Food supplies, grapes or otherwise,
were soon exhausted, for Buckingham had never planned to spend four

[34] *A Continued Iournall . . . August 30* (1627, ESTC S111538), 7; *A Continued Iournall . . . September 18*
(London, 1627 ESTC 111536), 3, 4, 7–8; *A Continued Iournall . . . October 2* (London, 1627 ESTC
S24743.2), 5–6; and *A Continued Iournall . . . November 2* (London, 1627 ESTC S111541), 3, 8–9.

[35] BL, Harleian MS 390, fo. 299; *The Diary of John Rous* (1856), 11; *The Diary of Thomas Crosfield* (1935),
15; *Holles Letters*, II, 362, 367, 369; PRO, SP 16/76/2.

months in front of the Citadel. A massive resupply operation having failed, the number of serviceable troops rapidly dwindled as quarrels among the officers escalated. In late October, when the badly weakened and divided army attempted to embark, an unexpected French attack produced a bloodbath from which less than a third of the force emerged alive. This bloody outcome, however, should not overshadow the expedition's very real accomplishment – never before had the government ever accorded any military or naval operation such lavish coverage. In 1596, after Essex captured Cadiz, the most that he could get into print was a map. Buckingham, in contrast, could point to his own map as well as his *Manifestation*, a broadside detailing the expedition's strength, and seven issues of the first government-sponsored periodical, one of which ran into a second edition. Indeed, 1627 seemed a good year to publish William Hubbocke's prayers for the 1596 Cadiz expedition, one of the items that Essex had failed to get into print.[36]

VI

The slickest PR could do little for the popularity of a general who lost most of his men and dozens of regimental flags, which ended up decorating Notre-Dame Cathedral. Thus, 'the Dukes fame', Wotton observed, 'did still remain more and more in obloquie among the mass of people', but since these popular 'judgments are only reconciled with good success', Buckingham immediately began preparing for another expedition.[37] In the interim, he experimented with another public relations novelty.

The expedition urgently required money, which the parliament-men could best provide. Yet standing in the way of a generous supply were not only bitter memories of the 1626 session and the Ré expedition, but also the regime's pronounced tilt in favour of 'innovation' in 1626–7, and the constitutional implications of the resulting Forced Loan haunted many parliament-men. The leadership in the Commons, however, decided that a repetition of another direct clash with the government might well compel the king to explore further 'innovations'. Instead, they agreed to correct only general abuses and, most importantly, to vote supply before considering redress of grievances. Therefore, on 4 April, the Commons approved five subsidies to be collected in one year, the largest

---

[36] William Hubbocke, *A Prayer used in Private . . . for the prosperous seccesse of the voyage then to Cales* ([1627], ESTC S93075).

[37] Wotton, 'A View of the Life', 111.

grant in parliamentary history. Given the care with which the government followed the progress of the all-important subsidy bill, the timing of this vote was no surprise, and while the parliament-men prepared to discuss the issue, Buckingham made his own preparations. Rather than the parliament-house, the duke chose the council chamber at Whitehall as the venue for his latest, more intimate performance. Once the news of the grant reached Charles, he proclaimed that he was 'in love with Parliaments'. Indeed, 'this day, he thought that he had gayned more Reputation in Christendome, then if he had wonne many Battailes'. In return, he promised to summon frequent sessions and to grant the members 'as great immunitie and freedom' as they had ever enjoyed. Such a customary, albeit gracious, royal address then gave way to a thoroughly extraordinary speech from the duke.

More as an old comrade than a royal minister, the duke observed 'mee thinkes I now behold you a great King'. What followed was a classic display of Buckingham's 'naturall and proper Dialect'. Praise rained down on the parliament-men, whose affection for Charles 'did move them all to ioyne with like love in this great Guift', which was 'more then ever Subiects did give in so short a time'. Charles had begun the session suspecting 'that your People loved you not', but now the members 'have taken your heart, drawne from you a declaration that you will love Parliaments'. In addition to making Charles 'loved at home, and now to bee feared abroad', they also had stopped 'from approaching your eares those Proiectors and Inducers of Innovation'. Public concerns then gave way to personal ones. 'I must confesse,' he confided, 'I have long lived in paine, Sleepe hath given mee no rest, Favours and Fortunes no content,' since many regarded him as 'the man of Seperation' and 'the evill Spirit that walked betweene a good Master and a loyal Peoples for ill offices'. Consequently, 'this day I account more blessed unto me then my birth, to see you brought in love with Parliaments, to see Parliament expresse such love to you'. He ended with an exhortation; 'love them I beseech you, and God so love me and mine, as I ioy to see this day'. This emotional conclusion, however, was not as striking as an earlier paradox worthy of Donne himself: 'I who have had the honour to be your Favourite, may now give up my title unto them, they to bee your Favourite, and I to be your Servant.' Having come to appreciate the power of a timely message, the regime released this performance both as a manuscript separate and as a printed tract.[38]

---

[38] *Aprill 4. The proceeding the Parliament this day related to the King...* (1628, ESTC S113916), (sig. A–A4). For the circulation of the tract, see Hampshire RO, Jervoise MSS 44M69/L23/18;

VII

As the Ré expedition neared its climax, fears of the duke's death overcame his wife, and she begged a friend to persuade her husband to return
by telling the Lord Admiral that 'by this action he is not any whitt the
more popular mane [sic] then when he went.'[39] Although unsuccessful
in her goal, the duchess did illustrate the importance that the duke set
on being 'more popular'. Notwithstanding the fear and loathing with
which many regarded him at the end of his life, Buckingham in 1624
enjoyed the most widespread and fervent popularity of anyone outside
the royal family in the early seventeenth century. To be sure, his standing rapidly eroded, but he never accepted the situation. In the 1625
and 1626 parliaments, he attempted to cut a dominant figure, as he had
done in 1624. This much at least was predictable; more novel, however, was the duke's willingness to experiment. Modern spin-doctors
would easily recognise his 1628 performance at the Council Table as a
carefully scripted media event; contemporaries, however, would have
been hard pressed to think of a precedent for it. They would have
no luck at all in recalling another occasion like the Ré expedition;
between throttling the *Mercurius* and then mounting its own coverage
of the campaign, replete with the first government-controlled periodical,
the government choreographed a war with a skill that would have made
Lyndon Johnson envious. Paradoxes in short abound with Buckingham,
but few are more profound than the fact that the quest for popularity
prompted James's last favourite to explore hitherto taboo areas of public
relations.

In the 1626 impeachment charges, Sir Dudley Digges compared
Buckingham to a blazing star. Thus the parliament-men, like 'learned
mathematicians were troubled to observe the irregular motions, the
prodigious magnitude, the ominous prognostics of that meteor'. Likewise, 'it cannot be marveled at if the poor commons gaze and wonder at
the comet'. Nearly four centuries later, historians are still marvelling as
they trace the various influences which this meteor from Leicestershire
had on the political nation. Irregular motions in warfare, 'high' politics and religious policy have long attracted scholarly attention to
'Buckingham's Commonwealth', but with the recent new interest in both

Northamptonshire RO, Isham MSS IC 3578. For manuscript accounts, see Inner Temple
Library, Petyt MS 538, vol. 18, fo. 45; Centre for Kentish Studies, Knatchbull MSS U951/
O10/11.

39 PRO, SP 16/82/42. See also P. E. J. Hammer, 'Myth-making: politics, propaganda and the
capture of Cadiz in 1596', *HJ*, 40 (1997), 633–5.

political culture and 'minister-favourites,' it is also well worth gazing and wondering at the impact of his quest for popularity. To be sure, no early modern politician's passing prompted such widespread celebrations. Yet this fact should not obscure the importance of Clarendon's recollection of the duke: 'never Man studied more to apt [sic] himself, nor descended to meaner Arts to give general Content.'[40]

[40] Jansson and Bidwell, *Proceedings in Parliament 1626*, 1, 409; and Clarendon, *Character of Robert Earl of Essex and . . . Buckingham*, 25.

11

Charles I and popularity[1]

Richard Cust

'Whatever his virtues', Charles I was 'unfit to be king' and this lack of fitness was a crucial factor in the causes of the English Civil War.[2] Conrad Russell's verdict has been widely endorsed. In an age when much depended on a monarch's personal qualities Charles is seen as lacking the attributes a ruler needed to succeed. Where his father was subtle, flexible and patient, he is viewed as rigid and inept. John Reeve has described him as 'not in any sense a political man', S. R. Gardiner as 'lacking in that elemental quality of veracity' and Michael Young as 'a stubborn, combative and high-handed king who generated conflict'.[3] There is a good deal of substance in these verdicts, but they have tended to produce a rather one-dimensional view of Charles. Russell himself provides the corrective in his essay on 'the Man Charles Stuart'. It is a subtle and revealing study of an individual's political personality. Russell acknowledges that Charles had strengths – or, at least, positive attributes – as well as weaknesses. He was not stupid, but he did suffer from what Russell calls 'a tunnel vision', which made it very difficult for him to understand anyone's perspective other than his own. Nor was he particularly duplicitous – at least no more so than any other politician with a long career – but he was capable of creating this impression through appearing to compromise whilst not actually changing the ultimate objectives of his policy. And although he may have lacked the kingly quality of being able to unite and reconcile, Russell points out that he could be a very effective party leader. Many of the king's defects, he suggests, can be traced back to a sense of personal inadequacy which explains, for example, Charles's

[1] This paper is the result of a dialogue with Conrad Russell about Charles's political beliefs which goes back to the time when I was his research student. I am very grateful for the stimulus which his never-ending willingness to debate this, and other, topics has provided for my work. I also wish to thank Ann Hughes and Peter Lake for commenting on early drafts of this paper.

[2] C. S. R. Russell, *The Causes of the English Civil War* (Oxford, 1990), 207.

[3] L. J. Reeve, *Charles I and the Road to Personal Rule* (Cambridge, 1989), 4; S. R. Gardiner, *History of the Great Civil War 1642–1649*, 4 vols. (1893), IV, 328; M. B. Young, *Charles I* (1997), 70.

nagging doubts about the loyalty of his people or 'his readiness to stake his authority where prudent kings might have kept it in reserve'.[4] Russell presents a compelling portrait of a complex and many-sided character. But there is one element in Charles's personal make-up which is worth exploring further: his ideological perspective.

Relatively little attention has been given to this in recent work. Kevin Sharpe is very much the exception with his analysis of the efforts Charles made to match himself up to the ideals of Renaissance kingship.[5] But he has been mainly concerned with the 'positive' side of the king's self-image. Much less has been written about his fears and prejudices. Russell has made a start with his discussion of the role of 'conspiracy theory' in the make-up of both Charles and his principal opponent John Pym. He argues that each was driven by 'phobias' which put them on a collision course and that each needed the other 'to validate their demonologies'. However, whereas he has provided a seminal account of the importance of anti-popery for Pym's world-view, he has stopped short of investigating the king's 'demonology'.[6] Yet, arguably, this is just as important as defects of character in explaining Charles's political style. If he suffered from 'tunnel vision' then this may be explicable through the ways he perceived the actions of those he was dealing with; and if he could only be half-persuaded to take moderate advice this may have been a function of particular views on the responsibilities of kingship. The aim of this essay, then, is to pick up where Russell left off and explore further the king's 'demonology'. The main focus will be on contemporary notions of the threat from popularity and the role played by these in Charles's personal and ideological formation. It will be argued that these provided a discourse – or framework of assumptions and ideas – through which the king processed political experience and reached his decisions about policy.[7]

[4] Russell, *Causes of the English Civil War*, ch. 8.
[5] K. Sharpe, *The Personal Rule of Charles I* (1992), 182–97; K. Sharpe, 'Private conscience and public duty in the writings of Charles I', *HJ*, 40 (1997), 643–65.
[6] C. S. R. Russell, *The Fall of the British Monarchies 1637–1642* (Oxford, 1991), 527–8; C. S. R. Russell, 'The parliamentary career of John Pym', in *Unrevolutionary England* (1990), 211–17, 221–8. Russell does offer some shrewd comments on the importance of Charles's anti-puritanism, but does not go much beyond these: *Causes of the English Civil War*, 196–8, 210.
[7] Malcolm Smuts offers a highly illuminating account of the role of popularity within the elite culture and philosophy of the early Stuart period. He approaches the whole topic from a different direction to the one I have adopted, analysing popularity in terms of the violent and destablising passions which contemporaries believed to be inherent in nature. This is an important dimension of Charles's own thinking on the subject and Smuts's discussion anticipates several of the arguments being put forward here: R. M. Smuts, *Court Culture and the Origins of a Royalist Tradition in Early Stuart England* (Philadelphia, 1987), 253–62.

A graphic illustration of how ideas about popularity became tied in with practical politics is provided by a memorandum addressed to Charles in the latter stages of the 1626 parliament. It apparently originated from within the Duke of Buckingham's circle at court and it argued his case by portraying him as the victim of a popular conspiracy. The basic premise was that opposition was 'stirred up and maintained by those who either maliciously, or ignorantly and concurrently, seek the debasing of this free monarchy which, because they fynd not yet ripe to attempt against the king himself, they endeavour it through the duke's sides'. The origins of this campaign could be traced back to the Presbyterian programme in the 1584–5 parliament which was described as 'against the king's government which they would have extinguished in matter ecclesiasticall and limited in temporal'. The campaign gathered strength during the latter years of Elizabeth when amongst 'innovators, plebicolae and king haters' it had become fashionable to pray for the state as well as the queen, 'this word (state) . . . learned by our neighbourhood and commerce with the low countries, as if we were or affected to be governed by states'. And its consequences were fully apparent by the time of James's first parliament, when lawyers, puritans and 'medling and busie persons' 'stood strong against him under colour of parliaments and parliamentary priviledges', even though 'those popular speeches' 'were never suffered as being the certain symptoms of subsequent rebellions, civil wars and the dethroning of our kings'. Troublemakers in the Commons had gained the upper hand to such an extent that 'no honest patriot dare oppose them, lest he incur the reputation of a fool or a coward in his countrie's cause'. James had attempted to strengthen himself 'ever with some favourite', but now parliament was turning on this royal safeguard. Events had reached such a critical stage that if the king allowed the duke to 'be but decourted it will be the cornerstone on which the demolishing of monarchy will be builded. For if they prevail with this they have hatched a thousand other demands to pull the feathers of royalty.'[8]

Whether Charles himself ever read the memorandum is unclear; but he was certainly prepared to follow the logic of its argument. In the months following the 1626 parliament, rather than expose the crown to the threat of further assaults, he resorted to unparliamentary taxation in the shape of the Forced Loan.[9] This tended to confirm what was implicit

[8] 'To his sacred Majesty, Ab Ignoto', printed in *Cabala Sive Scrinia Sacra* (3rd edn, 1691), 255–7. For the context for the memorandum, see R. P. Cust, *The Forced Loan and English Politics 1626–1628* (Oxford, 1987), 13–30.
[9] R. P. Cust, 'Charles I, the Privy Council and the Forced Loan', *JBS*, 24 (1985), 208–35.

in the memorandum – that in court circles soon after Charles's accession there existed a well-developed theory of popular conspiracy which politicians could appeal to and manipulate for various ends. This theory focused on the idea that various groups of factious and self-interested troublemakers were seeking to play on the irrational and destructive impulses of the people and pull down the monarchy. Their aim was to create a state of anarchy or rebellion in which all notions of hierarchy and unitary authority would be demolished and they themselves could seize power. The anonymous author traced the roots of the conspiracy back to the latter part of Elizabeth's reign when, John Guy has argued, alarm about the 'threat from popularity' became 'obsessional'.[10] However, it had been a well-established theme of political thought long before this.

Popularity, and in particular the destructive force wielded by popular demagogues, was a central preoccupation of the historians of ancient Greece and Rome.[11] Their writings served as a constant reminder to Tudor political theorists of the hazards of democracy which of the three classical forms of government – democracy, aristocracy and monarchy – was seen as much the most dangerous.[12] Sir Thomas Elyot in *The Book Named the Governor* (1531), for example, provided an extended discussion of the chaos which ensued where 'the multitude of people have overmuch libertie'. He harked back to the democracy of post-Periclean Athens where popular demagogues, in pursuit of their own ambitious ends, had exploited an irrational and unstable people. They had done their best to 'order everything without justice', secured the banishment of 'the best citizens which by their virtue and wisdom had profited the publick weale' and selfishly served their own private ends. The end result had been anarchy followed by tyranny, as those in power desperately sought to tame this 'monster with many heads'. The only remedy, Elyot went on to argue, was the rule of a wise monarch, supported by virtuous magistrates.[13] Elyot was more sensitive than most to the threat posed by 'the multitude'; none the less his work reflected a general alarm which permeated much of Tudor propaganda and political thought.[14] It was

[10] J. A. Guy, 'Introduction. The 1590s: the second reign of Elizabeth I', in J. A. Guy (ed.), *The Reign of Elizabeth I. Court and Culture in the Last Decade* (Cambridge, 1995), 1, 11, 18–19.
[11] *The Oxford Classical Dictionary* (1949), 'Democracy'; for an illuminating discussion of the role of the demagogue in the writings of Plutarch, see A. Wardman, *Plutarch's Lives* (1974).
[12] J. P. Sommerville, *Royalists and Patriots. Politics and Ideology in England 1603–1640* (2nd edn, 1999), 61–2.
[13] Thomas Elyot, *The Boke Named the Governour* (Everyman edn, 1962), 7–8, 9–20.
[14] A. Fletcher and D. MacCulloch, *Tudor Rebellions* (4th edn, Harlow, 1997), 5, 7–12; C. Hill, 'The many-headed monster', in *Change and Continuity in 17th century England* (1991 edn), 181–92; L. Stone, *The Crisis of the Aristocracy 1558–1641* (Oxford, 1965), 29–35.

the events of the 1580s and 90s which brought this to the forefront of contemporary consciousness.

As the author of the anonymous memorandum indicated, the initial reason for this was the reaction against Presbyterian proposals for church reform. The association of presbyterianism with a popular threat to monarchy and hierarchy had first been outlined in detail during the Admonition Controversy of the early 1570s. John Whitgift had argued that the election of ministers by their congregations, as propounded by Thomas Cartwright, represented a dangerous intrusion of popularity into both church and civil society. Fallen man needed to be kept in a state of obedience, not encouraged to interfere in government. The 'common sort' were 'ignorant and unlearned and inapt' and their involvement could only lead to 'discord' and 'contention'. The surest guarantee of order and stability, Whitgift insisted, was to accept the rule of a godly prince. His arguments helped to establish the view that Presbyterianism and, by implication, puritanism, were inherently threatening to the existing hierarchy.[15] This was restated with much greater vigour in the response to the Marprelate tracts and the Presbyterian classical movement during the late 80s and early 90s. Richard Bancroft took the lead in a series of polemical works which portrayed the Presbyterians as populist firebrands. Again he highlighted the perils of allowing 'the multitude' to participate in church government; but this time added a chilling account of how such a policy had been exported from Calvin's Geneva to France, Scotland and now – through the classical movement – to England. Once established it would promote resistance theory and principles of consent which had the potential not only to sweep away bishops in the church, but also destroy monarchy and nobility. Sovereign power would reside with 'the multitude' and the world would be 'set all upon liberty'.[16] This shocking prospect was given added plausibility by political events.

Here, as the memorandum suggested, concern was perhaps triggered initially by increasing usage of the term 'state' in the political vocabulary of the 1580s and 90s and the closer contacts with the Netherlands which resulted from Leicester's expedition of 1585–6.[17] However, a more

[15] P. G. Lake, *Anglicans and Puritans? Presbyterianism and English Conformist Thought from Whitgift to Hooker* (1988), 59–65; P. G. Lake, 'Anti-popery: the structure of a prejudice', in R. P. Cust and A. L. Hughes (eds.), *Conflict in Early Stuart England* (Harlow, 1989), 84.

[16] Lake, *Anglicans and Puritans?*, 11–13, 130–1; P. G. Lake, 'Conformist clericalism? Richard Bancroft's analysis of the socio-economic roots of presbyterianism', in W. J. Sheils and D. Wood (eds.), *The Church and Wealth* (Studies in Church History, 24, 1987), 219–29.

[17] S. L. Adams, 'The patronage of the Crown in Elizabethan politics: the 1590s in perspective', in Guy (ed.), *The Reign of Elizabeth I*, 42–3. There is a good deal of comment in the early Stuart

immediate cause of concern about popularity was the activities of the
Earl of Essex. Essex was viewed in some quarters as an example of precisely the sort of ambitious demagogue that writers like Elyot warned
against. He was a military leader, lionised by the people, whose arrogant
determination to secure his due appeared to be plunging the court into
political strife.[18] The earl and his advisers were conscious of this charge
and sought to deflect it. In the aftermath of Cadiz expedition of 1596,
for example, when Essex's popular reputation was at its height, Francis
Bacon urged him 'to take all occasions, to the queen, to speake against
popularity and popular causes vehemently, and to tax it in all others'.[19]
However, the earl was never entirely able to shake off his reputation as a
demagogue and following the failure of his rebellion in February 1601, it
became firmly established within contemporary political idiom. William
Camden portrayed him in the *Annals of Elizabeth* as the flawed military
hero, lured to his destruction by ambition, lack of judgement and a misplaced faith in 'the vulgar'; whilst James Howell, looking back on the
earl's career at the time of the 1626 parliament, warned Buckingham
against being drawn down the same path: for it was said 'that [Essex]
was growen so popular that he was too dangerous for the times and
the times for him'.[20] The turmoil caused by Essex, then, again focused
attention on the dangers of the popular.

   Politics became less fraught in the early part of James's reign, but the
habits of thinking established in the 1580s and 90s persisted, and they

period about subversive ideas spreading from the Netherlands after the close association formed
in the 1580s: for example, see the views of George Abbott (Lake, 'Anti-popery', 90) and Francis
Bacon (J. Spedding (ed.), *The Letters and Life of Francis Bacon*, 7 vols. (1861–74), VI, 158.) I am
grateful to Simon Adams for guidance on this issue.

[18] S. Brigden, *New Worlds, Lost Worlds* (2000), 338–9; N. Mears, '*Regnum Cecilianum*? A Cecilian
perspective of the Court', in Guy (ed.), *The Reign of Elizabeth I*, 55, 63. The fashion for 'politic'
history during the 1590s accentuated this view of Essex and the concern with popularity more
generally. Drawing on the writings of Tacitus, in particular, it sought to analyse the mysteries
of state and identify the forces which might undermine virtue and order in politics. Ambitious
demagogues and the depraving and destabilising influence of 'the multitude' were seen as playing
very significant roles in this respect: R. M. Smuts, 'Court-centred politics and the uses of Roman
historians, c.1590–1630', in P. G. Lake and K. Sharpe (eds.), *Culture and Politics in Early Stuart England*
(Basingstoke, 1994), 21–43; R. M. Smuts, *Culture and Power in England 1585–1685* (Basingstoke,
1999), 66–9; Smuts, *Court Culture*, 106–8. For a collection of early Stuart commonplaces about
the dangers of 'popularity', drawing mainly on Tacitus and others writing in the same sceptical
tradition, such as Guicciardini, see Kent Archives Office, U269/F35.

[19] This is cited in M. Peltonen, 'Bacon's political philosophy', in M. Peltonen (ed.), *The Cambridge
Companion to Bacon* (Cambridge, 1996), 297.

[20] M. E. James, 'At a crossroads of the political culture: the Essex revolt, 1601', in *Society, Politics and
Culture* (1986), 450–3, 457; William Camden, *The Historie of the Princess Elizabeth* (1630), 167–77;
James Howell, *Epistolae Ho Elianae: Familiar Letters*, ed. J. Jacobs (1890), 232–4; Smuts, *Culture and
Power*, 69. On parallels with Essex and the dangers to Buckingham in becoming too popular,
see also Cogswell, ' "The People's Love"; the Duke of Buckingham and popularity', above,
212–13, 216.

were encouraged by the king himself. His views were set out at length in his advice book for Prince Henry, the *Basilicon Doron*, which probably played an important part in shaping Charles's own ideas on the whole subject of popularity. He was always enormously respectful of his father's opinions and the *Basilicon Doron* was reissued in 1616, as part of James's collected works, with a preface enjoining the young prince to imitate 'the good presidents of a good father' and to let the advice 'lie before you as a patterne'.[21] Much of the book consisted of conventional guidance on how to become a virtuous ruler; but in Book 2, 'Of a king's duetie in his office', James included an analysis of the sedition he had faced in Scotland during the late 1580s and 90s.[22]

The origins of this, he argued, could be traced back to the character of the Scottish Reformation, 'wherin many things were inordinately done by a popular tumult and rebellion . . .' At an early stage,

some fierie spirited men in the ministerie got such a guiding of the people . . . as finding the gust of gouvernment sweete they begouth to fantasie to themselves a Democraticke forme of gouvernment . . . [and] fed themselves with the hope to become *tribuni plebis* and so in a popular gouvernment by leading the people by the nose to beare the sway of all rule.

Their efforts had helped to destroy the rule of his grandmother and his mother, and during his own minority had succeeded in overwhelming the loyal majority in the church and interposing 'paritie, the mother of confusion and enemie of unitie'. More alarmingly still, he recognised the danger highlighted by Whitgift and Bancroft that 'once established in the ecclesiasticall gouvernment, the politicke and civill estate should be drawn to the like'. 'Take heed therefore', he urged his son, of

such puritanes, verie pestes in the church and common-weale . . . breathing nothing but sedition and calumnies, aspiring without measure, railing without reason and making their own imaginations . . . the square of their conscience . . . suffer not the principals of them to brooke your land if ye like to sit at rest.[23]

James's perception of the popular threat in Scotland focused mainly on puritan ministers. Once in England he extended it to include lawyers and 'free speakers' as well. In a 1616 speech in Star Chamber, for example, he warned the judges to beware of common lawyers, led on by

[21] *The Workes of James, King of Great Britaine, France and Ireland, published by James Bishop of Winton* (1616), 'the epistle dedicatorie'.
[22] 'Basilicon Doron', in J. P. Sommerville (ed.), *King James VI and I. Political Writings* (Cambridge, 1994), 1–61.
[23] Sommerville, *James VI and I. Political Writings*, 25–7.

a 'vaine popular humour', who 'thinke they are not eloquent and bold
spirited enough except they meddle with the king's prerogative'. He also
denounced those who 'shewed themselves too bold of late in the lower
house of parliament'. They

cannot be content with the present forme of gouvernment, but must have a kind
of libertie in the people . . . and in every cause that concernes prerogative give a
snatch against monarchie, through their puritanicall itching after popularitie.[24]

As Andrew Thrush demonstrates in his essay on James's personal rule,
this association of members of the Commons with a 'popular' challenge
to monarchy can be traced back to the parliament of 1610.[25] James's
exasperation at the end of the session provided the cue for Lord Keeper
Ellesmere to draw up a memorandum which analysed the House's actions in terms of classic popular conspiracy theory. He asserted that
'the popular estate ever since the beginning of his Majesty's gracious
and sweet government hath grown big and audacious', opening up
'breaches . . . upon the regality and supreme prerogative of the crown,
under pretext of lawful liberty and ancient privileges'. If this was allowed
to continue, 'it will not cease until it break out into democracy'.[26]

Ellesmere's memorandum is a measure of the extent to which, well
before the 1620s, popularity had become the basis for a conspiracy theory which could be used to explain the actions of almost anyone who
appeared to be challenging royal authority. It was a theory which divided
the world between positive and negative characteristics and allowed certain trends to be labelled as subversive of good government. There were
strong parallels, as Peter Lake has demonstrated, between fear of popularity and fear of popery. Just as popery could be presented as a negative
image of true religion, so popularity was seen as an inversion of right
government. Each negative characteristic imputed to it could be taken
to imply a positive attribute of monarchy. And where monarchy, and the
virtues associated with it, came under threat, it became entirely rational
to identify popularity as the root cause and adopt measures which would
counteract it.[27]

This had a direct impact on Charles's thinking about politics. As we
shall see, James's account of popularity in *Basilicon Doron* appears to have
provided a template for his son's understanding of the origins of disorder

---

[24] *Ibid.*, 213, 222.   [25] A. Thrush, 'The personal rule of James I, 1611–1620', above, 84–5.
[26] 'Special observations touching all the sessions of the late Parliament, anno 7 Regis and etc.', in
    L. B. Knafla, *Law and Politics in Jacobean England* (Cambridge, 1977), 254–62.
[27] Lake, 'Anti-popery', 72–97.

and rebellion. But, beyond this, it also helped to shape his positive views on the nature of kingship. This can be illustrated by an analysis of Sir Robert Filmer's *Patriarcha*, most of which was probably written in the late 1620s and early 30s with Charles's government very much in mind.[28] Filmer's case for an authoritarian patriarchal monarchy rested on an extended discussion of what he took to be its polar opposite, democracy or 'a popular estate'. His book is subtitled 'The Naturall power of kinges defended against the unnatural liberty of the people' and it proceeds to catalogue the many iniquities associated with 'this beast of many heads'. The opinions of the people were 'variable and sudden as tempests'. They were constantly 'desirous of new stirs and changes and . . . enemies to quiet and rest'. They rejected the rule of the virtuous, as had happened in Athens, where 'the wicked [were] always in greatest credit'. They encouraged a spirit of selfishness, where 'each man hath a care of his particular and thinks basely of the common good'. And they promoted 'sedition', with 'that damnable conclusion which is made by too many that the multitude may correct or depose their prince if need be'. Filmer's verdict was that it was necessary to reject any mixture of 'popular and regal power', even though this might be the type of government favoured by a majority of his contemporaries. The only secure and natural basis for rule was absolute authority vested in a patriarchal sovereign.[29]

Filmer's view of popularity was entirely conventional and drew on many of the standard classical sources used by others to discuss the issue. What is interesting about it is the way in which it was juxtaposed with his notion of good government. He systematically portrayed popularity as the very antithesis of everything he valued. It promoted the pursuit of private greed instead of the public good; it pulled down and destroyed men of wisdom and virtue when these were essential for the state to flourish; it encouraged faction and sedition in place of loyalty and obedience, innovation and disorder in place of peace and harmony. In short, it was a complete inversion of right order which, in turn, served to validate his particularly uncompromising version of patriarchal kingship.

---

[28] Robert Filmer, *Patriarcha and Other Writings*, ed. J. P. Sommerville (Cambridge, 1991), xxxiii–iv; for the context in which it was produced see, Sommerville, *Royalists and Patriots*, 235–7, 249, 257. Charles appears to have denied Filmer's request in 1632 that *Patriarcha* be licensed for publication. Anthony Milton has suggested, very plausibly, that this was because the king recognised that sponsorship of such an openly absolutist tract at this juncture would be damaging for the image of royal government: A. Milton, 'Thomas Wentworth and the political thought of the Personal Rule', in J. F. Merritt, *The Political World of Thomas Wentworth, Earl of Strafford, 1621–1641* (Cambridge, 1996), 134–5.

[29] Filmer, *Patriarcha*, 1, 24–33.

Whether Charles actually read *Patriarcha* is uncertain. But there is no doubt that he sought to embody most of the positive attributes of monarchy which Filmer pointed to, and anathematise the vices he associated with popularity.[30] In this respect, the work appears to have been drawing on assumptions and ideas which were entirely familiar to the king.

The importance of popularity was firstly, and most immediately, apparent in his attitude to parliaments. Charles's dislike of parliaments and, in particular, his suspicions of the House of Commons, are often seen as a product of his experiences during the late 1620s. However, there is a strong suggestion that he had absorbed some of the implications of his father's rhetoric as early the parliament of 1621. During the second session, he became infuriated when the Commons prepared a petition denouncing his proposed marriage to the Spanish Infanta and urged that the 'seditious fellows' who were responsible be 'sett fast' and 'made an example to others'. This picked up on James's own denunciation a few days earlier of 'fiery and popular spirits' debating 'matters far above their reach or capacity, tending to our high dishonour and trenching upon our prerogative royal'. The prince's intervention appears to have helped persuade the king to dissolve the parliament and then imprison, or exile, the leading troublemakers.[31] Already, it would seem, Charles shared his father's belief that the root cause of disruption in parliament was 'popular spirits'.

This became clearer during the parliament of 1626 when the Commons attempted to impeach Buckingham. Charles became increasingly exasperated at their conduct and gave vent to his feelings in a speech delivered on his behalf by the Lord Keeper on 29 March. He warned that the Commons was failing to maintain the 'difference between counseling and controlling, between liberty and abuse of liberty'. Whilst he accepted that the majority of the House consisted of 'wise and well tempered men', they were in danger of being led astray by 'the irregular humors of some particular persons'. This had become apparent in their determination to hound Buckingham, in spite of his own assurances that the duke was simply doing his bidding. The Commons' real objective, he suggested, was 'to wound the honour and government of his Majesty

---

[30] See references above, footnote 5.
[31] Bod. Lib., Tanner MS 73, fo. 79 (There are problems over dating this letter which are discussed in my forthcoming article, 'Prince Charles and the second session of the Parliament of 1621'); C. S. R. Russell, *Parliaments and English Politics 1621–1629* (Oxford, 1979), 135–44.

and his late blessed father'. The speech ended with a stark warning: 'Remember that parliaments are altogether in my power for the calling, sitting and continuance of them. Therefore as I find the fruits either good or evil they are for to continue or not to be.'[32]

This was a pivotal moment in Charles's reign, signalling publicly his acceptance of the view that parliament was in danger of being taken over by a popular faction. It provided the cue for the memorandum on popularity and numerous attacks by courtiers on the loyalty and obedience of the subject over the following months.[33] At this stage, however, it was not a view which was fixed or permanent. The Commons could still redeem themselves, as far as the king was concerned, by loyal support and prompt offers of supply; and he continued to accept that it was the duty of a good king to unite with his subjects in acts of mutual love and support. None the less, from this point onwards his suspicions tended to be uppermost when he was dealing with parliament. He expected them to co-operate on his terms and display a suitably docile and submissive attitude. When they did not he was quick to infer disloyalty and subversion.

It was in this frame of mind that Charles approached the parliaments of 1628 and 1629. He was willing to give the Commons another chance – and, of course, he was in desperate need of money which, as Andrew Thrush shows in his essay, tended to concentrate royal thinking on the positive aspects of the assembly.[34] However, throughout the meetings he was on the look-out for signs of 'popular spirits' at work and, following the disruptions of the 1629 meeting, he appears to have decided that enough was enough. He explained his reasoning in a declaration issued soon after the dissolution of the parliament. It emphasised throughout his moderation and determination to abide by traditions of good kingship. He had made numerous concessions and allowed the Commons unprecedented latitude in debating grievances, but he had been confronted by 'turbulent and ill affected spirits' who had intimidated 'the sincerer and better part of the house' and sought to 'infuse' 'rumours and jealous fears' into his people. 'Their drift', the king claimed, 'was to break, by this means, through all respects and ligaments of government and to erect an universal over-swaying power to themselves.' It was now

[32] M. Jansson and W. B. Bidwell (eds.), *Proceedings in Parliament 1626*, 4 vols. (New Haven, 1991–6), I, 391–5.

[33] Cust, *The Forced Loan*, 13–72.

[34] R. P. Cust, 'Charles I, the Privy Council and the Parliament of 1628', *TRHS*, 6th ser., 2 (1992), 25–50.

manifest the duke was not alone the mark these men shot at but was only as a near minister of ours taken up on the by and in their passage to their more secret designs which were only to cast our affairs into a desperate condition, to abate the powers of our crown and to bring our government into obloquy that in the end all things may be overwhelmed with anarchy and confusion.[35]

The only rational response was a period of calm reflection in which royal authority could be re-established and the effects of the turmoil allowed to subside. Meanwhile, as Charles announced in a proclamation of 27 March 1629, 'we shall account it presumption for any to prescribe any time unto us for parliaments'.[36]

The king's open espousal of the discourse on the evils of popularity helped create a climate in which his privy councillors found it increasingly hard to push for a resummons. Throughout the late 1620s council discussions about parliament were overshadowed by the issue of whether the Commons could be trusted to refrain from assaults on the prerogative. In the post-mortem which followed the Oxford Parliament of 1625 blame for breakdown was laid on what Lord Keeper Williams referred to as 'stirring men' bent on pursuing 'the popular way'. However, it was said that, at this stage, the king was taking a relatively relaxed view and was determined that 'for the distemper of 5 or 6 men he would not be angry with his people, but still undertook to preserve and love them'. Similar discussions took place prior to the parliaments of 1628 and 1629. In each case moderate councillors managed to persuade Charles that the 'distempers' amongst 'the people' had settled sufficiently for it to be safe to hold another meeting.[37] However, the Commons' conduct in 1629, together with the winding down of the war effort, made such arguments far harder to sustain; and under the terms of the March 1629 proclamation Charles was clearly established as ultimate arbiter of when, and whether, another parliament should be summoned. The consequences were apparent in December 1631, when the foreign situation seemed to demand a meeting to subsidise Gustavus Adolphus's efforts to recover the Palatinate. Charles was able to rule it out in council discussion by

---

[35] S. R. Gardiner (ed.), *Constitutional Documents of the Puritan Revolution 1625–1660* (Oxford, 1889), 83–99.

[36] P. L. Hughes and J. F. Larkin (eds.), *Stuart Proclamations*, 2 vols. (Oxford, 1973–83), II, 226–8.

[37] For 1625, see J. Hacket, *Scrinia Reserata. A Memorial of John Williams D. D.*, 2 parts in 1 vol. (1693), pt. ii, 17, 20 and PRO, SP 84/129, fo. 28; for 1628, see Cust, *Forced Loan*, 72–85; for 1629, PRO, SP 99/30, fos. 180–1. Discussions about the dangers of the 'popular party' in the Commons also appear to have had a part in the council debates about a resummons during the 1610s referred to by Andrew Thrush (above, 85–101): Spedding, *Life and Letters of Bacon*, IV, 366–73; V, 181, 190; VII, 116.

pointing out Sir John Eliot was continuing his efforts to stir up sedition. If there was a defining moment on the road to personal rule, then, as John Reeve has argued, this was surely it.[38]

The prospects for parliament diminished rapidly from this point onwards. In 1634 Charles famously described the assembly as 'that Hidra' and urged Lord Deputy Wentworth to be particularly careful in handling its counterpart in Ireland, 'for you know that I have found it as well cunning as malicious'.[39] Where such hostile rhetoric could be applied to parliament it became very difficult for royal councillors to push the case for another meeting. Lord Keeper Coventry tried to do so in 1633, but it was said that 'the king so rattled [him] that he is now the most pliable man in England'. And when a council committee suggested that there was 'no other way' if England was to mount an effective war effort against the Scots in 1639, Charles silenced discussion by simply telling them he would not 'hear of a parliament'.[40] Entering a major war without a summons of parliament was almost unprecedented in England. But it was the logical consequence of the hostility which had been developing within the royal court since at least 1610. And in the emergence of this climate of opinion popularity played a critical role.

Fear of 'popularity' also did much to shape Charles's religious policy. Uppermost in his mind were the puritans, whom he saw as presenting a constant threat to his vision of the Church of England. This view was summed up in the preface to the Canons of 1640, which was issued in his name.[41] Here the puritans were seen as operating in much the same way as the 'ill affected' in parliament. Under the 'mask of zeal and countefeit holiness', they had spread their 'poisoned conceits' among 'the weaker sort who are prone to be misled by crafty seducers.' They had encouraged the king's 'good subjects' to 'take offence' at the rites and ceremonies used in the church and sought to discredit Charles himself with suggestions that 'we intend to bring in some alteration to the religion

---

[38] PRO, C 115/M35/8387; Reeve, *Road to Personal Rule*, 275–91.

[39] W. Knowler (ed.), *The Earl of Strafforde's Letters and Dispatches*, 2 vols. (1739), I, 233. For an excellent discussion of the context for Charles's remarks, see Milton, 'Political thought of the Personal Rule', 142–9.

[40] Knowler, *Strafforde's Letters and Dispatches*, I, 141; II, 246.

[41] W. Laud, *The Works of the Most Reverend Father in God, William Laud D. D.*, 7 vols., eds. W. Scott and J. Bliss (1847–60), v, 609–13. Laud was the likely author of the preface, but as with other statements issued in his name it would probably have been carefully scrutinised and approved by Charles himself: K. Fincham and P. G. Lake, 'The ecclesiastical policies of James I and Charles I', in K. Fincham (ed.), *The Early Stuart Church, 1603–1642* (Basingstoke, 1993), 36.

established'. What was needed, the preface insisted, was 'a return unto the true former splendour of uniformity, devotion and holy order' which had been achieved under Elizabeth.

Charles's efforts to restore this vision, in the face of the puritan threat, provided the basis for his ecclesiastical policy in England.[42] It also had important implications in Scotland, where his efforts to impose a new prayerbook, and especially his handling of the rebellion which followed, again owed a good deal to his perception of the 'popular' threat. This was explained at length in *The Large Declaration* which was published in February 1639. Most of the text was ghost-written by Walter Balcanquall, but the king 'owned it from the beginning as his own' and parts of it contained extensive marginal annotations which he made himself.[43] Even allowing for the work's polemical purpose – which was to tar the Scottish Covenanters with the brush of extremism and prepare the English nation for war – it provides a valuable insight into Charles's thinking.

The Large Declaration portrayed the prayerbook rebellion in similar terms to those used in *Basilicon Doron*. It traced the origins back to the self-governing and democratic principles of the Presbyterian kirk which, like his father, Charles regarded as an encouragement to 'popularity' and sedition. He was alarmed by the reduced role accorded to bishops which he regarded as incompatible with an acceptance of monarchical authority in the state.[44] He also found the lack of set forms of worship and intrusive lay influence in Scotland both aesthetically and ideologically repugnant. It led to a situation described in *The Large Declaration*, where

preachers or readers and ignorant schoolmasters prayed in the church sometimes so ignorantly as it was a shame to all religion to have the Majestie of God so barbarously spoken unto, and sometimes so seditiously that their prayers were plaine libels, girding at soveraigntie and authoritie.[45]

These tendencies, according to the declaration, provided the driving force behind a conspiracy which involved 'factious spirits' amongst the Presbyterian ministry and the Scottish nobility. It had begun at the start of Charles's reign with opposition to the Act of Revocation and developed

---

[42] Fincham and Lake, 'Ecclesiastical policies of James I and Charles I', 36–49; J. Davies, *The Caroline Captivity of the Church* (Oxford, 1992), 13–14.

[43] *A Large Declaration Concerning the Late Tumults in Scotland by the King* (1639); Russell, *Fall of the British Monarchies*, 44n; for Charles's marginal notations, see *Large Declaration*, 320–4 (comments on the Acts of the Glasgow Assembly), 337–50 (comments on the Covenanters' answer to Hamilton), 375–401 (comments on the Protestation of the Glasgow Assembly).

[44] Russell, *Fall of the British Monarchies*, 53, 57; *Large Declaration*, 371.   [45] *Large Declaration*, 16.

through the troubles in the Scottish parliament of 1633 and the treason of Lord Balmerino. Charles had attempted to counteract these tendencies by reforming the Scottish kirk in ways which would make it more like the Church of England. But the opposition had finally burst through all restraints in the summer of 1637 when the new prayerbook was rejected and, with encouragement from above, the 'base multitude' rioted on the streets.[46]

Agitation followed a familiar pattern. 'Unquiet spirits', operating through 'the seditious prayers and sermons of some preachers suborned by them for the purpose', had infected 'our good, but simple and seduced people'. They had persuaded the Scots of the king's 'inclination to popery' and presented themselves as the defenders of 'true religion'.[47] However, the ultimate aim of the rebellion was not religion at all: it was, in the words of a proclamation which accompanied *The Large Declaration*, 'to shake of all monarchicall government and to vilifie our regall power justly descended on us over them'.[48] As evidence of this Charles pointed to the groundless nature of rebel claims that the prayerbook represented 'popery and innovation'. This was self-evidently nonsense since English Protestants had been martyred in defence of a very similar liturgy under Mary.[49] He also picked up on the 'strange and damnable positions' maintained by the rebels, which included open espousal of resistance theory. In one of his marginal comments he noted that the Covenanters had appointed Robert Blair Professor of Divinity at St Andrews after he 'was expelled from Glasgow University for teaching his scholars in his lectures upon Aristotle that monarchicall government was unlawfull'. In another he pointed out that the claims to spiritual sovereignty put forward by the General Assembly of the kirk were comparable to those made by the Jesuits on behalf of the Pope, echoing terms used by James in denouncing the Commons' actions in 1621.[50]

The full extent of the Covenanters' ambitions had, according to *The Large Declaration*, become apparent at the Glasgow Assembly which began in November 1638. They had used subterfuge and 'secret instructions' to exclude moderate ministers; then proceeded to assert the supremacy of the lay elders even in spiritual matters, such as the status of the bishops; and finally used 'the Tables' (the standing committees of the Assembly) to interfere in every aspect of justice and government.[51] In

---

[46] *Ibid.*, 6–15, 30–1, 34–40.   [47] *Ibid.*, 106–7, 124–5, 155–7, 184, 403–4.
[48] Hughes and Larkin, *Stuart Proclamations*, II, 633. See also *Large Declaration*, 2, 428.
[49] *Ibid.*, 18–20.   [50] *Ibid.*, 324, 397, 410–15; Sommerville, *James VI and I. Political Writings*, 257.
[51] *Large Declaration*, 413–15, 428.

spite of their progress, however, Charles believed that the 'mutineers and rebels' reflected the views of no more than a small minority of his Scottish subjects – 'a private and schismaticall part though never so many' 'who had led the rest by the nose.'[52] If he could communicate with the loyalist majority, he remained confident that they would return to the fold.

Charles's perception of the rebellion as a 'popular' conspiracy, and the conclusions he drew from this, did much to structure his policy towards Scotland in the late 1630s. It helps to explain, for example, his determination not to give way over the prayer book even when it became obvious that it was unenforceable.[53] Charles appears to have firmly believed that the religious objections to the new liturgy were simply a cloak for more sinister designs against monarchy. If he gave way, it would be interpreted as a sign of weakness which would simply encourage his opponents. Far better to make a stand and rally the supposedly loyal majority. This appears to have been the thinking behind the disastrous proclamation of February 1638, which informed the Scots that he had 'read and approved' the prayerbook, that there was nothing in it detrimental to true religion and that if its opponents continued in their display of 'preposterous zeal' they would be dealt with as traitors.[54] Unfortunately, it had the opposite of the effect intended, backing protesters into a corner from which their only escape was to escalate opposition by subscribing to the National Covenant. The whole episode clearly demonstrates Charles's lack of political judgement, his inability, as Russell puts it, 'to read the political map'.[55] However, it also shows something more than this – that Charles's 'misjudgements' were often a consequence of his particular understanding of the aims and motives of his opponents.

The same point can be made about his determination, from the moment the Covenant was signed, to teach his Scottish subjects a lesson in obedience. This was what undermined the patient efforts made by Hamilton to reach some sort of settlement with the Covenanters during 1638. Charles approached the negotiations with the belief that opposition was the work of few 'factious spirits' and that it would collapse if he stood firm and rallied loyalist support. He was also conscious that the 'popular' conspiracy in Scotland embraced English puritans as well, and any allowances he made might be used against him south of border. In these circumstances, he was willing to support Hamilton's concessions,

---

[52] *Ibid.*, 378, 384.   [53] Russell, *Fall of the British Monarchies*, 49–51.
[54] *Large Declaration*, 48–50.
[55] D. Stevenson, *The Scottish Revolution 1637–1644* (Newton Abbot, 1973), 79–87; Russell, *Causes of the English Civil War*, 208.

as a means of buying time and dividing the Covenanters. But when it came to the point of delivery, just before the Glasgow Assembly, he backed off and withdrew his offer to allow discussion of the full range of religious grievances.[56] This episode illustrates Russell's point that Charles 'was open to counsel about means, but never open to counsel about his "grounds"'.[57] But it also helps to explain why he adopted this approach. Given his perception of the 'popular' threat, compromise was always going to appear to him as a very risky way of resolving a political crisis.

This approach was reinforced by Charles's view of his kingship as the antithesis of 'popularity'. As far as he was concerned the first duty of a king was to uphold standards of virtue and honour and fulfil the obligations of his conscience and his calling. Compromise and negotiation – which he described in other contexts as 'policy' – were not what he was supposed to aspire to. He might legitimately engage in such actions as means to his ends; but, in the final analysis, if he failed to uphold his vision of royal authority then – as he explained in *The Large Declaration* – he would 'betray the trust which the king of kings hath reposed in us for the maintenance of religion and justice amongst all his people whom he hath committed to our charge'.[58] Such high-minded rigidity not only encouraged him to stand firm; it also helped to close his mind to the necessity of acknowledging that his policies might not be acceptable to a majority of his subjects. This was another obstacle in the way of councillors trying to persuade him to adopt a realistic approach to the problems he faced. In the Scottish context, it explains why even in late 1640 he refused to give up trying to fight the Bishops' Wars long after most politicians had concluded that they were unwinnable.[59]

A third area where 'popularity' exercised an important influence was in Charles's efforts to defeat John Pym and 'the junto' during 1641. Once the king had abandoned the policy of bridging appointments in late February 1641, his strategy for regaining the political initiative was twofold: firstly, to build a royalist party which could defeat Pym both inside and outside the House of Commons; and secondly, to remove 'the junto' leadership by force. For much of the period he ran the two policies in tandem, presenting an accomodating public face in an effort

---

[56] For an excellent account of the negotiations in 1638, see J. J. Scally, 'The political career of James Third Marquis and First Duke of Hamilton (1606–1649) to 1643', Ph.D. thesis, University of Cambridge, 1992, ch. 6.

[57] Russell, *Causes of the English Civil War*, 194; Russell, *Fall of the British Monarchies*, 89–90.

[58] Sharpe, 'Private conscience and public duty', 48–9; *Large Declaration*, 5.

[59] C. S. R. Russell, 'Why did Charles I call the Long Parliament', in *Unrevolutionary England*, 253–61.

to build moderate support and working covertly behind the scenes to prepare a coup against his enemies should the need, or the opportunity, arise.[60] In each case 'popularity' played an influential role.

Charles's party-building relied to a considerable extent on presenting Pym and his godly allies as the vanguard of a 'popular' conspiracy against the crown. This was the theme of the declaration which he issued after the dissolution of the Short Parliament in May 1640. In terms reminiscent of the late 1620s, the king insisted that the parliament had been undermined by 'some few seditiously affected men' whose 'malice' had led astray the loyal majority and threatened 'to bring ruin and confusion to the state, and render contemptible this glorious monarchy'.[61] The same theme was highlighted in some of his comments at court and also in a draft petition from the army which he approved for presentation to parliament in June 1641.[62] When linked with fears of destructive interventions by 'the multitude' and puritan/Presbyterian domination of the church, this provided a powerful platform for building royalist support.

As early as February 1641, in debates about root and branch reform of episcopacy, members of the Commons were expressing alarm about petitioning 'by tumultuous assemblies of the people' and the prospect of bishops being replaced by a Presbyterian 'pope' in every parish. 'If we make a parity in the church,' Sir John Strangeways told the house, 'we must come to a parity in the commonwealth.'[63] Such concern increased with demonstrations on the London streets and efforts to dismantle the structures of the Church of England during the spring and summer; and it came to a head during debates on the Grand Remonstrance in November, when speaker after speaker protested against 'the junto's' resort to demagoguery. 'I did not dream', Sir Edward Dering lamented, 'that we should remonstrate downward, tell stories to the people and talk of the king as a third person.'[64]

Perhaps the most cogent and lucid expression of this view was provided by the small group of Scottish nobles, led by the Earl of Montrose, who emerged as royal supporters at the start of 1641. Montrose's brother-in-law and former tutor Lord Napier drew up a statement of their objections

[60] For the best account of Charles's approach during 1641, see Russell, *Fall of the British Monarchies*, chs. 6–9.
[61] *His Majesties Declaration to all his loving subjects of the causes which moved him, to dissolve the last parliament* (1640), printed in J. Rushworth, *Historical Collections*, 7 vols. (1659–1701), III, 1160–7.
[62] *CSPV 1640–2*, III; Edward, Earl of Clarendon, *The History of the Rebellion and Civil Wars in England*, 6 vols., ed. W. D. Macray (1888), I, 323–5.
[63] Gardiner, *History of England from the Accession of James I to the Outbreak of Civil War, 1603–1642*, 10 vols. (1895–9), IX, 276–87.
[64] Russell, *Fall of the British Monarchies*, 427–9; S. R. Gardiner, *History of England*, X, 76–9.

to Covenanter rule, known as the 'Letter on Sovereign Power', which was a classic account of how a balanced polity could be destroyed by 'ambitious designs of rule in great men'. Their 'designs', it predicted, would lead to 'a tyranny of the subjects', 'the most fierce, insatiable and insupportable tyranny in the world – where every man of power oppresseth his neighbour without any hope of redress from a prince'.[65] These statements – and the evidence from Cheshire discussed in Peter Lake's essay – demonstrate that there was a ready-made constituency, extending well beyond the royal court, which shared the king's concern with 'popularity'. Had Charles stuck to a policy of building on this he could well have gained the upper hand over Pym during 1641. However, his efforts were consistently undermined by his propensity for plotting.

Russell has demonstrated that Charles was closely involved in the First Army Plot of March–May 1641 and that the revelations about his role were disastrous for his attempts to build moderate support. He presents a similar picture of 'the Incident' in Edinburgh in early October.[66] If one adds evidence of preparations for a coup in November 1640 – forestalled by the sequestration and imprisonment of Strafford – the Earl of Antrim's claims about Irish Army Plots in April–May and September–October 1641 and, of course, the attempt on the Five Members in January 1642, then it appears that the king was involved in a sequence of failed plots which lasted for well over a year.[67] This dismal record has been interpreted by most historians as yet another indication of his ineptitude and lack of judgement. Given the legal and constitutional constraints which operated within English political culture, his actions are generally seen as desperate gambles by a politician who was incapable of recognising the strength of his own position and was increasingly subject to the influence of his wife.[68] There is, of course, a good deal in this verdict. But it is also important to remember that there is a case to made for Charles

---

[65] Stevenson, *The Scottish Revolution*, 224–7, 365–6n; M. Napier, *Montrose and the Covenanters*, 2 vols. (1838), I, 397–409.

[66] C. S. R. Russell, 'The first Army Plot of 1641', in *Unrevolutionary England*, 281–302; Russell, *Fall of the British Monarchies*, 322–8.

[67] Gardiner, *History of England*, IX, 231–6; J. H. Ohlmeyer, 'The Antrim plot of 1641 – a myth?', *HJ*, 35 (1992), 905–19; J. H. Ohlmeyer, 'The Antrim plot of 1641: a rejoinder', *HJ*, 37 (1994), 431–7. There has been considerable debate about whether Antrim's claims were true. For the case against believing them, see M. Perceval-Maxwell, 'The Antrim plot of 1641 – a myth? A response', *HJ*, 37 (1994), 421–30; C. S. R. Russell, 'The British background to the Irish Rebellion of 1641', in *Unrevolutionary England*, 274–6. The balance of probability, I would argue, supports Antrim's claims. Apart from the reasons adduced by Ohlmeyer, an Irish Army Plot would have been entirely consistent with Charles's approach during 1641.

[68] Young, *Charles I*, 149; Gardiner, *History of England*, x, 129–33; A. Fletcher, *The Outbreak of the English Civil War* (1981), 181.

behaving the way he did; and as far as he was concerned his actions were both rational and legitimate.

The reasoning behind his attempt on the Five Members, which was the culmination of this approach, was outlined in 'His Majestie's Declaration to all his Loving Subjects concerning the proceedings of this present parliament'. Again one has to allow for its polemical purpose – and a certain amount of retrospective justification of the king's actions, since this was issued at York on 12 August 1642 to accompany the raising of the royal standard.[69] But since the account it offers is entirely consistent with earlier declarations, and since Charles firmly believed that a monarch should explain things to his people as he saw them – as part of his duty to educate and enlighten[70] – it seems legitimate to treat it as an insight into the king's thinking.

The declaration tells a familiar story which was taken back to the start of the Long Parliament. Charles had set out with the intention of winning 'the hearts and affections' of his subjects, but had found himself opposed by a 'faction of a few ambitious, discontented and seditious persons' who had set out 'to ruine the government of the kingdome and to destroy us and our posteritie'. An integral part of the conspiracy was to 'startle the people' with 'false reports' of plots and stir them to 'rage and fury through seditious preachers and agents'. This had been alarmingly effective, producing 'great multitudes' who had 'trained down to Westminster . . . with swords and clubs', intimidating bishops, peers and anyone else who stood by the king. At first Charles had refrained from responding directly, hoping that 'the better sort' would recognise the malicious intent of 'the malignant party'. However, the naked appeal to the people in the Grand Remonstrance finally persuaded him to bring treason charges against the leadership, so that 'all the world might see what ambition, malice and sedition had been hid under the vizard of conscience and religion'.[71]

Viewed in these terms the arrest of the Five Members was a logical attempt to expose, and cut off the head of, 'the malignant party' before it could do any more damage. It was a policy which made sense if one presumed that the opposition consisted of a few factious troublemakers who had hoodwinked 'the better sort'. As we have seen, this was precisely what Charles believed had happened. It was also a policy which was

---

[69] 'His Majesties Declaration to all his loving subjects concerning the proceedings of this present parliament, Aug 12 1642', in *An Exact Collection of all Remonstrances, Declarations, etc. . . . formerly published by the King's Majesties Command . . .* (1643), 514–62.

[70] Sharpe, 'Private conscience and public duty', 646–54.

[71] 'His Majesties Declaration . . . Aug 12 1642', 514–35.

workable if the treason charges against the Five Members could be made to stand up in court. Again, the king seems to have had no doubts on this score and Russell has pointed out that in strictly legal terms the case against them was rather stronger than that against Strafford.[72] It appeared to him that, in the circumstances, inaction was more dangerous than action. The demonstrations around Westminster in the last week of December, and the vote against the bishops' protest in the Lords on the 28th, could be taken as warnings that if he hesitated he would lose control of both the London streets and the upper house. The coup against royal authority which had been long anticipated in the rhetoric of 'popularity' seemed about to happen and Charles's attempted counter-coup was a logical response.[73] This did not, of course, make it any less disastrous. The attempt on the Five Members destroyed the immediate possibilities of building a royalist party, lost him his capital and made civil war highly probable. But it does show that there was a reasoning process going on behind actions which to some historians have appeared so ill-judged as to be almost nonsensical; and this process had its origins in the fear of popularity.

Fear of popularity played a role in Charles's thinking which extended well beyond the three areas highlighted here. Under his auspices, it became one of the defining features of court culture during the 1630s, emerging, for example, in the masque, where anti-masque characters pitted against the virtue and wisdom of the king regularly took the form of seditious puritans, leaders of popular rebellion or simply the swirling and destabilising forces of 'the multitude'.[74] It was also evident in his efforts to reform certain urban corporations whose constitutions lent themselves to 'disordered elections' and 'popular tumults'.[75] And it helped to shape his more fundamental attitudes towards the political order and constitutional arrangements in England.

---

[72] Russell, *Fall of the British Monarchies*, 447–9.

[73] Charles's tendency to see the actions of 'the malignant party' as part of a continuous 'popular' conspiracy which he had been facing since the late 1620s is, perhaps, indicated in the decision to include Denzil Holles in the list of those whom he charged with treason. Holles was not one of the most prominent or outspoken of Pym's allies in the Commons, but, like William Strode, he had been among the MPs involved in the disturbances in the 1629 parliament: *DNB*, 'Holles, Denzil'.

[74] Smuts, *Court Culture*, 253–62; M. Butler, 'Reform or reverence? The politics of the Caroline masque', in J. R. Mulryne and M. Shewring (eds.), *Theatre and Government Under the Early Stuarts* (Cambridge, 1993), 144–51.

[75] R. P. Cust, 'Anti-puritanism and urban politics: Charles I and Great Yarmouth', *HJ*, 35 (1992), 1–2, 23.

This emerges from a fuller examination of Napier's 'Letter on Sovereign Power'. Although written in the context of Scottish politics in early 1641, it took the form of a generalised discussion of the nature of political systems and the various threats to their integrity. What it said was just as applicable to England as Scotland. The discussion was based on the premise that sovereign power was ordained by God as something sacred and indivisible. This power could take various forms, ranging from republicanism to monarchy, but in each case its purpose was to unite ruler and people and provide government which was in the public interest. This generally happened when the sovereign power was 'possessed with moderation' and guided 'by the laws of God, of nature and the fundamental laws of the country'. However, it was susceptible to two particular weaknesses: when it was either 'extended beyond the laws whereby it is bounded', or 'restrained of these essential parts'. The former tended to occur when princes were led astray by evil counsellors. In this case the subject should seek his remedy in parliament, relying on 'good counsel' to persuade the ruler of the error of his ways. For 'if parliaments be frequent and rightly constituted' then evil counsellors would be deterred and laws could be passed to protect the liberties of the subject. The latter was generally a result of the malign influence of popular demagogues. 'Ambitious designs of rule in great men, veiled under the specious pretext of religion and the subjects' liberties, seconded with the arguments and false positions of seditious preachers' were perhaps the greatest threats to the delicate balance of trust and responsibility which bound together ruler and people. They sowed 'the spirits of division', stirred up jealousies against the nobility and led to that 'tyranny of the subjects' which was so abhorrent. Here the only remedy was the virtuous rule of a strong prince, utilising his 'prerogative . . . to protect his subjects from oppression and maintain their liberties entire'.[76]

There was little here which, in public at least, either Charles or his opponents would have disagreed with. Recognition that sovereign power was divinely ordained, respect for the rule of law, acknowledgement of the beneficial effects of a parliament and awareness of the disruptive

---

[76] Napier, *Montrose and the Covenanters*, 1, 397–409. For a comparable analysis of the nature of the political system, again ending with a vivid description of the chaos which would ensue if 'democracy' was allowed to triumph over monarchical authority, see the middle passage of 'His Majesties Answer to the Nineteen Propositions' from June 1642: *An Exact Collection of all Remonstrances, Declarations, Votes . . . formerly published by the King's Majesties Command or by Order from One or Both Houses of Parliament* (1643), 320–22. Authorship of this has been attributed to Sir John Culpepper and Lord Falkland: M. J. Mendle, *Dangerous Positions. Mixed Government, the Estates of the Realm and the Making of the Answer to the xix Propositions* (Alabama, 1985), 5–7.

effects of evil counsellors and 'popular' demagogues were all commonplaces of contemporary political thought. But within this thought much
depended on where the emphasis was placed, where the balance was
struck. If the main threat was seen as lying in evil counsellors encouraging the prince to overreach himself then the stess tended to be on using
legal and parliamentary means to curb 'the exorbitancy of a prince's
power' and ensure that it would 'run in the even channel'. If the basic
problem was ambitious demagogues and the anarchic tendencies of the
people then priority had to be given to bolstering the prince's 'prerogative' so that he could protect his subjects and maintain order.[77]

Broadly speaking, the former was the view of parliaments in the late
1620s and early 1640s and the latter the view of Montrose's party and, of
course, the king. Indeed, it was a view which appeared to go to the heart
of Charles's understanding and analysis of politics. He was particularly
sensitive to the popular threat. He had been taught about it by his revered
father and experienced it at first hand in the early years of his reign. It
seems to have constituted the stuff of his nightmares and evoked a deep,
visceral loathing, visible in his remarkable description of parliament as
'that hydra'. And it appears to have been fundamental to his perception
of his kingship. Malcolm Smuts has argued, very persuasively, that ultimately Charles conceived of popularity as an elemental force, a natural
feature of human existence, which stirred up violent and unstable passions and fomented disorder. As a divinely ordained monarch, it was his
duty and his destiny to confront this force and subdue it; and this was
one of the roles he acted out in the court masque.[78]

The preoccupation with popularity is an aspect of Charles's ideological make-up which has been underplayed in most recent accounts of his
kingship, perhaps because it appears to be at odds with the revisionist
stress on the consensual nature of contemporary political language.[79] In
fact, fear of popularity helps to explain how Charles could talk a common language, but pursue lines of policy which – to borrow Russell's
description of his religious position – were decidedly 'off centre'.[80] Thus,
he could accept the principle that parliaments were a desirable means
of achieving unity with the subject and yet become so suspicious of the
popular aims of the Commons that he refused to summon them; and

---

[77] Napier, *Montrose and the Covenanters*, I, 400–406.
[78] Smuts, *Court Culture*, 253–62. As Smuts indicates, the 1640 masque *Salmacida Spolia* was the key
text in this respect; but it was not alone: Butler, 'Reform or reverence?', 144–51.
[79] For a notable exception, see Milton, 'Political thought of the Personal Rule', 133–56.
[80] Russell, *Causes of the English Civil War*, 196.

he could recognise the need to be bound by law, custom and tradition, whilst concentrating so exclusively on the preservation of his prerogative that he appeared to be doing his best to destroy them. Charles's 'tunnel vision', his refusal to abandon ultimate policy objectives and his insistently partisan approach to issues of allegiance all owed a good deal to his fear of popularity.

12

Puritans, popularity and petitions: local politics in national context, Cheshire, 1641

Peter Lake

I

On 27 February 1641 Sir Thomas Aston presented a petition to the House of Lords in defence of the episcopal government of the English church. It came with over 6,000 names attached and, having been signed, it was claimed, 'by all the lords that were not popishly affected and by most of the best of the gentry', was delivered in the name 'of the county palatine of Chester'. Almost a year later, on 21 December 1641, Aston repeated the trick, for, on that day, via the Lord Keeper, the king referred to the Lords another Cheshire petition – this one in favour of the book of common prayer and signed by some 8,000 hands.[1] Here we might conclude, with Dr Maltby, was a central strand of English provincial opinion – 'prayer book protestantism' – coming into its own through the largely spontaneous emergence from the provinces of mass petitions and protests against the extremities of both Laudian and puritan innovation. And here, too, was Sir Thomas Aston – a moderate man in increasingly extreme and fractious times – playing a central role in this process.[2] Of course, all this positioning and petitioning was taking place in the midst of one of the greatest political crises in English history and there was accordingly a both local and national politics to these developments and it is precisely with these politics and the interactions between them that this paper is concerned.

---

[1] *LJ*, 4, 174, 482. The texts of the petitions are printed in J. Maltby (ed.), 'Petitions for episcopacy and the book of common prayer on the eve of the civil war, 1641–2', in Stephen Taylor (ed.), *From Cranmer to Davidson; a Chuch of England Miscellany* (The Church of England Record Society, 1999), 116–18, 133–4.

[2] J. Maltby, *Prayer Book and People in Elizabethan and Early Stuart England* (Cambridge, 1998), chapter 4. Dr Maltby's account of these events is, in turn, based on the political narrative provided in John Morrill, *Cheshire 1630–1660, County Government and Society During the English Revolution* (Oxford, 1974), chs. 1 and 2.

II

For even Aston's initial, pro-episcopal petition was not the product of a united county community. To understand the personal and political divisions and conflicts in which it intervened (and which, in fact, it served considerably to worsen) we need to turn briefly to the events of 1640 and in particular to the elections to the Short and Long Parliaments. County politics, and certainly the parliamentary representation of the county, had been dominated (if not monopolised) by a group of gentry led by Sir Richard Grosvenor, Sir Richard Wilbraham and Sir George Booth. Strongly anti-Catholic, with close links to the local godly clergy, suspicious of court corruption and the influence of evil counsellors and Arminians in high places, these men were, in their own eyes, fathers of their country, archetypical commonwealthsmen, 'patriots'. To their enemies – like Aston and his friend and confidante, the Chester lawyer John Werden – they were 'popular patriots' – a far less complimentary term. (During the Short Parliament campaign Werden accused them, under cover of a 'bare pretence of the public good', of pursuing their own 'ambition' and 'profit' to such an extent that they had become 'adversaries to the peace' 'of their country'; and all 'to advance their own interests and popularity'.)[3] By the time of Short Parliament Grosvenor was too old and indebted to stand and in the Short Parliament elections this group was probably represented by the candidacy of the sons of Wilbraham and Booth.

But, in the end, the old county political establishment was outflanked in 1640 by two younger men – Sir Thomas Aston and Sir William Brereton, who appear to have done some sort of electoral deal. Aston and Brereton were odd bedfellows. Aston was a courtier – a gentlemen of the privy chamber and an active ship-money sheriff, while Brereton had a considerable following amongst the local godly. Aston talked the language of anti-puritanism in his election letters, while Brereton employed the language of the commonwealthsman and patriot. Aston was backed by Viscounts Cholmondeley, Kilmorey, Lord Brereton and Earl Rivers, the latter a Catholic with considerable court connections.[4] Both, however, could claim to have opposed ship money; Aston because, despite

---

[3] PRO SP Dom. 16/448/43, Werden to Thomas Smyth, 20 March 1639/40 and SP Dom. 16/44 9/14, Werden to Smyth, 27 March 1640. R. P. Cust and P. G. Lake, 'Sir Richard Grosvenor and the rhetoric of magistracy', *Bulletin of the Institute of Historical Research*, 54, 1981 and R. P. Cust (ed.), *The Papers of Sir Richard Grosvenor, 1st Bart. (1585–1645)* (The Record Society of Lancashire and Cheshire, 1996).

[4] University College of North Wales, Mostyn MS 9082/19.

his devotion to the service, he had prosecuted with vigour the county's disputes over assessment with the city and Brereton because at a crucial moment he had encouraged his tenants not to pay. The 'popular patriots', members of the county establishment and deputy lieutenants, may at this date also have been tainted with their association with the military charges associated with the Bishops' War.[5] Either way, Aston and Brereton were s/elected.

But then, between the Short and Long Parliaments, something happened. For when Aston stood again, in a contested election, Brereton and Peter Venables, the Baron of Kinderton, a close associate of the 'patriots', were chosen. It may well be that in the interim Aston's bona fides as a straightforward critic or opponent of the Personal Rule had been called into question. At a meeting of quarter sessions in October 1640, probably orchestrated by Booth and Wilbraham, at which the county's grievances over ship and coat and conduct money were debated and a petition for redress to be sent to parliament drawn up, Aston had had to clear himself from allegations of malfeasance and extortion during his time as sheriff. On his own account, at a crucial juncture during the Short Parliament Aston had tried to persuade the House to vote supply to the king, on remarkably open-ended terms. His connections to the court can have been no secret nor can the presence of papists and crypto-papists (Earl Rivers) amongst his local backers. Indeed, it seems that at some point in 1640 rumours about his religious opinions were circulating. Why else did Aston, in Holborn on 8 December 1640, 'freely and of his own accord' take the oath of allegiance from a Middlesex JP?[6]

Either way, the Long Parliament opened with something like normal service resumed in Cheshire; with two parliament-men returned for the county with close links to the Booth-Wilbraham-Grosvenor group and the political initiative firmly in the hands of the godly, who now, no doubt under the influence of national events and wider currents of opinion, proceeded to overreach themselves. Calvin Bruen and other puritans from around Chester raised a petition amongst the freeholders of the county for root-and-branch reform of the church. This was presented to the House of Commons by Brereton on 19 February 1641.[7] And it was in response to this that Aston raised and presented to the Lords his petition in favour of episcopacy.

---

[5] Peter Lake, 'The collection of ship money in Cheshire during the sixteen thirties: a case study of relations between central and local government', *Northern History*, 17 (1981).

[6] J. Maltby (ed), *The Short Parliament (1640) Diary of Sir Thomas Aston* (Camden Society, 4th ser. 35, 1988), 143–4; PRO SP Dom. 16/432/35.

[7] *CJ*, 89, 123.

Explaining his conduct retrospectively early in 1641, Aston claimed that a 'clamorous petition in the name of the freeholders' against episcopacy had been doing the rounds in Cheshire in December 1640. Circulated amongst the people but not the gentry, this so-called 'freeholders' petition' nevertheless still 'injuriously assumed' 'the name of the whole county'. Staying in Derbyshire over Christmas, Aston had been alerted to its existence by Roger Wilbraham, 'who writ to me full of passionate distaste of it'. Later on a trip to Cheshire,

> passing by my Lord Kilmorrey's, Thomas Cotton's, Sir Thomas Brereton and Lord Colmondeley I found them all full of dislike of it, holding it not only fit but necessary to take some course to vindicate the country from the injury of such a clamour. I was desirous to offer once more to draw both ends together, presuming where public interest was all private respects would be set apart.

Throughout, therefore, Aston presented himself as having acted as an honest broker to the county gentry to arrange a unanimous repudiation of the freeholders' anti-episcopal petition as a genuinely representative expression of Chesire opinion. In doing so, of course, he was also seeking to challenge Brereton – the man who had presented the freeholders' petition to the Commons – for the role of the true representative of 'the county'; a claim which, having lost a parliamentary election which his rival Brereton had won, he now sought to substantiate by organising and presenting on the national political stage (albeit to the Lords not to the Commons) a petition in favour of episcopacy so massively backed by both elite and popular county opinion that it would make Bruen and Brereton's puny effort look both unrepresentative and silly. Accordingly, Sir Thomas initiated a series of discussions with other groups of gentry, the while collecting, parish by parish, as many signatures as he could. Despite what he claimed were considerable efforts on his part, Aston failed to gain the support of the group of gentry led by Sir Richard Wilbraham, Sir George Booth and Sir Richard Grosvenor – Werden's 'popular patriots' from the Short Parliament election. After protracted negotiations had proved fruitless, Aston and his friends decided to go it alone.[8]

The petition as presented took a studiedly moderate view of the central issues, opening with genuflections towards the need for reform. Thus,

---

[8] BL, Additional MS 36913, fol. 66r, Aston to an unknown correspondent – a signatory of the Attestation explaining his conduct over the petitioning campaigns. This is very likely a draft of a round robin letter sent to any or all those who had signed the Attestation whom Aston felt he could detach from the Booth-Wilbraham connection.

the petitioners proclaimed that 'we, as others, are sensible of the common grievances of the kingdom and have just cause to rejoice at, and acknowledge with thankfulness, the pious care which is already taken for the suppressing of the growth of popery, the better supply of able ministers and the removing of all innovation'. It then made a plea for further reform of the workings of the church courts. But that was the extent of its reformist 'anti-Laudianism'. Thereafter the petition got down to the business of defending the episcopal goverment of the national church and denouncing puritan schemes for reformation.

Of the institution of episcopacy itself the petition gave an exaltedly moderate account, claiming

that bishops were instituted in the time of the apostles; that they were the great lights of the church in all the first general councils . . . that to them we owe the redemption of the purity of the gospel we now profess from Romish corruption; that many of them, for the propagation of the truth, became such glorious martyrs; that divers of them (lately and) yet living with us have been so great asserters of our religion against its common enemy of Rome; and that their government hath been so long approved, so oft established by the common and statute laws of this kingdom; and as yet nothing in their doctrine (generally taught) dissonant from the word of God or the articles ratified by law.

By the standards of the 1630s this was a decidedly downbeat, studiedly un-Laudian defence of the institution. It retreated from the dominical account of epsicopacy as not only apostolic but directly divine in origins. While it might gesture at it, the petition did not even embrace an explicitly apostolical account of those origins. Moreover, rather than centre the case for episcopacy on a visible institutional succession linking the present church to that of the apostles through the church of Rome, Aston chose to highlight the role of the martyr bishops of Mary's reign in vindicating the doctrinal truths upon which the post-Reformation English church was founded. All in all, this was a position carefully crafted to avoid the dominant Calvinist conformist, erastian and moderate puritan critiques of Laudian episcopacy as incompatible with the royal supremacy of crown in parliament and as the Trojan horse through which popish or Arminian doctrine and ceremonial innovation had been introduced into the church.

But if the petition's treatment of episcopacy was 'moderate', the same cannot be said of its approach to puritanism. The petition, just as Werden and Aston did in their private correspondence, sought to run together all sorts of puritan behaviour and belief to create a picture of a levelling Presbyterian threat to all order:

When we consider the tenor of such writings, as in the name of petitions, are spread amongst the common people; the tenets preached publicly in pulpits, and the contents of many printed pamphlets, swarming amongst us; all of them dangerously exciting a disobedience to the established form of government . . . we cannot but express our fears that their desire is to introduce an absolute innovation of presbyteral government.

Through these means 'such popular infusions spread as incline to a parity'. Instead of the present government by twenty-six bishops, England would be exposed to 'the mere arbitrary government of a numerous presbytery, who together with their ruling elders will arise to near forty thousand church governors'. Such a system would represent a serious danger to all order in church, state and society. A Presbyterian church would be neither 'reducible by parliaments' nor 'consistent with a monarchy'. On the contrary, it was 'dangerously conducible to an anarchy', all too likely to 'produce an extermination of nobility, gentry and order, if not of religion'. The result was a remarkably political (even in some sense secular) defence of the ecclesiastical status quo, conducted more in terms of the likely political and social consequences of further reformation than of any very developed positive account of the spiritual benefits likely to be conferred on the nation by episcopacy.[9]

The moderation of much of its tone and content and the mass support it was able to garner renders it all the more remarkable that Aston's petition was the product of a fractured gentry community; a situation which left the door open for a counter- (anti-episcopal) petitioning campaign. In April Werden wrote to Aston telling him of efforts by the local puritans at 'an exercise at Neston' and 'amongst the brethren on the Wirall' 'to inveigh against our petition and to exhort the godly to certify against it and to make a collection'.[10] These local efforts culminated in 'a petition put into the House of Commons' 'by one Calvin Briant [or Bruen] with some few more of mean condition, which petition scandaliseth that which was preferred to the Lords and rather clamours unjustly than is able to prove truly those assertions they cast upon it'.[11] This was presented to the Commons on 19 April 1641 and referred on the 23rd to 'the committee for the ministers' remonstrance', which 'shall have power to send for parties, witnesses, papers and records . . . to examine the misdemeanours expressed in that petition', to further which purpose the House ordered

[9] Maltby, 'Petitions for episcopacy', 116–18.
[10] BL, Additional MS 36913, fol. 210r, Werden to Aston, April 1641.
[11] BL, Additional MS 36913, fol. 205r, unnamed local correspondent to Aston; also see BL, Additional Mss 36914, fol. 214r, Werden to Aston, Good Friday, 1641.

that 'Mr Boswell, Sir Nathaniel Barnardiston, Mr Purfrey, Mr Rowse (Rous), Sir William Brereton, Sir Dudley North, Mr Whitakers' should be 'added to the committee as to this particular petition only'.[12] In short, the committee that was to hear Aston's case was being packed with hardened puritans and supporters of root and branch, headed, of course, by Aston's local rival, the enemy against whose both local and national standing his own complaints were ultimately aimed – Sir William Brereton.

At this point, with things going against him at Westminister and his local enemies carrying damaging rumours about him down to the county and sending new allegations back to the centre, some of Aston's enemies overreached themselves by producing a printed petition to the Commons which purported to have been signed by precisely twice the number of persons in precisely the same social categories as had signed Aston's petition. This was, of course, a fraud; in Aston's later indignant words 'never any such petition seen in Cheshire, never presented to the house, no such persons ever signed it'.[13] Aston then proceeded to reply to this petition with a second of his own, again directed to the Lords. Therein, Aston asked that the Lords 'attach and bring before' them 'the several persons whose names are in your paper annexed'. For by interrogating them Aston felt sure that their Lordships would 'find out the authors, dispenser and stationers that have contrived and divulged this libel' and thus be enabled to inflict 'exemplary punishment upon the delinquents'. According to a later printed petition, Aston went so far as to use this second spurious root-and-branch petition as a pretext to get some of those involved in the earlier freeholders' petition – the petition that Brereton himself had presented to the Commons – imprisoned. 'Hath he troubled and caused to be imprisoned myself and some others who protest before your honours that we had no hand at all in it.' Their only crime had been the public expression of their zealously anti-episcopal views, views which they were proud to own.[14] According to his enemies, at least, Aston was seizing on the spurious printed petition as an instrument with which to discredit the earlier root-and-branch petition and legally to harass his local puritan enemies. The only trouble was that he was doing all this with an equally spurious petition of his own, which, just like the puritan petition it was denouncing, had never been seen or circulated in Cheshire.

---

[12] *CJ*, 123, 126.
[13] Thomas Aston, *A Remonstrance against Presbytery* (1641) sig. A2r, 'to the reader'.
[14] *A Humble Remonstrance to the Right Honourable the Lords in the High Court of Parliament*, BL, Thomason Tracts E178 (4).

Even in the more conservative House of Lords Aston's counter-attacking complaints about the 'anti-petition' met with considerable opposition. In the words of one diarist, Aston had asked the Lords

to give him leave to make enquirey of the authors of the mock petition and of the printer that so they might receive condign punishment and in case they would not he then would protest against it. Whereupon the zealous party said a loud he must be brought upon his knees before the house for wronging the honour of it, others contradicting, it came to vote and he carried it by three or four voices. My Lord of Essex, seeing he could not carry it, would have protested their dissenting from the rest but my Lord of Holland told him that those who had voted the contrary were as sensible of the honour of that house as he and that if they went to protest their disagreement they would do the like for their consent.

In the end, Aston was allowed to stand and, he 'having explained himself', 'the Lords were pleased to pass the offence'.[15]

In the Commons, too, things came to a similarly equivocal conclusion. As Aston explained to the Cheshire gentleman William Moreton, while, on the one hand, his accusers 'after two days hearing were by committee adjudged to have proved nothing that could by the honour of the house be taken as a charge to anybody', on the other, the committee refused to allow Aston to turn their proceedings into an enquiry into the conduct of his enemies, who, he claimed, had 'injuriously sought to breed a difference betwixt the houses, pretending a breech of privilege'. Arguably, of course, this was to impute to his enemies precisely what Sir Thomas himself was trying to do to them. At that point, the committee, 'being strongly inclined to preserve the complainants from punishment', tried to bring the matter to a close but by a ruse Brereton prevented it, hoping thereby to live to fight another day by bringing yet more lies and half-truths up from the country to defame Aston before the parliament.[16]

III

Frustrated at the centre, as he claimed, by the political connections and dirty tricks of Sir William Brereton, Aston's precipitate submission to the Lords of his second petition also exposed his flank back in Cheshire. There the Wilbraham-Booth-Grosvenor connection took the opportunity offered by Aston's failure to consult gentry opinion in Cheshire to revive their credentials as the true spokesmen for the county. This

[15] BL, Sloane MS 1467, fol. 26r; *LJ*, 4, 205, April 1641.
[16] BL, Additional MS 33936, fol. 232r–v, Aston to William Moreton, 28 May, 1641.

was a role that had been (temporarily) usurped during the exchanges described above by the petitioning campaigns of Aston and his adversaries in London and Cheshire and now the old political establishment, the 'commonwealthsmen' of the county, wanted it back. They were also (surely knowingly) giving the campaign to discredit Aston being waged in London by Brereton, 'the zealous party' in both houses and the Cheshire godly – a campaign which, as we have seen, was, for the moment, in abeyance – a helping, indeed a reviving, hand. To these ends they produced the so-called Attestation, yet another 'anti-petition', this time addressed to the House of Commons and signed by (amongst fifty or so others) Wilbraham, Booth and Grosvenor. Werden reported the meetings that produced this document in what were becoming (on both sides) typically personalised and polarised terms. 'Mr Hugh Wilbraham yesterday reported to a good friend of mine that Sir George Booth and Mr Richard Wilbraham, meeting with many other gentlemen at Nantwich on Monday next, they all signed some protestation or petition against you which (to use his own words) as he said was very tart and rough.'[17]

Without conceding any shred of legitimacy to the puritan petition to which, much like Aston, they referred as 'the late printed libel in answer to his former petition, which we disclaim as never approved or seen in this county till the press made it common', the Booth-Wilbraham group still managed utterly to repudiate Aston's second petition. 'We, who, in respect of our interests, hold ourselves to be a considerable part of this shire, do utterly mislike that any one man should take so much power upon himself, without public trust and appointment, [Aston had, after all, lost the Long Parliament election] to use the name of the county.' Nor did they stop there but went on, without commenting on either document's substantive pro-episcopal contents, to use Aston's, in effect fraudulent, second petition to cast doubt upon the legitimacy and representativeness of his first.

And though hitherto we have been silent (as unwilling to nourish discontents in our country by excepting against his former petition) yet now, when we see one man assume so much boldness to himself and such confidence to petition their lordships in the name of the gentry and inhabitants of this county, when none of us were held worthy by him to be consulted withal nor to be made acquainted with his intent, it is high time to express our dislike of this, his voluntary act, not holding it safe to refer to any of so forward a disposition the managing of any business in the name of the county nor him fitting to do it without the

[17] BL, Additional MS 36914, fol. 215v, Werden to Aston, Good Friday, 1641.

approbation of those that the country hath instructed as knights for our shire. So that hereby we make bold to disclaim this last petition of his to their honours and to leave him to justify his own undertakings. And for the substance of his former petition, with the managing thereof and the manner of acquiring hands thereto, we think it not fit for us to interpose our censures but in all humility, as becomes us, shall leave it wholly to the discussion of this honourable house when it shall be thither referred by the House of Lords.[18]

Thus, explicitly denied any claim to speak for the county or the public, his second petition utterly repudiated by some of the most influential of his provincial peers and with grave doubts having been cast upon the legitimacy and representativeness of his first, Aston was left to twist in the wind, his fate depending on the tender mercies not merely of the House of Commons, but of the committee on the ministers' remonstrance where, of course, the influence of his enemy and chief rival, Sir William Brereton, and his allies in 'the zealous party' was considerable.

In the course of a long news letter to Sir Richard Grosvenor of late May 1641 the MP for Chester, Francis Gamul, described how

the baron [of Kinderton, Peter Venables, Brereton's colleague as knight of the shire] hath profoundly put in your attestation, which was read in the house and referred but all to no purpose. Sir William Brereton is gone into Cheshire we hear to obtain new matter and that committee is not like to remain unless he come with new force out of Cheshire.[19]

As Gamul's emphatic use of the term 'your' shows, the Attestation was Grosvenor and his friends' instrument in a struggle to put Aston in his place and Gamul and Venables, as well, of course, as Brereton, were all part of a virtual campaign both in the Commons and the county, dedicated to precisely that end.

Nor were the authorities in, or parliamentary representatives of, the city of Chester any more sympathetic to Aston's cause. Aston did indeed succeed in interesting the House of Lord's committee of religion in events in Cheshire and, in particular, in the city of Chester. But this was an action for which he received scant thanks from the city fathers. On 20 April 1641 the House of Lords responded to reports of

some tumults and disorders within the county palatine and city of Chester whereby divine service hath been disturbed and disquieted or otherwise ne-glected' with an order that 'the divine service be performed and as it is ap-pointed by the act of parliament of this realm and all such as shall disturb that

---

[18] BL, Additional MS 36913, fols. 63r-64r.
[19] BL, Harleian MS 2081, fols. 93r-v, Gamul to Grosvenor, 25 May 1641.

wholesome order shall be severely punished, according to the law and that the parsons, vicars and curates in several parishes shall forebear to introduce rites or ceremonies that may give offence otherwise than those which are established by the laws of the land.

This missive drew from the mayor, alderman and leading clergy of the city a bland *omnia bene*, coupled with a counter-complaint against those who had been telling the Lords such scandalous lies about Chester, 'whom we humbly leave to be ordered according as your honours in prudence and justice think meet'.[20]

Indeed, even after the case against Aston the petitioner had collapsed in the Commons, the case against Aston the ship-money sheriff and tax farmer seems to have picked up again. On 18 June 1641 Aston was summoned to attend the House of Commons 'on Monday next'. His failure to comply led to his being 'sent for as a delinquent by the serjeant at arms'. The cause appears to have been a case brought against Aston by 'divers merchants and citizens of Chester' which, along with Aston's counter-petition, was referred to the 'committee for customers' on 20 July. In a letter of 7 August a group of prominent Chester men wrote to the city MP, Sir Thomas Smith, thanking him for his expedition in 'the business of Sir Thomas Aston' and for his 'care' in the 'sudden preferring of the petition and the speedy getting of the same committed'.[21]

All of which might be taken to imply that many leading gentlemen in both the city and county, none of them radical puritans of the Calvin Bruen or even William Brereton sort, felt able to distinguish, as Aston did not, between different types of puritan activity, refusing to assimilate any and all acts of iconoclasm or nonconformity to a unitary populist, radical puritan, indeed Presbyterian, threat to all order in church, state and society. Indeed, on this evidence, they appear to have found Aston's own efforts to defend the county from puritanism more divisive, more threatening to the unity and order of local society and their own authority as local magistrates than anything the puritans were doing.[22] Neither Venables nor Gamul nor Smith – all eventual royalists – were puritan firebrands, indeed in the same letter to Grosvenor in which he described Venables' efforts against Aston in the Commons Gamul revealed himself

---

[20] HLRO, Main Papers, 20 April 1641, 31 May 1641.

[21] *CJ*, 179, 189, 218; PRO, SP 16/483/25, William Gamul, Thomas Thorpe, William Ince *et al.* to Sir Thomas Smith, 7 August 1641. Clearly Aston's local enemies in county and city were not about to leave him alone.

[22] Bodleian Library Nalson MS, vol. 13, fols. 66r–71v. Also see BL, Additional MS 36914, fols. 224r–225r, petition from Cholmondeley, Kilmorrey *et al.* to the Lords endorsing Aston as a spokesman for 'the county' and complaining about puritan excesses in Cheshire and Chester.

as decidedly lukewarm on the topic of ecclesiastical reform. If men of this temper were opposed to him, Aston was not going to get much change out of either the House of Commons or the middle group of Cheshire gentry opinion.

But if that was how some sections of Cheshire opinion responded to Aston's efforts, another group (of forty-two county gentry) stood four-square behind him. This connection, which was to form the kernel of the Cheshire royalist party in 1642, was led by Aston's old allies from the Short Parliament election, Cholmondeley, Kilmorrey and Cotton. They both wrote a formal letter of support to Sir Thomas and petitioned the House of Lords to 'testify your great care and diligence for the country and our approbation thereof' and to 'acknowledge your good service here for your country and your merit from the inhabitants thereof, who stand well affected either to his majesty or the good and peaceable government of this kingdom'. They had, they wrote, recently received printed copies of a fraudulent petition 'which vile and machiavellian petition we perceive was never preferred to neither house but dispersed maliciously and seditiously to stir up discord and tumult'. This Sir Thomas' second petition to the Lords had been designed to allay and although it had indeed never circulated in the county, they, the undersigned, remained convinced that, if it had been, all 'those many thousands who subscribed our remonstrance, preferred by you, which found so gracious acceptation both with his sacred majesty and the Lords to whom it was preferred', would have signed it, as would 'many thousands more of this county whose hands could not, by reason of shortness of time, be gotten'. They encouraged Sir Thomas to continue, in the county's name, to press the Lords to 'check the further growth of these seditious insolences and attempts to cast aspersions upon our local intentions and disturb the peace of our church and state government'. The situation was urgent; 'here are daily more innovations by the importunity of the authors of these schisms and factions' and they could see 'that much ill is to be feared if a timely prevention be not given to the growth thereof'.[23]

This praise for Aston from his local supporters echoed, in part, Sir Thomas's own justification of his conduct to the Cheshire gentleman William Moreton and the authors of the Attestation, to both of whom Aston claimed to have been motivated by his obligations to 'the county' and the need to prevent 'the scandal' that the county might suffer from

---

[23] BL, Additional MS 36914, fol. 222r–v.

a counterfeit petition being published and disseminated in its name. In taking action to avert that, Aston claimed, he had not been acting only as a private man. 'For any man to assume the name of the county to advance any private business of his own or to set on foot any public business for the county without warrant from the county were a just cause of dislike,' Aston conceded. But he had been far from commiting such an offence. For not only did he conceive 'it the duty of every man that is a member of a county to vindicate his country from scandal', Aston himself had not entered the fray as simply a private man. 'There was no forwardness in me than became one so far instructed, as I was, in the delivering of the first petition'. On Aston's account, through his role in organising the pro-episcopal petition, he had taken on a public persona, as some sort of representative of the county, a role and a duty intensified and compounded when others directly attacked, indeed contradicted, that petition's bona fides, in the process claiming fraudulently to speak in the county's name.

When confronted with the 'printed libel', fathered on the county by persons unknown, Aston explained, he had been placed in a quandary. 'To prefer no petition but to let that libel pass uncontradicted had been to let the bastard disinherit the right issue of very many considerable persons . . . To have preferred a petition in the name of half had been to vindicate them and leave the others as countenancers of that libel. To stay till all that were worthy to be acquainted with it had been sent to at this distance had certainly been to give way to the dispersing many thousands' of copies of the counterfeit petition, which otherwise might easily enough have been 'suppressed'. Since it would have been 'impossible to recall them, if once out' this would have amounted to 'a ridiculous neglect'. So Aston had decided to proceed without further consultation with the gentry of and in Cheshire – but not before consulting what we might term the virtual, 'representative', reality of the county, that is to say the county as it was embodied, not by the gentry or even the substantial inhabitants and freeholders of Cheshire, but by its elected representatives at Westminister.

I did acquaint the baron [of Kinderton, i.e. Peter Venables, one of the county MPs], Sir Thomas Smith and Mr Gamul [the members for Chester] with it and desired them to prefer a petition or join in it with me and they all approved of it as fit to be done, though they conceived not by them, seeing the first petition was in the Lords' House and not in theirs and it was questionable whether, being of the lower house, they might join in a petition to the Lords. Therefore, it was thought more proper for me to do it, they professing, if they were called, they would be ready to testify how much they thought the county injured in it.[24]

Of course, the one person representing the county in Westminister whom Aston had not consulted, indeed the one name conspicuously absent from Aston's account of the whole affair, was that of Sir William Brereton. It was as though, for Aston, merely by presenting the freeholders' root-and-branch petition to the Commons as an accurate representation of Cheshire opinion Brereton had foregone or forefeited his role as a real representative of the county, a role for which Aston, despite his defeat in the Long Parliament election, was now making a renewed bid, on the basis of a mass petitioning campaign that represented the real will of 'the county' and thus validated Aston's claim to be able to represent that will.[25] It appears that Aston was using the topic of episcopacy and the conduct of the godly in, as he claimed, misrepresenting the opinion of the county on that issue as a wedge with which to divide Sir William from his erstwhile allies in the middle group and to attach that group to his own reconstituted notion of what the county stood for and how and by whom its opinions and preferences should be represented. If that was indeed Sir Thomas's aim, on the evidence presented here, for all the considerable support he had had raised in the county – express backing of forty-two gentlemen and the other 6,000 signatures – he had signally failed to achieve it.

IV

In his account to William Moreton of why he had failed to win over Wilbraham, Booth and Grosvenor and their friends, Aston had remained silent on whatever points of substance might have divided the parties. Discussions had kicked off with a preliminary meeting between Aston and his friends and Sir Richard Wilbraham and his kinsman Thomas Wilbraham. Despite Sir Richard's claim 'that no man's more forwardness than Sir Richard Wilbraham, no greater sense of such an affront to the country' could be found 'in any man than in him', he then proceeded to 'take many exceptions to what had been with the assistance of very good advice well drawn'. Wilbraham proposed that a general meeting of the gentry be called where the matter could be thrashed out and

---

[24] BL, Additional MS 36913, fols. 63v–64r, 71v–72r, 73v. Aston's reply to the Attestation.
[25] BL, Additional MS 36914, fol. 224r, Cholmondeley, Kilmorrey *et al.* to House of Lords.

a general response agreed; a suggestion to which everyone assented. The next morning Aston and a man of Lord Cholmondeley's called on Wilbraham at his seat at Woodhay to tell him that 'if it pleased him to send to those gentlemen he had most usual recourse to my lord would assume to bring all his friends and give meeting in any part of Cheshire where they would'. So that names could go on being collected in the meanwhile, Aston claimed, a version of the petition 'languaged as near the dictamen of his [Wilbraham's] will as was possible' was put into circulation. For reasons which remained unspecified in Aston's account, a general meeting of the gentry proved impossible to arrange. Aston and his friends went on circulating the petition which was now 'conceived without exception, if Sir George Booth might see it and were pleased to approve of it'. While signatures were still being collected, the petition was sent to Booth who returned answer that 'when he saw Sir Richard Wilbraham's hand to it, he would dispatch it'. 'It was then returned to Cholmeley and again a meeting of many gentlemen at which time it pleased Sir Richard Wilbraham to make some new exceptions to it.' It was again 'framed to his mind' and all seemed set fair for the petition's general acceptance, except that now it was to be sent 'to Chester to Sir Richard Grosvenor for his approbation'. This proved the sticking point. While, Aston claimed, Grosvenor's approval 'truly was heartily wished', this was one delay too many. 'But being three weeks time was spent and the matter not contradicted . . . this was but to be tossed from hand to hand and we advanced nothing' and so Aston and his associates went ahead collecting signatures hundred by hundred, expecting, even at the last, to get Wilbraham's assent – which, strangely, never came.[26]

According to Aston, then, everyone essentially agreed with what his petition said but, for mysterious reasons of personal pique and *amour propre*, the likes of Booth, Wilbraham and Grosevenor had never been quite able to bring themselves to sign the thing; the only differences separating him and his friends from the Booth-Wilbraham connection were personal and procedural rather than ideological or substantive, but, then, since Aston was desperate throughout to present his petition as the expression of the united view of the county (papists and puritans excepted), he would say that, wouldn't he? In fact, even in Aston's own account, Wilbraham is quoted as only having agreed to the proposition that the anti-episcopal petition was a fraud whose claims to represent the opinion of 'the county' had to be repudiated. That, of course, did not necessarily

[26] BL, Additional MS 36913, fol. 66r, Aston to an unnamed signatory of the Attestation.

imply agreement with the sharply anti-puritan and determinedly epis-
copalian bent of Aston's petition as it was presented to the Lords.

Luckily, for all that we have only Aston's account of these negotiations,
there are some other bits and pieces of evidence that allow us at least
to glimpse the sorts of arguments and discussions that were going on
behind the scenes in January and February 1641. In a commonplace
book containing a range of political materials generated during 1640–1
there is a copy of the Cheshire petition in favour of bishops with some of
the objections being raised in London against it appended. According to
these, the hands 'of the men of Cheshire were not underwritten to this
petition but to the subsequent brief declaration of the intent of the petition'. This ran, or so it was being alleged in London,

a petition to be presented to parliament against innovation in religion and alteration in church government, praying that both be settled as in the purest times
of queen Elizabeth and to regulate what was amiss either in church and state.
Whereunto your hands are required and being put to this paper will warrant
the inserting thereof into the schedule annexed into the original petition.[27]

If we turn to the actual text of the petition and the schedules of signatures
as they were turned over to the House of Lords we find considerable cor-
roboration for this claim. Potential supporters were asked to sign onto
schedules with a variety of different formulas at their head. Of these,
some were very sparely worded indeed, as in the following: 'we whose
names are underwritten give our consent to the petition agreed on by
the gentlemen of this county for settling the church government as it was
in the purest days of queen Elizabeth'; or again, 'upon consideration
of the copy of the petition agreed on by the nobility and gentry of this
county for the settling of church government as now it is by the bishops without alteration'. Others were more extended, as the following
presented to the parishioners of Sandbach: 'a petition to be preferred
in parliament against innovations in religion and alteration of church
government, praying that both may be settled as at in the purest times
of queen Elizabeth and to regulate whatsoever is amiss in ecclesiastical
courts'. In many cases these relatively brief forms of words were presented along with lists of the leading gentry and clergy who had already
endorsed them. There followed a list of the usual suspects at the centre of
the Cholmondeley-Aston-Kilmorrey connection. In one case the schedule came accompanied with a personal endorsement by Cholmondeley

[27] BL, Harleian MS 4931, fols. 118r–119r.

himself. This informed potential signatories that a petition was being prepared

> by myself and others of the nobility and gentry and inhabitants of this county to be preferred to the parliament house concerning the establishment of church government according to the practise of the happy days of queen Elizabeth and both myself and many of the gentry have already signed it and we desire that as much of the inhabitants as well freeholders as others of you . . . may join with us I desire you to subscribe your name to the paper enclosed.

This missive was signed 'your loving friend R. Cholmondeley'.[28]

In evaluating the precise meaning of these schedules, much turns upon what was meant by the phrase 'the purest times of queen Elizabeth'. As Gardiner himself pointed out, this was a phrase that, during the 1630s, had been used by Charles I to underwrite a high Laudian vision of the church – it figures prominently in fact in the preamble to the Canons of 1640. By 1641, however, Charles was using precisely the same term in order to repudiate Laudian 'innovation'. But by then similar references to 'the purest times of Elizabeth's reign' were also being deployed by many a moderate puritan to justify a variety of packages of ecclesiastical reform that, while they might fall short of the complete abolition of either episcopacy or the prayerbook, did not, however conservative the terms in which the were couched, in fact constitute a simple return to the pre-Laudian status quo ante.[29] There might, therefore, be all the difference in the world between signing off on a petition 'establishing the government of the church according to the purest days of queen Elizabeth' and one 'settling the church government as now it is by bishops without alteration'. Moreover, it appears that these potential discrepancies and ambiguities were something that the people who orchestrated the final presentation of the bundle of the various parish schedules collected during late January and early February to the House of Lords as a coherent statement of county opinion were only too well aware. For sometimes, confronted with schedules which featured the phrase 'according to the purest times of queen Elizabeth', they sought to close down the implications of moderate reform of church government that might be contained in that formula by adding, in a different hand and in a different ink, the

---

[28] HLRO, Main Papers, 27 February 1640–1.

[29] S. R. Gardiner, *History of England from the Accession of James I to the Outbreak of the Civil War, 1603–42*, 10 vols (1884), IX, 268. 'It was useless to tell them [the parliament] that he was ready to return to the church system of Elizabeth. They knew that in the days of his unquestioned power, he had professed to be following in the steps of Elizabeth, and that there was nothing to show that he meant to interpret her system otherwise than he had interpreted it then.'

further qualifying phrase 'without innovation in government' or, more simply, 'in government'.

We can, then, see inscribed in the composite body of the petition the dim outlines of the sorts of discussion about the precise content and tone of the final version of the petition that must have comprised the substance of the conversation between Aston and Wilbraham and his friends. We can also gain some sense of the range of disparate pitches whereby a variety of people were induced to sign off on the petition and watch those different messages being massaged into a univocal endorsement of what, after their negotiations with Wilbraham, Booth and Grosvenor had broken down, Aston and his friends had decided was to be the final purport of the petition. In short, we can reconstruct the process whereby the petition was assembled as a coalition-building exercise through which Aston and his allies sought to align as wide a range of persons and opinions as possible behind the defence of 'the church of England' against 'innovation' and 'puritanism'. It was merely that what was meant by any and all of these key terms might vary very considerably between the various strands of opinion whose support was being canvassed and whose expression was being framed and finessed by the various forms of words circulated around the county. In short, rather than an unproblematic articulation of some pre-existing 'prayer book protestant' tradition, a straightforward product of a stable middle ground, located between and defined by equally stable, Laudian and puritan, extremes, Aston's petition emerges from this material as the product of a relatively open-ended and unstable process of negotiation. Viewed in such 'political' terms, it can be seen as an attempt to create a pro-episcopal, anti-Presbyterian coalition that could or would encompass a spectrum of opinion running from conviction Laudians, anxious to save as much as possible of episcopal and monarchical government from the burning car wreck of the Personal Rule, through various sorts of Calvinist and erastian episcopalians, to encompass many an erstwhile moderate puritan, alarmed and alienated by the extremism of current puritan nonconformist behaviour and political agitation and by the imminent prospect of a genuinely Presbyterian church settlement.[30] On this basis, we might see the final

---

[30] By this date Charles himself had dropped both Laud and Laudianism and the archbishop himself was busy repudiating the policies that he had professed during the Personal Rule. Nor was the king alone in this; in January 1642 that leading lay Laudian and friend of the archbishop, Viscount Scudamore, was to endorse (presumably for tactical political reasons) an apparently anti-Laudian but virulently pro-episcopal petition being raised in Herefordshire. As Ian Atherton observes, given Scudamore's previous track record, 'one is left wondering what, in the church policy of

refusal of Wilbraham, Booth, Grosvenor and the others to sign off on Aston's version of the petition – moderate as its defence of episcopacy was – as a product not only of personal pique and misplaced *amour propre*, but also of real ideological differences about how they wanted the church and commonwealth to be 'settled' or 'established' and just as pressing doubts as to the wider, national political purposes to which Aston and his allies might put the petition once it was signed and sealed and sent off to Westminister. If the petition was intended as such a coalition-building enterprise, with the refusal of Wilbraham and his friends to sign on, it failed. But the failure was only a partial one; indeed this cloud had rather a shiny silver lining, since once Aston had taken his unilateral decision to break off negotiations he was free not only to adjust the final form of words to suit his own preferences and purposes but also to shape and time the petition's entry into the tense central political narrative then taking shape at Westminister and Whitehall. Small wonder, then, that after Aston and his friends had finished with it, 'some of those who have subscribed . . . the abstract were much distracted upon the view of the large petition'.[31]

V

Thus far we have largely concerned ourselves with the local dynamics of these interactions. But it seems unlikely in the extreme that either Sir Thomas or his local enemies and rivals were playing a merely or even mainly local politics. As Conrad Russell has observed, the anti-puritan, pro-episcopal reaction in which Aston's Cheshire petition played so prominent a part was, in fact, a national phenomenon. Moreover, on Russell's account, the moment in February at which Aston presented it to the Lords was a peculiarly pivotal one. It came in the midst of Commons debates about church government that were themselves a crucial part of negotiations between the Scots, the junto and the king over a projected settlement for the three kingdoms, a projected settlement broken in part over the issue of church government and from which the king felt able to extricate himself precisely because of the groundswell of anti-puritan and anti-Scots feeling then sweeping the nation.

the 1630s, Scudamore regarded as an excess or an exorbitance'. I. Atherton, *Ambition and Failure in Stuart England: the Career of John, First Viscount Scudamore* (Manchester, 1999), 222–3. See also, J. Walter, 'Confessional politics in pre civil war Essex: prayer books, profanations and petitions', *HJ*, 44 (2001), 677–701.

[31] BL, Harleian MS 4931, fols. 118v–119r.

In a speech at the Banqueting House to both houses of parliament
on 23 January 1641 Charles issued a public statement of what he was
prepared to yield and what he was not. Reform of the courts 'according
to the law'; removal of those aspects of his revenue that were deemed
oppressive or illegal; frequent, but certainly not annual, parliaments. 'He
would trust to the affections' of his subjects for supply and admitted 'that
often parliaments are the fittest means to keep a good correspondency
between me and my people, which I do much desire'. In general, he
professed his desire to effect 'the reformation of all innovations both in
church or commonwealth' in order 'to reduce all things to the times of
Elizabeth'. There were, however, limits to his reforming zeal and on the
issue of church government he made it clear that, while he might consider
preventing the bishops encroaching 'too much upon the temporality' in
future, such efforts would fall short of removing their places in parliament
and that such measures, whatever they might in the end amount to,
would be the extent of the reformation that he was about to allow in
the church. Indeed, this was the issue upon which Charles made his
stand, playing the order and anti-puritan cards hard, as he complained
vigorously about

the distractions that are at this present occasioned through the cause of parliament, though not by the parliament; for there are some men who more maliciously than ignorantly will put no difference between reformation or alteration
of government. Hence it cometh that divine service is irreverently interrupted
and petitions in an illegal way given are neither dismissed nor denied . . . There
are some very strange (I know not what to term them) petitions given in the
names of divers countries against the established government of the church

which contained 'great threatenings against the bishops, as they would
be but cyphers or at the least take them quite away'.[32]
    In effect, Charles was announcing episcopacy as the wedge issue with
which he was going to part the would-be parliamentary participants
in 'the projected settlement of 1641' from their erstwhile Scottish allies
or else use to break the settlement itself. He was also choosing anti-
puritanism as the ideological terrain upon which he was going to build
himself a party. Here, of course, was Aston's issue, Aston's language and
Aston's political programme; there was now something like a perfect
fit between Aston's attitudes and agenda and those of the crown. In a
peroration that followed closely the sentiments of the king's Banqueting
House speech, Aston proclaimed that

<hr />

[32] BL, Harleian MS 4931, fols. 106r–107r.

his majesty persevering in his gracious inclination to hear the complaints and relieve the grievances of his subjects in frequent parliaments, it will so unite the head and body, so indissolubly cement the affections of his people to our royal sovereign, that without any other change of government, he can never want revenue nor we justice.[33]

All that remained to bring such a much-to-be-wished consummation about, the petition implied (again echoing the king), was the active suppression of the puritan campaign for further reformation and it was that – 'to stop the torrent of such spirits before they swell beyond the bounds of government' – that the House of Lords was being petitioned to do.

Moreover, Aston was able to introduce the Cheshire petition into the cockpit of national politics on what Russell has identitifed as the crucial day. For Aston presented his petition to the Lords on 27 February, the very moment when, in the House of Commons, 'in a debate forced with the skill of a modern question time', Hyde was trying to make the members of the junto choose between their alliance to the Scots and their attachment to a settlement with the crown with episcopacy at its heart. Introduced at precisely this moment into the Lords, as Russell laconically remarks, Aston's petition indicated 'that the king too had a body of public opinion to appeal to'. The salience and significance of Aston's intervention seems to have been recognised immediately by members of 'the zealous party' in the Lords who tried, if not to prevent then at least to delay, Aston's petition being read. According to one diarist 'Lords Say, Brook, Paget and Mandeville and others' all argued long and hard that it might be 'deferred the reading' and it was only after 'long debate' that 'it was at last admitted to be heard'.[34]

Small wonder: for on Russell's account

this debate seems to have brought the settlement scheme to an end. Charles had preferred his new Privy Councillors in order to persuade them to abandon the Scots and root and branch, and, at the first opportunity they had in public, some of their key allies had refused to do so. In forcing Hampden and others to make a declaration on the Scots' paper, Hyde had brought himself a degree nearer the king's favour, and civil war several degrees nearer. [A judgement, of course, that applies with equal force to Aston.] The king seems to have decided, probably within hours, on a change of policy. This was not just because his new councillors had let him down: it was also because the new wave of anti-Scottish and anti-puritan feeling for which Hyde, Culpepper, Strangeways, Hopton and Digby spoke on 27 February offered him the possibility of raising a party against a group of people whose outlook had always been profoundly distasteful to him.

---

[33] Maltby, 'Petitions for episcopacy', 117–18.   [34] BL, Harleian MS 6424, fol. 43r.

It offered him a chance, not to reunite a country much of which he disliked, but to underake what he always found the much more congenial task of leading a party.[35]

In building that party, of course, Charles needed not merely parliamentary spokesmen like Hyde, but local agents, mediators between events at the centre and the localities, and that was precisely what Sir Thomas Aston had now become (perhaps in a way had always been) as he transformed a petition that may well have been intended – certainly by those who in the end did not sign it – to have been an agent of conciliation, even an endorsement of some moderate process of further reformation and moderated episcopacy, into a far more subversively and divisively 'royalist' document.

Nor should such a close involvement on Aston's part in central politics surprise us. As we have seen, since 1635 he had been a gentleman of the privy chamber and acted as a ship-money sheriff of exemplary energy and ruthlessness. Also in the mid 1630s he had re-edified the church at Aston Chapel according to decidedly Laudian, altar-centred notions of the beauty of holiness. He also seems to have spent the crucial period of spring 1641 consistently in London rather than in Cheshire. John Werden and Lord Cholmondeley's letters, which were all designed to keep him abreast of events in the county, were addressed to him either at his brother John's lodging in Falcon Court, Fleet Street or at Mr Garland's house, Holborn. (His brother too was a fledgling courtier, holding the office of gentleman usher in the household of the Prince of Wales.)[36] Sir Thomas was, therefore, perfectly placed to pick up the nature and nuances of royal policy and propaganda from its very source, co-ordinating his efforts in the country with the statements and initiatives coming out of the court. Again, the nature of his subsequent campaign against Brereton, designed to set the Lords against the Commons and to play upon issues of privilege and fears in the Lords of puritan radicalism and disorder, fits perfectly with Charles I's wider political strategy during this period which, as

---

[35] C. S. R. Russell, *The Fall of the British Monarchies 1637–1642* (Oxford, 1991), 270.

[36] Lake, 'The collection of ship money in Cheshire'; Maltby, *Prayer Book and People*, pp. 137–41; for letters addressed to Aston in London see, for instance, BL, Additional MS 36914, fol. 197v, Werden to Aston, 13 March 1640/1 or *ibid.* fol. 200v; Cholmondeley to Aston, 20 March 1640/1, or *ibid.* fol. 210, Werden to Aston, 2 April 1641, or ibid., fol. 218r, Cholmondeley to Aston, 1 May 1641, all addressed to his brother John's lodgings in Falcon Court 'over against St Dunstan's in Fleetstreet'. For letters addressed to Aston 'at Mr Garland's house at Holborn' see *ibid.*, fol. 217v, Werden to Aston, March 1641, or ibid. 221v, Werden to Aston, 7 May 1641. For his brother's position in the household of the Prince of Wales see Bod. Lib., Nalson MS, vol. 13, fol. 74v.

Russell has described it, revolved around the exploitation of precisely the same structural, institutional and ideological forces and tensions.

A timetable set rather more by events in Westminister and Whitehall than by those in Cheshire and a political strategy dictated as much by exigencies of the politics of the parliament and the court as by those of the county would explain Aston's haste in pushing his first petition through without first securing Booth and Wilbraham's support. If it was needed for a concerted push on the issue of episcopacy in both Houses then time was of the essence. Such considerations might also explain Aston's (potentially disastrous) miscalculation in preferring his second petition to the Lords without reference back to county opinion. Seeing an opportunity to further both his own and his royal master's interests, he wanted desperately to push that advantage home. Taking a few liberties with Cheshire opinion probably seemed a price well worth paying for such a prize.

Certainly, such a bi-polar approach, playing off interests and divisions in the locality against the political needs and requirements of a variety of central authorities, using his clout at the centre to enhance his standing in the locality and his standing there similarly to enhance his status at the centre, was entirely familar to Aston, who, during the 1630s, had pursued just such a political strategy over ship money with energy and imagination. As a tireless defender of the shire's interests against the city in the matter of ship money, Sir Thomas had managed to raise his profile in the county sufficiently to challenge the scions of the old county elite in the Short Parliament election. From before the Short Parliament he had revealed himself as a conviction anti-puritan, and from early on his close associates in the county, some of whom, like Aston, had ties with the court, had revealed pronounced anti-Scottish feelings. Rebuffed at the county election for the Long Parliament, Aston seized on the issue of root and branch to intervene both in county and national politics. He did so through a petitioning campaign which, as we have seen, allowed him to claim a public representative role in defending the name of the county and the national church and episcopacy from populist, puritan assault. In so doing he was also attempting to dish his local rival Sir William Brereton and to establish or re-establish close links with the court and the political and polemical programme of the king. In many ways, Aston was trying to do here precisely what many members of the Long Parliament were also doing; shuffling, indeed trying to mediate, between the movements of local opinion and events and an even more volatile national, indeed British, political scene. It was just that Aston was trying to perform this trick from outside rather than from inside the parliament, basing his claims to be a 'public' or 'representative person' not on membership of the parliament, but on his petitioning activities and his politico-religious contacts and influence in both court and country. He was appealing to, and trying to manipulate, a variety of different points of central authority, in the process playing off the shifting loci of administrative and political power that were constantly coagulating and dissolving, forming and reforming, across Westminister and Whitehall, within and between king, Lords and Commons. This, of course, was also precisely what his opponents in the county and at Westminister were trying to do to him. In short, Aston was operating as a sort of one-man point of contact, a freelance public man and representative person, intervening in events at the centre on the basis of his local support base, his claimed capacity to speak for the county, and in the locality through the backing of whatever emanations of central authority he could successfully co-opt.

The ironies at work here were considerable; for here was the great opponent of puritanism and popularity appealing to 'the people' through the press and a mass petitioning campaign conducted with all the skill and commitment of any puritan firebrand. In so doing, just as much as the puritan godly Sir Thomas was responding to and seeking to bend to his purposes the fragmentation both of central authority and provincial opinion consequent upon a national (indeed an incipiently 'British') political crisis. Again, just like the puritans, he was seeking to co-ordinate and interconnect events at the centre and in the localities, appealing to 'the people', representing the county and the country to the centre and the centre to the county or country in ways likely to further his particular politico-religious agenda.

VI

And sure enough by March 1641 Aston had indeed managed to secure the overt support, indeed the personal endorsement, of the king himself. On 26 March Cholmondeley wrote to Aston to inform him that 'the king by a letter hath been pleased to acknowledge our petition'.[37] With typical acumen, Aston immediately moved to turn this token of royal regard to his political advantage in the locality. He sent the king's missive approving their petition to Werden for general distribution amongst the leading gentry. In April Werden reported that 'I have sent Mr Allen a

---

[37] BL, Additional MS 36913, fol. 201r.

copy of the king's letter which was before dispersed into every corner of the country and (as you presage) causes envy enough. There is not one of quality but they have a copy of the letter.'[38] At the assizes at Chester in May Werden set about dispersing either this or another letter from the king (Werden merely referred to 'his majesty's most gracious letter') more generally amongst the gentry. 'Beside the immediate presentation thereof to my good old lord I did yesternight show the letter itself and gave copies thereof to my Lord Brereton and to Sir Richard Wilbraham and Mr High Sherriff, so that a week's time in the vacation could not have so divulged it as this one night hath'. 'By it' [the letter], Werden reported,

I can perceive our neutrals and adversaries both awaked. I showed it to the judges likewise who much applauded it as a prop to their fidelities and orthodox professions of the religion established, which was very effectually pressed by our chief justice in his charge. I showed it to young Mr Grosvenor (Sir Richard languisheth at Eccleston of the gout) and he told me the certificate of the patriots [perhaps a reference to the Attestation] was gone, though by the reluctancy I observed in him and some others I can believe they will post after to stay the delivery. Mr Cotton and my Lord Cholmondeley even now write to me. I will come this night to tender the petition now sent to Sir Richard Wilbraham's subscription which if he give [?] I will hope it may prove a reconciler and gain myriads of more hands unto it.'[39]

At least in Aston's circle, the royal missive was received with rapture. In another letter of April 1641 Werden described its tonic effects:

I have no abilities to express the joy of this most honourable Earl [Rivers?] to whom I delivered his majesty's grace and from him I have transmitted it to the other Lords of whom I am able to say (particularly of my Lord Colmondeley) he hath a jubilee of joy ... The rest (I dare assure you) before this hour have all received his majesty's royal favour and the general dispersion is already made thereof in these parts, as none of quality (except our mayor who countenanced the seditious preacher) but they have testified an inexpressible comfort in his majesty's resolution and acceptance of their duties and devotions.[40]

[38] BL, Additional MS 36914, fol. 210r, Werden to Aston, April 1641.
[39] BL, Additional MS 36914, fols. 220r–v, Werden to Aston, 7 May 1641. This is almost certainly a reference to a very early draft of the petition in favour of the prayerbook, canvassed in the county during October and November 1641 and presented in the Lords on 21 December. This was Aston's finest hour – the point when he finally succeeded in attaching the Wilbraham/Booth/Grosvenor group to a defence of the ecclesiastical status quo. But even this petition was subject to a variety of competing interpretations and was to be (again) inserted by Aston into a crucial conjuncture of events at Westminister in such a way as to render it a far more overtly partisan, 'royalist' gesture than many of those who had signed it had very likely intended. I intend to deal with these events in more detail elsewhere.
[40] BL, Additional MS 36914, fol. 216r–v, Werden to Aston, late March 1641.

Werden himself went into ecstasies on the subject in a remarkable letter to Aston dated dated 'beatissimi dei':

The day is the most happy anniversary inauguration of the blessed reign of our gracious sovereign and this the first employment of that day wherein the opportunity adds fervency to my prayers, that God would lengthen his days as the days of heaven and protect him with a choir grand of angels that his wisdom may yet more appear as a ray of God's spirit. You have, Sir, honoured me with an employment whereof my life and fortune cannot be worthy both in showing me so blessed a resolution of his sacred majesty and making me the messenger of so acceptable an evangelium to my good old lord and those other noble men to whom this divine goodness is directed . . . For my part I have begged his Majesty's letter of my Lord that my dying prayer [Werden was obviously ill as he wrote the letter] may bless those happy characters and royal hand which gave us assurance of preservation from schisms and innovations . . . I do not know what could have added more cheerfulness from earth to my nunc dimittis than the promising blessings of his Majesty's goodness.[41]

With its liturgical and para-liturgical references, its constant slippage between divine and royal favour, between the word of God and that of the king, with its sense of the charismatic, almost talismanic, relic-like significance conferred on the holder by physical possession of a royal holograph written in such a cause, the letter breathes the language of sacerdotal kingship, of what one might term Laudian absolutism or rather it exists on a cusp dividing the culture of the Caroline court and that of later church and king Cavalier Anglicanism. It is all the more remarkable in a letter of March 1641 coming not from the court to the country but from an obscure provincial lawyer and man of business writing to a gentleman of the privy chamber.

Aston, too, seems to have collapsed his religious allegiances to the national church and episcopacy into his political allegiance to his monarch. Writing of the motives of the authors of the Attestation, Aston himself casually observed that 'I know not out of what zeal, whether against me or the cause would needs set this gin a work again.' The 'cause', of course, was 'the preservation of the church government' – something to which Werdon at one point referred simply as 'God's own cause'[42] – now seen as both an end in itself and as a token of or symbol for a wider sense of political loyalty. For since epsicopacy 'was so consonant with the word of God, the constant practise of all times (?) since Christianity came in and so acceptable to the king, as he hath declared himself, no loyal person

[41] BL, Additional MS 36914, fol. 216r–v.
[42] BL, Additional MS 36914, fol. 197v, Werden to Aston 13 March 1641.

should thus, maliciously, wrestle against it'.[43] Aston continued to pursue this line in his tract *A remonstrance against presbytery*, which was dedicated to the king, wore Charles' epistolary approval of the petition of February as a badge of honour, and repeated the argument that given the king's express support for episcopacy no genuinely loyal subject could continue to oppose it.[44]

Of course, Aston claimed to be motivated not only by his loyalty to 'the cause' , but also by his obligations to the service of 'the county' or 'the country'. He had, he asserted at one point, 'a real heart for my country's service'. In his dealings with the authors of the Attestation Aston presented himself not so much as an intransigent defender of 'the cause', but as the vindicator of both his own and, more importantly, 'the county's', honour from the fraudulent and seditious efforts of Brereton and the local puritans to hijack 'Cheshire' for their own pernicious and partisan purposes. Thus, even as Aston and his friends privately used the language of division and ideological polarisation, of loyalty and dis-loyalty, of orthodoxy and schism, of good Christians and 'precisians', so they and Aston continued, in public, to deploy the rhetoric of unity and consensus, of honour and shame, in the representation and service of what were traditionally taken as (but which were now rapidly ceasing to be) univocal notions of entirely compatible , indeed, of almost inter-changeable, entities that went variously under the names of 'the county', 'the country' , the 'public' and 'the cause'. As he told the authors of the Attestation,

tis true I have lately been upon the stage exposed to much censure but must wish you to examine your own hearts and satisfy yourself by this large quere, and if you find I have either injured you or any man living or have unjustly traduced any man, I shall confess to have deserved this and more from you. But if to be sensible of the violation of a professed friendship, of a breach of such a promise as engaged me into trouble, divided the country into factions or to avert the attempt of a public affront from myself be imputed as crimes, I shall forever be still. It hath ever been my first principle to do no wrong and my second to take none I can avoid.[45]

Here, in a tone of aggrieved innocence, Aston was presenting himself as the guardian of the honour, integrity and the unity of the county. In preferring his second petition he had merely been discharging his obligations to both county and commonwealth. It was those who, for

---

[43] B.L., Additional MS 33936, fol. 232 r–v, Aston to William Moreton, 28 May 1641.
[44] Aston, *A remonstrance*, dedicatory epistle, 'To the king's most excellent majesty'.
[45] BL, Additional MS 36913, fol. 77v.

their own private purposes, had refused to support his efforts who were, in fact, failing in their duty to the county and commonwealth. 'You might have done yourselves more right and more good to the commonwealth', Sir Thomas indignantly told the authors of the Attestation, 'by joining in [rather] than excepting against that petition.'[46] ''Tis the fate of all times,' he lamented, 'divisions have been and will be while there are men. But woe and sorrow to them by whom such divisions come.'[47] Thus was an entirely traditional positive language of unity and consensus, of loyalty and service to the county and commonwealth, of public professions and commitments publicly made and just as publicly kept, and an equally traditional negative language of division and faction, created by the preference of private respects to public duties, turned on the middle group by the very man whom they clearly regarded as having, for his own private, both personal and political, interests, divided the county by usurping a public representative role to which he had no right.

The county community is a palpable (albeit increasingly absent) presence in these exchanges, but it is so as a sort of 'imagined community', a bundle of moral and social norms and constraints, of tacit assumptions and expectations about one's own and other's conduct. On both sides, however, this traditional notion of how things should be was now being honoured at least as much in the breach as in the observance. But even as it was breaking down, the ideal of a 'county community' of publicly engaged and honourable gentlemen, united in the representation and service of the county and the commonwealth, retained considerable rhetorical or moral force, as the expectations and standards attached to this ideal now became available as sticks with which to beat and berate one's opponents, as both Aston and the signatories of the Attestation duked it out as representatives of 'the country'.

But the existence of such incipiently political, partly personal, partly ideological and partly structural divisions amongst the county's 'representatives' could not but have an effect on the ways in which core terms like 'county', 'country' and 'commonwealth' were construed and deployed. Thus, when large sections of the gentry county community made it quite clear that they did not care for Aston's style of vindication, indeed, that they did not wish to sign up for his version of what 'the county' was or stood for, his supporters responded by adjusting their definition of 'the county' accordingly. Thus, on May 1, 1641 Lord Cholmondeley wrote Aston a brief note of praise and encouragement:

[46] *Ibid.*, fol. 71v   [47] *Ibid.*, fol. 76r.

'noble Sir Thomas your faithful service, and exquisite pains and care for your county hath been such and so great that you have truly deserved the love of all good men in the county, for the rest they are neither worth wishing nor having and a great number that I know do acknowledge it'.[48] The more general and formal letter in support of Aston's second petition – the counter-Attestation, as it were – made much the same point in even more pointed language, speaking of the support Aston enjoyed as coming not so much from 'the county' or 'country' as from 'the inabitants thereof who stand well affected either to his majesty or the good and peaceable government of this kingdom'.[49]

The real object of loyalty, the true subject of vindication here was now no longer simply 'the county' or 'the country' so much as 'the good men in the county', those 'well affected to his majesty'. On this evidence that which was being represented and vindicated had become, for Aston and his associates, just as it surely had for Brereton and the puritan godly, not merely a function of what persons, even persons of substance, in the county wanted, but an amalgam of that and the demands of 'the cause', an ideologically defined version of what all true and loyal and orthodox English persons and Cheshire men would or should naturally want. Only thus could the complete compatibility of ideological rectitude, orthodoxy and loyalty, on the one hand, and an open-handed public canvassing and representation of the sense of the county or country, on the other, be maintained. That they were compatible remained, of course, axiomatic for Aston, just as it did, at the other politico-religious extreme, for Brereton. But in the presence of an ongoing political crisis at the centre and of what were rapidly becoming recognised as non-negotiable religio-political disputes about the nature of orthodoxy and loyalty conducted across the country and the social order, it was becoming increasingly difficult to both further 'the cause' (whatever it was) and to represent the interests and opinions of 'the county' or 'the country'.

Thus was 'religion' transmuted into 'politics', as different styles of piety and positions on church government shaded into other more 'political' debates about 'representation', 'order', and the nature and locus of authority throughout the polity. Certainly, many of the most serious divisions in play here could certainly be said to be 'religious' in origin, created by the contest for the leadership of the county between that zealous puritan opponent of episcopacy, Sir William Brereton, and his pro-episcopalian adversary, the no less zealous Aston. However, the issues

---

[48] BL, Additional MS 36914, fol. 218r.b.   [49] *Ibid.*, fols. 222r–223r.

around which the resulting debates were organised and the forms they took swiftly became 'political', concerned with the nature and appropriate forms of representation and order – with questions of who could speak for the county, how best to do it and to whom. The intensity of Aston and Werden and their friends' religious commitments to the prayerbook and episcopacy and their loathing for 'puritanism' is scarcely to be doubted (although there perhaps remains a question of how best to characterise those commitments). But even Aston chose to couch his assault on Presbyterianism and defence of episcopacy in terms of very wide, in part at least 'secular', notions of social and political order. Moreover, his petitioning activities are best seen not as simple statements of a pre-existingly coherent religious position – 'prayer book protestantism' coming, under the impact of political crisis and of puritan and Laudian attack, to full self-awareness – but as elaborate coalition-building exercises, in which a variety of strands of opinion were being aligned behind forms of words that could mean subtly different things to different people. This, of course, was an inherently political enterprise, as too was the nature and timing of Aston's subsequent deployments of the resulting statements of 'Cheshire opinion' into the central political narrative.[50]

Thus did the language of division, of 'the good men of the county', of 'the well affected' and their opposites, invade a political rhetoric still ostensibly dominated by the need for agreement, consensus and service to an entirely transparent and univocal public or common good. We can watch in these exchanges the fabric of the county community – the mutual bonds of trust, respect and restraint that kept that 'community' together – breaking down under, even as they were deployed to both resist and exploit, the pressure exerted by ideological disagreement, personal and political competition and the exigencies of a rapidly changing national political scene.[51] Thus, too, did national political issues and stances come to frame and colour what might appear at first sight to have been quintessentially local focuses of loyalty, identity and concern. Certainly, many of the forms, interests and causes being appealed to and defended throughout these transactions were intensely local – centred on the county of Cheshire, both name and thing. However, almost none of the succeeding political moves, manoeuvres and appeals took a straightforwardly 'localist' form. On the contrary, they involved the appeal to and manipulation (by a variety of local interests and connections,

[50] Cf. John Morrill, 'The religious context of the English civil war', in his *The Nature of the English Revolution* (1993).
[51] Cf. Mark Kishlansky, *Parliamentary Selection* (Cambridge, 1986).

invoking a range of national religio-political platforms and principles) of a number of nodes of central authority and the further massaging and manipulation of opinion in the county through (what could ever be only partially successful) partisan attempts to control the (often contradictory) waves of information, instruction and authority entering the county from the centre.[52]

---

[52] Cf. John Morrill, *The Revolt of the Provinces* (1976) and A. J. Fletcher, *The Outbreak of the English Civil War* (1979) and, of course, above all, C. S. R. Russell, *The Fall of the British Monarchies*.

A bibliography of the principal published writings of Conrad Russell, 1962–2002

Compiled by Richard Cust and Elizabeth Russell

1962

'The ship-money judgments of Bramston and Davenport', *EHR*, 77, 312–18 (reprinted in *Unrevolutionary England, 1603–1642* (1990), 137–44).

1965

'The theory of treason in the trial of Strafford', *EHR*, 80, 30–50 (reprinted in *Unrevolutionary England, 1603–1642*, 89–109).

1967

'Arguments for religious unity in England, 1530–1650', *JEH*, 18, 201–26 (reprinted in *Unrevolutionary England, 1603–1642*, 179–204).

1968

'The authorship of the bishop's diary in the House of Lords in 1641', *BIHR*, 41, 229–36 (reprinted in *Unrevolutionary England, 1603–1642*, 111–18).
'Justice Croke and the Hampdens', *N&Q*, 213 (October), 367.

1969

'The wardship of John Pym', *EHR*, 84, 304–17 (reprinted in *Unrevolutionary England, 1603–1642*, 145–64).
'Robert Cecil and his father's wardship leases', *N&Q*, 214 (January), 33.
'The date of John Hampden's birth', *N&Q*, 214 (March), 90.

1971

The Crisis of Parliaments: English History, 1509–1660 (Oxford: Clarendon Press).

1972

'English land sales, 1540–1640: a comment on the evidence', *EcHR*, 2nd ser., 25, 117–21.

1973

'Introduction' and 'Parliament and the king's finances' in *The Origins of the English Civil War* (London and Basingstoke: Macmillan Press), 1–31, 91–116.
'John Pym and the queen's receivership' (jointly with the late Miss Evelyn Gore), *BIHR*, 46, 106–7.

1976

'Parliamentary history in perspective, 1604–1629', *Hist*, 61, 1–27 (reprinted in *Unrevolutionary England, 1603–1642*, 31–57).
'Parliamentarianism 1604–1642', in W. Lamont (ed.), *Sussex Tapes*, 135–53, transcript of a tape-recorded interview, with Professor G. E. Aylmer.

1977

'The foreign policy debate in the House of Commons in 1621', *HJ*, 20, 289–309 (reprinted in *Unrevolutionary England, 1603–1642*, 59–79).
'The examination of Mr Mallory after the Parliament of 1621', *BIHR*, 50, 125–32 (reprinted in *Unrevolutionary England, 1603–1642*, 81–8).

1979

Parliaments and English Politics, 1621–1629 (Oxford: Clarendon Press).
'The parliamentary career of John Pym, 1621–9', in P. Clark, A. G. R. Smith and N. R. N. Tyacke (eds.), *The English Commonwealth 1546–1640: Essays in Politics and Society Presented to Joel Hurstfield* (Leicester: Leicester University Press), 147–65 (reprinted in *Unrevolutionary England, 1603–1642*, 205–228).

1982

'Monarchies, wars and estates in England, France and Spain, c.1580–1640', *Legislative Studies Quarterly*, 7, 205–20 (reprinted in *Unrevolutionary England, 1603–1642*, 121–36).

1983

'The nature of a parliament in early Stuart England', in H. Tomlinson (ed.), *Before the English Civil War: Essays on Early Stuart Politics and Government* (London and Basingstoke: MacMillan Press), 123–50 (reprinted in *Unrevolutionary England, 1603–1642*, 1–29).

1984

'Why did Charles I call the Long Parliament', *Hist*, 69, 375–83 (reprinted in *Unrevolutionary England, 1603–1642*, 253–60).
'Why did Charles I fight the civil war?', *History Today*, 34 (June), 31–4.

1985

'Charles I's financial estimates of 1642', *BIHR*, 58, 109–20 (reprinted in *Unrevolutionary England, 1603–1642*, 165–76).
'What is political history?', *History Today*, 35 (January), 12–13.
'The Catholic wind', in J. M. Merriman (ed.), *For Want of a Horse* (Lexington, Mass.: Viking Press), 103–7 (reprinted in *Unrevolutionary England, 1603–1642*, 305–8).

1987

'The British problem and the English Civil War', *Hist*, 72, 395–415 (reprinted in *Unrevolutionary England, 1603–1642*, 231–51), Inaugural Lecture delivered at University College, London on 7 March 1985.
'England's last poll tax', *History Today*, 37 (October), 9–11.

1988

'The First Army Plot of 1641', *TRHS*, 5th ser., 38, 85–106 (reprinted in *Unrevolutionary England, 1603–1642*, 281–302).
'The British background to the Irish Rebellion of 1641', *BIHR*, 61, 166–82 (reprinted in *Unrevolutionary England, 1603–1642*, 263–79).

1990

The Causes of the English Civil War (Oxford: Clarendon Press), The Ford Lectures Delivered in the University of Oxford, 1987–1988.
Unrevolutionary England, 1603–1642 (London: Hambledon Press).
'English Parliaments, 1593–1606: one epoch or two?', in D. M. Dean and N. L. Jones (eds.), *The Parliaments of Elizabethan England* (Oxford: Blackwell), 191–213.
'The Bourgeois Revolution – a mirage', *History Today*, 40 (September), 7–9.

1991

The Fall of the British Monarchies, 1637–1642 (Oxford: Clarendon Press).
'Issues in the House of Commons, 1621–1629: predictors of civil war allegiance', *Albion*, 23, 23–39.

1992

The Addled Parliament of 1614: The Limits of Revision (Reading: University of Reading), The Stenton Lecture, University of Reading, 1991.

1993

'The Scottish party in English parliaments, 1640–2 or the myth of the English Revolution', *HR*, 66, 35–52, Inaugural Lecture at King's College, University of London, 29 January 1991.
'Divine Rights in the early seventeenth century', in J. S. Morrill, P. Slack and D. Woolf (eds.), *Public Duty and Private Conscience in Seventeenth Century England: Essays Presented to G. E. Aylmer* (Oxford: Clarendon Press), 101–20.

1994

'The Anglo-Scottish union 1603–1643: a success?', in A. Fletcher and P. Roberts (eds.), *Culture and Society in Early Modern Britain: Essays in Honour of Patrick Collinson* (Cambridge: Cambridge University Press), 238–56.

1995

'Composite monarchies in early modern Europe: the British and Irish example', in A. Grant and K. J. Stringer (eds.), *Uniting the Kingdom? The Making of British History* (Routledge), 133–46.
'Whose supremacy? King, parliament and the church, 1530–1640', *Lambeth Palace Library Annual Review*, 53–64.

1996

'The Reformation and the creation of the Church of England, 1500–1640', in J. S. Morrill (ed.), *The Oxford Illustrated History of Tudor and Stuart Britain* (Oxford: Oxford University Press), 258–292.
'Sir Thomas Wentworth and anti-Spanish sentiment, 1621–1624', in J. F. Merritt (ed.), *The Political World of Thomas Wentworth, Earl of Strafford, 1621–1641* (Cambridge: Cambridge University Press), 47–62.

1997

'Thomas Cromwell's doctrine of parliamentary sovereignty', *TRHS*, 6th ser., 7, 235–46.
'Judicial independence in the early seventeenth century', *Graya Occasional Paper* (The Honourable Society of Grays Inn).
'Der Englische König Jacob I', in H. Duchardt (ed.), *Der Herrscher in der Doppelpflicht, Europäische Fürsten und ihre beiden Throne* (Mainz), 123–37.

1999

'Why did people choose sides in the English Civil War?', *The Historian*, 63 (Autumn), 4–9.

2000

'Parliament, the royal supremacy and the church', in S. Taylor and J. Parry (eds.), *Parliament and the Church* (*PH*, 19, pt 1), 27–37.

2002

'Bishop Berkeley at Westminster', in S. Clucas and R. Davies (eds.), *The Crisis of 1614 and the Addled Parliament: Literary and Historical Perspectives* (Aldershot: Ashgate Publishing).

Index

Abbot, George, Archbishop 78–9, 81, 100, 138, 240
Abbot, Robert, Bishop 205
Act of Revocation 248
Adams S. L. 6
admiralty 103–23
Admonition Controversy, the 239
Airey, Henry 82
Albigensians, the 166–7
Allen, John 113
altar policy 165, 170, 171, 172, 173, 174, 182, 185, 189, 193, 280
Alvey, Henry 145
Andrewes, Lancelot, Bishop 82, 165, 167
Andrews, K. R. 108
Angel, John 120
anti-nomianism 151
anti-popery 11, 32, 72, 79, 129, 134, 166, 168, 172, 175, 183, 186, 191, 196, 201, 204, 242, 260, 263
anti-puritanism 64, 165, 167, 168, 169, 176, 177, 180, 237, 241, 247–51, 252, 260, 274, 277, 278–9, 281, 282, 288
Antrim, Randal MacDonnell, 2nd earl of 253
Apsley, Henry 24
Arminianism 4–5, 8, 13, 17, 81, 145, 166, 167, 175, 176, 183, 198, 222, 224, 260, 263
Army Plot 253
Arundel, Thomas Howard, 21st earl of 113
Ashbourne, Derbys. 144
Ashford, Kent 197
Ashton, Abdias 144
Aston, Sir Thomas 17, 259–89
attorney general 127, 138, 139
Aylmer, G. E. 9

Babington, Gervase, Bishop 29
Bacon, Ann 70, 71
Bacon, Anthony 28

Bacon, Sir Francis, attorney general, lord keeper 50, 70, 91, 97, 100, 115–16, 216, 240
Bacon, Sir Nicholas, lord keeper 70
Bagg, Sir James 111
Balcanquall, Walter 176, 248
Ball, J. N. 5
Balmerino, James Elphinstone, 2nd Lord 249
Bancroft, Richard, Archbishop 23, 59, 62, 77, 78, 239, 241
Barker, Rowland 29
Barnardiston, Sir Nathaniel 265
Barnes, Michael 182
Barnes, T. G. 5
Barnet, Nathaniel 192
Barrat, Francis 123
Barrell, Robert 202–3
Barrett, William 145, 152, 153
Bastwick, John 163, 178
Bedford, Francis Russell, 2nd earl of 28–9
Beza, Theodore 29, 36, 155
Bible 147, 152
Billingsley, Sir Henry 40
Bing, William 113
Bishops Wars 251, 261
Blair, Robert, Professor 249
Blount, Richard 24
Boden, Joseph 191
Bolton, Edmund 224
Book of Sports 163, 165, 171, 172, 182
Booth, Sir George 260, 261, 266, 267, 272, 273, 276, 277, 281, 282
Boswell, Mr 265
Botero, Giovanni 65–6
Boughen, Edward 163n, 181
Bourne, Nicholas 227–9
Bowes, Robert 26, 27
Bowes, Sir William 24
Bowles, Edward 195
Braddick, M. J. 15, 125
Brampton Bryan, Herefs. 198, 201

295